Praise for *Natural Disasters in a Global Environment*

"*Natural Disasters in a Global Environment* serves as a much-needed respite from the glossy hyper-produced texts on environmental geology and natural disasters so prevalent today. Instead, Penna and Rivers couple delightful exposition, insightful comparative images, and historical anecdotes that together produce some of the finest science writing I've seen. This book not only could be an outstanding text for a course on the subject, but it also would be a fine read for anyone interested in how Earth 'works.'"

Donald Siegel, Syracuse University

"This is an impressive collection, wide ranging in time, place and discipline. The result stimulates new thinking both about history and about the ongoing role of catastrophe in the course of human society – altogether, an imaginative venture."

Peter Stearns, George Mason University

"Eco-anxiety sometimes makes us exaggerate our power over nature for good and ill. In an important, welcome and riveting collaboration between history and science, Penna and Rivers unfold a minatory drama of disasters – seismic, climatic, pandemic, atmospheric, meteoric – that humans can barely influence, let alone control."

Felipe Fernandez-Armesto, University of Notre Dame

"This skillful record of natural disaster – in climate, epidemics, and earth tremors – shows how society risks further disaster even in planning for safety."

Patrick Manning, University of Pittsburgh

"Appealing to both students of history and science, this study of natural hazards and vulnerable populations provides an enthralling guide to how disasters have altered the course of human history."

Greg Bankoff, University of Hull

"Interdisciplinary in methods and reach, *Natural Disasters in a Global Environment* surveys big ideas in concise and accessible form. This book is an indispensable introduction for everyone who wants to understand human response to disaster – scientists, disaster planners, historians, and policy-makers, students and senior researchers."

Conevery Bolton Valencius, University of Massachusetts, Boston

NATURAL DISASTERS IN A GLOBAL ENVIRONMENT

Anthony N. Penna and Jennifer S. Rivers

WILEY-BLACKWELL
A John Wiley & Sons, Ltd., Publication

This edition first published 2013

Wiley-Blackwell is an imprint of John Wiley & Sons, formed by the merger of Wiley's global Scientific, Technical and Medical business with Blackwell Publishing.

Registered Office
John Wiley & Sons Ltd, The Atrium, Southern Gate, Chichester, West Sussex, PO19 8SQ, UK

Editorial Offices
350 Main Street, Malden, MA 02148-5020, USA
9600 Garsington Road, Oxford, OX4 2DQ, UK
The Atrium, Southern Gate, Chichester, West Sussex, PO19 8SQ, UK

For details of our global editorial offices, for customer services, and for information about how to apply for permission to reuse the copyright material in this book please see our website at www.wiley.com/wiley-blackwell.

Library of Congress Cataloging-in-Publication Data
Penna, Anthony N.
Natural disasters in a global environment / Anthony N. Penna and Jennifer S. Rivers.
pages cm
Includes bibliographical references and index.
ISBN 978-1-118-25234-5 (hardback) – ISBN 978-1-118-25233-8 (paperback) – ISBN 978-1-118-32752-4 (emobi) 1. Natural disasters–History. 2. Environmental disasters–History. 3. Natural disasters–Environmental aspects. I. Rivers, Jennifer S. II. Title.
GB5014.P46 2013
363.3409–dc23

2012043158

A catalogue record for this book is available from the British Library.

Cover images: Main image: Hurricane on Earth © BSH_Stock/Image Source/Corbis. Above from left to right: Smoke and burnt wilderness emergency © Pgiam, Flooding in the Midwest © Curt Pickens, Tungurahua volcano eruption © Elena Kalistratova, Global warming © Tarek El Sombati
Cover design by Simon Levy

Set in Minion 10.5/13 pt by Toppan Best-set Premedia Limited
Printed and bound in Malaysia by Vivar Printing Sdn Bhd

1 2013

Anthony dedicates this book to the children in his blended family: Christina, Matthew, Olan, Trevor, Laura, Greg, and Brandon.

Jennifer dedicates this book to her father, Michael D. Rivers, who wanted to name her Aberfan as a memorial to the children who died in the Welsh landslide.

Contents

List of figures

The authors and publisher gratefully acknowledge the permission granted to reproduce the copyright material in this book. Every effort has been made to trace copyright holders and to obtain their permission for the use of copyright material. The publisher apologizes for any errors or omissions and would be grateful if notified of any corrections that should be incorporated in future reprints or editions of this book.

Preface

This book came about as a logical merging of our two disciplines, history and environmental science. Professor Penna taught environmental history both for history majors and as a requirement for environmental studies majors for many years. His interest in the subject of natural disasters came from two sources. First, he was invited to write three short essays for a volume titled *American Disasters* edited by his colleague in history, Ballard Campbell. The three essays were titled: "The 1935 Hurricane in the Florida Keys," "The Great Hurricane of 1938," and "The Mississippi Flood of 1927." These essays piqued his interest in the larger subject of natural disasters and his awareness that the subject of natural disasters and their environmental impact was becoming a topic of renewed interest by historians, social scientists, and the larger scientific community. Second, Hurricane Katrina exposed the vulnerability of citizens caught in this storm, and highlighted the failure of the immediate response by local, state, and national agencies. This event, more than any other, suggested to him that it would be worthwhile examining the subject from a historical point of view, yet with a solid scientific underpinning

Professor Rivers serves as Director of the Environmental Studies program at Northeastern University in Boston, USA. She teaches a variety of undergraduate courses including Natural Disasters and Catastrophes and Environmental Science in the Department of Earth and Environmental Sciences, both for science majors and for the larger university community. Chief among her interests as an environmental scientist is the role global climate change may have on disasters, including increasing both the severity and the frequency of atmospheric disasters as well as potentially increasing the severity and frequency of submarine earthquakes and tsunamis. In her very popular Disasters course she uses many case studies detailed in this book, such as the 1906 San Francisco earthquake and the 1755 Lisbon tsunami as a frame of reference by which to enable students to discuss engineering, city infrastructure, early warning, and emergency response mechanisms.

Thus, we were a logical pairing. Professors Penna and Rivers met for the first time in the spring of 2009 to discuss the possibility of writing this book. A series of meetings ensued, in which we developed a broad outline for the book based on the major categories of disasters which would become chapter titles, with three or more case studies that had societal implications beyond the immediate events. Based on the available historical and scientific material, we attempted to cut a wide path across geological and historical time frames. We sought uniformity for each chapter, but discovered that the scientific material specific to the older case studies we wished to use simply did not exist. As a result, we selected many cases from more recent nineteenth- and twentieth-century history.

Acknowledgments

At each step during the research and writing of this book, a number of students from the environmental studies program compiled preliminary bibliographies and articles from science and history journals. They included Mollie Stone, Alyssa Pandolfi, Ali Tarbous, Caroline Malcolm, and Jessica Feldish. Liam Madden made the imperial and metric systems consistent throughout the manuscript, and compiled a list of further readings for each chapter. Haley Oller and Lana Penn concentrated on photographic research, with Lana designing and revising a number of maps. Haley created an index for the manuscript that made the task of completing one for the page proofs much less onerous. A number of our students focused on a single task over the course of a semester, while others worked during the entire academic year.

Special thanks go to Karl Geiger, a retired engineer and Professor Penna's partner for almost twenty years at Habitat for Humanity, Boston, building low-income housing. They spent days discussing the structure and content of the manuscript. Karl scrutinized each chapter for scientific and technological accuracy and provided us with extensive commentary. Without his involvement, many errors would have made their way into the text. The few that may remain are ours only. Tom Detreth and Paul Goffer, two physicians who traveled with Professor Penna through Botswana and Zambia in August 2010, provided much-needed commentary on Chapter 7, Pandemic Diseases. Professor Penna's wife, Channing Penna, read the chapters with great interest and provided a loving home life that made this seemingly unending project worthwhile.

In order to identify reviewers of the pre-publication manuscript, the editorial staff asked us to provide names of scholars whose interests and research activity coincided with ours. Special thanks go to Joel A. Tarr, John R. McNeill, Pat Manning, Heather Streets-Salter, John Brooke, Ted Steinberg, Ken Hewitt, Ben Wisner, Mary Jane Maxwell, Paulette Peckol, Donald Siegel, and Robert Schmidt for identifying possible reviewers. To those anonymous readers, we owe special thanks for pointing out omissions, errors, and dubious interpretations. Peter Coveney, executive editor, guided this project with great skill and enthusiasm from the proposal writing stage to the manuscript's completion and publication. In the UK, Joanna Pyke, Caroline Hensman, and Jane Hammett provided much needed management, photographic research, and editing support, respectively.

Thanks to Deborah White for reading, reviewing, and editing the chapters on meteorites and tsunamis. Ryan Hill, senior technician in the Department of Earth and Environmental Sciences at Northeastern University, gave much appreciated technical support as we edited the manuscript and produced the images you see in this book.

Dr. Rivers would like to thank Anthony N. Penna for the honor of working together and for becoming a dear friend. Dr. Rivers gives special thanks to her sister, Julie A. Rivers, and her mother, Sally Rivers, for their boundless love and support. Thank you to Peter Rosen, Robert E. Schmidt, Paulette M. Peckol, and Donald I. Siegel for being mentors and friends.

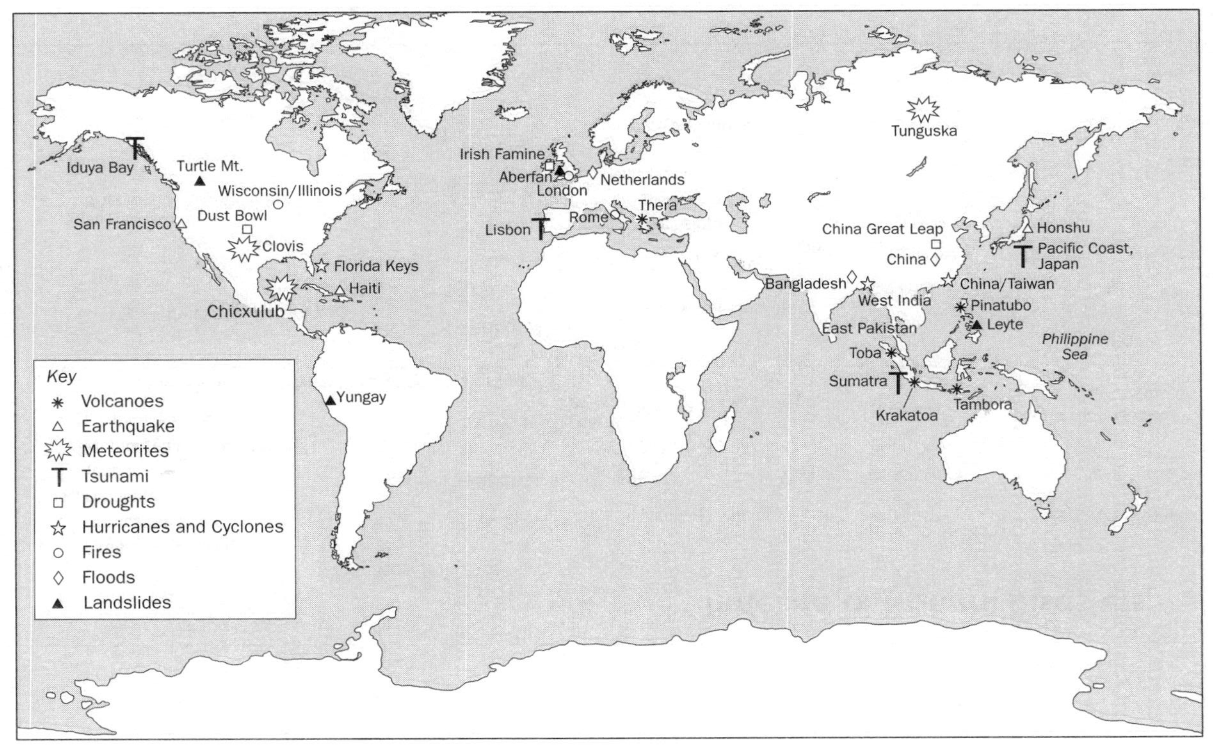
Iduya Bay
Turtle Mt.
Wisconsin/Illinois
Dust Bowl
San Francisco
Clovis
Florida Keys
Haiti
Chicxulub
Yungay
Irish Famine
Aberfan
London
Netherlands
Thera
Rome
Lisbon
Tunguska
China Great Leap
China
Honshu
Pacific Coast, Japan
Bangladesh
West India
China/Taiwan
Pinatubo
Leyte
East Pakistan
Philippine Sea
Toba
Sumatra
Krakatoa
Tambora
Key
Volcanoes
Earthquake
Meteorites
Tsunami
Droughts
Hurricanes and Cyclones
Fires
Floods
Landslides

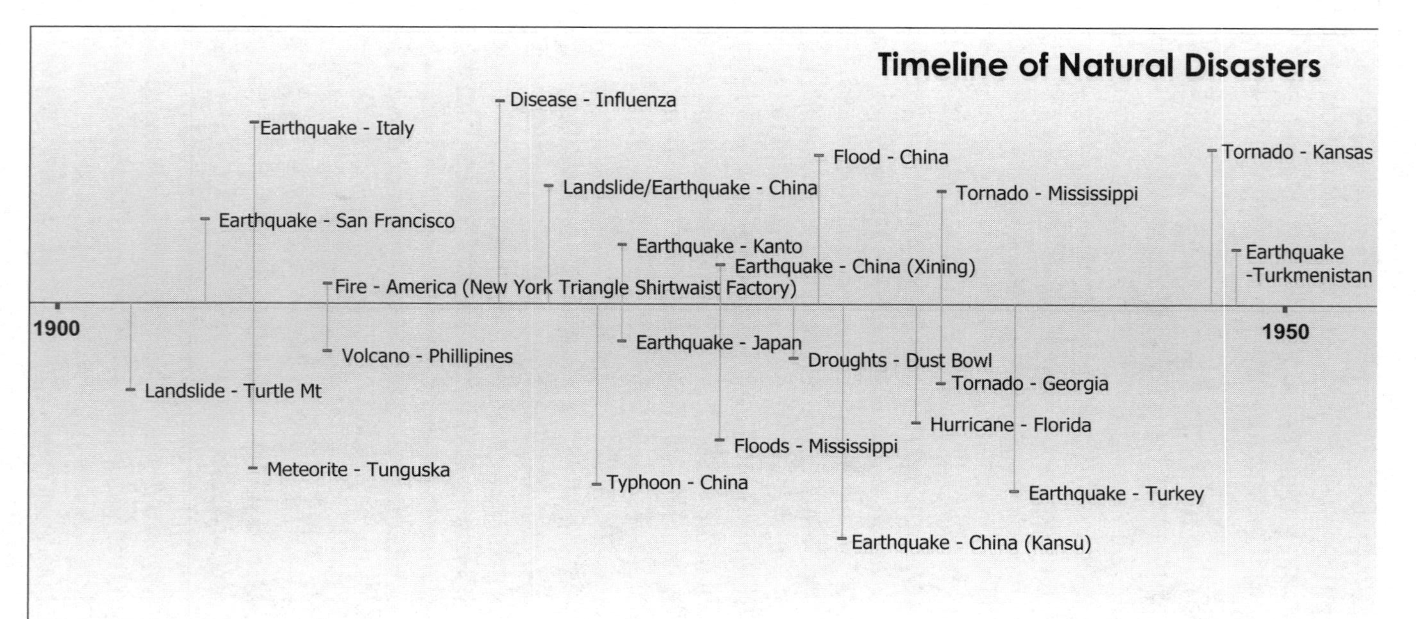

Timeline of Natural Disasters
1900
1950
Landslide - Turtle Mt
Earthquake - San Francisco
Earthquake - Italy
Meteorite - Tunguska
Fire - America (New York Triangle Shirtwaist Factory)
Volcano - Phillipines
Disease - Influenza
Landslide/Earthquake - China
Typhoon - China
Earthquake - Kanto
Earthquake - Japan
Earthquake - China (Xining)
Floods - Mississippi
Droughts - Dust Bowl
Flood - China
Earthquake - China (Kansu)
Hurricane - Florida
Tornado - Mississippi
Tornado - Georgia
Earthquake - Turkey
Tornado - Kansas
Earthquake
-Turkmenistan

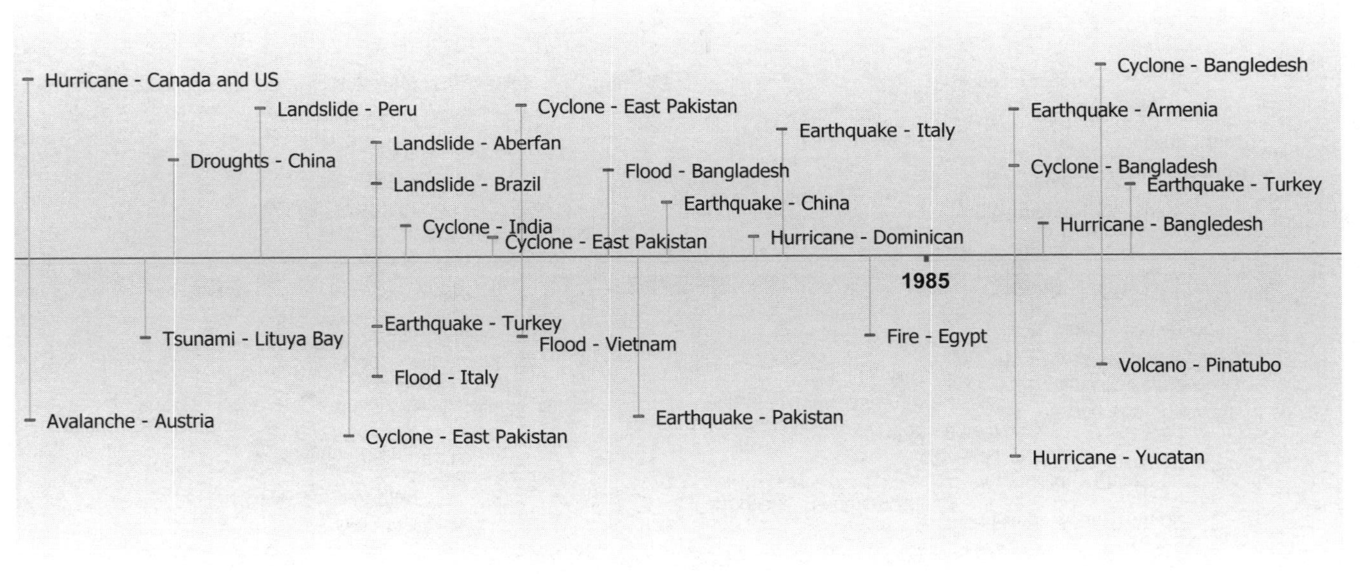

Hurricane - Canada and US
Avalanche - Austria
Tsunami - Lituya Bay
Droughts - China
Landslide - Peru
Cyclone - East Pakistan
Landslide - Aberfan
Landslide - Brazil
Earthquake - Turkey
Flood - Italy
Cyclone - India
Cyclone - East Pakistan
Flood - Vietnam
Cyclone - East Pakistan
Flood - Bangladesh
Earthquake - Pakistan
Earthquake - China
Hurricane - Dominican
Earthquake - Italy
1985
Fire - Egypt
Earthquake - Armenia
Cyclone - Bangladesh
Hurricane - Yucatan
Hurricane - Bangledesh
Cyclone - Bangledesh
Volcano - Pinatubo
Earthquake - Turkey

(*Continued*)

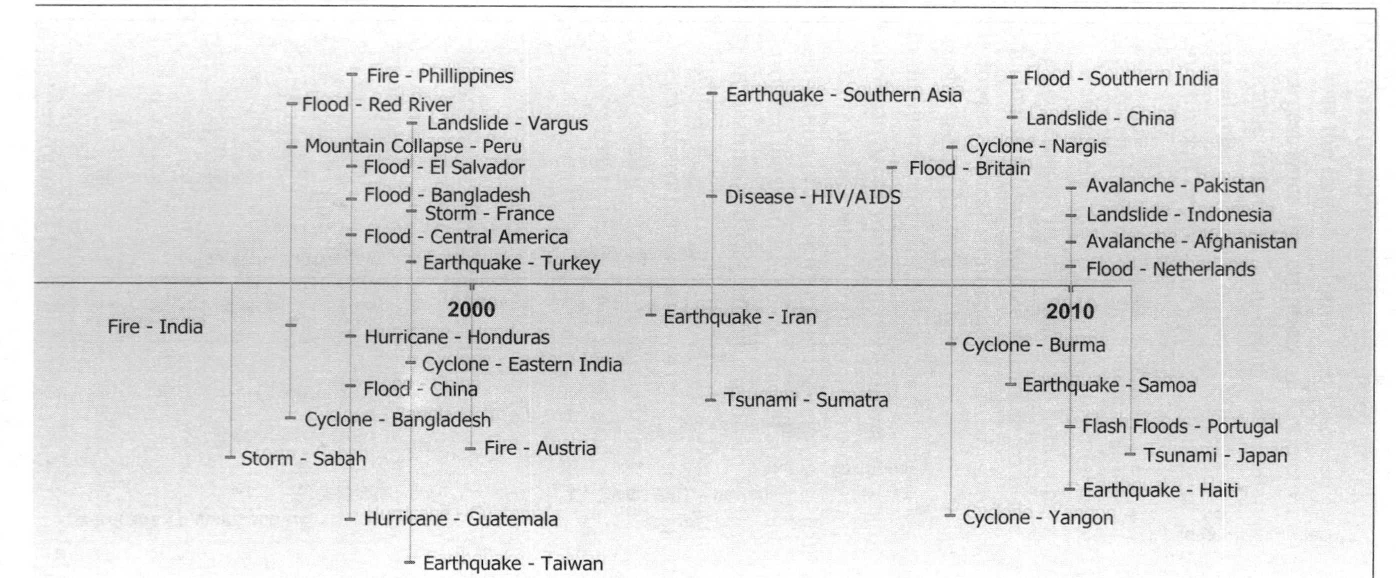
Fire - India
Storm - Sabah
Flood - Red River
Mountain Collapse - Peru
Cyclone - Bangladesh
Fire - Phillippines
Flood - El Salvador
Flood - Bangladesh
Flood - Central America
Hurricane - Honduras
Flood - China
Hurricane - Guatemala
Landslide - Vargus
Storm - France
Earthquake - Turkey
Cyclone - Eastern India
Earthquake - Taiwan
2000
Fire - Austria
Earthquake - Iran
Earthquake - Southern Asia
Disease - HIV/AIDS
Tsunami - Sumatra
Flood - Britain
Cyclone - Nargis
Cyclone - Burma
Cyclone - Yangon
Flood - Southern India
Landslide - China
Earthquake - Samoa
Avalanche - Pakistan
Landslide - Indonesia
Avalanche - Afghanistan
Flood - Netherlands
2010
Flash Floods - Portugal
Earthquake - Haiti
Tsunami - Japan

Introduction

> *It reminded me of something that tsunami survivors mentioned in the first days after the waves receded. Up and down the battered coast, they had rediscovered gnarled stone tablets, some of them hundreds of years old, which had been left by ancient ancestors at precise points on the shore to indicate the high-water marks of previous tsunamis. The inscriptions implored future generations never to build closer to the water again. "No matter how many years may pass," read one, "do not forget this warning." (Evan Osnos, "Letter from Fukushima: the fallout")*[1]

Natural disasters have the ability to seriously disrupt the functioning of society. They pose significant and widespread threats to life, property, and the environment. They are caused by accidents, nature, or human activities.[2] Though we have improved our disaster warning, response, and recovery systems, our engineered structures and effective emergency management and responses may have lulled us into a false sense of security. As we saw with the 2011 tsunami in Japan referenced in the above quote, people were standing on top of their "indestructible" sea walls as the tsunami waves came in, only to be washed out to sea, along with the rubble from sea walls, boats, and coastal housing.

Background

To examine natural disasters comparatively and across historical time involves focusing on macro forces. One of the most significant macro forces in the last century has been the four-fold increase in the human population. In 2012, the world's population exceeded seven billion people. With

Natural Disasters in a Global Environment, First Edition. Anthony N. Penna and Jennifer S. Rivers.

500,000,000 living in proximity to the world's coastal regions and with increasing numbers moving there, they become more vulnerable to coastal flooding caused by sea-level rise and hurricane storm surges. In addition, another one-half billion people live within a 60-mi (100 km) radius of volcanoes that have been active during the last thousand years. There, subsurface volcanic eruptions along the boundaries of the world's tectonic plates cause calamitous tsunamis.

Populations moving to coastal communities for work or play become more vulnerable to catastrophic events, including oceanic earthquakes that cause tsunamis and hurricanes that cause storm surge and coastal and inland flooding. For example, the land in the Bengali Delta sinks at a rate of one inch each year. Human action rather than natural processes is causing this land subsidence: "Surge and subsidence make a bad combination."[3] The 3.5 million people who live in and around the Delta extract millions of gallons of groundwater each year for household use and for irrigation, causing this sinking. In the rest of the country, land clearing and deforestation expands the nation's agricultural footprint, making it vulnerable to flooding from the major river systems that flow through the nation. This combination resulted in the devastation caused by the Bhola cyclone (a case study in Chapter 8), which was one of the most destructive natural disasters of the last century, with at least 300,000 casualties.

A population's poor becomes increasingly vulnerable because either no alternative living arrangements exist, as in the case in Dhaka, Bangladesh, or due to a false impression that engineered structures create safe havens atop unstable geologic substrate. Increasingly, people occupy regions vulnerable to earthquakes. The affluent knowingly move there for the amenities; a view, a woodlands, or a lake. In the event of a quake, they rebuild or go on to a safer haven. For the poor and more vulnerable, no such options exist. This trend, along with the decline in the capacity of ecosystems to provide a buffer to extreme events, has led to lost lives with rapidly rising economic losses from natural disasters.[4]

Probably the most common human action contributing to losses from disasters is the decision to fill wetlands, marshes, and mudflats along the world's coasts to create land for more affluent populations seeking the amenities of coastal living. They may not be aware of the consequences of their actions and as a result create their own vulnerability. By enlarging their geographical footprint, they fill wetlands with debris to accommodate larger populations, commerce, and industry. In so doing, many coastal cities and communities place their citizens in harm's way. In cities close to or on top of tectonic plates, such as San Francisco and Tokyo, earthquakes have been amplified by manmade land, filled with sediment and debris. Less dramatic but equally destructive effects of filling coastal wetlands include blocked drainage, compromised sanitation systems, the spread of infectious pathogens, and a declining population of fish and marine life which local people may depend on.[5] So, a number of factors contribute to "natural" and "human" disasters, with the most important ones related to a country's social system and its power structure. Although geophysical and biological events may trigger a disaster, we have attempted to place them into a complex framework of social, political, and economic environments.

In writing this book, we made a number of multidisciplinary connections. On the spread of pandemic diseases, Chapter 7 provides examples of disasters that were capable of changing the direction of world history. Environmental conditions, such as poor sanitation, contaminated drinking water, and poor hygiene, contributed to their outbreaks. For example, during the Bubonic Plague, infected fleas looking for blood hosts found rats first and then infected humans. Two of our case studies reinforce this conclusion. Many biologists and historians agree on the effects of Justinian's Plague (541–750 CE), with some suggesting that it may have been responsible, or partly so, for the end of the Ancient World and the beginning of Europe's Medieval Period.

Others note that the "Black Death" (1347–1351 CE) may be among the primary reasons for the demise of the Medieval and the beginning of the European Renaissance that ushered in the modern age. These may be defining episodes in world history, rather than dramatic isolated events. If this is correct, then we all need to re-evaluate the significance of natural disasters in past global and environmental history as major societal turning points. In all cases, people without access to medical or public health knowledge became vulnerable to rapidly spreading pathogens. In the past, there were no safeguards and certainly no ways to manage the risks. Running away from infected people, without knowledge of the disease vectors, spread the affliction.

According to environmental geographer Vaclav Smil, some of the disasters noted above fall into the category of sudden, unpredictable low-probability events.[6] The case studies of five supervolcanoes (Chapter 1) fall into this category. They were the Mt. Toba (Sumatra) super-eruption (73,000 years ago), the Thera (Santorini) super-eruption (circa 1,660 years before the common era; BCE), the Mt. Tambora (1815), Krakatau (1883), and Mt Pinatubo (1991) eruptions. One of the fascinating hypotheses suggests that the eruption of Mt. Toba explains the bottleneck found by geneticists as they mapped humanity's DNA (see Chapter 1). Santorini's explosions, according to some researchers, precipitated the decline of Minoan civilization in the Aegean Sea. In cases with such far-reaching outcomes, Smil's categorizing seems warranted.

Sudden high-probability disasters that occur more frequently than others include floods and cyclones. That cyclones, floods, and landslides top the high-probability list is predictable given the advances in global communication and reporting and, more importantly, the development of the science of climate change during the last decades. As the world's oceans warm, more water evaporates. The increased moisture in the atmosphere causes frequent torrential rainfall. Sudden flooding follows this surface and atmospheric exchange. Figure 0.1 details the rapid increase in these high-probability floods compared to the increase in cyclones and earthquakes in recent decades.

In the first years of the twenty-first century, storms and floods accounted for 70–75% of all natural disasters, with earthquakes, tsunamis, temperature extremes, fires, and blizzards following in terms of frequency. However, between 1970 and 2005 earthquakes and resultant tsunamis claimed the largest number of victims (over one million people) followed by cyclones and floods (approximately 550,000 people). Each year one single catastrophic event accounts for the majority of the fatalities. In 2003 and 2005, earthquakes in Iran and Kashmir (disputed land separating Pakistan and India) accounted for 80% and 85% of the year's total fatalities, respectively. The Sumatra–Andaman earthquake and tsunami were responsible for 95% of 2004's fatalities.[7] These "sudden discontinuities" (volcanoes, earthquakes, tsunamis, fires, and droughts), all topics in this volume, occur less frequently. What the future holds regarding the incidence of these events remains a topic of discussion based on projections about climatic conditions, enhanced reporting of events across the world, and disaster risk management. To avoid compartmentalizing natural disasters into discrete categories, repeated efforts to link them in meaningful ways has become a priority. One of the more dramatic examples of this linkage can be seen in the eighteenth-century drawing (Figure 3.1) of the Lisbon earthquake (1755) that destroyed the city, causing uncontrollable fires and a tsunami. Two recent disasters, the Sumatra–Andaman earthquake (2004) in the Sumatra Straits and the Japanese earthquake (2011) off the country's east coast, triggered two of the modern world's most destructive tsunamis.

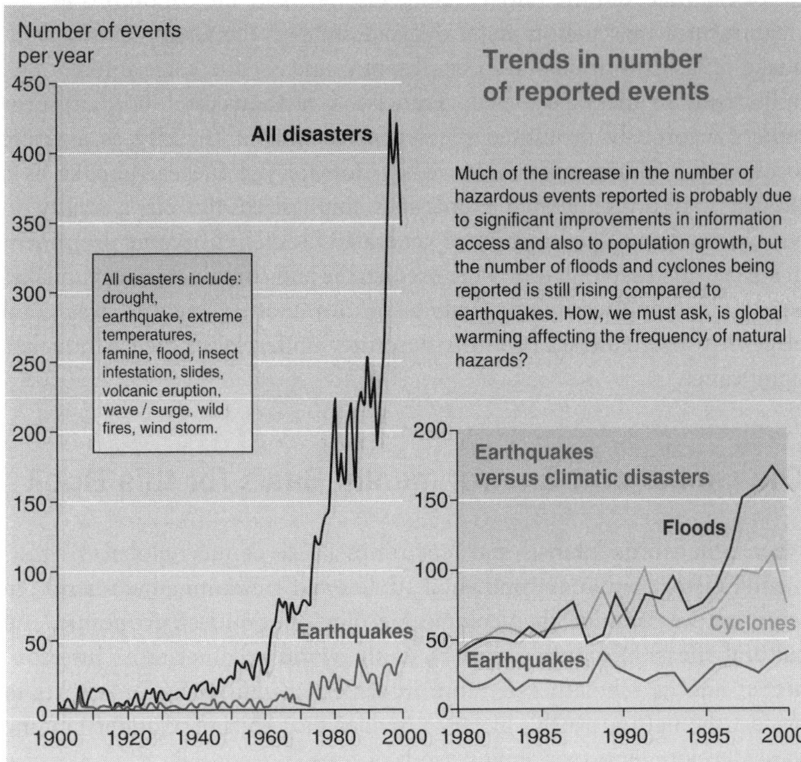

Figure 0.1 Trends in natural disasters.
Source: Centre for Research on the Epidemiology of Disasters (CRED). http://www.grida.no/graphicslib/detail/trends-in-natural-disasters_a899. Used by permission Emmanuelle Bournay, UNEP/GRID-Arendal.

Responses to Hazards and Disasters

Questions abound about individual and collective responses to geological, atmospheric, and biological processes. What caused these episodes? What were their effects? What constitutes their depth and breadth? How many died? Which government and nongovernmental organizations (NGOs) initiated relief and rescue missions, and how successful were they? Did a rebuilding effort create a safer environment, or did it replicate the previous built environment? How did society contribute to the disaster? What did society make of it? How did society confront it or even use it?[8]

For example, did the Bhola cyclone (1971) create the conditions for the creation of a new nation state, Bangladesh? Did the Great Kanto earthquake (1923) thwart Japan's liberalization and set the stage for renewed militarism? In the wake of San Francisco's earthquake (1906), city promoters vigorously promoted the reconstruction of the city as a viable location for future investments. They downplayed the earthquake as a sudden and unpredictable event and emphasized the city's ability to rebuild itself after the earthquake-generated fires. Fires became prominent in advertising material; they were predictable and containable, earthquakes were sudden and terrifying. A city at risk for another 'big one" was not a place that would attract investment, so they underplayed the earthquake's significance.

The Global and Environmental Basis for this Book

We use the words "global" and "environment" to connect global environmental history with environmental studies and environmental science. In doing so, we examine the geological, ecological, political, economic, and cultural effects of natural disasters. As the world becomes more interconnected and as scholars and more informed citizens focus on efforts to protect the natural world, history provides the vehicle for understanding these developments over long periods of time.

For global history, the publication of Fernand Braudel's *Civilization matererielle, economie et capitalisme, XVe–XVIIe siècle* (1979) became such a work. A number of scholars followed by examining the interconnections of material life and the environment. Later global histories focused on economic transnational linkages. Andre Gunder Frank[9] and Kenneth Pomerantz[10] brought to our attention economic developments in Asia during the last centuries. *ReOrient* and *The Great Divergence* by these scholars, respectively, extended our knowledge of global developments. As of the time of writing, the resurgence of China and other Asian countries in the twenty-first century can now be viewed within the historical perspective of many centuries, with the nineteenth and much of the twentieth century being periods of decline in Asia.

For environmental history, again a relatively new field, the seminal works include Alfred W. Crosby Jr.'s *The Columbian Exchange*[11] and *Ecological Imperialism*.[12] The title of the former has entered the lexicon of history to such an extent that it is now used without reference to Crosby's earlier work. In both studies, Crosby defined humans as biological entities interacting with the rest of nature. Both books transcend local and national boundaries, as does J.R. McNeill's *Something New Under The Sun*[13] and, with William McNeill, *The Human Web*.[14] David Christian's *Maps of Time*[15] views history through the lens of many disciplines and stretches both global and environmental history into the realm of "big history." To accomplish the merger of the global and environmental more effectively, we have connected environmental science and history. By doing so, we believe that our book becomes diverse, comparative, international, and historical.

The Emergence of Climate Science and its Relationship to Natural Disasters

The marriage of global and environmental history to environmental science breaks through a barrier erected by many modern historians who until recently did not incorporate natural disasters into their studies of political and cultural history. This was especially the case with studies written from the perspective of the national state. This separation of natural disasters from mainstream history "represents a stunning reversal from the sensibilities of pre-modern historians, to whom natural disasters were among the primary markers of chronological change."[16] Over the last decade, however, the number of scholarly books on natural disasters, recognizing their importance for historical and social scientific study, has grown markedly. Many reasons explain this growth but one stands out.

For the first time in recorded history, humans have become geological agents able to alter the global climate system, which in some instances can cause unpredictable sudden natural disasters. In a recent article, titled "The Climate of History: Four Theses," University of Chicago historian Dipesh Chakrabarty argued that the impact of humans, defined by Alfred W. Crosby as biological, has been extended to the geological realm.[17] Climate change casts in bold relief humanity's vulnerability to volatile weather systems.

Chakrabarty's conclusions draw on the growing body of research findings by climate scientists. As a historian of science, Naomi Oreskes pointed out in her review of the abstracts of 928 scientific papers published in peer-reviewed scientific journals between 1993 and 2003 that none refuted the growing body of research "over the reality of human-induced climate change."[18] As recently as 2010, William Anderegg conducted another meta-analysis of more recent studies that reaffirm her findings.[19] In November 2012, a leading climate-change skeptic, University of California at Berkeley's Professor Richard Muller changed his opposition to climate change projections and wrote, "[I] found that global land temperatures have increased by a remarkable 1°C (1.8°F) in just 60 years."[20] As the meta-analyses of these climate studies and Professor Muller's conclusions suggest, the separation of human history from natural history represents a false dichotomy.

Currently, scientists focus their research increasingly on efforts to connect the findings about anthropogenic climate change to the increase in natural disasters; for example, the probability that the 4% increase in atmospheric moisture caused by melting glaciers is a primary reason for recurrent torrential rainfall and devastating floods. Events such as these occurred in places that experienced them once in a century or once in a decade, but not on a yearly basis. Increased floods, landslides, and cyclones have become side-effects of a warming climate.

Studying slowly developing and sudden natural disasters strengthens the relationship between the natural sciences and history. Both require the use of specific meteorological, atmospheric, and geological knowledge, but not to the exclusion of knowledge from other disciplines including biology, anthropology, and human genetics – all of which are familiar terrain for historians and scientists.

Each chapter in this book contains case studies based on the available scientific and historical knowledge. We discuss disasters that have their origin in Earth's *sub-surface* (e.g. volcanoes, earthquakes, and tsunamis; Chapters 1–3), *surface* (e.g. floods, landslides, fires, and pandemic diseases; Chapters 4–7), and *atmosphere* (e.g. droughts and famines, hurricanes, cyclones, typhoons, and meteor strikes; Chapters 8–10).

Conclusion

Drawing from this range of disciplines and the three categories listed above, situating natural disasters in the context of cultures at risk seems appropriate. Learning about natural disasters in the context of specific cultures will allow readers to examine how humans faced calamities and attempted to protect themselves from their worst effects. The historical record provides many examples of humanity's resilience when facing catastrophes; and, at the same time, its vulnerability.

We have written a scientific and historical narrative based on a global and comparative examination of case studies. In doing so, we hope to prepare ourselves for an uncertain future. Mitigating natural disasters should become our collective goal, and protecting the environment is clearly the means to achieve this end. The following phrase, "Go green, be fair, and keep safe"[21] can summarize three of the means to achieve this end. "Going green" means that we make every effort to minimize our exposure to natural hazards. Here, we have described briefly the hazards of moving to coastal regions. Many more hazards will become apparent as you read further. "Being fair" means that we do not victimize already vulnerable populations by our actions, and that we acknowledge that they suffer most during and after natural disasters. They will need our assistance. Lastly, "keep safe" means assessing and managing risk by imposing high standards for the built environment. That means clear and enforceable construction codes for homes, levees, dams, and many other human structures.

If we elevate the status of natural disasters and reverse the historical trend of neglect, then they will neither be erased from memory nor relegated to sidebars and parentheses. Although the historical record provides many examples of efforts to erase or distort the memory of natural and manmade disasters (e.g. the San Francisco earthquake of 1906, the influenza pandemic of 1918), a number of case studies will demonstrate humanity's desire to honor those who lost their lives during and in the immediate aftermath of the catastrophes (see sections on the Irish Famine of 1851, the Great Kanto earthquake of 1923, and the Yungay landslide in Peru in 1970).

Notes

1 Evan Osnos (2011), "Letter from Fukushima: the fallout," *The New Yorker*, October 17, 48.

2 UN International Strategy for Disaster Reduction, "Terminology on Disaster Risk Reduction." At http://www.adrc.asia/publications/terminology/top.htm.

3 Robert R.M. Verchick (2010), *Facing Catastrophe: Environmental Action for a Post-Katrina World* (Cambridge, MA: Harvard University Press), 29.

4 Vaclav Smil (2008), *Global Catastrophes and Trends: The Next Fifty Years* (Cambridge, MA: MIT Press), 46.

5 Ibid.

6 Ibid.

7 Karen Sudmeier-Rieux, Hillary Masundire, Ali Rizvi, et al., eds. (2006), *Ecosystems, Livelihoods and Disasters: An Integrated Approach to Disaster Risk Management* (Gland, Switzerland: IUCN Press), 31.

8 Robert R.M. Verchick (2010), *Facing Catastrophe: Environmental Action for a Post-Katrina World*, 3.

9 Andre Gunder Frank (1998), *ReOrient: Global Economy in the Asian Age* (Berkeley, CA: University of California Press).

10 Kenneth Pomerantz (2011), *The Great Divergence: China, Europe and the Making of the Modern World Economy* (Princeton, NJ: Princeton University Press).

11 Alfred W. Crosby, Jr. (2003), *The Columbian Exchange: Biological and Cultural Consequences of 1492*, 30th anniversary edition (Westport, CT: Praeger).

12 Alfred W. Crosby, Jr. (1986), *Ecological Imperialism: The Biological Expansion of Europe, 900–1900* (Cambridge, UK: Cambridge University Press).

13 J.R. McNeill (2001), *Something New Under The Sun: An Environmental History of the Twentieth-Century World* (New York: W.W. Norton Publishing).

14 J.R. McNeill and William McNeill (2003), *The Human Web: A Bird's Eye View of World History* (New York: W.W. Norton Publishing).

15 David Christian (2005), *Maps of Time: An Introduction to Big History* (Berkeley, CA: University of California Press).

16 Vaclav Smil (2008), *Global Catastrophes and Trends: The Next Fifty Years*, 56.

17 Dipesh Chakrabarty, "The Climate of History: Four Theses" At http://pcc.hypotheses.org/files/2012/03/Chakrabarty_2009.pdf.

18 Naomi Oreskes (2007), "The scientific consensus on climate change: how do we know we're not wrong?" in *Climate Change: What It Means for Us, Our Children, and Our Grandchildren*, eds. Joseph F.C. Dimento and Pamela Doughman (Cambridge, MA: MIT Press), 73–74.

19 William R.L. Anderegg, James W. Prall, Jacob Harold, et al. (2010), "Expert credibility in climate change," *Proceedings of the National Academy of Science*, 107(27), 12, 107–109.

20 Richard Muller (2011), "Dr. Muller's Findings," *The New York Times*, November 4, A30.

21 Robert R.M. Verchick (2010), *Facing Catastrophe: Environmental Action for a Post-Katrina World*, 29.

Part 1

Internal Processes

Chapter 1

Supervolcanoes

All of a sudden there came a great noise. We saw a great black thing, a long way off, coming towards us. It was very high and very strong, and we soon saw that it was water . . . The people began to . . . run for their lives . . . There was a general rush to climb up in one particular place . . . You can see the marks on the hillside where the fight for life took place. Some . . . dragged others down with them. (A description of the eruption of Krakatau by a Javanese field hand, working 5 mi (8 km) inland on Monday, August 28, 1883 at 10:30 a.m.)[1]

Introduction

As a recent volcanic eruption demonstrated, air travel – a convenient, speedy, and affordable means of modern transportation – was brought to a standstill by the explosive emissions from Mt. Eyjafjallajökull in Iceland from which a tephra plume (consisting of ash, dust, and solid rock) reached 5.6 mi (9 km) into the stratosphere in April 2010. At no time since the end of World War II had air traffic in the northern hemisphere experienced such a disruption. Although this particular eruption was short-lived, others, which were of a longer duration, changed the global climate.

During the last 46,000 years, major eruptions have occurred on average of one every 80 years. Some volcanoes have erupted for several consecutive years and multiple times in a single year. They discharged millions of cubic kilometers of ash into the atmosphere. As these eruptions continued, sulfur dioxide (SO_2), the most active chemical agent emitted by volcanoes, combined with large quantities of emitted water vapor (H_2O) and oxidized into

Natural Disasters in a Global Environment, First Edition. Anthony N. Penna and Jennifer S. Rivers.

sulfuric acid (H_2SO_4) aerosols. These aerosols spread around the world, reflecting the sun's radiation and causing a decrease in global temperatures. So, an initial warming of the climate system caused by a volcanic eruption was soon followed by a cooling.

The radiative effect of volcanic aerosols generates general stratospheric (upper atmosphere) heating and tropospheric (lower atmosphere) cooling, and a tropospheric warming pattern in the winter.[2] This occurs because volcanic sulfuric aerosol clouds in the stratosphere absorb heat reflected from Earth while preventing sunlight from reaching Earth's surface. As a result, the stratosphere (upper atmosphere) heats up, while ash and pumice spread a haze across the troposphere (lower atmosphere), lowering global temperatures by a degree or more.[3] Unlike the ash residue from the combustion of wood, paper, and coal, volcanic ash is composed of jagged bits of rocks, minerals, and glass, often smaller than two millimeters in size. Breathing in such a substance is lethal to humans and animals alike, and when combined with moisture, it forms wet cement-type substance capable of obliterating everything in its path.

The case studies that follow explore natural world supervolcanic catastrophes: Mt. Toba (73,000 years ago), Santorini (circa 1660–1613 BCE), Tambora (1815 CE), Krakatau (1883 CE), and the most recent large volcanic eruption, Mt. Pinatubo, in 1991.

These five accounts of highly disruptive and lethal eruptions fall into the category of supervolcanoes, a rare geological event that may not occur for hundreds of thousands of years. Such rare events pose threats to life on the planet. The eruption of Mt. Toba on the island of Sumatra around 73,000 years ago falls into this category. The second supervolcano, on the island of Thera (modern-day Santorini), circa 1660–1613 BCE, may have accelerated the collapse of Minoan civilization, sending tsunamis across the Aegean Sea. Unlike Mt. Toba, planetary life remained intact. Thera's volcanic eruption, however, threatened the region's advanced commercial and economic life and its status as a thriving society. The third and fourth supervolcanoes erupted in the nineteenth century, Tambora in 1815 and Krakatau in 1883, both located in the Indonesian Volcanic Arc close to the Mt. Toba event many thousands of years before. Both disrupted atmospheric conditions in the northern hemisphere and were highly destructive to persons and property. The eruption of Mt. Pinatubo in the Philippines on June 15, 1991, destroyed property with minimal loss of life. This modern example of a supervolcano illustrates the importance of early warning systems and local people being alert.

The Mt. Toba Eruption (73,000 BP)

Supervolcanoes, those rare geological events, pose the most catastrophic threat to life on this planet. No super-eruption of Mt. Toba's magnitude has occurred during the Common Era (CE). It is the most studied of all known supervolcanoes in geological time, even though no precise measurements exist of its ejected material in either solid or gaseous states. Only cylinders of ice from the Greenland Sheet Project 2 (GISP2), measured for trapped gases, provide information about the magnitude of the Toba eruption.

The eruption was identified as the Younger Toba Tuff (YTT), to distinguish it from previous supervolcanoes at the same site. The Middle Toba Tuff (500,000 years Before Present; BP), the Oldest Toba Tuff (840,000 years BP), and the Haranggoal Dacite (1.2 million years BP) preceded it. The magma reservoirs from these older eruptions remained thermally stagnant for thousands of years, while the magma from the YTT began to accumulate and become more active for at least 100,000 years before its eruption.[4]

Its eruption expelled 6.7 mi^3 (2,800 km^3) of dense lava. The largest recorded eruption of Mt. Tambora in Indonesia in 1815 (whose effects historians have identified as "the year without a summer") was minimal when compared to the Younger Toba Tuff. Scientists estimated its explosive capacity at 3,500 times greater than the 1815 explosion. As fractures opened in the roof of YTT's magma chamber, massive outflows of dense magma covered 7,700 mi^2 (19,930 km^2) of Sumatra during a 9–14-day period. Combining the magnitude of the eruption with its intensity of around 7.8 million tons per second (7.1 billion kg/s), scientists estimated that the plume height was 20 ± 3 mi (32 ± 5 km).[5]

Once the plume became airborne, its gas content of H_2S (hydrogen sulfide) oxidized rapidly into H_2SO_4 (sulfuric acid). Approximately 3.8 million tons (3.5 billion kg) of H_2S would oxidize into 11 million tons (10 billion kg) of H_2SO_4. However, since these estimates are subject to re-evaluation with further research, they should be accepted cautiously.[6] Confirmation of such high readings in the atmosphere is recorded in the Greenland Ice Sheet. With an error margin of five years, these high readings about 70,000 years ago are greater than at any time in the 110,000-year record of the GISP2.[7]

Additional evidence of the magnitude of this monumental event is found in the deposits of Toba tephra ejected during the volcanic explosion and spread across a wide expanse of the Indian Ocean and the South China Sea and beyond, including the surrounding areas of Borneo, Sumatra, Sri Lanka, Malaysia, Vietnam, and the Arabian Sea. Mt. Toba deposited at least 1,000 yd^3 (765 m^3) of ash and several gigatons of volcanic gases across this vast expanse. Additional discoveries of YTT tephra appear as deep-sea drilling continues to date ash deposits of 4 in (10 cm) or more. These covered at least 1% of Earth's surface with 3,700 yd^3 (2,829 m^3) of dense rock equivalent (DRE). Researchers have uncovered as much as 35 in (90 cm) of ash in Malaysia. With each new discovery, the magnitude of this supervolcano grows and its estimated impact on the global climate system becomes clearer.

Scientists Michael R. Rampino and Stephen Self argued that the possible effects of the Toba eruption was the onset of a "volcanic winter" creating conditions suggested by the exchange of nuclear weapons that would create a cloud of ash caused by fireballs blocking out the energy from the sun. In the latitudes from 30° to 70°N, drops in temperatures ranging from 9–27°F (5–15°C) would have been possible, with deep freezes in the midlatitudes. Temperatures below normal in the range of 5.4–9°F (3–5°C) may have continued for several years. More snow and sea ice would have accumulated, thereby accelerating cool conditions and leading to decades of long winters and shorter summers.[8]

Evidence from the Vostok ice core from Antarctica indicates that the global drop in temperatures of 7.2°F (4°C) occurred between 80,000 and 75,000 years ago.[9] Although Rampino and Self acknowledged that global cooling had begun before the Toba super-eruption, they believed that the aerosol cloud accelerated the push toward full glacial conditions. Although the cloud cover would disperse in the short term, elevated levels of sulfuric acid (H_2SO_4) and the clouds that it created would remain in the atmosphere for at least five years after the eruption. The estimated amounts of stratospheric H_2SO_4 from the supervolcano range from 100 megatons (Mt) to 10 gigatons (Gt), with 6Gt of sulfuric acid remaining in the stratosphere for five years, a figure that coincides with the amounts found in the ice cores.[10]

The consensus among scientists suggests that the Toba supervolcano may have been a contributing factor to the instability of the climate. A decrease in ocean temperatures by 50°F (10°C) for the next millennium, explaining the expansion of ice fields in the northern hemisphere, a cooling in China and in the Pacific Ocean, all point to Toba as a causal factor.[11] More speculative is the suggestion that:

> climate change could have triggered the eruption via the impact of sea-level change on seismicity along the Great Sumatra Fault that runs the length of the island, accommodating oblique convergence between the Eurasian and Australasian plates. Major earthquakes have been implicated as eruption triggers and the location of Toba itself may be related to the apparent bend in the Great Sumatra Fault which could have promoted the development of large, long-lived magma reservoirs there in the first place.[12]

For example, one climate-change scientist has evaluated the 110,000-year record of the GISP2 and noted the correspondence of major volcanic eruptions with periods of changing climatic conditions. "These data support the suggestion that environmental change associated with climate change has the potential to increase volcanism."[13]

More recent research has suggested that even minor changes in climate can alter the position of Earth's tectonic plates and trigger volcanic eruptions and earthquakes. The conference on Climate Forcing of Geological and Geomorphological Hazards held in London in September 2009 suggested that climate change "could tip the planet's delicate balance and unleash a host of geological disasters."[14] Renewed focus has been directed at rising sea levels caused by melting glaciers as the global climate warms. Added weight puts pressure on the fluids in porous rock beneath the seabed. According to researchers, this minor change in pressure may be enough to alter the frictional force that stabilizes tectonic plates and holds them in place. A small change can have a significantly larger effect.

Since most of the world's volcanoes are located within a few miles of the shorelines of the world's oceans, the melting of large ice sheets into the oceans adding weight to them also increases the probability of volcanism by bending Earth's crust and allowing magma to reach Earth's surface (Figure 1.1). Since our knowledge about Earth's sensitivity to climate change is relatively new, the papers given at the London conference created a new challenge, that of modeling the kinds of effects described above. According to Bill McGuire of University College London (UCL), and organizer of the conference, "It's serious science, not scaremongering."[15]

The Mt. Toba eruption and the human bottleneck controversy

Unlike most past supervolcanic events, the YTT occurred when *Homo sapiens* had begun to emerge as the dominant human species on the planet, competing for dominance with *Homo neanderthalensis* in southwest Asia

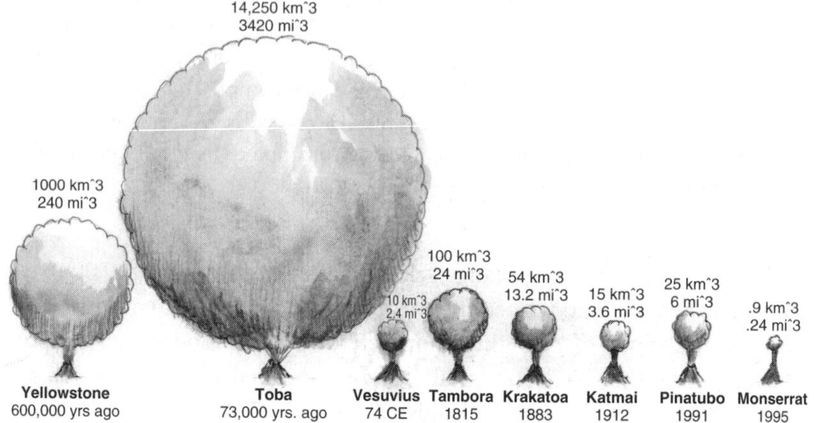

Figure 1.1 The Toba supervolcano compared to other supervolcanic events. *Source:* Reproduced by permission of Michael D. Rivers.

and Europe and quite possibly *Homo erectus* throughout the remaining Asian continent. A *Homo sapiens* population estimated to be between hundreds of thousands and a few million members during the YTT event seems plausible.

As suggested by one scientist, anthropologist Stanley Ambrose, the largest amount of atmospheric sulfur during the 110,000-year record of the GISP2 occurred during the YTT volcanic event with a peak spanning five or seven years. In the Greenland record, this peak was followed by abnormal amounts of atmospheric calcium, indicative of a 200-year period with high levels of wind-blown dust, probably caused by decreased vegetation. The exposure of land due to receding sea levels and a drop in Greenland temperatures of 10.8°F (12.5°C) were also contributing causes.[16] This decrease represented the largest drop in temperature during the Pleistocene Epoch and it coincided with the YTT eruption.

According to Ambrose, a significant reduction in population followed the YTT eruption, especially outside isolated tropical refuges, and resulted in a genetic bottleneck that lasted possibly longer than 500 generations. Bottlenecks can significantly reduce a population's genetic variation. The decimation of the human population during a volcanic winter allegedly caused by the YTT was conceivably large enough for founder effects and is consistent with the isolation of African tropical populations.[17]

Founder effects "occur when a new colony is started by a few members of the original population."[18] Evidence for the theory of a genetic bottleneck is the consistency with which it is identified in the human genome. Ambrose's theory suggests that "it most likely took place in response to three major climatic events over a 11,500-year period representing 550 generations. These events comprise the six-year volcanic winter at 73,000 years ago, the 1000-year instant ice age it apparently initiated, and the early glacial maximum, oxygen isotope stage 4 from 68 to 59.5 ka."[19]

An extended volcanic winter would have lowered sea surface temperatures by 5.4–6.3°F (3–3.5°C). At higher latitudes, temperatures declined by an estimated 21.6°F (17.8°C). Coupled with extended periods of snow cover that reflected solar energy, it created a feedback loop that turned months of frigid weather into years and even decades. For the human population living outside of the tropics, the reduction in biomass, plants, and ground animals would cause famine. While the ash fallout from the YTT would have killed humans at higher latitudes, the onset of an extended volcanic winter may have brought human groups weakened by the immediate impact of Toba to the brink of extinction.

In the wake of the YTT, isolated populations living in tropical African settings and outside of this protected environment may have experienced founder effects. In such a case, genetic diversity is either lost or significantly reduced. However, "a small, random subset of pre-existing genetic diversity is retained in each isolated population. If this remains the case for many generations, the genetic drift leads to the random loss of additional alleles (an alternative form of a gene, one member of a pair in which one is dominant and the other is recessive), reducing genetic diversity and increasing between-population differences even further."[20]

Struggling to survive the conditions of a volcanic winter that lasted a millennium during the last ice age, several isolated populations may have lived through genetic bottlenecks. As such, small founder populations would have retained a small amount of genetic diversity. However, if they remained isolated for many generations then genetic drift would lead to the random loss of some genetic characteristics and the fixation of others. The same would take place in other isolated populations where the random loss of some features and the fixation of others would take place. Globally, this would result in "increasing between-population difference even further."[21]

Conclusion

The YTT brings to mind the cataclysm to end all such happenings. The probability of a similar event occurring with any regularity remains low by any scientific standards. If Toba brought our species to the brink of extinction 73,000 years ago, an eruption of this magnitude today would have devastating global consequences and reveal the extent of humanity's vulnerability to nature's fury.

A topic like this one has attracted the attention of many geophysicists, who recently tested the hypothesis of a genetic bottleneck using climate model simulations. They concluded that although the Mt. Toba supervolcanic eruption may not have caused a "volcanic winter," its size and scope today "would have devastating consequences for humanity and global ecosystems. These simulations support the theory that the Toba eruption indeed may have contributed to a genetic bottleneck."[22]

The Thera (Santorini) Eruption in the Aegean Sea (1600 BCE)

Four thousand years BP, several major civilizations developed in the Aegean region, including Minoan (Crete), Mycenaean (Greece), and Anatolian (modern Turkey), all of which were precursors of early Greek and European civilizations. Each became integrated into a cultural and trading network that comprised the ancient Levant (a large area of south-west Asia) and Egypt. All existed within the tectonic region of the Hellenic Volcanic Arc where the convergence of the African and Eurasian plates and the Anatolian and Arabian platelets squeeze the land beneath the Aegean Sea, causing it to spring upward giving rise to the 39 Cycladic Islands that include Santorini. As one of the most tectonically active regions in the world, it produces as much as 5% annually of all of the energy released globally by earthquakes.[23]

The subduction of the African plate creates the conditions for volcanic activity in the Aegean. More than 100 mi (160 km) below the surface, Earth's mantle becomes molten. As molten rock penetrates faults caused by the stretching and bulging of the surface above, earthquakes and volcanoes release the energy created by the convergence of tectonic plates. As a result, this region, with the island of Santorini located on one of the Hellenic Arc's fault lines, has experienced earthquakes and volcanoes throughout its geological history. Major eruptions occurred 100,000, 54,000, 37,000, and 18,000 years BP. It was during the Bronze Age of Minoan civilization (2660–1400 BCE) that the supervolcano known to us as Santorini erupted.

Minoan civilization

Its edifices, its cultural artifacts, its trading networks, and its mythology of King Minos, the Minotaur, the Deucalion flood, and the travels of the Argonauts defined Minoan civilization. On the island of Crete, the center of its civilization, Minoans built a palace at the city of Knossos in approximately 1900 BCE. Within a hundred years it was completed. Two hundred years later, however, a supposedly large earthquake caused by the movement of these same tectonic plates in the Aegean sent destructive seismic waves throughout the ocean floor, creating tsunami waves across the eastern Mediterranean and reaching many shorelines. The seismic shocks and waves destroyed Knossos, its newly designed and spacious palace, and devastated Minoan civilization and the Mycenaean cities of Greece.

Undeterred, the Minoans rebuilt Knossos and an elaborate new palace that covered 5.4 acres and would mark the zenith of the New Palace civilization on Crete. During this New Palace period, 1700–1450 BCE, Minoan Bronze Age culture thrived with its elaborate palaces as centers of political and economic power. It brokered extended trading connections throughout the Levant and beyond. In addition to the palace at Knossos, Minoans built others at Mallia in the north, Phaistos in the south, and Zakros in the east.

As well as the central courtyards of the new palaces, colorful frescoes depicted rituals and scenes from nature. Sanitary facilities, sufficient lighting, and ventilation illuminated and cooled palaces and the more spacious Minoan houses. Their complex art became a symbol of cultural uniqueness with delicate pottery, vases, and vibrant fresco wall paintings depicting magical gardens, animals, and religious scenes. The catastrophic events that followed would change the course of Aegean civilization forever.

The Santorini eruption

Sometime between 1613 and 1600 BCE, according to the latest research, a Bronze Age supervolcano erupted in four phases, creating the current configuration of Santorini and its neighboring islands. The first phase ejected ash and pumice (light porous volcanic glass) into the atmosphere, which quickly settled onto Santorini and into the sea nearby. Today, those deposits measure 20 ft (6 m) on the island and 9.8 in (25 cm) on the small island of Aspronisi. With the collapse of the walls of the volcano, pyroclastic clouds of gases and dense magma covered Santorini, making it uninhabitable.[24]

Figure 1.2 Caldera created by the supervolcanic eruption of Santorini. *Source:* Shutterstock/Petros Tsonis.

A second volcanic phase began as seawater entered the crater through faults and mixed with molten magma, ejecting superheated steam and ash into the atmosphere. In addition, avalanches covered Santorini with 39 ft (12 m) of mud. A third and most destructive stage followed soon thereafter, as seawater mixed with magma causing blasts of ash, pumice, and dense rock fragments. Once the third and most explosive phase was complete, about 200 ft (60 m) of debris covered the land, with smaller amounts layering the sea floor (Figure 1.2).

> The explosions must have been loud enough to have been heard throughout southern Europe, northern Africa, and the Middle East. Undoubtedly they blew such large volumes of volcanic dust and aerosols into the atmosphere that sunlight was dimmed over much of the eastern Mediterranean region for several days. These assumptions are based on the comparison with the eruption on the islet of Krakatau on August 26–27, 1883 in the Sunda Strait between Java and Sumatra. That explosion, with an estimated VEI (volcanic explosivity index) of 6, was heard as far as 2,900 mi (4,600 km) away, and darkness in the region lasted for three days. Santorini's VEI is assumed to have approached a value of 7, considered "colossal" by volcanologists.[25]

A fourth and final phase included more pyroclastic flows of pumice and rocks that increased the depth of volcanic material on the land and sea floor.

After a 20-year hiatus, people returned to Santorini and Crete to rebuild the damaged structures.

The physical, social, and cultural meaning of this supervolcano

The publication of *The Volcanic Destruction of Minoan Crete* by the archaeologist Spyridon Marinatos[26] triggered debate regarding the full impact of the Santorini super-eruption. He rejected the suggestion that an earthquake could possibly cause the extensive damage found on the islands of Santorini and Crete. His excavations, however, led him to conclude ". . . that the disaster in Crete must be attributed to a tremendous eruption of the volcano on the neighboring island of Thera."[27] To support his argument he used two historical precedents, namely that (Thera) Santorini had erupted much further back in geological time as well as more recently in 726 CE and again in 1655 CE, the sound of the latter having reached southwest Asia.

The second important fact was the eruption of Krakatau in 1883, for which there was a detailed descriptive record. Although discussed in greater detail later in this chapter, Marinatos's comparison points out the difference in magnitude of the two super-eruptions. For him, the archaeological evidence suggested that the eruption of Santorini was much larger, with 75% more of the island submerged than Krakatau, 22.8 mi^2 (59 km^2) versus 83 mi^2 (215 km^2) for Santorini.

Yet, as Marinatos pointed out by implication, the global effects of Santorini dwarfed those of Krakatau. For example, the sound of Krakatau's eruption resonated 2,000 mi (3,200 km) in all directions, spanning one-twelfth of Earth's circumference. For 100 mi (160 km) and more, volcanic ash, pumice, and gases darkened the sky for days. Picked up by wind currents and enveloping Earth, the finest particles of ash rose 30 mi (50 km) into the stratosphere. The spectrum of colors at dusk that individuals wrote about in the months after the eruption represented telltale evidence of Krakatau's lingering effects.

Marinatos used the algebraic calculations of the Dutch observer R.D.M. Verbeek (the islands that today form the country of Indonesia were, until 1949, part of the Dutch colonial empire and identified as the Dutch East Indies). Verbeek witnessed the Krakatau eruption and explained the formation, speed, and destructive force of the tsunami caused by it. According to Verbeek, the speed of tsunami waves can be measured in proportion to the depth of the sea at any given point: the deeper the sea, the faster and greater the waves.

The tsunami born of the supervolcano was 90 ft (27 m) high, struck the shores of Java and Sumatra with devastating force, and moved inland as much as 1000 yd (900 m) at a height of 45 ft (14 m), destroying everything in its wake including towns, villages, crop lands, railroads, and ships, and most importantly killing 36,000 inhabitants. Almost 5,000 ft (1500 m) from the coast the waves were 49 ft (15 m) high. With Santorini's explosive capacity being 75% greater than the strength of Krakatau's, this led Marinatos to conclude that Santorini's supervolcano caused much greater and wider destruction.

With Crete, the center of Minoan civilization, only 62 mi (100 km) from Santorini and the sea separating them reaching depths of 1.2 mi (1930 m), an enormously destructive tsunami would hit the coast of Crete in less than one-half hour. His archaeological excavations revealed that all of the island's coastal settlements disappeared at the same time, and earthquakes would have devastated districts beyond the reach of the tsunamis. To Marinatos, the short-term effects of the eruption would have terrorized Crete's inhabitants, and forced them to retreat from the coastal zones and seek refuge on higher ground.

Some scientists have suggested that a major earthquake struck the Aegean between two and five years before the Santorini eruption and that a causal link exists between them. Such an earthquake would have disrupted life across a number of Aegean islands, including the developed societies of Crete and Santorini. With the super-eruption and the tsunami that followed, harbor installations would have suffered major damage to their docks, ships, and coastal warehouses. Covered in pumice from the eruption, the tsunami's waves would carry these volcanic materials to the coastal regions of surrounding islands, including Crete.

Deposits on the land as high as 105 ft (32 m) provide a historical record of the force with which the tsunami hit the north-facing regions of Crete. Without a doubt, agricultural productivity declined as a result of large deposits of volcanic ash on the land. Such an intrusion would have killed animals and humans. For surviving grazing animals seeking fodder from the land, ash residue clogged their digestive system. Water contamination from the fallout would result in the closing of some wells and require efforts to dig others. The prospect of volcanic winter lasting several years would trigger a subsistence crisis in Santorini, Crete, and many other Aegean islands. Famine, disease, and a degree of societal disintegration usually followed such events.

Conclusion

Many of the changes that occurred in the wake of the Santorini eruption and the destruction of Akrotiri, Santorini's largest city (sometimes referred to as the Minoan Pompeii), forecast the decline of Minoan Crete. The abandonment of villages, the depopulation of others, and the lack of centralized political control gave rise to local autonomy. The loss of Cretan influence and power over the larger Aegean network of trading partners culminated in a weakened Crete. Eventually it became incorporated into a larger Mycenaean Greek political, economic, and social world.[28] The physical and ecological damage placed additional stress on Crete's resources, making it vulnerable to invasion from the Mycenaean Greeks. "In time Crete sank further and further into decay,"[29] probably a victim of the greatest volcanic catastrophe of the Bronze Age.

Mt. Tambora (1815) and Krakatau (1883)

These two supervolcanic eruptions in the nineteenth century serve as a reminder that eruptions have global consequences. The explosions occurred at Mt. Tambora in April 1815 and Krakatau in August 1883, both located in the Indonesian Volcanic Arc and home to more than 130 active volcanoes. There, four tectonic plates meet: the Pacific, Eurasian, Philippine, and Australian. Constant volcanic and seismic activities among these plates comprise part of the Pacific Ring of Fire. Although dormant for 5,000 years, Tambora, located on the island of Sumbawa but existing in an active subduction zone, leaked dense magma slowly inside the mountain chamber, causing a build-up that reached its limits in 1815.

A first major eruption took place on April 5, sending an ash plume 15 mi (25 km) into the stratosphere. A second explosion occurred on April 10, with pyroclastic flow destroying villages in its wake. These continued until April 15, when a final supervolcanic eruption composed of lethal gases, rocks, pumice, and hot ash inundated the island, killing 10,000 people in Tambora Province. Once the flows reached the sea, they generated tsunamis that destroyed the neighboring islands, killing between 82,000 and 92,000 inhabitants. The aftermath of the super-eruption was felt for years to come. Its immediate impact was felt both on the island of Sumbawa, where sunlight was blocked for several days, and globally, where a cloud of ash lowered temperatures by 35.6°F (2°C). Tambora is remembered as causing "the year without a summer" in 1815, as the cloud reached the northern hemisphere causing crop failures, lowered temperatures with snow in June in New England, and frosty temperatures throughout the summer months.[30]

Much of the writing about the Krakatau volcano that lies in the Sunda Strait between Java and Sumatra has focused on its eruption in August 1883, which caused a series of destructive tsunamis killing approximately 36,000 people and destroying 165 coastal villages. The largest wave reached heights of 140 ft (42.67 m) above sea level and its tidal effects were recorded 4,050 mi (7,000 km) away. The first signs of an eruption were on May 20, and there were mild explosions throughout May and June. By mid-June, eruptions increased, with a series of new vents opening. By mid-July, pumice had flowed into the Sunda Straits between Sumatra and Java.

On Sunday, August 26 at 12:53 pm, Krakatau erupted with an ear-shattering blast accompanied by a darkening cloud of volcanic gases and dense magma that would quickly rise to a height of at least 22 mi (36 km). As the eruptions rose in intensity and the debris field widened, they threatened the coastal villages of western Sumatra, western Java, and the adjacent islands. At 5:30 am on Monday, August 27, as many as four more blasts culminated in one that destroyed Krakatau and ripped the island apart, with two-thirds of it disappearing below sea level. The pyroclastic flows from these calamitous blasts created enormous tsunamis across the Sunda Straits, some as high as 133 ft (40 m). They completely submerged many islands, stripping away the landscape and devastating the population. Much like other supervolcanoes, Krakatau's ash traveled as far as 1,500 mi (2,500 km) within a few days of the eruption. In a few weeks, a broad cloud of gases and fine ash rose into the stratosphere and remained there for years:

> The cloud contained large volumes of sulfur dioxide gas that rapidly combined with water vapor to generate sulfuric acid aerosols in the high atmosphere. The resulting veil of acidic aerosols and volcanic dust provided an atmospheric shield capable of reflecting enough sunlight to cause global temperatures to drop by several degrees. This aerosol-rich veil also generated spectacular optical effects over 70% of Earth's surface. For several years after

> the 1883 eruption, Earth experienced exotic colors in the sky, halos around the sun and moon, and a spectacular array of anomalous sunsets and sunrises.[31]

Passengers on the *Loudon*, a ship under the command of Captain Lindemann, described the arrival of a massive tsunami on Monday morning:

> Suddenly we saw a gigantic wave of prodigious height advancing toward the seashore with considerable speed. The ship met the wave head on and the *Loudon* was lifted up with a dizzying rapidity and made a formidable leap. . . . The ship rode at a high angle over the crest of the wave and down the other side. The wave continued on its journey toward land, and the benumbed crew watched as the sea in a single sweeping motion consumed the town. There, where an instant before had laid the town of Telok Betong, nothing remained but the open sea.[32]

Dutch authorities estimated that the number of dead reached 36,417, of whom 90% were killed by the tsunami. Months later, pumice floated in the sea, along with the charred remains of Krakatau's victims. Parts of the Sunda Straits contained so much debris that it hindered relief ships in their efforts to help survivors. By September 1884, the tides would carry dense pumice thousands of kilometers from Krakatau beyond the Java Sea and Indian Ocean to the northern coast of Australia.

Conclusion

Santorini, Tambora, and Krakatau, all supervolcanoes, possessed similar characteristics. They became the visible manifestation of Earth's volatile inner core of superheated dense magma. All were located in places where Earth's tectonic plates meet, and rub against each other until one subducts under the other, causing earthquakes and volcanic eruptions on the surface. These areas are called "volcanic arcs" and "rings of fire", and their geographies challenge growing populations living in their midst to prepare for catastrophes and adapt their built environments for eruptions. As each of these cases made clear, supervolcanoes have regional and sometimes global effects, changing climate conditions, causing tsunamis capable of reaching distant shores, disrupting air and oceanic transportation, and devastating civilizations. Despite its ability to destroy and disrupt various forms of communication and drive citizens from their homes and livelihoods, Pinatubo was different due to what it did *not* do.

The Mt. Pinatubo Eruption (1991)

The June 15, 1991 eruption of Mt. Pinatubo in the Philippines ejected 1.2 mi^3 (5 km^3) of ash and pyroclastic material including 20 to 30 megatons of sulfur dioxide (SO_2) and sulfuric acid aerosols (H_2SO_4) into the atmosphere in columns that were 11 mi (18 km) wide with heights reaching 19 mi (30 km). The temperature of the tropical lower stratosphere rose 39°F (4°C) because of the absorption of solar near-infrared radiation.

The Luzon earthquake – a harbinger

The earthquake that struck central Luzon Island in the Philippines on July 16, 1990 was comparable in size to the earthquake that struck San Francisco in 1906 (see case study in Chapter 2), and Sichuan, China in 2008, measuring 7.7 on the Richter scale. The quake followed the contours of the Philippine geological fault system and devastated cities and towns along its path. Located about 40 mi (65 km) north-northeast of Mt. Pinatubo, the Luzon earthquake has been cited by volcanologists as a possible cause for the mountain's eruption more than a year later in June 1991. Mt. Pinatubo is one of a chain of volcanoes sitting on the crest of a subduction zone known to geologists as the Manila Trench. Although no conclusive proof of a relationship exists, the temporal proximity of earthquakes, volcanoes, and tsunamis seems more than coincidental despite the absence of confirming scientific evidence.

On March 15, 1991, a series of earthquakes occurred, followed by the awakening of the Mt. Pinatubo volcano. From May 13 to May 28 the measured volume of daily sulfur dioxide emissions increased from 500 tons (453,592 kg) to 5,000 tons (4,535,923 kg). The decline in emissions that followed suggested that a blockage in the magma chamber would cause pressure to increase, leading to explosive eruptions. They began on June 3 with the prospect that more eruptions would follow. By that time, more than 100,000 people had evacuated the immediate area, including the 58,000 people living near the volcano who were evacuated by government agencies.

Those leaving included the 14,500 United States military personnel and their families living on Clark air force base about 10 mi (16 km) from the volcano and 50 mi (80 km) north of Manila. The US government closed the base permanently after the eruption and deemed it unusable for military or civilian operations. Layers of pumice covered the sprawling US Subic Bay naval station as well. Several buildings at both military locations collapsed under the weight of the ash and dense particulate material. On June 15, Typhoon Yunya struck the island of Luzon, mixing heavy rain with the ejected pumice and causing massive landslides. Much of Luzon, covering more than 50,000 mi^2 (130,000 km^2), descended into immediate darkness. The typhoon rains that followed turned both military stations into wastelands.

From June 12 to 15, a series of explosive magma eruptions took place, spreading pyroclastic flows across the landscape as far as 12 mi (19 km) from their origins in the lava dome. Although the evacuation of residents from areas directly affected by the eruption saved thousands of lives, the accumulated weight of wet pumice killed approximately 900 people. In the immediate aftermath of the eruption, the typhoon weakened the already compromised hillsides, causing the evacuation of more people. As disease spread through crowded relief camps, death from poor sanitation took the lives of hundreds of displaced residents.

Relief efforts

With 300 mi^2 (800 km^2) of rice-growing farmland destroyed and almost 800,000 livestock killed, a fertile landscape became barren. Displaced farmers witnessed the destruction of livelihoods practiced by generations of their families. The eruption destroyed 8,000 houses and damaged 73,000 more, as 364 communities, home to 2.1 million people, were damaged. The estimated cost of repairing the damage to the infrastructure, including healthcare facilities, schools, roads, and communication systems was estimated at US $500,000,000. A year after the eruption, 31,000 people were still in refugee camps, waiting to return to their rebuilt villages.

Another risk factor derived from the fact that concentrated sulfuric acid (H_2SO_4) reacts with solid sodium chloride (NaCl) in the cold atmosphere to produce hydrogen chloride (HCI) and sodium hydrogen sulfate ($NaHSO_4$). HCI is effective in destroying ozone (the layer of protection against ultraviolet radiation). It was customary to believe that because of its location in the troposphere (which is 6 mi (10 km) above Earth's surface), normal rainfall washed it away.

After the eruption, however, satellite data confirmed a 15–20% ozone loss globally and a greater than 50% loss over Antarctica. Volcanic HCI is, fortunately, short-lived as particles drift back to Earth in about three years.

The recovery of the protective ozone layer, however, after decades of destruction from manmade chlorofluorocarbons (CFCs), may be delayed by future volcanic eruptions. Satellite communication once again provided new and significant information about the global environmental effects of volcanism.

Monitoring the volcano begin in April 1999 by seismologists in the Philippines and in the United States. They recommended – and the government of President Corazon Aquino insisted – on the evacuation of about 20,000 indigenous Aeta highlanders who lived on the slopes of the volcano. Taking note of the government's order, people living on the lowlands left voluntarily. The US government ordered 15,000 American service personnel and their families stationed at Clark air base to leave the area as well.

The country's National Disaster Coordinating Council intervened immediately after the eruption, using civilian and military personnel in rescue and emergency relief operations. Victims and displaced persons received medical attention for injuries and emotional trauma. Public health agencies located at evacuation centers checked citizens for sore eyes and respiratory ailments caused by fine volcanic particles.

Within the first weeks after the disaster, a number of countries and nongovernmental organizations (NGOs) came to the aid of the Philippines government with contributions of money and supplies of food, medicines, and building materials. From Asia; Australia, China, India, Indonesia, Japan, Malaysia, Myanmar, Taiwan, Thailand, New Zealand, Singapore, and South Korea provided donations of goods and cash. From Europe; Belgium, Denmark, France, Finland, Germany, Italy, Malta, Netherlands, Norway, Spain, Sweden, and the UK did the same. From southwest Asia, came Saudi Arabia. From North America; Canada and the US provided assistance. Loans, grants, and technical assistance in varying amounts provided the Philippines with the resources to begin resettlement and reconstruction.

Rebuilding

Irrigation systems, roads, bridges, and public buildings including 700 schools needed repair or rebuilding. Housing that either collapsed during the eruption or fell victim to the mud flows of volcanic material followed. Monsoon rains turned flows into landslides. Unseasonably high winds carried ashfall greater distances in the Philippines, adding to the outbreak of chronic respiratory illness (Figure 1.3). With more than 100,000 homes destroyed, turning 1.2 million people into refugees, the rebuilding and

Figure 1.3 The ash and pumice cloud caused by the eruption of Mt. Pinatubo.
Sources: Photograph: Richard P. Hoblitt. Used by permission US Geological Survey.

relocation process was formidable. The Philippine National Red Cross (PNRC) engaged in a massive relocation process by placing families in newly constructed permanent villages that provided the occupants with sustainable occupations in aquatic and land-based farming, orchid production, and textiles.

Global effects

Powerful eruptions with enormous volumes of magma and ash inject significant quantities of aerosols and dust into the stratosphere. A month after

Mt. Pinatubo, a haze of sulfur dioxide encircled the globe. Volcanologists believed that it was the largest volume ever recorded by modern instruments and the largest since the eruption of Krakatau in 1883. As noted earlier, large volcanic eruptions can bring about changes in the global climate that extend over a number of years. Mt. Pinatubo's 1991 eruption provided the most recent example of a strong climate response to a major volcanic event.

When strong volcanic eruptions eject large volumes of sulfur dioxide into the lower stratosphere, they combine with water vapor and oxygen to form sulfuric acid aerosols. In the northern hemisphere, these aerosols disperse, producing significant winter warming from the equator to the Arctic. As the lower tropical stratosphere heated, strong westerly winds from the sub-polar region to the mid-latitudes created "continental winter warming" and the northward direction of storm tracts.[33]

A moderately warm Arctic winter in 1991–92 was one significant anomaly caused by the Mt. Pinatubo event. Another, and probably a more significant, one was the destruction of polar ozone in the few years that followed. The heating of the tropical lower stratosphere affected stratospheric circulation. These changes in heating and circulation combined to produce Antarctic ozone loss at altitudes of 6.2–7.5 mi (10–12 km).[34] Despite this, in the lower stratosphere, the northern hemisphere warmed to several degrees higher than normal. The normal amount of sunlight reaching Earth's surface declined by roughly 10%. This led to a global decline in temperatures of about 0.72°F (0.4°C) for almost eighteen months after the eruption.[35]

A Threatening Future Scenario

The case for an eruption in Yellowstone National Park in Wyoming, the USA, the home of one of the world's largest and most dangerous supervolcanoes, lies hidden just below the surface. Its most significant super-eruptions occurred 2.1 million years ago, 1.3 million years ago, and 640,000 years ago. To gain some perspective on the total volume of rock, pumice, and ash ejected from these three eruptions, they were enough to fill the Grand Canyon and spread a 20-ft layer of volcanic emissions over an area the size of California.[36] Globally, ash and dust would cover the planet, plunging it into a "nuclear winter." Today, Yellowstone is a major tourist attraction because it possesses one-half of the world's geysers and is home to numerous forms of hydrothermal activity, all of which are representative of the volcanic activity in the magma chamber 5–7 mi (8–11 km) below Earth's surface. Since more than half a billion years have elapsed since its last supervolcanic explosion, the question is not *if* another eruption will occur, but *when* it will happen, and what will be its magnitude? Will it be a series of smaller eruptions that have occurred many times in the past or will it be a supervolcano, "ejecting more than 240 mi^3 (1,000 km^3) of pumice and ash in a single event . . . Volcanoes form mountains; supervolcanoes erase them. Volcanoes kill plants and animals for miles around; supervolcanoes threaten whole species with extinction by changing the climate across the entire planet."[37]

The energy released by the eruption(s) would be equivalent to the explosion of 1,000 atomic bombs. The release of its pumice, ash, and aerosols would affect three-quarters of the USA. Its explosive effect would be ten million times greater than that experienced in Ground Zero on September 11, 2001. In zone one of the blasts of pyroclastic flow, the velocity and sound of the eruption would destroy everything within a 60-mi (100-km) radius and cover 3,000 mi^2 (7,800 km^2). An estimated mortality rate of 87,000 people or 19% of the population within this range is likely. In zone two, an extremely damaging cloud of ash, 6 in (15 cm) deep, would cover much of the continental USA, causing death by suffocation, collapsing structures, with rainstorms turning ash into mud flows. An estimated 500,000 deaths would be the result.

Within days, a fine layer of dust would reach Europe, with a finer cloak covering the planet. The stratosphere, the region above the highest clouds, would turn sulfur dioxide into sulfuric acid and remain there for years. Its effect on the global climate system would be profound, lowering temperatures in the northern hemisphere by an average of 12°F (–11°C). Snow would cover the ground all year round. In the tropics, the effect of a 15°F (–9.5°C) decline would end the monsoon rains, destroying agriculture and leading to mass starvation.

Summary

Supervolcanoes, in their global and environmental effects, are catastrophic and unpredictable in character. We know *where* future potential mega-events are likely to take place, but we do not know *when* they will occur, despite the technological revolution in monitoring and measuring seismic disturbances. What we do know is that all supervolcanoes eject enough sulfur dioxide (SO_2) (which oxidizes into sulfuric acid; H_2S0_4) into the lower stratosphere within weeks of an eruption, which is enough to cool Earth's surface temperature for at least three years by a minimum of 0.72°F (0.4°C). So, unlike other catastrophes such as earthquakes and tsunamis, the persistent atmospheric effects of volcanoes can last for years after the eruption.

Major volcanic eruptions produce large amounts of pyroclastic flow capable of crossing many miles of open sea and producing life-threatening tsunamis as the flows enter the water. On land such flows are capable of triggering mudslides that destroy homes and disrupt drainage and transportation networks by causing the build-up of sediments in rivers and harbors. On a global scale, the release of volcanic gases into the lower stratosphere, where these gases exist in extremely low amounts, and their transformation into acid aerosols will have a greater environmental impact than the fallout of volcanic ash across regional and continental boundaries.

Such fallout, however, because of its mineral composition, cannot be minimized. In the short term, as little as 0.39 in (1 cm) of ash can disrupt agricultural productivity during the growing season, leading to malnutrition, famine, and death. The longer-term implications of volcanic fallout seem to be quite different, however. At higher amounts, airborne ash will interfere with birds, air transport, and satellite communication systems. Roof collapses, poor drinking-water quality, failures in power generation from hydroelectric and nuclear plants because of ash interrupting water intakes are but a few of its effects. As noted in the case of Mt. Pinatubo, the discovery of the loss of ozone by acidic aerosols, permitting higher ultraviolet penetration to the ground in high- and mid-latitude regions, lasted for a few years after the eruption. As scientists and volcanologists probe further into the effects of these mega-events, we will learn more about their impact on the global climate and life on our planet.

As noted above, the short-term effects of volcanic fallout are quite devastating. The long term may offer some relief from these immediate impacts. In tropical areas, such as the Philippines, for instance, heavy tropical rainfall normally leaches nutrients out of the soil, diminishing agricultural returns. In the longer term, volcanic deposits can improve the soil's fertility and lead to gains in productivity. For example, despite the devastation caused by the volcanic eruption of Krakatau in 1883, within 25 years that region of Sumatra, poor before the eruption, became agriculturally fertile, the people prosperous, and the region more densely populated. On the island of Java, which has many active volcanoes, population density is ten times higher than other Indonesian islands, primarily because of its rich volcanic soil and high levels of agricultural productivity.[38]

Although none of these long-term gains will offer a ray of hope to those caught up in the mayhem and explosive terror of a volcanic eruption, volcanic deposits may be one of the many natural ways in which the planet renews itself after centuries of use and abuse. In the case of Mt. Pinatubo, its six or more eruptions in the last 35,000 years after lengthy periods of quiet may follow the rhythms of an ever-revitalizing Earth.

Notes

1 Littell's Living Age (1885), "The Krakatoa eruption," LII, 176.
2 Ingo Kirchner, Georgly Stenchikov, Hans-F. Graf, et al. (1999), "Climate model simulation of winter warming and summer cooling following the 1991 Mount Pinatubo volcanic eruption," *Journal of Geological Research*, 104, 19039.
3 Joel Achenbach (2009), "When Yellowstone explodes," *National Geographic*, 216(2) (August), 56–68.
4 Jorge A. Vazquez and Mary R. Reid (2004), "Probing the accumulation history of the voluminous Toba magma," *Science*, 305(5686), 994.
5 Clive Oppenheimer (2002), "Limited global change due to the largest known Quaternary eruption, Toba = 74kyr BP?" *Quaternary Science Reviews*, 21(14–15), 1593–1596.
6 Ibid., 1594.
7 Gregory A. Zielinski (2000), "Use of paleo-records in determining variability within the volcanism-climate system," *Quaternary Science Reviews*, 19(1–5), 423.
8 Michael R. Rampino and Stephen Self (1993), "Bottleneck in human evolution and the Toba eruption," *Science*, 262(5142), 1955.
9 Craig A. Chester, William I. Rose, Alan Deino, et al. (1991), "Eruptive history of Earth's largest Quaternary caldera (Toba, Indonesia) clarified," *Geology*, 19, 202.
10 Gareth S. Jones, Jonathan M. Gregory, Peter A. Stott, et al. (2005), "An AOGCM simulation of the climate response to a volcanic super-eruption," *Climate Dynamics*, 25, 728.
11 Clive Oppenheimer (2002), "Limited global change due to the largest known Quaternary eruption, Toba = 74kyr BP?", 1596.
12 Ibid., 1593.
13 Gregory A. Zielinski (2000), "Use of paleo-records in determining variability within the volcanism-climate system," 432.

14 Richard Fisher (2009), "Climate change may trigger earthquakes and volcanoes," *New Scientist*, 2727 (September 23). At www.newscientist.com/article/mg20327273.800-climate-change-may-trigger-earthquakes-and-volcanoes.html.

15 Ibid.

16 Stanley H. Ambrose (1998), "Late Pleistocene human population bottlenecks, volcanic winter, and differentiation of modern humans," *Journal of Human Evolution*, 34, 633.

17 Ibid., 231.

18 Bottlenecks and Founder Effects. At http://evolution.berkeley.edu/evosite/evo101/IIID3Bottlenecks.shtml.

19 Stanley H. Ambrose (1993), "Late Pleistocene human population bottlenecks, volcanic winter, and differentiation of modern humans," 644.

20 Ibid.

21 Ibid.

22 Bottlenecks and Founder Effects. At http://evolution.berkeley.edu/evosite/evo101/IIID3Bottlenecks.shtml.

23 Jelle Zeilinga de Boer and Donald Theodore Sanders (2000), *Volcanoes in Human History: The Far-Reaching Effects of Major Eruptions* (Princeton, NJ: Princeton University Press), 50–51.

24 Sturt W. Manning, Christopher Bronk Ramsey, Walter Kutschera, et al. (2006), "Chronology for the Aegean Late Bronze Age 1700–1400 BC," *Science*, 312(5773), 565–569.

25 Jelle Zeilinga de Boer and Donald Theodore Sanders (2000), *Volcanoes in Human History: The Far-Reaching Effects of Major Eruptions*, 55.

26 Spyridon Marinatos (1939), "The volcanic destruction of Minoan Crete," *Antiquity*, 13, 429–439.

27 Ibid., 430.

28 Ibid., 439.

29 Ibid., 438.

30 http://suite101.com/article/the-1883-eruption-of-the-volcano-krakatoa-a227100.

31 www.geology.sdsu.edu/how_volcanoes_work/Krakatau.html.

32 Littell's Living Age (1885), "The Kratatoa eruption," LII, 176.

33 Hans-F. Graf, Qian Li, and Marco A. Giorgetta (2007), *Atmospheric Chemistry and Physics*, 7, 4503–4511.

34 Simone Tilmes, Rolf Muller, and Ross Salawitch (2008), Whither geoengineering, *Science*, 320(5880), 1166–1167.

35 Brian J. Soden, Richard Wetherald, Georgly Stenchikov, et al. (2002), Global cooling following the eruption of Mt. Pinatubo: A test of climate feedback by water vapor, *Science*, 296, 728.

36 Ibid.,729.

37 Ibid., 730.

38 Fred M. Bullard (1984), *Volcanoes of the Earth* (Austin, TX: University of Texas Press).

Further Reading

Joan Marti and Gerald Ernst (2005), *Volcanoes and the Environment* (Cambridge, UK: Cambridge University Press).
This text is both comprehensive and accessible. Some of the world's foremost leading authorities on volcanology have contributed to it.

Cliff Ollier (1988), *Volcanoes* (Oxford, UK: Blackwell).
This book provides examples of research on the distribution of volcanic activity around the world correlated to tectonic activity.

Haraldur Sigurðsson, ed. (2000), *Encyclopedia of Volcanoes* (San Diego, Academic Press).
This multidisciplinary encyclopedia provides a comprehensive source of facts on the destructive and beneficial aspects of global volcanic eruptions.

Irasema Alcántara-Ayala and Andrew S. Goudie (2010), *Geomorphological Hazards and Disaster Prevention* (Cambridge, UK: Cambridge University Press).
This volume is a wide-ranging review of how society both manages and responds to volcanic hazards.

Peter Francis and Clive Oppenheimer (2003), *Volcanoes* (New York: Oxford University Press, 2nd edn.).
This book provides fascinating details about many particular eruptions, guiding the reader through the technical details without sacrificing the narrative.

Chapter 2

Earthquakes

All the cunning adjustments of a twentieth-century city had been smashed by the earthquake. The streets were humped into ridges and depressions, and piled with the debris of fallen walls. The steel rails were twisted into perpendicular and horizontal angles. The telephone and telegraph systems were disrupted. And the great water mains had burst. All the shrewd contrivances and safeguards of man had been thrown out of gear by thirty seconds twitching of the earth-crust. (Jack London, "The Story of an Eyewitness: The San Francisco Earthquake")[1]

Introduction

Unlike other natural disasters, including hurricanes, floods, and fires, earthquakes interrupt the normal flow of human activity suddenly and without warning. The movement of tectonic plates may last for only a few minutes, yet can cause massive death and destruction. During the twentieth century, the only century for which we have almost complete data, an estimated two million people died in earthquakes. For example, in 1976, China suffered a devastating earthquake that killed around 700,000 people. None of the cases in this chapter tells stories of earthquakes with similar death tolls, with the exception of the Great Kanto earthquake (1923) in Japan, which caused hundreds of thousands of casualties.

All three cases discussed in this chapter took place in the twentieth century: the San Francisco in 1906, the Great Kanto in 1923, and the Haiti earthquake of 2011. Each account will follow a similar pattern, including significant past events, the geological vulnerabilities of the region in question, the earthquake event, and episodes of relief and recovery in the aftermath. Fires would become major destructive forces that lasted for days

Natural Disasters in a Global Environment, First Edition. Anthony N. Penna and Jennifer S. Rivers.

in the San Francisco and Great Kanto quakes. In both, leaking gas lines and the preponderance of wooden construction material accelerated the spread of local fires. These countries differed greatly in their remembrance of these calamities, however. In San Francisco, city boosters, alarmed that an earthquake would suppress future investments in the city, denied the almost instantaneous destruction by the earthquake and replaced it with raging but controllable fires. In Japan, recovery from the Great Kanto earthquake, a national crisis, received proper commemoration, with a memorial honoring the bravery of the survivors and the sacrifice of its victims. Unlike San Francisco or Tokyo (Yokohama), Haiti and its capital city of Port-au-Prince were mostly populated by the poor and uneducated. The country lacked the resources to handle the earthquake's aftermath of infectious disease. Despite an outpouring of international aid, Haiti's present compromised condition cries out for succor from the international community.

The San Francisco Earthquake (1906)

In the twentieth-century history of the USA, the San Francisco earthquake that struck at 5:12 a.m. on Wednesday, April 18, 1906 would turn out to be the nation's worst earthquake disaster. When earthquakes strike densely populated areas with a modern infrastructure of water and natural gas lines, breakage caused by leaking gas can start serious fires. With an estimated cost of $500,000,000 in 1906 ($50 billion in modern terms), this earthquake was one of the most expensive natural disasters in the world.[2] Tectonic plate movement 6–9 mi (9.6–14.5 km) below the surface south of Lake Merced in San Francisco and on or near the San Mateo County coastline fractured, moving ten feet horizontally and three feet vertically. "A series of concentric seismic waves spread across the land and water at speeds up to three miles per second (4.8 km/s)."[3] Although the Richter scale was not invented at that time, to measure the energy unleashed by these tectonic disruptions, seismologists estimated that the earthquake would have measured 8.3.[*,4]

* The Richter magnitude scale was developed in 1935 by Charles F. Richter of the California Institute of Technology to compare the size of earthquakes. On the Richter scale, magnitude is expressed in whole numbers and decimal fractions. Because of the logarithmic basis of the scale, each whole-number increase in magnitude represents a tenfold increase in measured energy released.

The city's early history of growth and its susceptibility to earthquakes

Before the discovery of gold in 1848 in the Sierra Nevada Mountains and the gold rush that followed, the area that became San Francisco was an understated Mexican village of Yerba Buena with a few hundred inhabitants. With the discovery, prospectors, builders, store- and saloonkeepers and many others flocked to the area in search of riches. By 1851, the village had become a new city with a population of approximately 30,000, with growth continuing through the nineteenth century. When California was admitted to the Union in 1850, the state's population jumped from 15,000 to nearly 100,000 in less than a decade.

The need to standardize the currency of the new state became paramount since as a territory it had accepted currencies including Mexican reals, Indian rupees, English shillings, French louis, and Dutch guilders. With gold nuggets and dust extracted from the mines in and around San Francisco and valued in the millions, Congress authorized the construction of a mint in San Francisco to turn the region's gold into US coins.

The discovery of the Comstock Silver Lode in Nevada in 1859 catapulted silver into the debate over whether gold, silver, or both would become legal tender. In later years, gold and silver would compete with each other for primacy; this became an emotionally charged political issue in the presidential election of 1896, pitting the Republican William McKinley, who supported the gold standard, against the Democrat William Jennings Bryant, an advocate of silver whose "Cross of Gold" speech rallied his followers. McKinley's victory in that presidential election settled the issue at the time. Although gold, silver, and greenbacks were accepted as legal currency for much of the USA's history; it was not until 1971 that the "gold standard" ended. Under this order from President Richard M. Nixon (1969–75), paper currency was no longer exchangeable for gold.

With large quantities of gold and silver coins minted as legal tender, San Francisco became the country's premier western city with banking, agriculture, and trans-Pacific trade as its principal wealth-creating activities. Earthquakes and fires throughout the early years of the nineteenth century punctured the exuberant growth. Given the region's sparse population before the gold rush of 1849, earthquakes caused little damage or loss of life.

Seismologists believe that a massive earthquake struck Northern California and the Pacific Northwest about 1650. Today, such an event would destroy Seattle, Portland, and San Francisco. In 1838, an earthquake similar to that of 1906 sent shock waves through the sparsely populated Yerba Buena area. On October 8, 1865, entrepreneurial and fast-growing San Francisco experienced an earthquake that would become the harbinger of the "big one" in 1906. Eyewitnesses described it as "powerful and convulsive, with a frightful and roaring sound."[5] In the words of Mark Twain as he walked along Third Street on that Sunday afternoon, San Francisco's City Hall was "dismembered" by the shaking. In 1868, another earthquake east of San Francisco and centered on the Haywood Fault showed the vulnerability of the city's "made land." It turned the ground into a procession of moving waves that reduced structures to rubble.

In the city's weathered and tightly packed wooden buildings, sparks burst into flames and spread as fires. As with its earthquake history, city chroniclers catalogued the presence of fires and gave them a dollar value based upon the damage that they had inflicted on the built environment. There were five major fires, unrelated to earthquakes, during the gold rush period of the 1850s, with one large fire destroying 16 blocks in 1851. In each instance, the city rebuilt and moved on. Discussions about improving and enforcing building codes followed, but with little or no compliance.

The earthquake

The scene that morning at 5:12 a.m. was a familiar one in the country's ninth largest city and the American West's premier city of 410,000 people. Its major form of mechanical inter-urban transportation, the cable car, was brought to life by "an unseen hand in a faraway engine house turn[ing] a crank and thr[owing] a giant lever, and huge drums began to roll; and so began the clanking grind of steel, steel rope, and ever-turning steel wheels that was then, as it is now, one of San Francisco's most haunting and evocative sounds."[6] Accompanied by the smell of oven fires, baking bread, and the like, the city began another day. Then, the earthquake hit.

The seismic magnitude of the quake destroyed poorly constructed buildings and those built on landfill along San Francisco Bay. About 5,000 houses in this zone collapsed immediately as the "made land" liquefied into waves of debris: "The ground seemed to twist under us like a top while it jerked this way and that, and up and down and every way."[7] San Francisco crackled with the sounds of snapping timbers, crashing walls of brick and stone masonry, and the howls and anguished cries of people caught in this quickly disintegrating built environment. Adding to the mayhem were the

Figure 2.1 Horses killed during the San Francisco earthquake by falling bricks. *Source:* L. Tom Perry Special Collections, Harold B. Lee Library, Brigham Young University, Provo, Utah. MSS P 585 #41.

whinnies of hundreds of frightened, disoriented horses. They were responsible for transporting people and goods in the centuries before motorized vehicles. Many ran wildly through the streets, injured by falling wreckage, and were put out of their misery by bullets fired by the police (Figure 2.1). As cattlemen drove their herds to the stockyards, frightened cattle stampeded, becoming entangled in wires and debris. In their panic, they became moving lethal objects when they encountered people who were also trying to escape from the falling debris.

As police officer Edward Plume, who was working at his desk in the City Hall's small police office, described the scene:

> The noise from the outside became deafening. I could hear the massive pillars that upheld the cornices and cupola of the City Hall go cracking with reports like cannon, and then falling with crashes like thunder. Huge stone and lumps of masonry came crashing down outside our doors; the large

> chandeliers swung to and fro, and then fell from the ceiling with a bang. In an instant the room was full of dust as well as soot and smoke from the fireplace. It seemed to be reeling like the cabin of a ship in a gale. Feeling sure that the building could never survive such shocks, and expecting every moment to be buried under a mass of ruins, I shouted to Officer Dwyer to get out. The lights were then out and all was in darkness.[8]

In the era of pre-earthquake resistant buildings, loosely enforced building codes resulted in construction that the US Geological Survey described in the 1906 event as "flimsy and loosely built structures [that] collapsed like houses of cards under the terrific wrenching and shaking, and many of the structures which withstood the earthquake were subjected to a second test in a fire which surpassed all the great conflagrations of recent years."[9] Unreinforced brick buildings and unlined tall chimneys that were old and in poor repair rained down on those in adjacent buildings and on the alleys and streets below.

Cement construction with reinforced steel bars (rebars) used in many eastern cities had not yet reached cities in western USA. As a result, churches, hotels, stores, government buildings, gambling halls, saloons, jails, rooming houses, mansions, and museums shared a common fate during the earthquake and its aftershocks. They became in some instances thousands of tons of unrecognizable rubble of brick, masonry, and twisted iron. The worst was yet to come, however.

The fire

The first of many fires to envelop and destroy San Francisco occurred at 5:30 a.m., less than one half hour after the quake. Falling electrical wires and exploding natural gas lines that both illuminated the city after dark and provided cooking fuel for many of the city's households turned about 50 local fires into uncontrollable conflagrations. These localized fires overwhelmed the city's six hundred firefighters. Severed power lines disrupted telephone communication and disabled the city's fire alarm system. Police and firefighters communicated by message, either on foot, by horseback, or with that newly available motorized vehicle, the automobile. This chaotic system left all involved vulnerable to fast-moving and unpredictable fires.

Adding to their dismay was the knowledge that the earthquake had fractured much of San Francisco's system of water pipes. With little or no water, a jerry-built method of communication and an overworked fire department made their task nearly impossible. The absence of an experienced leader in Fire Chief Dennis Sullivan was exacerbated by the lack of manpower and the breakdown in communications. He lived with his wife in a third-floor apartment above Fire Engine Company No. 3. Brick and masonry from the collapsing five-story California Hotel crashed into their apartment. Although the chief's wife survived, he sustained life-threatening injuries and died four days later.

The cry of "no water" resonated throughout the city from Wednesday to Saturday. Although the earthquake had not disrupted the three main reservoirs outside of the city, its 3,000 distribution mains carrying water through 22,300 connecting pipes from the city's nine distributing reservoirs and tanks cracked, disrupting the water's flow. Many of these pipes broke because they crossed soft and made land. When city officials decided to use explosives to create the firebreaks needed to stop the spreading fires, they inadvertently destroyed a number of water pipes.[10] Using gunpowder rather than dynamite as a fire suppressant by the military magnified the dangers. Its use ignited more fires, causing them to combine and spread. Blowing up buildings without knowledge of their flammable contents, including chemicals and alcohol, added to the misery.

This decision turned a natural disaster into a human tragedy. Ironically, in the earthquake's aftermath, the city's boosters tried to diminish the role of the earthquake and elevate the fires to a position of prominence. Fires could easily be explained away as common occurrences facing all major cities, but earthquakes were another matter. They came without warning, they disabled a city's infrastructure quickly, and they destroyed lives and property swiftly. They proved unmistakably that San Francisco's businesses and commercial enterprises lived on a razor's edge in earthquake-prone geological zones. Fires, on the other hand, may have begun without warning and spread quickly but ultimately they either burned out or were managed and contained by firefighters. The boosters' narrative was that fires, which lasted for days, and not the earthquake, which lasted for a minute, destroyed much of the city. This orchestrated narrative, that appeared in the city's promotional literature, was intended to assure investors that San Francisco was not a disaster-prone location. San Francisco's 1915 Panama Pacific International Exposition, the city's first World's Fair, would be proof that the city was not only back on its feet but had entered a new and glorious stage in its history.

Relief efforts

The fires spread rapidly, aided by human error, the initial indecisiveness of city government, and a military decision to deny citizens a role in protecting their city. Headquartered in the city, Brigadier General Frederick Funston, commander of the US Army's Pacific command, filled the power vacuum. He concluded correctly that city officials would be preoccupied with providing relief medical and evacuation services to residents traumatized by the events of the day. With hundreds of soldiers under his command and with the advice and consent of San Francisco's mayor, Eugene Schmitz, he immediately took control of policing and firefighting functions. He ignored the availability of the city's police and fire departments. Without declaring martial law, which only the Californian governor or the president could do, he cordoned off fire-stricken areas with the purpose of keeping onlookers away. He secured the US Mint that held millions in currency and gold bullion and he issued "shoot to kill" orders regarding looters. Closing saloons, banning the use of unguarded candles, and suspending gas and electrical services were among his more benign executive orders.

Funston appealed successfully to the Secretary of War, William Howard Taft, for aid from the federal government. With authorization from President Theodore Roosevelt, the government engaged in its largest relief effort to date. Within a few days, a number of army bases dispatched equipment, including tents and medicine, while 200,000 rations were sent from barracks in Washington State. "Before long every single tent in the military's possession was in San Francisco, and the largest hospital train ever made was sent out from Virginia. A few weeks later fully 10% of the standing army was there as well as an enormous commitment of men and materiel, and an immense expenditure of federal funds."[11] Although attitudes had been changing about the role of the federal government from laissez-faire to intervention, the decision to intervene and provide aid to a disaster-stricken area represented a new role for government. With Theodore Roosevelt's leadership, Congress unanimously voted to donate $2,500,000 in disaster relief.

Fighting urban fires in the early years of the twentieth century lacked a defined scientific basis. Aside from the use of water cannons, hand-driven pumping devices, horse-drawn fire wagons, and the creation of firebreaks, professional fire-fighting remained a labor intensive and dangerous occupation. Lastly, denying citizens who had successfully fought fires with buckets of water, shovels, and wet gunnysacks an opportunity to join the battle prevented energized populations from contributing to the fight and eliminated large numbers of stakeholders in the city's survival. As one angry citizen stated, "The stories have but one beginning and one end. They begin with the criminal idiocy of the military; they end with the surmounting heroism of the citizen."[12]

The government employees working at the Post Office and the US Mint and those working for private companies took matters into their own hands. They saved their jobs and their buildings by fighting the fires with wet sacks and by pulling down buildings and removing the debris away from the advancing flames. "[An] improvised bucket brigade, working in the face of almost insufferable heat, saved their own valley from imminent destruction, and thus probably saved the greater part of San Francisco that survived the fire."[13]

The behavior of surviving citizens during and after the earthquake and fire was praiseworthy. They fed and cared for neighbors in the immediate aftermath of the disaster before government and non-profit relief agencies moved in to build tent communities, provide medical attention, and distribute rations. Their behavior became symbolic of a "civic temperament." City government provided these temporary communities with fresh water for cooking and bathing as well as makeshift sewers and drains.

Rebuilding

Many thousands of survivors left the city on trains provided by the Southern Pacific Railroad and by ferry. Many never returned. The city's population recovered quickly, however, as the number of registered residents reached 375,000 by July 1906.[14] It took only three years to complete the construction of a "new" San Francisco with 20,000 new buildings – only 1,700 of which adhered to the building codes of May 1906. The city's Real Estate Board replaced the phrase "the great earthquake" with "the great fire," implying that building codes would not only deter investments but also slow the rebuilding process. More than 8,000 "refugee houses" replaced the tents pitched immediately after the earthquake. They were wooden barracks to house multiple poor and working-class families, and remained in use for years after the disaster.

For the propertied classes and elites, loans and subsidies became available to relocate and rebuild by the summer of 1906. Both American and foreign insurance and reinsurance companies processed claims totaling

$250,000,000, with disputes over coverage for the earthquake or the fires being settled by litigation. About 80% of the claims were paid for fire damage with many insurers going bankrupt in the process. These banking policies drove the poor and working classes away from the downtown's prime real estate to the outer fringes of the city, creating a more socially segregated San Francisco.[15]

With the city in ruins, government officials and real estate developers saw this calamity as an opportunity to move the city's Chinatown from a prime location downtown to Hunter's Point, an undesirable location on a peninsula southeast of the city. Their efforts received a setback when China's Dowager Empress, Cixi, expressed her intention to rebuild the headquarters of her government's legation on China's property on Stockton Street. Her government also warned that a forced removal of Chinese would damage US/Chinese relationships and bring into question the continuation of friendly trade relations, a relationship that American commercial interests valued highly.

Although San Francisco's government rejected plans to transform the city with wider thoroughfares and open spaces, by 1911 the central business district had expanded, with finance, commercial activity, and hotels dominating the built environment. Manufacturing never recovered from the effects of the earthquake. By 1911, 100,000 fewer people lived within 3 mi^2 (7.8 km^2) of the central business district. The opening of the Panama Canal in 1909 and the celebration of San Francisco's recovery with its World's Fair in 1915 marked a new beginning for the city. The memory of the 1906 catastrophe faded into the background. With no memorial to honor the dead and remind future generations of this greatest of early twentieth-century American disasters, San Franciscans moved on without making preparations for an unpredictable future.

Conclusion

As noted earlier, city boosters and investors tried valiantly to manage the news about the city's catastrophe, describing it in news releases and promotional literature as the "Great San Francisco fire," not the "Great San Francisco earthquake." They cited daunting evidence to support their labeling. From the morning of April 18 to the morning of April 21, the fire destroyed 28,000 buildings. It destroyed City Hall, the city's largest building, the entire business district, all of the city's theaters and hotels, and more than half of all residences. Boosters attempted to minimize the number of deaths at 478 but research by a former city archivist, Gladys Hansen of the San Francisco public library in the 1990s, puts the figure at more than 3,000.[16]

The Great Kanto Earthquake (1923)

> "I had scarcely returned to my desk when, without warning, came the first rumbling jar of an earthquake, a sickening sway, the vicious grinding of timbers and, in a few seconds, a crescendo of turmoil as the floor began to heave and the building to lurch drunkenly. The ground could scarcely be said to shake; it heaved, tossed and leaped under one. The walls bulged as if made of cardboard and the din became awful. Slabs of plaster left the ceilings and fell about our ears, filling the air with a blinding, smothering fog of dust. How long it lasted, I don't know. It seemed an eternity; but the official record says four minutes. (Otis Manchester Poole, General Manager of Dodwell & Co. in Yokohama)[17]

Introduction

In the decade before the Great Kanto earthquake, Japan's conservative bureaucratic government faced an increasing number of strikes and disputes by laborers over hours, working conditions, and wages. A growing urban middle class demanded universal male suffrage while university students and faculty lobbied for shared governance and the liberalization of academic policy. All argued for an end to top-down decision-making and the replacement of bureaucratic control with freely elected political parties. Government officials who were reminded of the 1918 Rice Riots that disrupted the orderly functioning of Japanese society reacted to such protestations warily.

A decade of political activism was accompanied with social changes that bureaucratic elites found distressing. An urban middle class embraced the Western values of mass consumption of goods and entertainment. These materialistic and individualistic trends troubled Japan's elites. Social commentators wrote and spoke publicly about a withering away of traditional values of loyalty to the Emperor that included filial piety, benevolence and charity, sacrifice, courage and bravery, and obedience.[18]

As a result, this greatest of natural disasters in Japanese history provided an opportunity to deal with the immediate crisis and to re-commit the population to traditional Japanese values. Defining the task before them as the equivalent of fighting and winning a war, the government responded swiftly on both fronts – immediate relief to a hungry, thirsty, and destitute population and the reinvigoration of traditional Japanese values. This meant a retreat from Western influences of consumption and individualism. As one economist noted at the time: "I have only read about the European war [World War I] and never had the opportunity to witness the horrible situation of it, but I can imagine that the horrendous sights in Yokohama and Tokyo must be exactly what it was like in the European cities after the war."[19]

This background provides the context for Japan's 1923 earthquake. As an island country, its location along the "Ring of Fire" describes its vulnerability to earthquakes. The Ring extends in an arc from the coastal regions of the Pacific Ocean from Chile, the USA, Canada, and across the ocean to Japan and Indonesia. It links all these countries in an unpredictable dance with nature. The Pacific and Philippine Sea tectonic plates and the continental plate of Eurasia move constantly, creating stress and strain, and keeping Japan in a constant state of instability. The awareness of this linkage was not lost upon Japanese seismologists and architects, who visited post-disaster San Francisco in 1906. They came to assess the damage, examine the debris field, and strategize about ways to prevent a similar disaster from devastating Japan. With 10% of the world's seismic energy released annually under Japan, the phrase "earthquake nation" is a poignant one.[20] Because repeated tremors and devastating earthquakes hit Tōhoku in 2011, Niigata in 2004, Kobe in 1995, Fukui in 1948, Tokyo in 1923, Nobi in 1891, Edo in 1855 and 1703, and Hizen in 1792, the country has been aptly described as "earthquake nation."[21]

According to Japanese seismologist Fusakichi Omori, as many as 222 destructive earthquakes struck Japan from the fifth to the twentieth century. Given its history of earthquakes, Japanese inspection of damage to San Francisco's buildings suggested that steel framing, a recent invention in building technology, was vulnerable to seismic waves whereas buildings constructed of ferro-concrete, meaning concrete poured around a configuration of rebars, was more earthquake-resistant.[22] The Nobi earthquake of October 28, 1891 located on the Nobi Plain just north of Nagoya, had sent seismic waves across the main island of Honshu from Tokyo to Osaka, killing between 7,000 and 8,000 people, collapsing iron bridges and brick buildings designed in the traditional manner by architects and constructed by Japanese engineers trained in Western modes of construction.

The period from 1920 to 1923 were years of unusual seismic activity in Tokyo that inspired controversy rather than cooperation and preparedness. The earthquake of December 8, 1921, Tokyo's strongest since 1891, disrupted the city's water supply with the destruction of a vital conduit. The stronger April 26, 1922 earthquake cut phone service, damaged buildings, and destroyed a railroad line into the city. A minor quake occurred on January 14, 1923. In hindsight, these three were harbingers of the Great Kanto earthquake that struck at 11:58 a.m. on Saturday, September 1, 1923.

The earthquake

One group of the country's architects and seismologists had disputed the idea that these early earthquakes represented anything but the norm in Japanese seismology. Others, led by Imamura Akitsune, an assistant professor of seismology at Tokyo Imperial University, argued that the absence of seismic records for Sagami Bay south of Tokyo with its major north–south fault created a serious gap in the predictions of his opponents. He argued that the opposition's position was false in claiming that nothing out of the ordinary could be deduced from prior seismic events. They argued that the fault that lay beneath the water made mapping its seismic activity difficult, if not impossible.[23]

The imperial capital Tokyo and the primary commercial port city of Yokohama, with an estimated combined population of 3.7 million people, were reduced to rubble within a week after the magnitude 8.3 earthquake. More than 200 aftershocks followed in the Tokyo/Yokohama area from Sagami Bay on the first day. The next day, September 2, over 300 more shocks were recorded, with one major shock at 11:47 a.m. From September 3–5, an additional 300 aftershocks rocked Tokyo and Yokohama. The quake, fires, and aftershocks destroyed over 48% of homes (397,119 out of a total of 829,900) in Tokyo prefecture and over 90% in Yokohama. More than 694,000 houses were either completely destroyed or left standing but uninhabitable. Both cities were built on mostly alluvium or soft river soil deposits, adding to the region's vulnerability to seismic activity.

The disaster left 2.5 million people homeless. Estimates of the dead ranged from 120,000 to 140,000 persons, with more than 40,000 perishing in Yokohama alone. As the worst catastrophe in Japanese history, the estimates exceeded the 118,000 Japanese soldiers killed in the Russo-Japanese War (1904–05). But worse was to come. Broken gas lines, charcoal braziers lit in preparation for the midday meal, and explosions in industries producing chemicals and other flammable materials started more than 130 major fires. Most broke out within one half-hour of the first tremor in Tokyo's most congested low-lying districts built on made land. The population on higher grounds, away from the coastal areas, fared better.[24]

A unique feature of this earthquake was the upheaval of the ground, which rose about 24 ft (7.3 m) at Misaki and reshaped the shoreline. Six mi (9.6 km) below Sagami Bay, the Philippine Sea tectonic plate descended at a 45° angle toward Earth's fiery mantle, forcing up the Eurasian plate and releasing a fury of destructive energy.[25] The uplift lasted for six days before it began to subside by as much as 2 ft (0.61 m) each day. When it finally settled, a 5-ft offset remained, causing landslides that buried some towns and damaged others. Days later, the Japan's Fishery Institute and its Naval Hydrological Department surveyed the sea floor at some 600 to 800 fathoms (1,100–1,500 m) and verified that two earthquakes had erupted in Sagami Bay, one east of Hatsushima Island and the other to the north of Oshima Island. Their investigation noted that new ocean ridges, ranging in height from 180–300 ft (55–90 m) were caused by the collapse and uplift into a rift. These new ridges remained after the earthquake and extended for hundreds of miles in a south-southeasterly direction along the "ring of fire."

Swirling winds and burning wooden buildings caused urban fires in both cities to spread rapidly. The fires consumed residents, carrying their household furnishings, desperately trying to escape the inferno. Thousands of burned automobiles and hundreds of gasoline filling stations added to the debris field. Tokyo's inter-urban tramway system lost 2,000 cars, while the imperial railways lost 33 locomotives, 500 passenger cars, and 800 freight cars. The telephone service came close to disappearing in Tokyo with the burning of 60,000 out of 80,000 phones. In Yokohama, no phones survived. The calamity destroyed or crippled essential services, including oil and coal depots, merchandise warehouses, and docks. Public buildings suffered similarly, with the destruction of schools, universities, hospitals, museums, and most government offices that provided essential services, including holding vital records.[26]

About 7,000 factories that included four major textile and spinning factories, 264 dyeing factories, 148 that produced ceramics, 445 tool manufacturers, 1,438 flour mills and many others were destroyed by the earthquake and fires. As many as 45% of the working population became unemployed instantly. Adding to the misery of the population was the loss of household money, money in central banks and in branch offices. Of 138 central bank offices, only 17 remained, while of the 310 local branch banks,

98 remained functional. Death, injury, loss of housing, money, and massive unemployment quickly turned this natural disaster into a human catastrophe.[27]

Survivors described the scene and its impact on the Japanese population. For those who wrote about its impact, they believed that "[It] overturned Japan's culture from its very foundations." "[It was] a watershed between prosperity and decline of a nation." And for the many thousands of survivors who described the chaos of the earthquake, the aftershocks and fires, the following is a sample of their remembrances.

> The large house started to swing back and forth and make eerie noises. Then, while the shaking continued, the low rumble of the dwelling gave way to the almost deafening sound of roof tiles falling and shattering, light globes smashing, and whole walls collapsing in on themselves. Roof tiles, rush mats, corrugated iron sheets, and everything began to fall on top of us like a rain of stones. Soon after an enormous wall of fire like a tidal wave as if released from hell itself turned the air as hot as melting rock and ignited everything in its path including scores of trapped people.[28]

Six days after the earthquake and the inferno that it created, one chronicler wrote the following as he crossed the Ryogoku Bridge in Tokyo: "Swollen bodies with discarded belongings littered the water below bobbing in the waves. The air was heavy with the stench of the same being cremated on hastily built funeral pyres." In addition, he passed bodies "stacked just like piles of fish that fishermen would make on shore before fish brokers came to buy them." Another wrote, "The reality of the destruction is beyond our imagination. There is nothing left among the ruins. Everything has been burned completely. All that remains is twisted steel, stone, and bricks." Another recalled, "What I saw with my eyes was more devastating than what I had heard in rumors. The busy streets of the once prosperous city had been burned to the ground in a second" (Figure 2.2).[29]

Relief efforts

Approaching the disaster as an event equivalent to preparing and then recovering from a war and by casting the tragedy in these terms allowed the government to mobilize the country in ways similar to those used during the first Sino-Japanese War (1895–96) and the Russo-Japanese War (1904–05). First, the task of restoring order to a frightened, suspicious, and vengeful population became a primary goal. Mobs of vigilantes believed

Figure 2.2 Death and destruction caused by the Great Kanto earthquake.
Source: John Hay Library, Brown University Library, MS. 2011.015, Box 1.

that the minority population of Koreans living and working in menial occupations was in some way responsible for the outbreak of fires throughout the city. They used this propaganda to create further chaos, attacking and killing thousands of Korean immigrants. It seems preposterous now, but then it led to the posting of bills that claimed, "3,000 Koreans are looting and destroying Yokohama and coming toward the capital."[30]

A conservative estimate of the value of property destroyed by the earthquake and fires and calculated in 1923 dollars was placed at $4,586,000,000. Assuming that 50% of the private property lost, including houses and goods, was insured, the value of the loss was placed at $3,286,000,000. The total destruction of the Yokohama Naval Station was about $300,000,000, with other government losses costing more than one billion dollars. None of these calculations include the loss of life, life-threatening physical injuries, or emotional suffering, all of which led to countless lost hours of economic productivity.[31]

The earthquake and the consequent outbreak of hundreds of fires overwhelmed Tokyo's local government and its metropolitan police. Without consulting the city's mayor or anyone else in city government, Tokyo's police chief appealed to the central government for support from the army. On September 2, the government initiated the country's largest peacetime mobilization and declared martial law. It commanded troops from infantry and engineering battalions to restore order. In addition to anarchy and bands of vigilantes, the chaos was accentuated by the absence of information about the extent of the damage to the city. Information was missing about the number of casualties both dead and trapped in collapsed buildings. No one knew about the status of the built environment, which included its hospitals, the infrastructure of roads, bridges, water pipes and conduits, and the communication systems.

By mid-September, the government had deployed more than 52,000 troops in Tokyo and Yokohama. "In virtually every way, Tokyo not only resembled a city heavily damaged by war, it was an urban landscape under military occupation. Not surprisingly, in the weeks and months after 1 September, many individuals throughout Japan came to view this calamity as Japan's first national tragedy and a test of national character every bit as challenging as a war."[32] Descriptions of the disaster were disseminated in newspapers that also contained photographs of the dead and collapsed buildings. The reporting and the visual representations reminded readers of scenes from a battlefield and of a nation at war. To overcome this adversity everyone was reminded that recovery would require a national commitment to selfless sacrifice.

Japan's prime minister, Yamamoto Gonnohyoe, and his cabinet created an Emergency Relief Bureau with leaders drawn from municipal and military officers to decide on the priorities for relief ranging from food and shelter to medical assistance and donations. Much of this assistance continued into 1924 with food, water, shelter, and medical care becoming top priorities. The USA and France provided tents, while donations of tangibles including money flowed in from around the world. Only a few years before, the world's population would have waited weeks, if not months, to hear the details of the calamity and responded. By 1923, governments and private companies had invested in powerful wireless transmitters that sent clear signals halfway around the world. The age of global telecommunications had commenced.

Rebuilding

Naval units had to wait for repairs to be made to the infrastructure before much of the food and water could be distributed and temporary shelters built. Military personnel did much of the work. Naval units built and repaired 86 docks for unloading supplies while army regiments disposed of 3,000 damaged rail cars and repaired 52 mi (84 km) of track by October 10. The distribution of food and potable water, much of it from Japanese cities and farms spared from the disaster waited until army and navy personnel completed many of these repairs. Once finished, distribution became a national effort, similar to the effort that would be required in wartime. Over 2.5 million homeless people needed sustenance and shelter. The task was enormous but between September 16–21, 2,097,170 people received about 15.8 oz (450 grams) of rice. Once canned food began to arrive from other countries, more varieties of food became available to distribute in October.[33]

To insure that the generosity of the Japanese people was not borne by the few, on September 2 the Yamamoto cabinet issued Imperial Ordinance No. 396, titled 'Emergency Requisition Ordinance' for food, medical care, and vehicles. It required citizens to comply with requests and receive compensation based on average market prices calculated over a three-month period. Failure to do so could result in imprisonment for up to three years and a fine of up to 3,000 yen.[34] Once again, the central government appealed to the people in terms of national self-sacrifice, reminding them that although the earthquake represented a moment in time, it was a defining moment for the nation. As such, it would require a national mobilization and a commitment from every Japanese citizen to engage in a sustained and long-term period of relief, recovery, and reconstruction.

Invoking the image of a wartime effort of renewal, November 11, 1923 became the Day of Remembrance in Japan and it was no coincidence that the government chose this date, since it also commemorated the armistice that ended World War I. The Tokyo Earthquake Memorial Hall at Yakama Park, Hondo holds the ashes of its victims. That the victims of the fire bombings of Tokyo by Allied forces in World War II are placed next to the 1923 dead are a reminder that the Japanese people view both as wartime casualties.[35]

Conclusion

The decade of reform (1913–23) before the Great Kanto earthquake included a parliamentary system of government with civilian cabinets and more inclusive election laws. It also encouraged changes in the consumption patterns of an emerging urban middle class. Control by Japan's elites weakened during this decade, but was not eliminated. The calamity unleashed a wave of ethnic violence against Korean workers, as mentioned above, and elevated the status of the country's military during this period of national reconstruction. Elites and the military preached values of obedience to its divine right Emperor, Hirohito, and sacrifice for the nation. Within a few years after the disaster, liberalization initiatives ended with the arrest and murder of members of Japan's Communist Party, legalized in 1923 before the earthquake.

Emboldened, military influence within the government came to guide the nation's foreign policy, first resulting in an invasion of a weak China in 1931 and in establishing a puppet regime in Manchuria. Opposition by Japan's prime minister to these military adventures resulted in his assassination by young army officers. Although the role of the Great Kanto earthquake in awakening Japan's militarism remains a hypothesis, the year 1923 and the calamity that occurred resulted in a national initiative to reject Western consumer values and return to the vigorous life of self-sacrifice and physical preparedness advocated by Japanese social commentators and reinforced by the country's military.[36]

The Haitian Earthquake (2010)

> I saw a lot of people crying for help, a lot of buildings collapsed, a lot of car damage, a lot of people without help, people bleeding. I saw a movie theater, a supermarket, a cybercafé, an apartment building, which collapsed. There is no electricity; all the phone networks are down, so there's no way that people can get in touch with their family and friends. There are aftershocks every 15 to 20 minutes. They last from three to five seconds. The first shock was really strong; people were falling in the streets and buildings collapsed. (Carel Pedre, a Haitian radio DJ)[37]

Introduction

Earthquakes in the Caribbean are not uncommon, but ones that strike the island of Hispaniola (which Haiti shares with the Dominican Republic) arrive more frequently. Between 1618 and 1860 seven large quakes hit Haiti, with the one in 1860 centered in the capital seaport city of Port-au-Prince. It probably caused a tsunami. The largest earthquake (8.1 magnitude) in the twentieth century to strike the Dominican Republic occurred in 1946 killing approximately 1,790 people. However, the Haitian (magnitude 7) earthquake of 2010 dwarfs all others on Hispaniola in terms of death and destruction. It killed approximately 46,000 to 85,000 people (the lack of an accurate national census made it impossible to find out the real number of dead) and left more than one million homeless. Buildings destroyed numbered in the hundreds of thousands. The government lost one-third of its workers and most of its buildings, bringing government services to a halt. In a country of 8.1 million, 2.5–3 million of whom live in Port-au-Prince, as of 2012 many hundreds of thousands of Haitians were still living in tents distributed after the disaster.[38]

Hispaniola's geology

Why do earthquakes strike Hispaniola and, more specifically, Haiti? Plate tectonics with their unpredictable movement, many miles below Earth's surface, provide the answer. "Haiti lies squarely on the Gonave microplate, a thin sliver of the Earth's crust about six mi (9.6 km) below Earth's surface between the much larger North American plate to the north and the Caribbean plate to the south."[39] As the North American and Caribbean tectonic plates grind against each other in an east–west direction, they compress this thin sliver of crust. It extends about 100 mi (160 km) from the Dominican Republic through Haiti's western peninsula along the sea floor and into Jamaica, making this entire Caribbean region highly vulnerable to seismic activity (Figure 2.3).[40]

A 25-mile-long (40 km) rupture along this microplate caused the earthquake. Purdue University geophysicist Eric Calais, who has spent years studying the faults of Hispaniola, concluded that the region contains two parallel plate boundaries. "That is quite unusual and a wake-up call to me to try and understand this system,"[41] given the density of the island's population and the tourism business in the region. The depth and size of the faults varies according to the geology of the region, with the thin Gonave microplate closer to the surface than many others. Plates and faults with these characteristics cause Earth's surface to shake more violently than those deeper in the Earth's mantle. Until the 2010 quake, a section of the geological fault that ruptured near Port-au-Prince had been "locked" since 1751 when the last major quake struck this location. With a much smaller population then, casualties were much fewer. The location of this fault explains why the shaking described to the UN by Susan Westwood, a Scottish nurse working at an orphanage just outside Port-au-Prince, is representative of the shaking throughout the city.

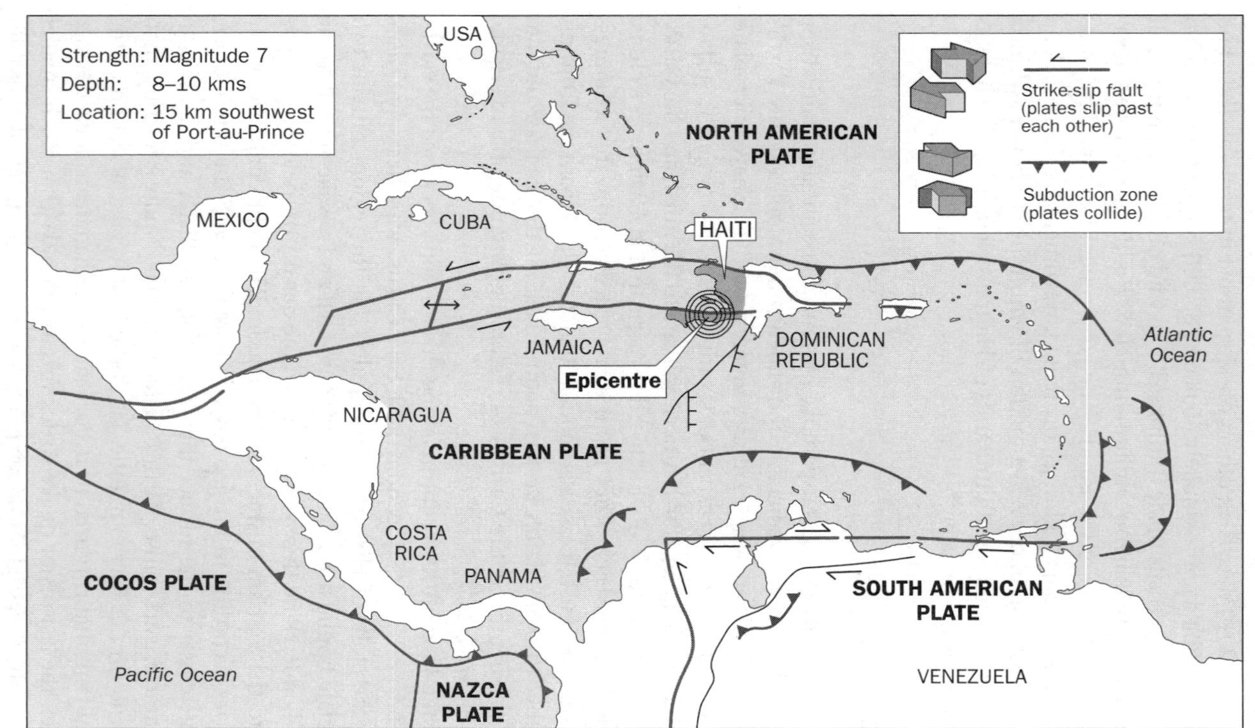

Figure 2.3 Haiti's vulnerability on the Caribbean tectonic plates.
Source: US Geological Survey.

> I was in the intensive care room looking after a nine-month-old baby girl when the earthquake hit. The floor started shaking violently and the whole building shook from side to side. It lasted about 45 seconds. After that there was a constant shuddering. The babies were really frightened and started to cry. Other staff and carers were screaming, they were so terrified . . . I couldn't stand upright so I dropped to my knees. I was able to keep hold of a baby girl and I grabbed hold of another baby. Objects were falling from shelves, there was debris crashing all around. I clung on to the babies and shielded them as best I could. Then came the aftershocks. It was impossible to even move. After a while we managed to take all the children out on to the driveway. We spent the whole night outside. It was chilly but we were OK. Some children are dehydrated now though because we couldn't get any medical supplies out of the building. There were eight aftershocks during the night, and we woke up every time. My children are terrified. Everyone is terrified.[42]

Haiti's history

Liberated from the yoke of French colonialism in 1804, Haiti became a republic with the promise that a resourceful and disciplined citizenry would build a successful democracy. The revolution destroyed the centralized slave plantation system. Replacing it was a thriving decentralized economy of small-plot sustainable agriculture known as inter-cropping, developed and maintained by former slaves. Inter-cropping involved planting crops close together including fruits, root vegetables, and coffee, the latter for a growing global market. This agricultural system of self-reliant farmers thrived in the nineteenth century. Immigrants including African-Americans flocked to the country to participate in this economic success.

However, the demand by the French government that Haiti pay reparations for its loss of property (slaves) and land (sugar and coffee plantations) drove the country into an abyss, stifling agricultural initiatives and economic development. A successful revolution against a colonial power would seem to negate the demand for such payments but that was not the case for Haiti. In contrast, at the end of the American Revolution (1775–83), the new government of the USA received $1,000,000 (reparation for previously captured US ships) from the UK in November 1794 as part of the Jay Treaty.

Political, social, and cultural transformations began with the overthrow of Louis XVI on July 14, 1789, a date signaling the beginning of the French Revolution. This period proved to be one of tumult with a revolution including a "reign of terror" within France, followed by the Napoleonic Wars in Europe, Napoleon's defeat in Czarist Russia (1812), and finally his arrest and deportation.

With the end of the Napoleonic Wars (1799–1815) and the end of its empire, France restored the Bourbon monarchy (1815–30), a constitutional regime. Unlike previous Bourbon kings who ruled France as absolute monarchs, the restoration required the participation of elected citizens. It was within this context of upheaval that a revolt erupted against the colonial government by Haiti's wealthy free men of color in May 1791. France's Revolutionary Convention in Paris, under the leadership of Maximilien Robespierre, who wanted to abolish slavery throughout the colonies, had granted them citizenship.

Plantation owners refused to obey this law, triggering an initial revolt among free men of color but which spread rapidly to slaves and plunged St. Domingue (France's name for the island) into open revolt on August 21, 1791. Within a week, slaves had taken control of the island's northern province and, with their numbers growing to 100,000, they plundered and destroyed hundreds of sugar, coffee, and indigo plantations. Since much of Europe had become addicted to the stimulants of sugar and coffee, the rebellion had a transatlantic economic and social impact.

Thirteen years later in 1804, French control over St. Domingue ended and independence was declared on January 1. The USA and Haiti became the only republics in the Americas. But unlike the USA, Haiti consisted of struggling masses in a country devastated by war. None of the great powers gave this new all-black republic diplomatic recognition, including the USA, where the power of its slave-owners dominated political discourse. Although a defeated France left the island, it wanted reparations as a condition of recognition. Payment would remain a yoke that strangled the Haitian economy and prevented the citizenry from rising socially.

With recognition granted in April 1825, King Charles X sent a squadron of 12 warships with 250 cannons to Haitian waters on July 3 to claim 150 million gold francs as repayment. France based this amount on the annual profits that plantation owners made selling sugar, coffee, indigo, cotton, and other commodities on the international market. The profits from these sales averaged 15 million gold francs a year, so after ten years this would total 150 million gold francs, the amount demanded by Charles X. The USA supported these French claims.

The arrival of France's warships posed a real threat to Haiti's independence since a failure to repay would result in a French takeover and the re-enslavement of the country. Reparations of this size amounted to ten times Haiti's annual revenues. In addition to the 150 million franc payment, France weakened Haiti's economy by imposing a 50% discount rate on all commercial goods entering and leaving Haiti.

With no means of paying such a large ransom, the Haitian government had no choice but to borrow 30 million francs from a French bank to pay the first installment on the indemnity. Once the bank had deducted its management fees from the face value of the loan and charged excessively high interest rates, Haiti was still 6 million francs short. "One study estimates the indemnity was 55 million more francs than was needed to restore the 793 sugar plantations, 3,117 coffee estates and 3,906 indigo, cotton and other crop plantations destroyed during the war for independence."[43]

Although France reduced the indemnity to 90 million francs in 1838, the debt ($21 billion in today's terms) made the country's escape from poverty nearly impossible. The final annual payment was not made until 1947! Debts paid to the French and to other foreign creditors in the twentieth century, such as the International Monetary Fund (IMF) and the World Bank, sapped Haitians of the financial resources needed to build a more livable society. In debt service alone, the interest payments and the management fees, Haiti spent millions each year. At its peak, the nation was paying 80% of its national budget to foreign creditors. Political instability thrived in a country struggling to escape the shackles of a punitive and retaliatory foreign power supported by its allies.

A long history of the brutal dictators followed, culminating in the second half of the twentieth century with the election of Francois Duvalier (1957–71). Upon his death his son Jean-Claude ruled from 1971–86, continuing his father's policy of state terrorism using its private army of killers known as the *Tonton Macoute* from 1957 to 1986. Military intervention by the USA that began in 1915 and was repeated for decades up to 1994 also contributed to the country's instability. All of the above crippled a country that was a once-wealthy colony. When the 2010 earthquake hit, it struck a weakened country of 8.1 million people, who survived on an average annual per capita income of $480.

Relief efforts

Aftershocks occurred frequently, causing further destruction and creating panic among a frightened and demoralized public. Months after the earthquake, its people suffered further from a series of intense storms that flooded whole towns, knocked out bridges, and made roads impassible. With one out of two buildings having collapsed in the capital, 447 *ad hoc* tent communities sprang up within days after the quake.

Haitians filled public parks, parking lots, and grassy fields, all spaces away from collapsed or weakened buildings. On government land near the suburb of Croix des Bouquets, 5000 Brazilian troops, flying the United Nations (UN) flag, began to level the ground to build a tent city for 30,000 people. Other sites in preparation were expected to provide temporary housing for another 100,000.[44]

Within 22 hours, the International Medical Corps, a relief organization that enters countries ravaged by war, disease, and natural disasters, began to deliver medical services to an injured and weakened population. Its first fixed base of operations opened at the damaged University Hospital in Port-au-Prince. In addition to its primary location in Port-au-Prince, it operated 15 mobile and fixed medical units in five locations hit hard by the quake. Three days after the earthquake, doctors and nurses were treating 1000 Haitians daily. Staffed primarily by volunteers, they provided round-the-clock coverage in the emergency room, pediatrics, and post-operative care. Although emergency assistance remained a critical component of its services, building a sustainable healthcare delivery system by training local healthcare workers about nutrition, maternal and child health, hygiene, sanitation, and communicable diseases became a vital aspect of its mandate.

Within 72 hours, 200 medical professionals from a number of other international search and rescue (SAR) teams had landed at the damaged Port-au-Prince airport. National field hospitals, equipped with sophisticated medical machinery and highly trained personnel, came from Israel, Germany, Belgium, Cuba, Venezuela, and Russia at the request of a dazed Haitian government. Israel provided surgical services to patients, beginning on January 16 and lasting for months. By the end of the first week, the USA's presence was visible with 17 ships, 48 helicopters, 12 fixed-wing aircraft, and about 10,000 sailors and Marines.

Church groups and unaffiliated individuals and small groups poured into Haiti in the immediate aftermath of the quake. Other volunteers came from Boston, London, and Sydney. With more than 300,000 injured Haitians, any number of volunteers seemed inadequate to the task of treating, rehabilitating, and placing the injured on the road to recovery. In addition to this international response, Haitians rescued the largest number of its citizens trapped in collapsed buildings and under earthquake rubble. They provided emergency first aid, carrying victims to aid stations on improvised stretchers, establishing shelters for children and adults, and pooling clean water and supplies. They took care of each other in the immediate aftermath of the quake and continued to do so once the international community had responded to the crisis.

With medical infrastructure in a state of collapse and a large number of healthcare workers either injured or dead, reconstruction and the education of new medical personnel became vital activities. As Dina Prior, head of the International Medical Corps (IMC)'s Emergency Response Team in Haiti, reported, "We are encouraged that critical lifesaving relief is reaching many of those who need it most. However, with the first heavy rains beginning since the earthquake occurred, we are extremely concerned about the hundreds of thousands living outside and in tent cities whose health will be severely compromised. Many still face little or no access to sanitation services and clean water."[45] Within a few months, hundreds of IMC doctors and nurses poured in from the USA working 14-day shifts to provide emergency medical services. Six months later, their focus changed from emergency care to concentrate on primary healthcare support.

Students from the University of Miami, there to assist in establishing community centers for Haiti's growing youth population in the capital city's slum of Cite Soleil, experienced the quake. One student, Kristina Rosales, recalled,

> We were in downtown Port-au-Prince when the earthquake struck. Fortunately, we were safe inside a car and did not get hit by any buildings. I have never seen such destruction and chaos. There were people crying and running, and it was heartbreaking to hear the voices of trapped people pleading for help. At the same time, it was inspiring to see how the Haitian people helped one another. The majority of Haitians we have helped in Cite Soleil are unaccounted for. More attention needs to be paid to the suffering of those in marginalized communities like Martissant and Cite Soleil where aid has been slow to arrive and most of the people trapped will probably die.[46]

As the poorest country in the western hemisphere, with an average life expectancy of 62 years, this catastrophe accentuated the repercussions of poverty beyond health and longevity. Without the financial resources to insure one's property, owners bear much of the reconstruction costs. To mitigate the costs, the prevailing low standards of construction warrant the use of unskilled day laborers, cheap materials, and an avoidance of building codes, when they exist.

The Insurance Information Institute calculated property losses at US$7.9 billion, or just over 120% of the country's gross national product (GNP) in 2009. Only about $20 million (about half of which was for automobile insurance) was covered by insurance. This knowledge led a number of insurers to make modest voluntary contributions to relief agencies. ACE Group (Zurich) donated $250,000 to the American Red Cross Haiti Relief and Development Fund, and matched employee donations dollar for dollar. Chubb Insurance (based in Warren, New Jersey) contributed $125,000 to Doctors Without Borders (Médecins Sans Frontières). Other insurers including Aetna (from Hartford, Connecticut) and Northwestern Mutual also made modest six-figure donations and matched employee donations.[47]

The statistics only begin to measure the shock and desperation of the Haitian people. Estimates of the total number dead have been revised downward to between 46,000 and 85,000 dead, although the true number may never be know, because mass graves created a final resting place for many thousands who died during the earthquake and many thousands more who perished in the rubble of collapsed buildings. The quake destroyed approximately 105,000 homes and damaged another 205,000. The homeless numbered 875,000 living in temporary housing settlements, with an additional 375,000 living under tarpaulins, in tents, and in makeshift wooden or cardboard shanties. Other edifices destroyed or severely damaged included 1,300 schools and colleges, and 50 hospitals and health care centers. For all practical purposes, the government ceased to exist, with the Presidential Palace, the court system, and most other government offices crippled.[48]

Rebuilding

The task is daunting and the clearing of debris from collapsed structures overwhelming. With thousands of cubic yards of concrete debris, a single Mack truck hauls about 9 yd^3 (3 m^3) in each trip. It travels about 8 mi (13 km) along the narrow and congested streets of the nation's capital to get to a dumpsite. At best, it will make four to five round trips a day. With no more than 100 such trucks in the entire country and about 150 Caterpillar excavators, the problem of removal became monumental. The UN's assessment unit estimated that 310,000 collapsed or damaged structures will produce 30–78 million yd^3 of rubble in the form of crushed cinderblocks and tangled metal. The Haitian government's plan to complete the removal by 2012 was overly optimistic.

The government's reconstruction plan called upon the international community to contribute US$3.9 billion for the first phase of recovery and stabilization, which was planned to last 18 months. It would house 1.3 million homeless Haitians and rebuild 1,300 schools and 50 hospitals. In addition, the airport at the nation's capital would be rebuilt along with two new regional airports, in an effort to create new zones of economic opportunity, thereby taking pressure off of Port-au-Prince with its population of between 2.5 and 3 million people, and also stopping the internal migration to the city. The first phase planned for five opportunity zones were to be located in Cap Haitien, Les Gonaives, St. Marc, Hinche, and Les Cayes.

A second, ten-year, investment of US$7.2 billion would focus on economic growth and the reduction in poverty where 75% of the population lives on less than two dollars a day, with 56% of people living on less than a dollar a day. Building upon the expected success of phase one, this second phase would focus on the revitalization of Haiti's regional economies in agriculture, tourism, and the textile industry. Funds for these initiatives would come from contributions from the world's developed countries, the World Bank, and the IMF. Unfortunately, money pledged does not always turn into cash contributions, as other priorities intervene abroad. A weakened Haiti was in no position to make demands on international agencies or developed countries.

Conclusion

A year and a half after the devastating earthquake, most of the 10,000 troops sent by the USA to provide relief, maintain order, and protect food distribution returned home. Those remaining troops protect the docks at the port and assist with reconstruction projects. Many of the emergency medical hospital ships have left Haiti. Those medical units that remain engage in establishing permanent healthcare facilities and proper sanitation. They fight to prevent the spread of infectious disease. Their efforts are hampered by a primitive wastewater system, much of which was destroyed in the earthquake and its many aftershocks. The spread of cholera caused by drinking contaminated water is the greatest threat. It appeared early and today remains a public health menace. Antibiotics and a salt and sugar serum injected into patients are the only known ways to fight the microbes that cause diarrhea, vomiting, and dehydration. Without them, death follows.

As of early 2012, more than 6,000 people have died in Haiti from cholera since October 2011. The disease has affected more than 420,000 people since the time when sewage from a UN camp city located north of Port-au-Prince poured into the Artibonite River, contaminating drinking water. In the aftermath of the devastating earthquake, international agencies including the UN's Pan-American Health Organization have failed to wage a more aggressive campaign against this dreaded disease. Not only are clean water and proper sanitation required, but also antibiotics and a cheap cholera vaccine that would alleviate the suffering of many thousands of people and prevent the spread of cholera. Currently, however, only 400,000 doses of the vaccines are available worldwide. So, an accelerated manufacture of more doses would provide a much-needed benefit to Haitians.

The immediate prospects for a rapid solution to the country's physical reconstruction and the personal health of Haitians has been stymied by the inability of its new president, Michel Martelly, to form a government from the country's divisive political parties. To exacerbate Haiti's inability to accomplish its many goals, the non-appearance of pledged donations from the international community of developed countries have created bottlenecks in the country's rebuilding plans.

The president has been unable to get Parliament to extend the mandate of the Interim Haiti Recovery Commission that is responsible for approving reconstruction projects. The mandate expired on October 21, 2011. The future remains bleak unless the Haitian government develops a national strategy for creating permanent housing, jobs, and convincing powerful landowners that resettling people out of Port-au-Prince serves the national interest. Hundreds of thousands still live in makeshift tent cities, despite the fact that one-half million cubic feet of debris has been removed from the capital city and its surrounding towns, so rebuilding can begin.

Summary

Each of these three earthquakes took place in locations made highly vulnerable by the convergence of tectonic plates. Each was situated in a coastal region that will become increasingly vulnerable as the climate changes and the sea level rises, from the increase in glacial meltwater. As noted earlier, one hypothesis currently being evaluated is that future earthquakes may have a climatic component. With hundreds of millions of tons of rising seawater piling up on the continental shelves, this added weight may increase the instability of tectonic plates. If evidence is found to prove a relationship between climate change and earthquakes, then increasing numbers of coastal residents living near or on geological faults will become vulnerable to future earthquake and tsunami events.

The San Francisco earthquake of 1906 and the Great Kanto earthquake of 1923 have become part of each nation's cultural memory. In the former, it was memorialized in the 1936 film version (*San Francisco*) of the earthquake, starring Clark Gable, Janette MacDonald, and Spencer Tracy. As a saloonkeeper, "Blackie" Norton (Clark Gable) lives life in the fast lane, does not believe in God, but befriends Tim Mullen (Spencer Tracy), a Roman Catholic priest. Mary Blake (Janette MacDonald), a singer in Blackie's saloon, leaves to become an opera singer in the city. Secretly "Blackie" loves Mary. The earthquake hits, fires rage, people run for their lives. When "Blackie" learns that Mary has survived, he falls to his knees in prayer. The movie ends with a culturally diverse group of citizens marching and singing "The Battle Hymn of the Republic," noting that the city will be rebuilt bigger and better.

With no memorial in San Francisco to honor the dead and injured, the film became the filter through which Americans understood this catastrophe. In the 20 years leading up to the making of the film, the guardians of the city's political culture downplayed the earthquake's devastation and focused on the fires without acknowledging their primary cause. By renaming the calamity the "Fire of San Francisco," they diverted attention away from the devastation caused by the earthquake. They thwarted efforts by geologists, who recommended standards for earthquake-proof buildings. In this way, they promoted the city as a safe environment for living and investing. They succeeded by denying one cultural memory and creating another. The not-so-hidden message was clear: Fires were containable while earthquakes were quick, devastating, and uncontrollable.

In terms of memory, the Great Kanto earthquake represented an opposite to the San Francisco quake. The loss of life in Tokyo and Yokohama dwarfed the number of casualties in San Francisco. The public, in Japan, with prompting from the government and the military, viewed the disaster as equivalent to war. No effort was made to minimize its impact. The government and the military publicized death and destruction as an opportunity to reform and rebuild society along traditional Japanese values. To sear the memory of this calamity into the national conscience, the government built the Tokyo Memorial Hall in Ryogoku, Toyko at Yokoamicho Park, a central place to honor those who lost their lives. To reinforce the imagery of war, those Japanese who died in the Allied bombing of the city during World War II have a similar memorial close by.

The case of the Haitian earthquake is an unfinished one, having occurred in 2010, but it is different in many ways to both the San Francisco and the Great Kanto earthquakes. Haiti's history diverged greatly from that of the USA. It was a slave colony that won political independence but remained a captive of the developed world for most of its history. Its people have suffered through the centuries without relief: from poverty, disease, and failed and dictatorial leaders, reinforced by a lack of educational progress. That the Haitian people have shown the resilience and fortitude to continue despite these hardships remains awe-inspiring.

Notes

1 Jack London, "The Story of an Eyewitness: The San Francisco Earthquake." At http://grammar.about.com/od/60essays/a/erathqkessay.htm.

2 Christian Pfister (2011), "The monster swallows you: disaster memory and risk culture in Western Europe, 1500–2000," *Rachel Carson Center Perspectives* (Munich, Germany), 13.

3 Philip L. Fradkin (2005), *The Great Earthquake and Firestorms of 1906* (Berkeley, CA: University of California Press), 52.

4 Christoph Strupp (2006), "*Dealing with disaster: the San Francisco earthquake of 1906*," Institute of European Studies, University of California, Berkeley, 2–5. At http://escholarship.org/uc/item/9gd2v192#page-2.

5 Philip L. Fradkin (2005), *The Great Earthquake and Firestorms of 1906*, 10–11.

6 Simon Winchester (2005), *A Crack in the Edge of the World: America and The Great California Earthquake of 1906* (New York: Harper Collins Publishers), 241.

7 Philip L. Fradkin (2005), *The Great Earthquake and Firestorms of 1906*, 53.

8 Simon Winchester (2005), *A Crack in the Edge of the World*, 247.

9 Ibid., 281.

10 Ibid., 72.

11 Ibid., 311.

12 Rebecca Solnit (2009), *A Paradise Built in Hell: The Extraordinary Communities That Arise in Disaster* (New York: Penguin), 43.

13 Ibid.

14 Gordon Thomas and Max Morgan Witts (1980), *The San Francisco Earthquake* (New York: Stein and Day), 200–201.

15 Christoph Strupp (2006), "Dealing with disaster: the San Francisco earthquake of 1906," 32–34.

16 Ibid., 8 and "Who Perished," a list of people who died in the 1906 San Francisco earthquake. At www.Sfmuseum.org/perished/index.html.

17 Otis Manchester Poole (1968), *The Death of Old Yokohama in the Great Japanese Earthquake of September 1, 1923* (London: George Allen and Unwin). The quotation can be found at http://nisee.berkeley.edu/kanto/tokyo1923.pdf.

18 Janet Borland (2006), "Capitalizing on catastrophe: reinvigorating the Japanese state with moral values through education following the 1923 Great Kanto earthquake," *Modern Asian Studies*, 40(4), 895.

19 J. Charles Schencking (2009), "1923 Tokyo as a devastated war and occupation zone: the catastrophe one confronted in post-earthquake Japan," *The Journal of Japanese Studies*, 29(1), 111.

20 Andrew Robinson (1993), *Earth Shock: Hurricanes, Volcanoes, Earthquakes, Tornadoes and Other Forces of Nature* (New York: Thames and Hudson), 76.

21 Gregory Clancey (2006), *Earthquake Nation: The Cultural Politics of Japanese Seismicity, 1868–1930* (Berkeley, CA: University of California Press).

22 Ibid., 214–215.

23 Ibid., 216–217.

24 J. Charles Schencking (2008), "The Great Kanto earthquake and the culture of catastrophe and reconstruction in 1920s Japan," *The Journal of Japanese Studies* 34(2) (Summer), 296.

25 Joshua Hammer (2006), *Yokohama Burning: The Deadly 1923 Earthquake and Fire That helped Forge the Path to World War II* (New York: Free Press), 87.

26 Thomas A. Jagger (1923), "The Yokohama–Tokyo earthquake of September 1, 1923," *Bulletin of the Seismological Society of America*, 13(4) (December), 131.

27 J. Charles Schencking (2009), "1923 Tokyo as a devastated war and occupation zone," 114.

28 Ibid.

29 Ibid.

30 Sonia Ryang (2003), "The Great Kanto earthquake and the massacre of Koreans in 1923: Notes on Japan's modern national sovereignty," *Anthropological Quarterly*, 76(4) (Fall), 733.

31 Thomas A. Jagger, "The Yokohama–Tokyo earthquake of September 1, 1923," 130.

32 J. Charles Schencking (2009), "1923 Tokyo as a devastated war and occupation zone," 119.

33 Ibid., 125.

34 Ibid., 124.

35 Ibid., 127.

36 Joshua Hammer (2006), *Yokohama Burning*, 239–270.

37 United Nations (2010), "UN officials give eyewitness accounts of the moment Haiti quake struck." At www.un.org/apps/news/story.asp?NewsID=33487&Cr =haiti&Cr1=14 January 2010.

38 Margaret Webb Pressler (2011), "Haiti still suffering a year after quake," *The Washington Post*, January 12, C10.

39 Simon Romero (2010), "Haiti lies in ruins; grim search for untold dead," *The New York Times*, January 14, A1.

40 Faye Flam (2010), "Future shocks? Haiti sits on several active geological faults, so the risk of more earthquakes is high. Where and when remains a mystery," *The Philadelphia Inquirer*, January 18, Daily Magazine C01.

41 Peter N. Spotts (2010), "The geology underlying the devastating Haiti earthquake," *The Christian Science Monitor*, January 13. At http://www.csmonitor.com/World/Americas/2010/0113/The-geology-underlying-the-devastating-Haiti-earthquake.

42 United Nations (2010), "UN officials give eyewitness accounts." At www.un.org/apps/news/story.asp?NewsID=33487&Cr=haiti&Cr1=14 January 2010.

43 Jean Damu (2010), "Haiti makes its case for reparations." At www.nathanielturner.com/haitimakescaseforreparations.htm.

44 Ray Rivera and Damien Cave (2010), "Haiti struggles to find tents to put over heads of its displaced masses," *The New York Times*, January 22, A4.

45 Rebecca Milner (2010), "International Medical Corps; one month after Haiti's devastating earthquake, relief efforts robust but rains bring more misery," *Biotech Business Week*, February 22, 4185.

46 Kristina Rosales (2010), "A plea for the stricken in Haiti," The *New York Times*, January 20, 20.

47 Anthony O'Donnell (2010), "Haiti quake presages others," *Insurance and Technology*, March 1, 8.

48 Olivia Ward (2010), "Who will be left to rebuild country?" *The Toronto Star*, January 15, A16.

Chapter 3

Tsunamis

It was a wall of water, straight up and down, about 200 ft tall (60 m), and it was black – totally black from the soil and trees. It was traveling about 70 mph (110 km/h), but it was strangely silent. It was snapping these spruce trees along the side of the bay. They were big spruce trees, probably 400 years old, and it was hitting them so hard, it was cutting them off at the stump. There was no way my boat was going to make it over that wave.[1]

Introduction

The 2004 catastrophe in Sumatra and disastrous tsunami in Japan in 2011 brought the world's attention to the devastating nature of tsunamis. Although relief efforts were swift, many gaps were discovered in tsunami prediction, warning, and evacuation efforts. "Tsunami," from the Japanese word meaning "harbor wave," is a series of high-speed waves resulting from the displacement of ocean water by earthquakes, volcanoes, landslides, or meteorite impacts. The large amount of economic activity occurring in ports, coupled with the fact that 40% of the world's population lives within 60 mi (100 km) of a coast, means a tsunami is capable of bringing life to a standstill where one strikes.

This chapter examines the Lisbon tsunami, which was the largest natural disaster in Europe in 500 years, and looks at a serious gap in disaster planning in this fallible portion of Europe. It also looks at the Lituya Bay, Alaska, tsunami as the tallest tsunami wave ever recorded; the deadliest tsunami – the Sumatra–Andaman event; and Japan's most recent catastrophe and how it caused the world to rethink nuclear power.

Natural Disasters in a Global Environment, First Edition. Anthony N. Penna and Jennifer S. Rivers.

Lisbon, Portugal: The Quadruple Disaster (1755)

> At 9:45 in the morning, the earth shook, but in such a weak manner that everyone imagined that it was nothing more than a carriage passing at high speed. This first tremor lasted two minutes. After an interval of two more minutes, the earth shook again, only with such violence that the majority of houses began to crack and roar. This second earthquake lasted approximately ten minutes. The dust raised was enough to obscure the sun. Again there was an interval of two or three minutes. As the thick dust settled, there was sufficient air and light for us to breathe and to see around us. Then there came a shock so awful that the houses, which had resisted the previous tremors, collapsed with a crash. The sky again grew dark and the earth seemed to want to revert to chaos.[2]

A monster earthquake with an estimated moment magnitude of up to 9.0 (M_w, a logarithmic scale of energy release which has a correction factor so that the Richter scale, designed to be used only in California, can be used globally) struck Lisbon in 1755 leaving the city in ruins as fires raged, buildings toppled, and chaos reigned. To escape the fires and falling debris, people fled towards the shore thinking they would be safe, only to see the waters rise up over 50 ft (15 m) and engulf everything. The death toll was estimated to be over 100,000, though it is impossible to determine how many died from each disaster. When all was finished, one of the largest and wealthiest European cities of the time was completely destroyed.[3] Despite this catastrophe, to this day there remains a gap in the planning and response capabilities of the Portuguese government that underscores the need for tsunami warning and response plans in Europe and around the globe.

In 1755, Lisbon was one of the most influential cities in the world. Its thriving economy was based on colonizing South America and Africa, enslaving its people, and exploiting its natural resources. Coupled with a gold rush in Brazil,[4] the spoils were to wage war on Spain, France, and Turkey as Portugal sought to colonize as much of the known world as possible. At the time, Portugal was a pious country populated with devout Catholics who feared repercussions from a God angry with those among them who sinned. Indeed, popular tales abound foretelling the smiting of Portugal by impending disasters, leaving its inhabitants fearing for their lives. It was therefore prophetic that the 1755 earthquake hit shortly before 10 a.m. on All Saints Day, Saturday, November 1, one of the most important Catholic festivals of the year. Fearful that another catastrophe would destroy the built environment, Portugal's king, Joseph I, spent most of the rest of his life in a complex of tents in the foothills of the Ajuda Mountains.

The earthquake

The first earthquake killed many residents including worshipers who filled the churches to capacity. In all, 30 out of 40 churches collapsed. Minutes later, a second earthquake caused many of the structurally unsound buildings weakened by the first earthquake to collapse as well. The final major aftershock, minutes later, leveled the city of Lisbon completely, and left the metropolis in ruins.

The tremors impacted not only Lisbon but also much of Europe and parts of North Africa in a serious and lasting manner. The coasts of Algeria, Spain, France, Gibraltar, and Italy suffered much damage from seismic waves. In Morocco, synagogues, churches, and many other buildings were razed, including the convent, church, and hospital of Saint Francisco, which collapsed completely, with numerous casualties reported.[5]

The fire

Shaking and damage from the earthquakes caused small fires used for cooking or heating to escape from their fireplaces and rage out of control when the buildings in which they were burning collapsed. Fire, when provided with oxygen and fuel, generates heat that knows no boundaries. Oxygen in the atmosphere was sufficient to fuel these fires, and wood, cooking oil, fabrics, and other materials provided ample fuel to sustain a temperature above the point of combustion. Fires destroyed major portions of the leveled city. It is impossible to know how many people died in these fires from the combination of being trapped in toppled buildings and being burned alive. "As the clouds of dust and lime settled and the darkness lifted, the morning light revealed a city in flames. The candles that had illuminated Lisbon's altars and the well-stoked fires that had burned in thousands of hearths and stoves throughout the city were now blazing out of control. To make matters worse, the early morning breeze had risen to violent gusts and the wind only fanned the flames."[6]

The tsunami

Those who were able to escape earthquake-damaged buildings and fire-ravaged areas went in search of a safe haven from the collapsing buildings and smoke. They were drawn to what would otherwise have been a logical location, the banks of the Tagus River. Here, there were no structures to topple and no major source of fuel to burn. The people there, lulled into a false sense of security after having been through so much, were about to experience more trauma, for it was then that the tsunami hit.

> All of a sudden I heard a general outcry. 'The sea is coming in; we shall be lost.' Upon this, turning my eyes toward the river, which in that place is near 4 mi (6 km) broad, I could perceive it heaving and swelling in a most unaccountable manner, as no wind was stirring. In an instant there appeared at some small distance a vast body of water, rising as it were, like a mountain, it came on foaming and roaming, and rushed toward the shore with such impetuosity that tho' we all immediately ran for our lives as fast as possible many were swept away.[7]

The tsunami was generated by the three strong earthquakes and took 30 minutes to arrive at Lisbon's port. These waves traveled up the Tagus River and into the port with run-up heights of 15–50 ft (5–15 m).[8] The swirling chaos of waves impregnated with debris from boats, piers, homes, and other structures dealt a deadly blow to any structures left standing and to the people who had survived the earthquake and fires.

Heavy destruction from the tsunami occurred along the coasts of Portugal, Spain, and Morocco. Tsunami effects were observed on the coasts of France, the UK, Ireland, Belgium, the Azores, and Holland with seiches (standing waves in enclosed seawater) occurring as far away as Finland. Damage was immense along the coast of Portugal, where the tsunami dismantled some coastal fortresses and leveled houses as waves crested at more than 100 ft (30 m).[9] The tsunami crossed the Atlantic Ocean, reaching the Antilles, Antigua, Martinique, and Barbados where waves over 3 ft (1 m) were observed. Much of the world felt at least minor impacts from the giant tsunami that mauled the coastline of Portugal that holy day (Figure 3.1).

Scientific and religious thought and the birth of modern seismology

The prevailing thought at the time was that this disaster was of divine origin. God was smiting the Portuguese for their sins. That the devastation coincided with All Saints Day did not escape the notice of the religious, as many of the faithful were killed including 204 members of the religious community, 63 nuns, 600 churchgoers attending the mass at the Franciscan

Figure 3.1 The Lisbon tsunami, earthquake, and fire.
Source: SPL / Photo Researchers, Inc.

convent, 400 parishioners at the Santa Trindade Church, 300 of the devout in the Convent of Nossa Senhora da Penha de França, and 137 members of the Sé Cathedral, though they all had the consolation of expiring on sanctified ground. Many likened the scale of the destruction to Jericho, Babylon, Nineveh, or Sodom and Gomorrah.[10] It was, however, a turning point for some officials and philosophers of the day. The Lisbon earthquake was the first modern disaster that compelled the state to oppose the notion of supernatural causation and to accept responsibility for the reconstruction of the city.[11]

The 1755 Lisbon earthquake is considered by some as the birth of modern seismology and to this day scientists continue to investigate and design new methods for pinpointing the intensity of quakes. The Lisbon earthquake was detailed in an exhaustive engineering study of earthquakes and tsunamis as a case study to determine how to categorize past earthquakes and tsunamis by today's scales.[12]

Thus, the Lisbon earthquake of 1755 was the cradle of modern seismology with a political eye towards earthquake disaster management including societal responsibility. "Although earthquakes were beginning to be understood as natural phenomena by some, the notion of natural disasters having supernatural overtones had to be overcome against strong resistance. The opposition, calling for humility towards God, proved an impediment for disaster management."[13] Indeed, the political theorist Judith Shklar has stated: "The modern age has many birthdays. One of them, my favorite, is the Lisbon earthquake of 1755. What makes it such a memorable disaster is not the destruction of a wealthy and splendid city, nor the death of some 100,000 to 150,000 people who perished in its ruins, but the intellectual response it evoked throughout Europe. It was the last time that the ways of God to man were the subject of general public debate and discussed by the finest minds of the day."[14]

This change was aided by reports coming back to Portugal that not only was the Lisbon earthquake felt throughout Europe and North Africa but also the tsunami that had devastated Lisbon had spread throughout the Atlantic, reaching London, the shores of Norway, Africa, the Canary Islands, and the Caribbean. Indeed, Earth's vibrations made church bells in Paris ring, and seiches were reported in Scotland, England, and Finland. Therefore, many Portuguese citizens reasoned, these catastrophes were not caused by God to punish Portugal, but rather, were a widely experienced natural phenomenon.

With the birth of modern seismology, scientific inquiry took off all over Europe. Immanuel Kant (an important eighteenth-century philosopher best known for placing humans at the center of both moral and logical worlds) published three tracts on earthquakes, regarding the events as a scientific rather than a moral phenomenon.[15] Kant supposed shifting underground pockets of gases caused the earthquake. Though Kant's supposition proved false, the notion of natural causes provided considerably more comfort than that of a vengeful God. Further, though the Catholic Church viewed this earthquake as the work of God, philosopher Voltaire wrote about the Lisbon earthquake in his novella *Candide*, saying the quake was not the wrath of a vengeful deity. For this and other reasons, the Catholic Church banned his writings as blasphemous.

Eventually, people began to accept the idea of earthquakes as natural phenomena. Science impeded the spread of the religious zealot's idea of a vengeful God and replaced it with the notion that humans were victims of a natural disaster. They replaced guilt with happenstance and repentance with an incentive to rebuild their beloved city and engage in a life of renewal. If religious dogma was capable of making survivors cower with the threat of damnation and the promise of redemption, science could uncover the principle workings of the natural world and liberate the ignorant and credulous from centuries of fanaticism.[16] This was a profound transition in eighteenth-century thinking.

Another by-product of this earthquake was the influence and the power of print:

> The earthquake became the subject of commentaries, cautionary tales, speculation, and heated debate in churches, salons, universities, civil institutions, and the street. To complement the terror-fraught narratives of the disaster that were appearing in the press, images were soon included – mostly copperplate engravings – that brought home the tragedy with chilling if not always accurate detail. Most of the unsigned engravings, published in broadsheets all over Europe, especially England, France, Holland, and Germany, were churned out by the sweatshop engravers in record time to satisfy the public appetite for a visual reference of a calamity that seemed to defy description. Rigor in rendering the architectural or natural landscape of Lisbon accurately counted for little.[17]

Relief efforts

The earthquake and tsunami were also the first modern disasters in which international relief was offered. Given Lisbon's function as a global center of trade, the earthquake was recognized as a catastrophe by London, Amsterdam, Hamburg, and Venice, all of which had invested considerable sums in Lisbon. Prior to 1755, for reasons of national pride and a jealous sense of sovereignty, the notion of foreign relief would have been unthinkable. By 1755, military and political alliances, mutual commercial interests, and improvements in travel and communications had made the states of Europe increasingly interdependent, and the Lisbon earthquake struck a chord of universal compassion.[18]

Relief poured in from all over in the form of money, food, clothing, and tools. Lisbon's losses were staggering; over half of the city was gone. People began to see the world as interconnected, and since the financial fate of one country was tied to another, it became important to much of the world that Portugal rebuild and recover from this disaster.

Rebuilding

Immediately following the quake, the prime minister Sebastião de Melo (the Marquis of Pombal) sent out questionnaires to parishes in Portugal asking about their experience during the earthquake. These questions included the following:

1. At what time did the earthquake begin on November 1, and how long did it last?
2. Did you perceive the shock to be greater from one direction than another?
3. How many buildings were ruined in each parish? Were there notable buildings among them, and in what state did they remain?
4. How many people died? Were any of them distinguished? Did you notice what happened to the sea, to fountains, and to rivers?
5. Did the sea rise or fall first, and how many hands did it rise above normal? How many times did you notice the extraordinary rise or fall, and did you notice how long it took to fall and rise?
6. Did any earthquakes occur after that of November 1? If so, when and what damage did they cause? And if fire broke out, how long did it last, and what damage did it cause?

Answers to these questionnaires were compiled, and this led to a change in the school of thought regarding earthquake engineering. Engineers built models of buildings and had soldiers march around them to test them against shaking. The resultant buildings comprising the Baixa Pombalina ("New Downtown") are the first buildings in Europe constructed to withstand earthquakes. The buildings were built together in a compound. The external walls were composed of limestone with lime mortar joints and were linked to an internal structure made of wood. The internal walls were constructed perpendicular to the external walls, had no openings, and extended above the roofs so they could completely divide the space and prevent the spread of fire. The first floor was constructed entirely of stone and contained arches and columns that strengthened the building and prevented fire from spreading. The floors were leveled by rubble remaining from the buildings that had been destroyed in the 1755 earthquake.[19]

This style of building then spread to other cities in Portugal. Ramos and Lourenço tested the buildings for seismic safety as recently as 2003 and have determined that although the construction does not comply with today's building codes, there is evidence that this type of construction was beneficial for the seismic behavior of the "Pombaline" downtown buildings.[20] In this way, Lisbon was rebuilt, and many of the buildings still stand today.

Conclusion

The Lisbon earthquake and tsunami, the largest natural disasters in Europe in 500 years, serves as a reminder of past natural disasters. A present-day occurrence of a moderate-to-intense tsunami would produce societal disruption and economic loss, orders of magnitude greater than those of previous events in history.[21] There exists a serious gap in the planning process in much of Europe to predict, prepare for, and respond to future earthquakes and tsunamis. Future disasters are likely, given the tectonic setting of this region in which the Atlantic and Eurasian plates converge.

Today, the area in Portugal that could, potentially, flood would put approximately 221,845 inhabitants at risk. Portugal remains, seismically, a geographic region to watch, and many buildings are not up to code. Portimão, a southern coastal town, 113 mi (180 km) from Lisbon, attracts thousands of tourists annually. Its population of 50,000 doubles during the height of the tourist season. Seismologists estimate that 5,000 buildings including hotels would be destroyed or severely damaged in an earthquake.[22] In a natural disaster, rescue and security forces would be flooded by appeals from police, airport personnel, the prison system, and the Red Cross. Their effect on the network of roads and other communications systems would be severe.[23]

The Lituya Bay Mega-Tsunami (1958)

A mega-tsunami (a tsunami with wave heights over 330 ft (100 m)) or iminami (Japanese for "wave of purification") occurred in 1958 in Lituya Bay, Alaska, and produced the highest wave ever recorded. It reached a height of 1,742 ft (530 m). The height of this run-up was incomparable to any other event; it was five times as high as the highest run-up ever previously observed. If a wave the size of the Lituya Bay tsunami had occurred in a populated region, there would be few, if any, survivors. Thankfully, Lituya Bay is largely unpopulated, thus only two fishermen were killed. The wave was sensationalized in the *New York Times* with headlines that read:

"Tremors break off glaciers and lift part of an island – Juneau Buildings rocked" and "Moviegoers watching *The Bridge on the River Kwai* were ordered by an authoritative voice to 'Keep your seats'."[24]

The earthquake

A Moment Magnitude (M_w) 8.3 earthquake occurred along the Fairweather fault between the Pacific and North American tectonic plates in southeastern Alaska at approximately 10:16 p.m. on July 9, 1958. This was likely due to the bottom of the Gilbert and Crillon Inlets moving northwest (and possibly up) relative to the northeast shore at the head of the Bay, on the opposite side of the Fairweather fault.[25] Four distinct shocks were felt, with additional tremors throughout the night.[26] The shaking from this quake lasted for approximately four minutes.

The landslides

The earthquakes triggered landslides and avalanches approximately one minute after the shaking began. These landslides were possibly because low deltas of gravel had built out onto the Gilbert Inlet at the southeast and northwest margins of the Lituya glacier front.[27] Bystanders referred to a "moving glacier" which was likely a mass of rock, snow, ice, and clouds of dust. When the landslide, composed of 40 million yd^3 (30 million m^3) of debris, hit Lituya Bay, the instantaneous displacement of water in the bay created a wall of water which traveled southward and obliterated millions of trees over 5 mi^2 (13 km^2).[28]

The tsunami

As the wave propagated outward from the landslide, its effects were colossal. Marine plants and marine invertebrates attached to rocks or burrowed in the mud or sand were destroyed by the wave. Barnacles and mussels that had been previously covering rocks were washed away; not one living clam was found post-tsunami. Freshwater organisms in local lakes were probably killed by the ingress of salt water.[29]

Three fishing boats were located in the Bay. One, a 55-ft (17 m) fishing trawler anchored in the harbor, was dashed against a cliff. No trace of the boat or its two passengers was ever found.[30] Another fishing boat, the *Badger*, was lifted up by the wave and carried across the La Chausse Spit, riding stern-first just below the crest of the wave, like a surfboard so that the pilot, Mr. Swanson, could look down on the trees growing on the spit before the boat hit the bottom.[31]

Fisherman Howard Urlich, out on the third boat with his young son when the tsunami hit, described the scene:

> Out of the corner of my eye, there was an explosion of water sending up a splash 1,700 ft high (550 m). And then the wave started coming. . . . The engine was wide open trying to get up that wave. And then it was on us. It snapped the anchor, and the chain whipped around and hit the pilothouse door. It carried us 100 ft (30 m) up, but we couldn't see anything but water and trees. It was pushing us backward and I was sure it was going to break and swamp us. Then, it was breaking around us, on either side, but not quite where the boat was. And somehow we got on top of it and to the other side. The wave crashed on the land behind us, but I didn't look back because we weren't out of it yet. There were swells up to 30 ft (9 m) high coming from all different directions. They'd toss the boat around, almost straight up in the air, with trees and ice floating around. Finally, we made it to the exit of the bay and out into calmer water. There had been two other boats in the bay. One was swamped, but the people survived. The wave spit them out into the ocean. The other boat just disappeared.[32]

Lituya Bay historical accounts

Giant waves have occurred in Lituya Bay up to five times during the past 150 years.[33] Ship logs of the famous French explorer LaPerouse, credited with the discovery of the Bay in 1786, commented on the lack of trees and vegetation on the sides of the Bay, "as though everything had been cut cleanly with a razor blade." Indian legends exist about a possible giant wave in 1853 or 1854. Evidence can be found from the trimline of old trees (the line where the trees were all chopped (trimmed) off at the stumps from the power of the wave) to support such an occurrence.Accounts by fisherman tell of catastrophic floods in 1890 and 1928. Another wave in 1899 destroyed a native village and fish saltery near the mouth of the Bay. All occurred after earthquakes. A 1936 wave was not due to a landslide or an earthquake, and its cause remains a mystery; it may have been caused by a surge caused by large pieces of glacier falling into the sea, a submarine slide, or the breaking of an ice dam after an unusually heavy rainfall.

One of the most impressive aspects of the 1958 tsunami was the thoroughness of its destruction of the forest. Extending to the upper limit of inundation, the suggested destroyed area is best conveyed by photographs, showing that in most places bare ground suggested that the tsunami washed away the trees.[34]

Modeling efforts fail

Interestingly, the mechanism that generated the giant wave run-up of 1,720 ft (525 m) above sea level has been a mystery baffling scientists. The wave was so high that computer models failed to produce output that matched geologic and environmental evidence left by the wave, such as tree removal and sediment deposition. Scientists have doubted on theoretical grounds that such a giant wave is possible.Several scientists have pointed to the evidence – trimline, washed area, and upturned trees – as evidence of a landslide rather than a tsunami.

On the other hand, attempts at modeling concluded that the amount of water displaced by a simple landslide or an earthquake at the head of the bay was insufficient to cause the observed tsunami wave.[35] Some researchers have conceded that the existing tsunami models would require advanced technology similar to that required for asteroid-generated waves. In 1999 when the modeling was done, it appeared that the computer modeling technology would not become available for many decades.[36] Nevertheless, field evidence such as the absence of vegetation in the wave run-up zone confirms to other researchers that this event was indeed the largest tsunami in recorded history.[37]

Later modeling efforts showed the event was divided into two main stages, a landslide impact and penetration combined with the forming of an air cavity. The air cavity collapsed with landslide run-out and debris, causing a mixing of water and landslide debris.[38] The entire event, pieced together by geologist Don Muller, was supported by a 1:1,000 scale model created by Robert Weigel, who experimented with many possible wave sources to determine the most likely scenario to have produced a wave responsible for the near-total destruction of the forest.[39]

Relief and rebuilding

What are the odds that such a mega-tsunami will happen again in Lituya Bay? These waves have occurred five times within the past 110 years, or approximately once every quarter of a century. The possibility of a large landslide and tsunami happening again has been increased by the creation of several rock fractures by the 1958 earthquake and by the removal of vegetation. The erosion of unconsolidated deposits further undermined the steep and unstable slopes around Lituya Bay.[40] In effect, Lituya Bay is the perfect setting – steep slopes, unconsolidated sediments, glaciers, and an active fault zone – for such catastrophic waves to occur with regularity, though we may take comfort in knowing the area is unpopulated and therefore loss of life on a large scale is unlikely. Past tsunamis have not led to discernible loss of life and therefore rebuilding and relief efforts were unnecessary, but the Lituya Bay tsunami provided a wealth of scientific data necessary to further tsunami modeling efforts, which may have saved lives in the past, and may continue to do so in future.

The Sumatra–Andaman Earthquake (2004)

> It was horrible. The waves were floating around me and I got pulled under the water. I hung on to a fridge and then a nail got stuck in my foot but I managed to get out. I managed to get hold of my son's hand and reach safety. There are about 30 of us Europeans stuck here with water all around us, with crocodiles and the like surrounding us. We can't get out. No one knows we are here[41] (Eyewitness Duncan Ridgeley, from Hertfordshire, UK, speaking from Sri Lanka after the tsunami.)

What happens when a large wave such as Lituya Bay's tsunami disrupts and destroys a populated region? Unfortunately, the world found out on December 26, 2004. This tsunami killed up to 250,000 people and completely destroyed much of the coast ringing the Indian Ocean. Though there was some warning, given the travel time of the wave, the remote nature of the coastal fishing villages made it impossible to warn inhabitants. Fishermen, sunbathers, scuba divers, and people involved in commerce in the many ports were unaware until the first wave was upon them, and by then, it was too late. When it was all over, hundreds of thousands of bodies floated in a churning, debris-filled sea.

The earthquake

A 1,000-mile-long (1,600 km) rupture along the subduction zone between the Eurasian plate and the Indo-Australian plate, thought by scientists to be dormant, generated a colossal earthquake of a magnitude of 9.3, the longest ever recorded at eight minutes. The earthquake was followed by a second earthquake that measured over 9.0, the largest aftershock ever recorded.[42]

Instrumentation picked up seismic vibration from this megathrust fault globally for a full seven days after the event occurred. This earthquake was so powerful that the entire Earth shook in its orbit by nearly one-half an inch. For scale, if one sums all the energy released by earthquakes in the past 100 years, approximately 12.5% was from this quake alone. Total work done (a physics measure of energy release) by this quake was estimated at 4.0×10^{22} joules (a measure of heat needed to do work, where 1,000 joules = 1 British thermal unit), which is equivalent to 9,560 gigatons of TNT, 550 million times stronger than the Hiroshima atomic blast in World War II, and equaling about 370 years of energy use in the USA.[43]

The main earthquake triggered aftershocks so large (one registered 8.7) that they themselves had aftershocks. Earthquakes were triggered globally as stuck plate boundaries were jarred loose as far away as the Aleutian Islands. The island of Simueleu in Indonesia was tipped sideways by the force. Embayments on the west side of Simueleu were drained while coral on the east side that had been submerged for thousands of years suddenly rose above sea level. The 50-ft-high (15.25 m) main rupture caused the sea floor to rise instantaneously, and created secondary faults in long narrow sections. These sprung-up blocks of sea floor further disturbed ocean water and added fuel to already displaced ocean water. This was a gargantuan earthquake with global effects.

The tsunami

The earthquakes displaced 7.2 mi^3 (30 km^3) of water in the form of a tsunami that affected 46 countries as it radiated outward along the entire 1,000-mile-long (1,600 km) fault. In many countries, waves traveled up to 1.5 mi (2.4 km) inland. The waves were so powerful that they were observed 16 hours and 5,300 mi (8,530 km) away in South Africa, where the sea level rose by 5 ft (1.5 m). In Antarctica, a 3 ft 3 in (1 m) rise in sea level lasted several days.[44] Closer to the epicenter, in places such as Thailand, Malaysia, and Sri Lanka, 33-ft (10 m) waves caused absolute destruction and complete chaos.

> We heard a roaring noise and could see ripples of frothy water bubbling up fast from the beach. Two or three minutes later the waves smashed into the

> hotel, breaking the windows and hitting the tables. Then, all of a sudden, the bay emptied of water, and we were able to return to our room on the first floor. But then the sea started charging ahead again, and for the next two or three hours we were hit by massive waves every 45 minutes or so. It knocked the hell out of the hotel – which was shuddering – smashing everything on the ground floor to bits. Great big swathes of the beach are completely washed away, the peninsula has huge gaps where hotels used to be, and the coconut palms are 5–6 ft (1.5–2 m) under water.[45]
>
> When the first wave hit the sea wall, the muddy water came in very quickly. It was thick, grey with filthy mud. We started to make our way out of the restaurant. The second wave came very fast on the heels of the first, and within seconds we were waist-deep in this horrible grey mud. We lost two children when they were completely submerged, and found them by desperately fumbling in the thick mud. We made our way through falling walls, breaking glass, and upturned furniture out of the restaurant. Our passage was blocked by falling kitchen equipment and vehicles that had been washed away . . . Chaos then ensued, as no one seemed to know what had happened. Passers-by in cars stopped to enquire what had happened – no help was offered in spite of pleas from the children in my party. Emergency services did not arrive until an hour after the waves struck.[46]

Indonesia was the hardest hit of the countries affected, with up to 250,000 dead or missing.[47] The island of Sumatra was the first hit; 30 minutes after the earthquake began, 65–100-ft (20–30 m) waves stripped the land of vegetation and swept boats inland. Tens of thousands of people perished on this island in approximately 10 minutes.[48] In Indonesia, 80-ft (24 m) waves led to an estimated 168,000 deaths and 83,000 missing people. The waves then reached Thailand where, tragically, the sea first retreated and many tourists walked out on the sea floor to view this strange sight. These tourists were hit with a 30-ft (9 m) wall of water and successive giant waves, killing 8,000 people.

While these waves were mauling the Thai coastline, deadly waves just 1 ft high (0.3 m), yet traveling at speeds of over 500 mph (800 km/h), were moving towards Sri Lanka. As the tsunami waves reached shore, they refracted, or bent, around the coastline and killed over 4,000 people as they continued northward to India where 10,000 people perished in the waves.

The island nation of Maldives, which was the next hit, could have been demolished. As the lowest-lying country on Earth, the Maldives is made up of nearly 2,000 islands, inhabited by 300,000 people. Miraculously, the tsunami killed only 108 people due to the volcanic nature of the islands. Tsunami waves are low and fast-moving in deep water, and since the Maldives have no continental shelf and therefore no shallow water, the 14-ft (4.2 m) waves ripped through the islands without losing speed and gaining height. These islands were also saved from more intense destruction due to many intact coral reefs and mangrove swamps which attenuated the wave energy. Massive damage did occur, however, totaling US$400 million in a country with a GDP (gross domestic product) of only $1.6 billion.[49]

Next, the tsunami, now 2,800 mi (4,500 km) from its source, hit Somalia and killed over 300 people and displaced over 50,000. By the time the waves reached Kenya, only one person perished due to drowning. Several other countries experienced fatalities including Myanmar (up to 600), Malaysia (approximately 75), Bangladesh (2), the Seychelles (10), South Africa (13), Tanzania (approximately 30), and Yemen (1). Australia, Madagascar, and Mauritius suffered damage, and 30 countries lost nationals who at the time were tourists visiting the affected countries. Sweden lost 543 of its citizens, and 51 US citizens were killed.

The destruction of coral reefs and mangrove forests played a role in the death toll throughout the Indian Ocean. Though coral grows very slowly, it can develop into large reefs surrounding islands or mainland that are capable of buffering the massive amounts of energy that come ashore as waves. When the Sumatra tsunami hit, areas with intact coral reefs and mangrove swamps experienced a lower death toll. For example, on Surin Island, where coral reefs had been left intact, the reefs buffered the impacts of the tsunami and fewer people died. Coral reefs and mangrove swamps do not make good shrimp farming habitat, and shrimp farming is a major industry in Indonesia and Thailand.[50] Many Asian countries, including Indonesia, have destroyed coral reefs with dynamite to make way for shrimp farms and for large boats, which ship materials into and out of these countries. The death toll was much higher in regions where coral reefs had been destroyed for shrimp farming, coastal development, or shipping.

Media reports were swift and sensational. Television images showed bodies floating in muddied waters, cars floating out to sea, boats beached on the land, and snorkelers being dragged onto the beach as sunbathers disappeared into the sea; first-hand accounts abounded, including those by S. Muthukumar, "The water came with no warning. We see the sea come forward. Everybody was running, but God saved little."[51] Reports detailed Hindus drowning during ritual bathing, lighthouses toppling into the water, a prison wrecked with inmates escaping, dead bodies strewn in treetops, and people impaled on fences.[52] Cultural monuments along the entire rim of the Indian Ocean were also destroyed or damaged, including the Old Town of Galle and its fortifications in Sri Lanka, and the Mahabalipuram and the Sun Temple of Koranak in India.[53]

Relief efforts

The Sumatra tsunami was the most generously funded relief effort ever, which makes sense given the scale of this tragedy (Figure 3.2). Damage was estimated at $10.73 billion, and though the official death toll was placed near 300,000 the total is likely to be much higher.[54, 55] Over 3 million people were injured and/or displaced and 1.5 million people lost their jobs. The ratio of women and children to men killed was 3:1, in part because so many men were out at sea fishing and the women were home caring for children.

International aid agencies mobilized as quickly as possible to limit the suffering of the tsunami's survivors, but there were delays in distributing

Figure 3.2 Street in downtown Banda Aceh after the 2004 tsunami.
Source: © Michael L. Bak/Department of Defense/Handout/Reuters/Corbis.

the necessary food, medicine, and temporary housing. Immediate health threats included diarrheal and respiratory diseases caused by various bacteria and viruses spreading rapidly because of poor sanitation and the absence of clean water.[56] Dehydration and heat stroke occurred. Injuries from stepping on nails, broken glass, and other debris were common, and the possibility of death by electrocution from downed wires added to the misery of the tsunami's survivors.

Doctors Without Borders (Medécins sans Frontières) experienced delays receiving medicines and materials due to the lack of available planes. Relief reached Banda Aceh international airport swiftly, but was unable to move forward for several days, efforts being hampered by lack of trucks and fuel, washed out roads and bridges, and power failures.[57]

Rebuilding

Rebuilding efforts have proceeded at different paces. In Thailand, whose economy is heavily dependent on tourism, rebuilding was swift. After meeting the urgent needs of survivors, longer-term recovery efforts focus on rebuilding livelihoods, restoring crucial infrastructure, and getting the tourism industry back on track as fast as possible.[58] Phuket Island, a main tourism destination, recovered fully in one year; however, neighboring Khao Lak has yet to recover, and land-use problems continue to plague Ko Phi Phi Don.[59]

Grabbing land poses a serious problem. In India, Thailand, and Sri Lanka, both predatory and strategic land grabs by developers and the government proceeded at a rapid pace.[60] The Sri Lankan government wanted to centralize its governance during redevelopment, but many citizens felt centralization would lead to corruption and bureaucracy due to this increase in government power.

Overall, however, completely obliterated coastal towns and villages have been rebuilt: "Coming up on five years now, by and large, the obvious effects of the tsunami have been kind of taken away visually. A lot of the urban areas are rebuilt. Houses are back up, buildings are back up," said Jeff Wright, a humanitarian affairs adviser at World Vision.[61]

"Aceh province was closest to the epicenter of the 2004 earthquake and hardest hit, with its capital Banda Aceh left largely in ruins. Today the city is almost entirely rebuilt with infrastructure better and more durable than what existed previously. All that is left to be done is finish [the] repair of a coastal road. Save for particular sites, I cannot recognize the Aceh of today as the one I saw in January 2005 myself," said Rod Volway, program director for Mercy Corps' Aceh, Indonesia, project.[62]

As a result of this disaster, efforts by countries to strengthen warning systems and disaster response strategies have become priorities. Thailand and Indonesia have installed warning towers on beaches, Sri Lanka has established "Tsunami Protection Villages," and India has spent $27 million to establish a regional warning center. Indonesian officials, however, stated that vandals have destroyed buoys off the Mentawai Islands that were there to give tsunami warnings.[63]

Conclusion

Where natural disasters strike, gaps in planning, warning measures, and responses quickly become exposed. Many such gaps were discovered after the Sumatra tsunami. Although waves swamped parts of the Sumatran coast and nearby islands within minutes, there would have been time to alert more distant communities if the Indian Ocean had a warning network like the Pacific Tsunami Warning System (PTWS), located in Honolulu, Hawaii, and supported by 26 nations in the Pacific basin.[64] It provides tsunami warning information to all member nations. Indeed, when Japan suffered from the 2011 tsunami, the potential death toll was greatly reduced due to the infrastructure of Japan's technologically advanced warning systems.

Immediately following the quake in 2004 and as the Indian Ocean tsunami approached the coastlines, scientists running the PTWS placed frantic calls from Honolulu to countries in the danger zone. Unfortunately, these calls failed to reach most countries in time. Many people feel the death toll was unnecessary: "There's no reason for a single individual to get killed in a tsunami. The waves are totally predictable. We have travel-time charges covering all of the Indian Ocean. From where this earthquake happened to hit, the travel time for waves to hit the tip of India was four hours. That's enough time for a warning," said expert Tad Murty.[65]

The Tōhoku (Japan) Tsunami (2011)

> Machines and other equipment lay scattered around factories at the port having been tossed here and there by the surging waters. Floating oil was

> forming spiral patterns offshore . . . The town of Kuji, Iwate Prefecture, once nestled in the curve of a bay, had been swept away by a tsunami. The ground was soaked in seawater and shining as it reflected the sunlight . . . [Yamadamachi in Iwate Prefecture] was swallowed up by seawaters . . . The flat land [of Ofunato, Iwate Prefecture], which extends into the sea like a cape, was totally swallowed . . . leaving no trace that a town was there. The next town south was Rikuzen-Takata, but almost no buildings were to be seen where the town should have been located. It seemed as if the port town had suddenly vanished. . . . Piles of rubble were scattered even as far as wooded areas several kilometers away from the coastline . . . The city of Kesennuma [in Miyagi Prefecture] smoldered beneath clouds of white smoke. The fishery town was ravaged by a tsunami during the day and suffered intense blazes at night. As if nothing burnable was left, the tragic area was filled with only rubble. Black smoke also boiled into the sky at Kesennuma, on a part of the coast where heavy oil was flowing from damaged tanks. Inland urban areas were still covered with seawater, and white smoke was rising in some places as if the areas had been destroyed by air raids.[66]

Introduction

The world watched in horror on March 11, 2011 as endless real-time video and photos depicted entire villages on Japan's northern coast disappearing under a wall of water. Unlike any other region in the world, Japan has long been known as a geological focus for tsunamis and earthquakes. More than any other nation, Japan has engineered its buildings to handle such catastrophes. Unfortunately, Japan's dependence upon nuclear energy produced one of the worst natural and man-made disasters to date.

The earthquake

Incredibly, officials warned of a strong earthquake a minute before Earth's great undersea megathrust earthquake created bedlam on March 11, 2011. It was a six-minute-long 9.0 moment magnitude scale (M_w) earthquake located 43 mi (69 km) east of Tōhoku.[67] Like the 2004 Sumatra quake, this earthquake was so powerful that it caused Earth to move on its axis by 4–10 in (10–25 cm), widened parts of Japan, and moved it 13 ft (3.9 m) closer to the USA.[68] Unlike Sumatra, several large foreshocks preceded the Tōhoku earthquake, including four between 6.0–7.2 M_w on March 9, as well as over 900 aftershocks of 4.0–7.9 M_w.[69] Although these aftershocks will continue for several years, they are likely to decrease in magnitude.

The exact cause of the earthquake puzzles scientists, since Japan is located at the junction of four major plates. Which plate, or combination of plates (Pacific, North American, Philippine, and Eurasian), was responsible for this earthquake remains unanswered. For scale, the Tōhoku earthquake released $1.9 \pm 0.5 \times 10^{17}$ joules of surface energy or approximately double that of the 2004 Sumatra earthquake.[70] Japanese authorities also reported land subsidence of over 2 ft (0.6 m) in some regions.

The tsunami

The wall of water that crashed into Japan's coastline as a result of the earthquake was up to 130 ft (40 m) high and traveled as much as 6 mi (10 km) inland, flooding 180 mi^2 (466 km^2).[71] One man, Yasumasa Miyakawa, described his narrow escape. A wave was barreling at him, about a half-mile away, in the bay, he said. He jumped in his car, and by the time he could turn the key and put it in gear, the wave was almost upon him. He said he sped out of town chased by the wave, rising in his rearview mirror. "It was like one of the ridiculous scenes from an action movie, except it was real," said Mr. Miyakawa, his hands quivering. "I was going at 45 mph (70 km/h) and the wave was gaining on me. That's how fast it was."[72]

Warnings went out to 50 countries globally which evacuated 11,000 coastal residents in response to the warning.[73] Alaska and Chile experienced 6-ft (2 m) waves. Guatemala, Mexico, and the west coast of North and South America were struck as well: 8-ft (2.4 m) waves crashed into California.[74] The tsunami waves in Japan were unexpectedly high and the nearly 40-ft (12 m) sea walls built to withstand such an assault proved to be inadequate. They were no match for these waves. They completely submerged and obliterated 17 towns.[75]

In Taro, home of one of the tallest, longest, and strongest tsunami walls, residents climbed on top of the wall to watch the tsunami, and were washed away when the wave destroyed the inner and outer walls. Residents of this community were secure in their belief that the sea wall would protect them, but it had not been built to withstand such a high wave.

The combined earthquake and tsunami killed nearly 16,000 people and destroyed over 125,000 buildings in Japan.[76] Of the casualties, nearly 95% drowned. In many of these towns on the west coast of Japan, no built structures or natural landscapes survived the forward motion of the waves, that picked up all movable objects including ships, boats, and vehicles and carried them along with the wave, smashing them into buildings. The tsunami destroyed roads, bridges, dams, gas, power and phone lines,

Figure 3.3 Aerial view of the flooding and fire caused by the Japanese tsunami. *Source:* U.S. Navy Photo 1100312-N-0000X-003 (Released).

cellular towers, and historic landmarks in its path, including 15 major ports (Figure 3.3).[77] For days after the initial catastrophe, aftershocks kept citizens alert but fearful. In addition, rolling blackouts plagued the afflicted cities and towns, which lacked the bare essentials of clean water, basic food, and temporary housing.[78]

Nuclear disaster

Japan derives one-third of its energy from nuclear power, from 52 power plants nationally. Immediately following the earthquake, managers gave orders to shut down 12 reactors and to activate generators to run the water pumps to cool the reactors. The tsunami damaged at least three Japanese nuclear power plants, including causing a Level 7 meltdown at the Fukushima reactors, where a 46-ft (14 m) tsunami breached sea walls designed to protect against a maximum 19-ft (5.8 m) wave.[79] The floodwaters reached the generators and destroyed their electrical capacity. Without electricity, cooling pumps ceased to function, causing the reactors to overheat. A full meltdown followed, and with it came hydrogen explosions, fires, and the spread of radioactive material into the atmosphere.[80] This disaster was only the second (Chernobyl being the first) to receive a Level 7 danger rating since humans began harnessing nuclear energy.[81] Although the only remaining and active nuclear reactor in Fukushima was officially shut down in May 2011, the effects of radioactivity will continue for years to come. Within the next few years, radiation released from Fukushima will travel across the Pacific Ocean and hit the coastline of the USA. Concentrated pulses of radiation are also expected to continue forming as the radiation moves on ocean currents, which could result in highly radioactive waves of ocean water striking the West Coast of the USA. And the situation at the Fukushima plant itself still appears to be highly problematic, as reports indicate that radiation levels at reactor 1, the fuel rod of which sustained 70% damage as a result of the disaster, are the highest they have ever been. According to the Tokyo Electric Power Company (TEPCO), which owns the Fukushima plant, levels of radiation at reactor 1 reached 10 times higher than levels recorded at reactors 2 and 3.

The evacuation zone from disabled reactor 1 was placed at 12 mi (19 km) and for reactor 2 at 6.2 mi (19 km), even though the USA cautioned its nationals to evacuate a 50-mile (80 km) radius from both plants. As the most complicated nuclear meltdown ever, it ignited fires and caused explosions in Fukushima. Later, radioactive water leaked into the region's surface soil, causing it to become contaminated with the radioactive element cesium (Cs). Highly radioactive water from a damaged maintenance pit began to leak into the sea.[82] To cool the reactors and to prevent additional fires and explosions, fire-fighters pumped hundreds of tons of seawater a day into the plant, with a significant portion of the water escaping as dangerous runoff into the sea. Scientific tests detected elevated levels of radioactive material in spinach and milk,[83] while the government banned fishing in the radioactive waters.[84] The USA and Canada detected tiny, trace amounts of radiation in rainwater in British Columbia and in milk from cows in Washington State.[85] Workers on-site have suffered negative side-effects, such as radiation burns to those who step in the water from the cooling ponds adjacent to the reactor.[86]

Relief efforts

After the tsunami, 4.4 million homes lacked electricity and 1.5 million had no water.[87] The tsunami struck during the working day, with hundreds of thousands of people either at work or at school. In the Buddhist tradition, people are cremated after death, not buried but, given the death toll, the Japanese abandoned this practice. Instead, dead bodies, many of them badly damaged or dismembered, were quickly buried in mass graves.[88]

Nearly 350,000 evacuees overwhelmed shelters, with many dying in or on the way to the shelters. These additional deaths were due in part to the lack of adequate medical care and basic necessities such as food, with some evacuees receiving only one meal a day.[89] As of May 2012, there remained a dire need for temporary housing. To meet the ongoing needs of the homeless, the towns of Iwate, Miyagi, and Fukushima are currently constructing 38,000 temporary shelters. With each passing day, sanitary conditions in the existing shelters fail to keep up with the needs of their occupants. As Atsuko Fujisawa, a spokeswoman for Iwate Prefecture, said, "There is no time frame for when people can go home," she said. "Their homes are wiped away."[90]

International aid was swift and generous. Over 100 countries and 28 international aid agencies sent funds or equipment. A partial list includes Taiwan, which donated US$243 million, the highest amount in the world, rescue teams, generators, sleeping bags, blankets, clothes, foods, drinks, materials, shelters, and assistance in relocating. Thailand donated US$18.6 million, 15,000 tons of rice, canned goods, blankets, clothing, search-and-rescue teams, officials, and search-and-rescue dogs. China gave almost US$5 million, a 15-member rescue team, 20,000 tons of fuel, 10 tons of drinking water, a mechanized water-pump, and sent engineers and consultants to assist with the overheating and radiation problems of the Fukushima power plant.

Generous contributions were also offered by corporations, nongovernmental organizations (NGOs), and private individuals. Interestingly, when Japan published a thank-you announcement, Taiwan was not listed, perhaps due to fears of angering China. When questioned, foreign ministry officials said, "they did not decide the thank-you list by the amount of donations received but by the size of the country and the impact it may have on its neighbor countries."[91]

Rebuilding

The effects of the disaster will be felt for several years, but estimates put the clean-up and recovery costs at well over 2.3 trillion Japanese yen

(US$300 billion).[92] Secondary to suffering and the loss of human life is the immediate impact on the global economy. While Japan's decade-long economic recession has resulted in its fall from second to third place in the world economy, it remains a significant participant in the global economy. This disaster has further compounded the global economy's thirst for short-term profits and just-in-time (JIT) inventory that allows companies to receive parts, products, and services at the point of need during manufacturing. With little to no inventory, many companies throughout the world became dependent upon certain Japanese-manufactured goods. Now, some scramble to continue operations due to a lack of surplus materials and finished products.

Planning and reconstruction efforts are currently underway, but it will take ten years to relocate people, remove the estimated 24 million tons of debris, create a reconstruction budget and administer the funds, plan new cities, and construct permanent housing and infrastructure. Many people are still living in temporary housing as policy-makers and architects design and suggest sustainable, earthquake- and tsunami-proof future cities.[93] The search for missing persons continues; the Fukushima power plant still leaks radioactive material; and many Japanese remain psychologically traumatized by the loss of family members, neighbors, personal possessions and familiar landmarks, including shops, places of worship, and the like. Reconstruction is an ongoing and uphill battle for this aging population.

Japan's energy future

Included in reconstruction efforts is planning for how to meet Japan's future energy needs. Until the Fukushima crisis, Japan's plans were to increase the amount of energy generated by nuclear to 50% of its total energy by 2030, compared to 30% currently.[94] Now, the government has cancelled plans for 14 new plants by 2030 (which were needed to meet the country's goal of 50% nuclear power). Japan's prime minister, Naoto Kan, has also recommended that the Hamaoka reactor, which will come back on line in two years, be protected by a new sea wall but in the long term be shut down permanently because it exists on a fault line with an almost 90% chance of experiencing another earthquake within 30 years. Japan has asked Russia for more power as it struggles to meet its current needs.

Will Japan be a test case for alternative energy efforts globally, even while the country serves as a leader in nuclear energy? Tetsunari Iida, executive director of the Institute for Sustainable Energy, says the traditionally close ties between the nuclear industry, politicians, and safety agencies – what he calls Japan's "nuclear village" – have hidden the true costs of atomic power plants. "On the outside we are told it's very safe and cheap, but inside it's rubbish," he said. "That's the nature of the Japanese nuclear community."[95] The true cost of nuclear power would be obvious if there was a tangible way in which to store, or to dispose of, nuclear waste. Many argue that this disaster has given Japan a reason to rebuild its economy and emerge as a global leader in clean, renewable energy.

A recent poll revealed that 40% of respondents said the nation's dependence on nuclear power is unavoidable, while 41% supported a cut in the number of plants. Only 13% said the industry should be shut down altogether. Despite this catastrophe, the poll suggests that Japanese citizens remain ambivalent about the role of nuclear energy as a power source.

Conclusion

Fortunately for Japan, its high economic output allows for investment in structural engineering, early warning systems, and disaster response mechanisms while many less developed countries ringing the Indian Ocean did not have such advantages. Many scientists, humanitarians, and scholars called into question why the Sumatra tsunami had few warning systems in place, while Japan, with its technological innovations, had a 30-minute warning in which to prepare for the onslaught of the wave. However, ultimately, the sheer size of the wave meant there was little that could have been done to prevent this massive destruction and loss of life.

Japan's dependence on nuclear energy made the 2011 Japan earthquake distinct from prior natural disasters. It assumed that nuclear energy was a proven and safe energy source. Its thirst for energy to power its technological society put its citizens and future generations at risk and sent a message to all nations that are committed to nuclear power or contemplating its use. A separate threat is the far-reaching impact of radiation in the disaster. When the USA carried out nuclear tests on the Bikini Islands in the Pacific Ocean from 1946–50, radioactive fallout due to wind carrying the radiation over a large area was far greater than anyone anticipated. We continue to monitor radiation levels from that 1946–50 testing. What was thought would be regionally contained nuclear testing spread radiation, some of it life-threatening, across the planet.

Summary

Often after a loss of life and property of this magnitude, gaps in preparedness and response are identified, and plans may then be strengthened for the next disaster, which is the case in Sumatra. For example, UNICEF developed a "Building Back Better" initiative through which many schools have been rehabilitated, and teacher-training centers have been created. To date, 28 childcare centers and 59 healthcare facilities, as well as a water service that now serves 700,000 people, have been opened. Over 1.2 million children in devastated regions have been immunized against measles, and essential drugs and vitamins have reached three million children. Through the devastation and death, some good has come for the surviving children in this area. The 2004 Sumatra tsunami changed the way many relief agencies operate by making them more efficient. These agencies have recognized the importance of timely action and that coordinated efforts will go much farther when the next tsunami puts these agencies to the test.

Over the next few decades, we may expect one or two great earthquakes and tsunamis, as devastating as the 2004 Indian Ocean and the 2011 Japanese tsunami.[96] Given the remote nature of many communities ringing the Indian Ocean, many scientists favor the education of local people on how to recognize a tsunami and what simple measures they can take to stay safe, such as locating escape routes, rather than creating sophisticated monitoring and warning systems that may end up underfunded, broken, untended, and useless. Tsunamis like the one in Lituya Bay are important for research, as they do not cause massive loss of life but contribute greatly to our understanding of mathematical models of these events.

Kerry Sieh identified five points that would substantially reduce death tolls: (1) basic science to understand the cyclic geological processes that generate these huge earthquakes, (2) the need for emergency response preparedness to deliver immediate assistance for search-and-rescue and medical aid, (3) a warning capability to alert people far in advance of the waves reaching a given population, (4) educating populations on how to act ahead of and during a tsunami, and (5) changes in infrastructure that protect people in the path of damage and destruction.[97]

Following the nuclear crisis at Fukushima and reviews of its own nuclear power systems, on May 30, 2011, Germany announced it will reverse its current policy and phase out all nuclear power plants by 2022. The news came shortly after Switzerland announced that it was also planning on phasing out nuclear power by allowing its nuclear power plants to reach the end of their operating life, but it would not replace them afterwards. Japanese television allowed the world to witness the chronicling of this disaster, but the footage neither captures nor puts into perspective the impact that dependence on nuclear energy will have for humanity. As of the time of writing, we have little understanding of how this disaster will affect future generations of Japanese citizens, as well as the wider world population.

In the case of tsunamis, it is difficult to implement an early warning system for many of the isolated areas in the Pacific and Indian Oceans. When emergency response systems improve and people are warned earlier of impending disasters, relief will become easier as well. However, even the most in-depth historical analysis of natural disasters is incapable of capturing the human factors that contribute to these tsunami disasters, and the stories and suffering that come from them.

Notes

1 Howard Ulrich (2011) as told to James Kendall, "What it feels like . . . to survive a tsunami," *Esquire* magazine, 11 March. At www.esquire.com/features/what-it-feels-like/tunami-japan-12788.
2 Ibid.
3 Alvaro S. Pereira (2009) "The opportunity of a disaster: the economic impact of the 1755 Lisbon earthquake," *The Journal of Economic History*, 69(2), 466–499.
4 Nicholas Shrady (2009), *The Last Day: Wrath, Ruin, and Reason in the Great Lisbon Earthquake of 1755* (New York: Penguin).
5 Jan T. Kozak and Charles D. James (1998), "Historical depictions of the 1755 Lisbon earthquake," *National Information Service for Earthquake Engineering*, 12 November. At http://nisee.berkeley.edu/lisbon/.
6 Ibid.
7 Harry Fielding Reid (1914), The Lisbon earthquake of November 1, 1755, *Bulletin of the Seismological Society of America*, 4, 53–80.
8 Roy Barkan, Uri S. ten Brink, and Jian Lin (2009), "Far field tsunami simulations of the 1755 Lisbon earthquake: implications for tsunami hazard to the US East Coast and the Caribbean," *Marine Geology*, 264(1–2) (August), 109–122.
9 Ella Mudie (2010), "The spectacle of seismicity: making art from earthquakes," *Leonardo*, 43(2), 133–139.
10 Nicholas Shrady (2009), *The Last Day*, 85.

11 Karl Fuchs (2006), "The great earthquakes of Lisbon 1755 and Aceh 2004 shook the world. Seismologists' societal responsibility," *European Review*, 14(2), 207–219.
12 Emanuela Guidoboni and John E. Ebel (2009), *Earthquakes and Tsunamis in the Past: A Guide to Techniques in Historical Seismology* (New York: Cambridge University Press), 590.
13 Karl Fuchs (2006), "The great earthquakes of Lisbon 1755 and Aceh 2004 shook the world," 207–219.
14 Judith N. Shklar (1990), *The Faces of Injustice* (New Haven, CT: Yale University Press), 51–55.
15 Nicholas Shrady (2009), *The Last Day*, 143.
16 Ibid.
17 Ibid.
18 Ibid.
19 Luis F. Ramos and Paulo B. Lourenço (2003), "Seismis analysis of the old town buildings in 'Baixa Pombalina' – Lisbon, Portugal," North American Masonry Conference, June 1–4, Clemson, South Carolina, 932–941.
20 Ibid, 941.
21 Shrady, *The Last Day*, 167.
22 F. Tedim Pedrosa and J. Gonçalves (2008), "The 1755 earthquake in the Algarve (south of Portugal): What would happen nowadays?" *Advances in Geosciences*, 14, 59–63.
23 Ibid.
24 Lawrence Davies (1958), "Severe earthquake jolts Alaska; 5 believed dead, several hurt; tremors break off glaciers and lift part of an island – Juneau Buildings rocked," *The New York Times*, July 11, 46.
25 Don J. Miller (1960), "Giant Waves in Lituya Bay." US Geological Survey professional paper, issue 354. United States Government Printing Office, Washington, DC.
26 Lawrence Davies (1958), "Severe earthquake jolts Alaska," 46.
27 Hermann M. Fritz, Fahad Mohammed, and Jeseon Yoo (2009), "Lituya Bay landslide impact generated mega-tsunami – 50th anniversary," *Pure and Applied Geophysics*, 166(1–2), 153–175.
28 George Pararas-Carayannis (1999), "Analysis of mechanism of tsunami generation in Lituya Bay," *Tsunami Hazards: The International Journal of The Tsunami Society*, 17(3), 193–206.
29 Don J. Miller (1960), "Giant Waves in Lituya Bay."
30 John Finney (1958), "Scientists reconstruct events of July 9 Alaska earthquake," *The New York Times*, December 1, 31.
31 Don J. Miller (1960), "Giant Waves in Lituya Bay."
32 Howard Ulrich (2011) as told to James Kendall, "What it feels like . . . to survive a tsunami."

33 Don J. Miller (1960), The Alaska earthquake of July 10, 1958: Giant wave in Lituya Bay, *Bulleti*n of the Seismological Society of America, 50(2), 253–266.

34 Ibid.

35 Charles L. Mader and Michael L. Gittings (2002), "Modeling the 1958 Lituya Bay mega-tsunami, II," *The Science of Tsunami Hazards,* 20(5), 241–246.

36 Ibid.

37 Don Tocher and Don J. Miller (1959), "Field observations on effects of Alaska earthquake of 10 July, 1958," *Science*, 129(3346), 392–395.

38 Hermann M. Fritz, Fahad Mohammed, Jeseon Yoo (2009), "Lituya Bay landslide impact," *Pure and Applied Geophysics,* 166(1–2), 153–175.

39 Don J. Miller (1965), "Giant wave in Lituya Bay: the biggest splash in history," *Mineral Information Service* 18(12), 217–220.

40 Don J. Miller (1960), "Giant Waves in Lituya Bay."

41 "Eyewitness accounts: Britons caught up in the sea surges across south and east Asia tell their stories," BBC News, 27 December 2004. At http://news.bbc.co.uk/2/hi/asia-pacific/4126183.stm.

42 Marsha Walton (2005), "Scientists: Sumatra quake longest ever recorded," CNN, May 20. At http://edition.cnn.com/2005/TECH/science/05/19/sumatra.quake/index.html.

43 US Geological Survey (2004), "USGS energy and broadband solution: Off W coast of Northern Sumatra." At http://neic.usgs.gov/neis/eq_depot/2004/eq_041226/neic_slav_e.html

44 Hydrographic and Oceanographic Department, Japanese Coast Guard, "Indian Ocean tsunami at Syowa, Antarctica." At www1.kaiho.mlit.go.jp/KANKYO/KAIYO/KOUHOU/iotunami/iotunami_eng.html.

45 Ibid.

46 Ibid.

47 Marsha Walton (2005), "Scientists: Sumatra quake longest ever recorded," CNN. March 31.

48 Helen Lambourne (2005), "Tsunami: anatomy of a disaster," BBC News, March 27. At http://news.bbc.co.uk/2/hi/science/nature/4381395.stm.

49 International Monetary Fund (2012), Maldives information. At www.imf.org/external/pubs/ft/weo/2010/01/weodata/weorept.aspx?sy=2007&ey=2010&scsm=1&ssd=1&sort=country&ds=.&br=1&c=556&s=NGDPD%2CNGDPDPC%2CPPPGDP%2CPPPPC%2CLP&grp=0&a=&pr.x=53&pr.y=18.

50 Kandasamy Kathiresan and Narayanasamy Rajendran (2005), "Coastal mangrove forests mitigated tsunami," *Estuarine, Coastal, and Shelf Science,* 65(3), 601–606.

51 Amy Waldman (2004), "Thousands die as quake-spawned waves crash onto coastlines across Southern Asia," *The New York Times*, December 27. At www.nytimes.com/2004/12/27/international/asia/27quake.html?pagewanted=all.

52 Robert D. McFadden (2004), "Walls of water sweeping all in their path: families, communities, livelihoods," *The New York Times*, December 27. At http://www.nytimes.com/2004/12/27/international/asia/27vignettes.html.

53 Yoshiaki Kawata, Yoshinobu Tsuji, Yoshio Sugimoto, et al. (2005), "Comprehensive analysis of the damage and its impact on coastal zones by the 2004 Indian Ocean tsunami disaster." At www.tsunami.civil.tohoku.ac.jp/sumatra2004/report.html.

54 Philip L.-F. Liu, Patrick Lynett, Harindra Fernando, et al. (2005), "Observations by the International Tsunami Survey Team in Sri Lanka," *Science*, 308(5728), 1595.

55 "Indonesia quake toll jumps again," BBC News, January 25, 2005. At http://news.bbc.co.uk/2/hi/asia-pacific/4204385.stm.

56 Lawrence K. Altman (2004), "International agencies mobilize in effort to limit health risks posed by disaster's aftermath," *The New York Times*, December 28. At www.nytimes.com/2004/12/28/health/28disease.html.

57 Robert D. McFadden (2005), "Relief delivery lags as deaths pass 140,000," *The New York Times*, January 1. At http://www.nytimes.com/2005/01/01/international/worldspecial4/01quake.html.

58 David Zurick (2011), "Post-tsunami recovery in South Thailand, with special reference to the tourism industry," in Pradyumna Prasad Karan, *The Indian Ocean Tsunami: The Global Response to a Natural Disaster* (Lexington, KY: University of Kentucky Press), 163.

59 Poh Poh Wong (2012), "Impacts, recovery and resilience of Thai tourist coasts to the 2001 Indian Ocean tsunami," Geological Society London, Special Publications, January 1, 361, 127–138.

60 Erik Cohen (2011), "Tourism and land grab in the aftermath of the Indian Ocean tsunami,", 11(3), Special Issue of *Scandinavian Journal of Hospitality and Tourism:* "Tourism in a Decade of Terrorism, Disasters and Threats – Some Lessons Learned."

61 Nathan Gronewold (2010), "Lessons from 2004 tsunami will guide redevelopment effort in Haiti," *The New York Times*, January 22. At www.nytimes.com/gwire/2010/01/22/22greenwire-lessons-from-2004-tsunami-will-guide-redevelop-88506.html?pagewanted=all.

62 Ibid.

63 " 'No alert' in Indonesian tsunami," BBC News, October 27, 2010. At www.bbc.co.uk/news/world-asia-pacific-11635714.

64 Andrew C. Revkin (2004), "With no alert system, Indian Ocean nations were vulnerable," *The New York Times*, December 27. At www.nytimes.com/2004/12/27/science/27science.html.

65 Ibid.

66 Koji Yasuda (2011), "Whole towns gone – no cars or people seen," *Daily Yomiuri Online*, March 13. At www.yomiuri.co.jp/dy/national/T110312004789.htm.

67 Peter Foster (2011), "Alert sounded a minute before the tremor struck," *The Montreal Gazette*, March 11. At http://www.telegraph.co.uk/news/worldnews/asia/japan/8377510/Alert-sounded-a-minute-before-the-tremor-struck.html.

68 Kenneth Chang (2011), "Quake moves Japan closer to US and alters Earth's spin," *The New York Times*, March 13. At http://www.nytimes.com/2011/03/14/world/asia/14seismic.html.

69 Richard A. Lovett (2011), "Japan earthquake not the 'Big One'?," *National Geographic Daily News*, March 14. At http://news.nationalgeographic.com/news/2011/03/110315-japan-earthquake-tsunami-big-one-science/.

70 US Geological Survey (2011). Information: USGS Energy and Broadband Solution Near East Coast of Honshu, Japan. At http://earthquake.usgs.gov/earthquakes/eqinthenews/2011/usc0001xgp/neic_c0001xgp_e.php.

71 "Japan earthquake: tsunami hits north-east," BBC News, March 11, 2011. At www.bbc.co.uk/news/world-asia-pacific-12709598.

72 Martin Fackler and Michael Wines (2011), "In remote coastal towns, survivors give witness to a wave's power," *The New York Times*, March 16. At http://query.nytimes.com/gst/fullpage.html?res=9902E4D7103EF935A25750C0A9679D8B63.

73 "Tsunami from Japanese quake prompts evacuation of 11,000 residents on Russia's Sakhalin Island," *The Guardian*, March 11, 2011. At www.570news.com/news/world/article/195950–tsunami-from-japanese-quake-prompts-evacuation-of-11-000-residents-on-russia-s-sakhalin-island.

74 "Tsunami warnings and advisories remain across Pacific region," CNN, March 11, 2011. At http://edition.cnn.com/2011/WORLD/asiapcf/03/11/tsunami.warning/index.html.

75 The towns of Kuji, Ofunato, Rikuzentakata, Kamaishi, Miyako, Otsuchi, Yamada, Namie, Soma, Minamisoma, Shichigahama, Higashimatsushima, Onagawa, Natori, Ishinomaki, Minamisanriku, and Kesennuma were all completely destroyed in the tsunami.

76 National Police Agency of Japan (2011), "Damage situation and police countermeasures associated with 2011 Tōhoku district – off the Pacific Ocean earthquake." At www.npa.go.jp/archive/keibi/biki/higaijokyo_e.pdf.

77 "Japan earthquake: tsunami hits north-east," BBC News, March 11, 2011. At www.bbc.co.uk/news/world-asia-pacific-12709598.

78 Ken Belson (2011), "As routines falter, so does national confidence," *The New York Times*, March 16. At http://query.nytimes.com/gst/fullpage.html?res=9A04E6DB103EF935A25750C0A9679D8B63.

79 Yomiuri Shimbun (2011), "TEPCO details tsunami damage/waves that hit Fukushima plant exceeded firm's worst-case projections," *The Daily Yomiuri Online*, April 11. At www.yomiuri.co.jp/dy/national/T110410003477.htm.

80 "Three nuclear reactors melted down after quake, Japan confirms," CNN, June 7. At http://edition.cnn.com/2011/WORLD/asiapcf/06/06/japan.nuclear.

meltdown/index.html?eref=rss_topstories&utm_source=feedburner&utm_medium=feed&utm_campaign=Feed%3A%2Brss%2Fcnn_topstories%2B(RSS%3A%2BTop%2BStories)&utm_content=Google%2BInternational.

81 Yomiuri Shimbun (2011), "TEPCO details tsunami damage/waves that hit Fukushima plant exceeded firm's worst-case projections."

82 Joe Burgess, Amanda Cox, Sergio Peçanha, et al. (2011), "Assessing the radiation danger, near and far," *The New York Times*, April 2. At www.nytimes.com/interactive/2011/04/02/world/asia/assessing-the-radiation-danger.html.

83 Ken Belson and Hiroko Tabuchi (2011), "Japan finds contaminated food up to 90 miles from nuclear sites," *The New York Times*, March 20. At http://query.nytimes.com/gst/fullpage.html?res=9A0DE2D61631F933A15750C0A9679D8B63.

84 Jae Hur (2011), "Food contamination set to rise as Japan fights radiation crisis at reactor," Bloomberg News, March 27. At www.bloomberg.com/news/2011-03-27/food-contamination-set-to-rise-as-japan-fights-radiation-crisis-at-reactor.html.

85 Joe Burgess, Amanda Cox, Sergio Peçanha, et al. (2011), "Assessing the radiation danger, near and far."

86 James Glanz and William J. Broad (2011), "US sees array of new threats at Japan's nuclear plant," *The New York Times*, April 5. At www.nytimes.com/2011/04/06/world/asia/06nuclear.html.

87 "Millions of stricken Japanese lack water, food, heat," NPR News, March 14, 2011. At http://www.npr.org/2011/03/18/134527591/millions-of-stricken-japanese-lack-water-food-heat.

88 Michael Wines (2011), "As tsunami robbed life, it also robs rite of death," *The New York Times*, March 23. At www.nytimes.com/2011/03/24/world/asia/24burial.html.

89 *Naoko Fujimura and Kana Nishizawa (2011),* "Quake evacuees survive on rice balls, bread, seek to avoid contracting flu," Bloomberg, March 26. At www.bloomberg.com/news/2011-03-26/japan-s-evacuees-battle-flu-survive-on-rice-balls-and-bread.html.

90 Naoko Fujimura (2011), "Japan moves to relocate quake victims after meeting food, clothing targets," Bloomberg, March 29. At www.bloomberg.com/news/2011-03-28/japan-starts-to-rebuild-after-quake-as-evacuees-told-to-avoid-power-plant.html.

91 Jimmy Chuang (2011), "Japan omits largest donor Taiwan from thank-you note," *WantChina Times*, April 16. At www.wantchinatimes.com/news-subclass-cnt.aspx?cid=1101&MainCatID=11&id=20110416000057.

92 Victoria Kim (2011), "Japan damage could reach $235 billion, World Bank estimates," *Los Angeles Times*, March 21. At http://articles.latimes.com/2011/mar/21/world/la-fgw-japan-quake-world-bank-20110322.

93 David Cyranosk (2012), "Rebuilding Japan: after the deluge," *Nature*, 483, 141–143. Volume:

94 Andrew Pollack (2011), "Nuclear future in the balance," *The New York Times*, May 10. At http://query.nytimes.com/gst/fullpage.html?res=9C03E0DD103AF933A25756C0A9679D8B63.

95 Andrew Pollack (2011), "Nuclear future in the balance."

96 Kerry Sieh (2006), "Sumatran megathrust earthquakes: from science to saving lives," *Philosophical Transactions of the Royal Society*, 364(1845), 1947–1963.

97 Ibid.

Further Reading

Jeff Kingston (ed.) (2012), *Natural Disaster and Nuclear Crisis in Japan: Response and Recovery after Japan's 3/11* (Oxford: Routlege).

Kingston gives important insights into the consequences of the Japanese tsunami and the ensuing nuclear disaster, and he challenges mainstream media views and misperceptions on the handling of this disaster.

William W. Lace (2008), *The Indian Ocean Tsunami of 2004 (Great Historic Disasters)* (New York: Chelsea House Publications).

This detailing of the Indian Ocean tsunami of December 26, 2004 looks through both a macro and micro lens and succeeds on both levels.

Gerard K. Sutton and Joseph A. Cassalli (2011), *Catastrophe in Japan: The Earthquake and Tsunami of 2011* (Hauppauge, NY: Nova Science Publications Inc.).

In this book, Sutton and Cassalli explore the catastrophe in Japan with a focus on economic and trade effects, as well as the food and agriculture ramifications of the Fukushima nuclear crisis.

Edward Bryant (2010), *Tsunami: The Underrated Hazard* (New York: Springer).

This is an introductory-level book on tsunamis, and discusses examples from all over the globe.

Charles Brooks (1994), *Disaster at Lisbon: The Great Earthquake of 1755* (Long Beach, CA: Shangton Longley Press).

This is a comprehensive treatise on the Lisbon earthquake and tsunami, from scientific and policy points of view.

Part 2

Surficial Processes

Chapter 4

Fire

Terrified, shrieking women, helpless old and young, people intent on their own safety, people unselfishly supporting invalids or waiting for them, fugitives and lingerers alike – all heightened the confusion. When people looked back, menacing flames sprang up before them or outflanked them. Finally, with no idea where and what to flee, they crowded on to the country roads, or lay in the fields. Some who had lost everything – even their food for the day – could have escaped, but preferred to die."[1] *(The Burning of Rome, July 19–24, 64 CE)*

Introduction

This chapter focuses on large fires in ancient Rome, pre-modern London, and nineteenth-century Chicago, Illinois and Peshtigo, Wisconsin in the USA. While the first three fires occurred where large urban populations reside, it was the Peshtigo fire that revealed the vulnerability of a self-contained rural logging and lumbering community to the ravages of an unstoppable conflagration. Rural and forest fires are most likely to happen when natural forces such as lightning strikes and sparks from falling rocks ignite natural materials such as trees and grasses. In theory, more preventable urban fires have human agents whose actions may foster the conditions for incendiary activities. The burning of Rome, London, and Chicago resulted in massive damage to the built environment, with minimal losses of human life. Human agents played a primary role in causing these fires, which spread from open pits and cooking ovens to devastate entire communities.

Natural Disasters in a Global Environment, First Edition. Anthony N. Penna and Jennifer S. Rivers.

The forest fire that spread to the lumber and milling town of Peshtigo from neighboring towns caused massive damage to both natural and built environments. Slash left on the ground, a by-product of clear-cutting, and numerous piles of sawdust adjacent to lumber mills in the towns, added much fuel to the fires. The origin of these forest fires remains a mystery. A lightning strike during an unseasonal hot and dry summer seems plausible, with ash from a cigarette, cigar, or pipe a likely cause. Later in this chapter, an alternative explanation suggests that a different culprit from a distant part of the solar system may have provided the ignitable material that burned Chicago and Peshtigo on the same day.

The Burning of Rome (68 CE)

The fire

Extensive fires burned portions of Rome in 6 and in 12 CE, the latter destroying the city's courts of law, the Basilica Julia, and the Roman Forum. In 22 CE, the site of Julius Caesar's assassination in 44 BCE, the Theater of Pompey was razed by fire. In 26 CE, a fire on the Caelian Hill, originally an old-growth forest of oak trees that became a real-estate development project, destroyed every structure. As a harbinger of the fire that was to come, a fire erupted in the Circus Maximus in 36 CE and, riding swift winds, swept across the Triumphal Way to the Aventine Hill, destroying single houses, tenements, bathhouses, and shops. In the aftermath of each destructive fire, a building program (often financed by the emperor) commenced, rebuilding a more elaborate and fire-resistant environment for the city's elite, removing tenements and haphazard shacks.[2] In the process, it banished poor residents of Rome to more undesirable living quarters. Rome's governing bodies passed neither fire prevention laws nor design or building regulations. As such, the city's 55 miles (89 km) of narrow and winding streets with wooden tenements and its zigzagging pedestrian lanes became a congested environment made for urban flames (Figure 4.1).

Circus Maximus

Circus Maximus was a long U-shaped wooden stadium for horse-racing and chariot races. Rebuilt after the fire in 36 CE, it became the largest wooden stadium in Rome, attracting as many as 300,000 fans during racing

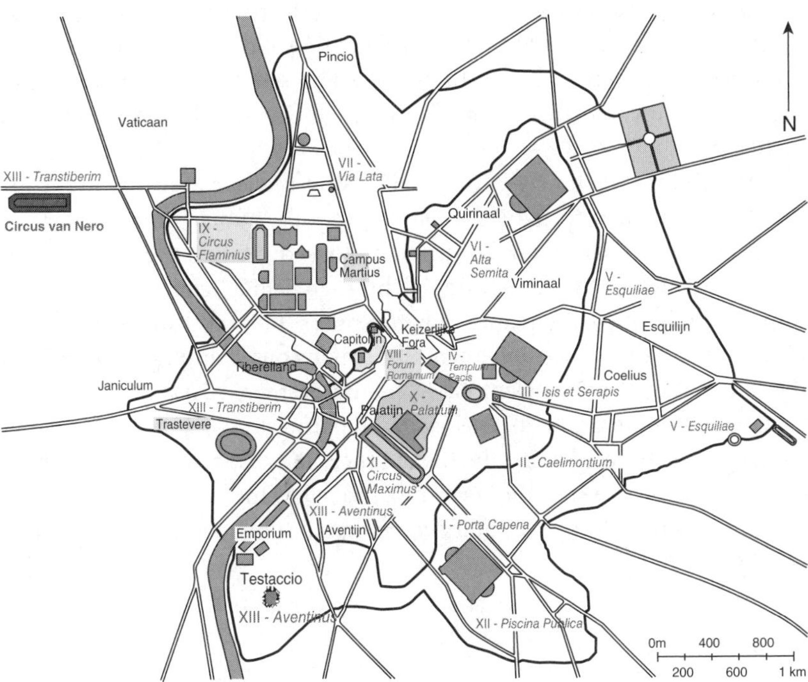

Figure 4.1 Map of Rome during the time of Emperor Nero.
Source: ColdEel. Wikimedia Commons.

holidays and religious festivals. On July 19, a blistering hot day in the city, crowds from surrounding towns and residents from its teeming tenements streamed into the neighborhoods surrounding the Circus. As night approached, carts filled with produce, fish, and game to feed these masses entered the city. At the same time in the open space below the Circus, bakers, pastry cooks, and hot-food vendors tended their fires, preparing carry-out breakfast and snack foods for those entering the stadium.

During the hot summer night, with cool breezes blowing in from the surrounding hills, sparks from fires for cooking may have escaped through the wooden porticos and spread quickly to shops that housed the vendors and to the wooden stands of the Circus above. This vast dry wooden structure burst into flames from end to end and the fire entered the blocks of tenements to the south. Fire bells alerted Rome's *vigils*, its local fire-fighters, to assemble and try to stop this wind-swept blaze from spreading beyond the districts closest to the fire. Given the primitive nature of their equipment (buckets of water), their second line of defense entailed knocking down buildings to create firebreaks. The speed with which the fire moved and the narrow streets in which they moved made firebreaks ineffective.

With nothing at the *vigils'* disposal to stop the spread of the fire, confused residents had to fight the blaze without a human support system, facing fire and collapsing buildings that blocked their escape. For six days and seven nights, the fire, whipped by high winds, changed directions unpredictably, moved up and down Rome's hills destroying not only blocks of tightly packed tenements but mansions, temples, and shrines, the landmarks of this ancient city. The fire destroyed 70% of Rome. The 27-year-old emperor, Nero, was away preparing to compete in a singing contest in Antium (Anzio). In his absence, the responsibility for taking control of efforts to stop the spreading fire fell to the city's prefect, Flavius Sabinus, a hero of Rome's military campaign to subdue recalcitrant Britons in 43 CE.

Relief efforts

One of Flavius's first acts was to dispatch Praetorian riders to inform Nero of the unfolding disaster. A second dispatch detailed a fast-moving fire that threatened the heart of Rome and the emperor's latest construction project, the massive *Domus transitoria*. It was "a long, colonnaded building that ran from the Palatine all the way across the city to the Gardens of Maecenas, which occupied the Esquiline Hill."[3] At this news, Nero decided to return to Rome. By the third day, the fire had become a firestorm and the *Domus* had become one of its victims. As he climbed to the top of the Esquiline Hill, Nero observed that all the buildings on the fringe of the Gardens had been destroyed to create a much-needed firebreak.

Nero commanded that more firebreaks be created to stop the spreading fire and that all public buildings safe from the fire be opened to the fire's refugees. As a result, the Campus Martius become the site of temporary structures to handle hundreds of thousands of the dispossessed. To feed residents, Nero ordered that food be brought from all the towns near Rome and be provided at reduced cost to the needy. The price of grain was lowered substantially, so bakeries could provide affordable bread for the masses. The fire continued to burn out of control until it reached a clear area approaching the Esquiline. As Tacitus reported, "the violence of the fire was met by clear ground and an open sky."[4] Weary Romans thought that the end was in sight, only to witness another outburst from the smoldering embers of a seemingly spent firestorm.

For two more days, a revitalized fire ravaged the hillside of the Capitoline Hill and down its reverse slope. As the wind dropped, the fire reached an already-burnt district and finally ended. In its wake, the fire left only four of its 14 districts untouched while completely destroying three others. The remaining seven districts suffered severe damage to most structures.

Rebuilding

Once the fire ended, Nero imposed new building regulations, reviving many instituted by his predecessor, the emperor Caesar Augustus, to limit the height of buildings, restrict the use of timber as a construction material, and the number of shared walls by adjoining structures. To replace timber usage, fire-resistant stone became the preferred alternative building material. The historic congestion of tenements was to be alleviated by incorporating courtyards and porticoes into the architectural plans of residential housing. Roads were widened to further lessen congestion. Prior to 64 CE, roads and pathways accommodated the movement of a single cart, with few exceptions. Creating open space and eliminating congestion would mean that the population density of Rome would decline, with fewer houses and tenements to accommodate a city of one million people.

He paid for the removal of rubble from Rome and used it to fill the marshes on the coast near Ostia, eliminating a valuable natural habitat for coastal birds and amphibians. To compensate owners of damaged properties in Rome itself, Nero encouraged them to sell their holdings and to purchase "made land" created by debris from the fire on the filled swamps and marshes.[5] His plan to build a canal through this "made land" connecting Ostia to Rome never got beyond the planning stage. Its goal of delivering harvested corn from Ostia to a rejuvenated Rome to feed the city's masses would have entailed considerable ecological costs.

Much of the reconstruction was left to private investors who were rewarded with the rights of Roman citizenship by spending at least 100,000 *sesterces* for building a house. Nero, however, quickly rebuilt the Circus Maximus, a number of religious shrines, and public buildings using his own imperial wealth rather than levying a tax on Rome's beleaguered fire-weary inhabitants.

Conclusion

Rome's glory was reflected in its public buildings and spaces. The massive reconstruction effort that the emperor planned and paid for was intended to return the imperial city to its zenith (although much of the wealth to undertake this effort came from Nero's treasury, which was replenished by tribute and taxes paid to him but seldom, if ever, deployed to alleviate the wretched living conditions of the masses). The rebuilding of Rome was not completed in the remaining four years of Nero's reign. Civil unrest, court intrigue, assassinations, and general mayhem ultimately reached Nero, who committed suicide rather than be whipped to death by his captors in 69 CE. The fire of 64 CE and the extravagance of his plans to reconstruct Rome in his image defined his life.

The Great Fire of London (1666)

> Many people, awakened from sleep by the heat of the flames or the warning cries of their friends, escaped with little more than the clothes they wore. Others had to abandon their carts and wheelbarrows when streets became impassable. Some streets were blocked by debris from houses pulled down in the path of the flames; in others, the roadway had been torn up in the rush to uncover and breach water pipes; and at street junctures soldiers were already posted in an endeavor to seal off the fire. To avoid hold-ups, many refugees took to the side streets and side alleys which, within hours, were as badly blocked.[6]

Introduction

The Great Fire of London of September 2–7, 1666, followed in the wake of a plague that struck London, Europe's third largest city with an estimated population of 500,000, with a vengeance in May 1665, killing 68,596 persons. "Now death rides triumphantly on his pale horse through our streets and breaks into every house almost where any inhabitants are to be found. Now people fall as thick as leaves from the trees in autumn, when they are shaken by a mighty wind."[7] Despite periodic outbreaks of plague, wealthy Londoners did not feel safe enough to return to their homes in the city until February 1666.

Under the best of circumstances – and these were hardly the best – city life in London was crowded, noisy, and filthy. Butchers disposed of carcasses' rotting remains by throwing them into congested alleys and open pits. Human and animal waste clogged open drains and added to the city's constant stench. This urban chaos was magnified by the haphazard and shoddy construction of shops, taverns, and dwellings that sprang up without even the semblance of urban planning, public safety, and health. Visible disorder and confusion in the built environment complemented the characteristics of an insolent, noisy, and unruly population.

The Great Fire of London began after midnight on Sunday morning, September 2, 1666, amidst gale-force winds blowing across southeast England and reaching the city in the early morning, knocking over chimneys and dislodging thatch from rooftops. In Pudding Lane, a dark, narrow street, "the king's baker" Thomas Farriner, who baked an unleavened biscuit for the king's navy, rose at midnight to check his oven in preparation for the morning's labor. Discovering that no fire remained in the oven, he struck a match, added kindling to the firebox and went back to bed. Whether the gale-force winds (a natural occurrence) or negligence on the part of Farriner (human error) or some combination of the above created the conditions for the conflagration remain a mystery.

What is known is that medieval cities like London, comprised of haphazard wooden buildings, were packed together so tightly that sunlight and fresh air were amenities unknown to their residents. In other words, fires were common and the loss of life an unfortunate by-product. Also, what is known was that the baker's helper, living and sleeping close to the oven, was awakened, gasping for air, as smoke filled the bakery. Alerted, Farriner roused his daughter, Hanna, and his maidservant, and escaped via the rooftops. The maidservant's fear of falling traumatized her, causing her to lose her balance and fall to her death. Their escape across the adjoining rooftops was not without its perils, as a severely burned Hanna survived but would live the rest of her life with scars inflicted on that fateful night. Farriner fared much better, escaping unharmed.

The rapid spread of the fire should be seen in the context of a long summer season characterized by excessive heat, a debilitating drought, and the attendant lack of water from the numerous aqueducts, conduits, and wells. An eighteen-month drought parched the land. Gale-force winds from the southeast fanned the fire and accelerated its spread. An ongoing war with the Dutch only added to the misery faced by citizens during this oppressive summer. A built environment of mostly wooden medieval structures made the city as vulnerable, as one can imagine, to the dangers of fire emanating from cooking and baking ovens, torches, candles, and the like.

A chaotic array of debris-strewn narrow alleys, rows, and lanes connected the neighborhoods. A surface of oyster shells pressed into the mud was smothered with stinking layers of horse manure, kitchen waste, ashes, and the contents of chamber pots thrown from the windows of upper-level bedrooms. Only a handful of structures were built of stone and brick; the majority of dwellings "were a sprawling rookery built of little more than sticks and mud. Clinging to every inch of space, stacked and cantilevered upon each other, stood ruinous tenements, shacks and hovels, cramped garrets, and damp dark cellars."[8]

These conditions made the alleys an onerous and barely passable network for humans and animals – but not for the roaring flames. In fact, Pudding Lane had formerly been named Red Rose Lane but after the reign of Richard II (1367–1400) was renamed Pudding to reflect the *puddings*, a euphemism for the intestines of butchered carcasses, carried down the lane and dumped into the Thames River at low tide.

Consequently, fire visited medieval wooden London repeatedly after prolonged hot droughts from 1611–16 CE, 1630–35, and 1653–57. But great fires extended back into centuries past to 798 CE, 982, and 989, followed by others in 1212, 1630, and 1633. The causes were similar to those of the Great Fire. "Many dwellings were little more than tar-paper shacks, thrown together around a timber frame that was sometimes prefabricated away from the site. Walls were made either from beech laths covered with mud and mixed with the hair of animals; the poor use very finely chopped straw."[9]

Despite this long history, efforts to impose construction codes using less flammable building materials failed at the implementation stage. Almost five centuries of edicts from city mayors and kings banning the use of thatch as roofing material and wooden chimney flues and demanding that stone construction replace wood went unheeded. Smoke and sparks continued to emanate from the furnaces of foundries, metal smiths, glassmakers, gunsmiths, and the like, making fires a constant hazard.

Knowledge of these hazards did not go unheeded, as London city laws required churches to possess ladders, buckets, axes, and fire hooks and to have them at the ready in the event of an outbreak. Barrels filled with water were to be located at every doorway during the summer months. Local residents borrowed ladders, buckets, and fire hooks, however, and never returned them. They also failed to fill barrels of water and in some instances they found other uses for them. Such were the conditions that not only made fire possible but probable. Overcrowding, faulty construction, poor maintenance, and the inadequate enforcement of fire laws created conditions conducive to fire.

The fire

Efforts to suppress the fire in Farriner's bakery with the help of neighbors carrying buckets of water failed, as the flames jumped from garret to garret fanned by the wind and fast-moving updraft. Sparks and burning debris encircled residences, buildings, and stables and within a few minutes Pudding Lane and Fish Street Hill were consumed by the inferno as it entered Thames Street and raced toward the river and London Bridge. The bridge, 910 ft (277 m) long and supported by 20 stone arches, contained a number of fashionable homes with stately facades and interior woodwork and paneling.

The fire swept across the bridge undeterred, engulfing the bridge's tower and houses. As burning timbers crashed to the bridge's roadway, residents scrambled from their beds to the safety of the Southwark bank. Burning and blowing embers ignited alleys and lanes hundreds of feet away from the bridge along the waterfront. Wooden waterwheels built to provide water for the waterfront district during low tide and much-needed succor during a conflagration collapsed under the assaulting flames.

The speed of the fire trapped almost everyone and everything in its path. The flames consumed primitive fire equipment and engines. The hot wind preceded the flames, carrying with it dense smoke and searing dust and ash. It roared like thunder as it approached buildings already covered in a rain of sparks, burning embers, and ash. Then, they burst into flames, 50 ft (17 m) high in some instances. The flames rumbled through the passageways as though a volcano had just erupted. Crowds of people, crushed under the burden of carrying their belongings, and covered in burning ash, became the fire's immediate victims.

The fire melted metalwork, burned wooden facades and structural timbers, shattered glass, and fractured stone supports. The lack of water to fight the fire only made matters worse. Given the extended drought, many wells were dry and the conduits bringing water from the Thames and from the new River Head at Islington failed for a similar reason. Fear and flames raged through the population, and the prospect of death by burning and suffocating or by being trampled in the stampede of flight served to terrify those who were fleeing. The swirling wind and the intensity of the fire confused and disabled those caught in its grip. As one terrified onlooker described it:

> The wind blew equally to the right and to the left, and caused the fire to burn on all sides, which persuaded many that the fire was miraculous. I myself remember that going into the streets at that time and having the wind impetuously in my face, I was in the hope that at my return I should have it at my back, but it was all one. The noise and crackling and thunder of the impetuous flames, the shrieking of women and children, the hurry of people, the fall of towers, houses and churches was like a hideous storm.[10]

Compounding the chaos created by the raging fire was the rush and crush of people trying to escape with their carts and wheelbarrows loaded with belongings and the influx of men trying to enter with empty vehicles of all kinds. Their intentions were well known: to take advantage of the crisis by charging exorbitant fees to carry away the prized possessions of merchants and upper-class individuals and families. Carrying these possessions away from the site of the conflagration and the chaos to the city's suburbs did not mean that their belongings would eventually be delivered to their rightful owners. The scene would be easy to visualize – a physical clashing of thousands of people pushing in opposite directions. While some tried desperately to leave the city and save their belongings, others attempted to enter the city to capitalize on the confusion of those who weighed their personal safely against their desire to protect their possessions.

"The weight of the traffic tore up the cobbles. Some roads had great holes dug in them where the water supply had been cut and in these the horses stumbled and fell. The roar and crackle of burning rafters, the falling sparks, the clouds of blinding acrid smoke like a dense black fog, the coughing, the cries of pain, the screams and curses turned the streets leading to Moorgate and Cripplegate into scenes of hopeless confusion."[11]

By Friday, September 7 London's medieval built environment located behind its 35-ft-high (10.7 m) and 10-ft-thick (3 m) walls had all but disappeared, the results of a rapidly spreading inferno. The fire destroyed five-sixths of London, approximately 373 acres (1.5 km^2) within the walls, and an additional 63 acres (0.25 km^2) beyond (Figure 4.2). Only 75 acres (0.31 km^2) within the city escaped the fire. Over 13,000 houses, 87 churches, and 52 livery stables had disappeared. Most of the city's jails burned to the ground, releasing hundreds if not thousands of convicts into the general

Figure 4.2 The Great Fire of London (1666).
Source: Third Day of the Great Fire of London 1666 by Rita Greer (history artist) from her collection of paintings of the life and times of Robert Hooke. Oil on board, 2007.

population. Civil administrative buildings also fell victim to the blaze including the Royal Exchange, the Customs House, and the Guildhall. Twenty wharves for coal and wood as well as one hundred boats and barges and stairs down to the Thames suffered a similar fate.

London's ability to deliver mail, print the news, and sustain its formerly thriving markets for food and local goods was suspended until the city had literally cooled down. Many local fires reignited once smoldering cellars, warehouses, and stores were exposed to the air. In the absence of professional fire-fighters, brigades of volunteers with buckets worked around the clock to keep the fire from spreading. Their efforts and the fact that much of the combustible material had already burned ultimately led to the Great Fire's demise.[12]

Since neither hastily-formed fire brigades nor the forces of nature seemed capable of quelling the blazes, the Lord Mayor, Bludworth, reluctantly accepted the plan to create firebreaks by demolishing houses with barrels of gunpowder. Despite the destructive capacity of a rampaging fire, delay in arriving at this decision was dictated by an ancient city law that made those who destroyed a person's house responsible for its rebuilding. Only the king acting with the consent of his Council could absolve citizens of this responsibility. By the time King Charles II gave his consent, London's very existence hung in the balance. "London, so famous for wisdom and dexterity, could now find neither brains nor hands to prevent its ruin."[13]

Rebuilding

Once the fire was extinguished and with 80% of London's 300,000 population homeless, the daunting task of building the city anew would cut it off from its medieval past and make the city safer from fires and the outbreaks of contagious diseases, with wider, cleaner, and airy streets. The losses estimated by the architect Christopher Wren were staggering, and the costs of rebuilding by contemporary standards would be immense. He estimated that losses of stores of wine, tobacco, sugar, plums, etc., were £1,500,000, house wares, money, and movable goods at £2,000,000, it cost £2,000,000 more to move possessions out of the city, and the houses destroyed were valued at £3,900,000 or £300 each. Of the original estimate of 15,000 dwellings inside the city walls, only 1,800 remained standing.[14] A daunting estimated figure of £11 million was given to rebuild London and the expenditure would require the imposition of stringent labor rules that eliminated the ancient privileges of medieval guilds.

Free laborers, including carpenters, bricklayers, plasterers, and other workers would have their wages fixed by judges appointed by the king. Judges possessed the power to imprison workers for a month if they left work unfinished and to impose fixed costs on construction materials. Fortunately for tenants and in some instances the owners, fire courts composed of 22 judges adjudicated claims by tenants and landlords over overdue rents and claims over property boundaries, and the chaos created by the loss of landmarks. Its intention was to get the parties to agree to the terms of the Rebuilding Acts of 1667 and 1673. The courts discovered that shared costs, reduced rents, extended leases, and a moratorium on quarterly rent payments proved to be a complicated yet effective way to get reconstruction underway.

In addition, to begin to pay for the enormous cost of renewal, the Rebuilding Act of 1667 imposed a tax on coal entering the city. The king's decision to suspend the Hearth Tax (property tax) for seven years on any new house built in the city offset its costs. After six years of rebuilding, a lecturer at Gresham College wrote to Christopher Wren claiming that "the Fire however disastrous it might be to the then inhabitants, had prov'd infinitely beneficial to their Posterity; conducing vastly to the Improvement and Increase, as well of the Riches and Opulence, as of the Splendor of the City."[15]

Despite these incentives from the king, rebuilding was so slow that by the end of 1670 workers had rebuilt none of the 84 destroyed churches. So few houses were rebuilt for commoners that those finished were reserved for workers and tavern-keepers who provided entertainment for said workers. The substantial civic buildings, including the Customs House and the Guildhall, remained unfinished, as did the city's gates, prisons, and the foundation for St. Paul's Cathedral, redesigned by Christopher Wren. It was not completed until 1711.

The replacement of public works damaged or destroyed by the fire became civic priorities and resulted in a surge of employment in the construction trades. However, the shortages of craftsmen caused delays in the rebuilding of private residences. Recovery remained a slow and arduous process, with reconstruction a patchwork of renewal. New residences appeared randomly without a plan and amidst a burned cityscape of empty, debris-covered lots. Once the pace of reconstruction quickened, sales failed to respond to the availability of new homes. By 1673, as many as 3,423 new homes remained unoccupied, with entire streets devoid of residents: "No person so much as asks the price of any."[16]

Leasehold tenants defined the relationship that most Londoners had with property owners. Most leases contained the same clause that required tenants "to sufficiently sustain, maintain, uphold and repair the premises, cause the pavement to be repaired and the privies to be cleaned."[17] Since leases were written for a specific time period, tenants were obligated to return the property in the "pristine" condition that they received it. If the property was damaged or destroyed, as 80% of it was during the Great Fire, the tenant was obligated to pay rent for the full term of the lease. Without savings and property insurance, an unknown vehicle for protection against casualty in the seventeenth century, many tens of thousands of London's citizens, including wealthy merchants, went bankrupt after the fire with no means of support. Destitution was exacerbated by the bitter winter that followed the inferno and the absence of a relief effort to alleviate the miseries of a starving, poor population.

Conclusion

The Great Fire sparked a wave of reform in urban construction, first in England but eventually in northern and central Europe. Streets were widened while advances in the engineering technology of fighting fires with better pumps, hoses, and fire engines restricted a fire's reach. Fire insurance became commonplace as companies offered property owners protection against losses. The passage and enforcement of fire codes and the replacement of thatch with brick and masonry reduced urban fires significantly. "Between 1700 and 1900 the number and size of English cities expanded dramatically but the size and frequency of conflagrations shrank. The cities grew faster than they burned. The control of urban fire, it is argued, augmented the size of investment capital. The industrial revolution not only put fire into machines but removed it from heavily capitalized cities."[18]

The Chicago and Peshtigo Fires (1871)

> I jumped out of bed and pulled on my pants. Everyone in the house was trying to save as much as possible. I tied my clothes in a sheet. With my clothes under my arm and my pack on my back, I left the house with the rest of the family. Everyone was running north. People were carrying all kinds of crazy things. A woman was carrying a pot of soup, which was spilling all over her dress. People were carrying cats, dogs and goats. In the great excitement people saved worthless things and left behind good things. I saw a woman carrying a big frame in which was framed her wedding veil and wreath. She said it would have been bad luck to leave it behind.[19]

Introduction

The movement of glaciers in the last Ice Age carved the geography of the Great Lakes region, creating the largest lakes in North America and the abundant woodlands that provided the lumber to build many of the country's Midwestern cities, of which Chicago was the first. The connection between this region as the nation's primary source of timber and Chicago's role as a lumber capital during the second half of the nineteenth century made the city "nature's metropolis."[20] By 1870, over 200 boats carrying lumber arrived in Chicago daily. Docks and yards were piled 12 ft (3.7 m) high with white pine, much of it used in the construction of cheap balloon-framed housing in which pine boards are nailed together to make a frame. Two huge fires consumed the lumber towns of Peshtigo, Holland, Manistee, and Port Huron in Michigan and Wisconsin and Chicago, Illinois, on the same night: Sunday, October 8, 1871.

The region's abundance of forests, cut logs, lumber, bark, and sawdust, its long drought, the appearance of a cyclonic windstorm in the American Midwest with a temperature difference of 40°F (4.4°C) on each side of the storm – all these factors provided the conditions for fires. Under normal circumstances, fire in forests and farming communities was commonplace; most were anthropogenic fires set by clearing fields for planting. Lightning and sparks caused only a few fires. During this fall season, smoke was ubiquitous and its smell was everywhere.

Chicago, on the other side of the lake, "served as the chief lumber market on Lake Michigan, but its role went much further than just buying and selling wood. Chicago capital often directed the movement of white pine from forest to mill to final consumer."[21] It was also a city where wood was almost everywhere, making Chicago a potential tinderbox. As the source for construction materials for public buildings, housing, stables, and liveries, it also provided planking for sidewalks, alleys, and roads. The city's built environment contained 56 mi (90 km) of wooden-block pavement and 651 mi (1,047 km) of wooden sidewalks. In addition, tightly packed wood-framed dwellings, some mere shanties, used sawdust, wooden shavings, and bark piled in backyard sheds along with coal to ignite fires for household use.[22] Urban fires confined to open hearths, fireplaces, furnaces, and lanterns sometimes went out of control, either through neglect or accident.[23]

During the particularly dry fall season of 1871, numerous autumn fires on the prairies and in the forests of Wisconsin and Michigan burned over an area larger than farmers and loggers could remember. Strong winds only accelerated their spread and forced some residents to vacate their homes. Weather in Chicago mimicked that on the prairies; drought and strong hot winds were common. Local fire brigades quickly extinguished small anthropogenic fires in the city; except on Saturday, October 7, when a fire erupted at the Lull and Holmes Planing Mill on South Canal Street and spread to the adjacent paper-box factory, lumber yard, and pinewood housing. When brought under control by fire-fighters laboring for 72 hours, four blocks of houses had burned, displacing hundreds of families and destroying 16 acres (0.65 km^2) of supplies of lumber and coal. In the eyes of Chicagoans, it was the city's Great Conflagration.[24] Such a characterization was short-lived, however, because the next evening an exhausted fire brigade would be confronted by the Chicago Fire.

In a world made of wood, urban and rural fires threatened to erupt without warning. In Chicago, the sound of a fire bell announcing another outburst was as familiar to residents as the sound of factory whistles signaling the beginning and the end of a work shift. In Peshtigo and its sister mill towns in the days before the fire, the presence of smoke not only irritated one's eyes but reduced visibility on some days such that ships on Lake Michigan approaching Green Bay used their foghorns to warn incoming and outgoing traffic of their presence. When the smoke was thick enough, only the sun was visible at midday. For the most part, city and mill town fires, however familiar and present, were containable. Such was not the case on October 8, 1871, however, with the almost simultaneous outburst in different locations of two fast-moving fires. Was the timing of these events a coincidence, or was there a cause for their outbreak that could be identified?

The Chicago fire

On or about 9:30 p.m. on Sunday, fire bells announced the outbreak of another fire, the origin of which remains in dispute. Inciting anti-immigrant sentiments, one report alleged that it began in the city's shanty district of Irish immigrants in a barn owned by Patrick O'Leary on Chicago's West Side. This allegation has turned into the legend of Mrs. O'Leary's cow kicking over a lantern, which sparked the fire. Other reports identify the outbreak at the rear of the old armory building across from the city's gas works. Regardless of who or what caused the fire, human error seems likely. At any rate, the fire spread rapidly, pushed by a howling wind that showered cinders and ashes on wooden structures, humans, and animals.

Within hours, it had jumped the Chicago River and burned to the south and north of the city. Escape across the river's many bridges became futile not only because of the fire but also because people, carrying whatever possessions they could, were rushing ahead of the fire from both directions.

In addition, some bridges rotated to allow ships passage to Lake Michigan, causing delays for escaping citizens. By midday on Monday, October 9, much of the city lay in ruins. A sleep-deprived and physically exhausted brigade of 185 fire-fighters, having yet to recover from the massive fire on Saturday, October 7, its twenty-ninth fire of the week, proved to be no match for this devastating, fast-moving blaze. The wind was the enemy of fire suppression, so despite the efforts of fire-fighters, superheated columns of air behaved like twisting tornadoes. Humans were no match for 100-ft-high flames that ripped through buildings and cast movable objects, including furniture, house wares, and appliances skyward.

As the fire moved east and north, it enveloped the city's downtown district of fashionable homes, hotels and boutiques, a courthouse with a basement prison, theaters, banks, and newspaper buildings with offices for managers and reporters. Their printing presses ran both morning and evening to give the public the latest news. As the fire consumed the city's water tower, its connection to Lake Michigan and as such its source of potable water for drinking, washing, and for combating fire, all seemed lost. In response, blowing up buildings to create the kind of firebreak familiar to foresters became a last-ditch strategy to stop the fire's spread.

Its success was modest, however, as the fire had already leaped over the Chicago River and begun its assault on the North Side business district, where it destroyed more buildings than on the South and West Sides combined. Of 13,800 buildings and homes, about 500 remained standing, leaving 74,450 residents homeless. On the West Side, flames destroyed about 500 structures leaving 2,250 people homeless, and on the South Side fire consumed 3,650 buildings and homes leaving about 21,000 more homeless. Almost 300 persons lost their lives, though many more were unaccounted for, suggesting that the actual figure may have been much higher. Property losses amounted to US$400 million, displacing about one-third of the city's population.[25] The material devastation to the city's built environment, though great, failed to reflect the terror and pandemonium that residents faced as they rushed to escape the flames among a sea of unrecognizable faces blackened with smoke.[26]

Relief efforts

The response to the chaos caused by this fire that burned itself out by Monday, October 10 was significant. The outpouring of charitable giving and relief items exceeded all previous responses to natural disasters in the USA. Citizens from across the country raised almost $4,000,000. The US army loaned Chicago 50,000 tents to house the destitute, while the city's mayor, Roswell Mason, commissioned the city's Relief and Aid Society to collect and distribute charitable donations. Within days of the conflagration, in a frenzy, Chicago began to rebuild.

With winter looming, workers built 5,000 wooden single-family shanties for the city's homeless, while primitive barracks were constructed for the city's burgeoning population of poor residents. The construction of thousands of wooden-framed houses began as well. Few, however, would withstand another great fire, since wood remained the construction material of choice.

Agencies set up to assist the homeless and the dispossessed in Chicago provided relief. In addition, Lieutenant General Philip Sheridan, a Union Army hero during the Civil War, arrived with five companies of infantry from Omaha and Fort Leavenworth to maintain the peace, although no acts of violence, rioting, or looting had taken place. Martial law was enforced for two weeks with the support of Mayor Mason but opposed by Illinois's governor, John M. Palmer, who believed that the state's militia and local police were able to maintain domestic tranquility and that Sheridan's involvement represented an intrusion of the federal government into the state's affairs.

Almost a week after the fire, a "General Plan" was devised by Chicago's Relief and Aid Society to provide shelter for the homeless, find employment, deliver food, clothing and medical services, and to arrange for transportation out of the city. Their responsibilities would tax the efforts of most benevolent societies. Conflicts within the bureaucracy established by the Society's Executive Committee would become commonplace, as would disputes between agency staff and members of the community.

One fundamental belief seemed to unify the Society and its staff: that aid was not an end in itself but a means to help citizens to become self-sufficient. Conflicts over how and when self-sufficiency would appear pitted formerly hard-working Chicagoans, now destitute and homeless, against bureaucrats who regarded work as a necessity, despite one's current condition. Pleas for financial assistance to rebuild collapsed or damaged dwellings were sometimes ignored, as the following case demonstrates: "I spent every dollar I had and borrowed some besides. It is three months since I started to build. I tried every way to finish it before I sent for any help, and now I am called upon for taxes . . . I will be obliged to live in that cold house without a chimney or anything if you do not send me some help."[27]

To exacerbate matters, the Society refused to continue aiding families financially whom it deemed to be unworthy, despite holding more than $1 million. This decision not only brought it into conflict with Chicago's needy but also Cook County's Board and the city's Common Council. Refusal to turn these funds over to the city meant that the Society discontinued aid to the needy in mid-1873, with $600,000 still unspent. This surplus would eliminate its need to fund-raise for over ten years.

Rebuilding

A "Great Rebuilding" that mobilized the city's labor, capital, material resources, and financial acumen began with much fanfare. The task of rebuilding the city began even as the embers from the fire cooled. Homeowners who had lost everything in the conflagration began assembling the prefabricated housing provided by municipal relief. Commercial property owners on the North Side reached out to the thousands of unemployed workers who had lost their livelihood to the fire's devastation and hired them to clear away the debris. With thousands of pick- and shovel-wielding men and boys at the ready, they knocked down the walls of buildings weakened by the fire and began the labor-intensive job of picking through the rubble to salvage usable bricks and iron. They loaded the remaining debris onto hundreds of horse-drawn wagons and daily dumped about 5,000 loads into Lake Michigan. Although carpenters erected temporary wooden commercial quarters on these sites, the goal was to build permanent structures. By December 1871, masons were building as many as 212 brick and stone structures on the city's South Side.[28]

A breathtaking two-year building boom was cut short by the Panic of 1873 when Cooke's Bank in New York City failed, sending shockwaves through the financial system of the country and contributing to a six-year depression. With lending and borrowing curtailed, real-estate development came to a screeching halt across the country, with Chicago suffering mostly in the wake of the fire. To make matters worse, poorly enforced building codes and the continuing use of wood for construction led to the Little Fire of 1874, which burned much of the city again. A second opportunity to rebuild came once the depression ended in 1879. This time, building codes were a priority.

Conclusion

A revitalized banking system provided the capital to begin the rebuilding of the city which the city's major daily newspaper, the *Tribune*, applauded with enthusiasm. It reported that the construction of four- to six-story commercial buildings would go forward with the greatest of speed. Speed it was, with one completed every day for the 200 working days from April 15 to December 1, 1872. These buildings of iron, brick, and stone did not include the thousands of wooden homes and structures built during the same period. A year and a half after the fire, the city's boosters and entrepreneurs rightfully claimed that commercial Chicago had rebuilt and rebounded from its greatest fire. Their boasts did not include the impact of the fire on the lives and future prospects of Chicago's poor and working class, however.

Figure 4.3 shows the areas affected by the Peshtigo and Chicago fires.

The Peshtigo fire (1871)

> The air was no longer fit to breathe, full as it was of sand, dust, ashes, cinders, sparks, smoke, and fire. It was almost impossible to keep one's eyes unclosed, to distinguish the road, or to recognize people, though the way was crowded with pedestrians, as well as vehicles crossing and crashing against each other in the general flight. The neighing of horses, falling of chimneys, crashing of uprooted trees, roaring and whistling of the wind, crackling of fire as it ran with lightning-like rapidity from house to house – all sounds were there save that of the human voice. People seemed stricken dumb by terror. Nature alone lifted up its voice and spoke.[29]

Introduction

In Peshtigo, Wisconsin, lumber entrepreneurs from Chicago led by William B. Ogden established the Peshtigo Company on Green Bay, dredging the harbor and expanding its docks to accommodate his lumber business. The company's railroad carried cut logs from the forests to its mill in Peshtigo, one of the largest in the state, cutting an average of 150,000 board ft (45,720 m) of lumber each day using its 97 saws. The town itself was a beehive of manufacturing activity, producing sashes, doors, and blinds. A machine shop, a gristmill, a large store, a company boarding house, and company-owned rental housing dominated the village. A smaller sawmill, a foundry, blacksmith and shoemaker shops, livery stables, grocery, dry

Figure 4.3 Map outlining the Peshtigo and Chicago fires of 1871.
Source: Reproduced by permission of the designer, Lana Penn.

goods, several boarding houses, and a hotel were owned independently. Two churches and a schoolhouse completed the town's built environment.

To give some semblance of the town's importance to the economy of the region, its wooden wares factory employed approximately 200 workers who used multiple and different saws, lathes, planers, and hoop-cutters. It may have been the largest factory of its kind under one roof in the USA, measuring 341 ft (104 m) long. The main building was four stories high and 60 ft (18 m) wide, with a three-story sawmill and a two-story shingle mill. In addition, there were 16 brick kilns, a four-story storehouse, and a two-story paint-grinding mill. In all, about 800 of Peshtigo's 2,000 residents worked wood in one capacity or another. Between January and mid-September of 1871, the mills sawed 5,690,384 board ft (1,734,429 m) of lumber, leaving vast piles of sawdust almost everywhere in the town, and slash and brush on the forest floor.[30] Peshtigo was a pulsating and thriving economy and an important link to Chicago, its urban neighbor on Lake Michigan but also another populated tinderbox, made so by human activity.

The fire

During the last week of September, fast-moving timber and brush fires spread across western Minnesota, "leaping roads, burning underground, curling back on them, rolling along at frightening speed."[31] By Thursday, October 5, high winds drove "the fire forward with lightning rapidity and it was burning fiercely in the woods around Glencoe, Leseni, Mankato and New Ulm, Minnesota."[32] Although these fires seemed to be far enough away from Peshtigo to create a safe distance, the "Great Woods" of the Michigan, Minnesota, and Wisconsin were an interconnected environment. Fed by gale-force winds from as far away as Texas, and creating their own wind, smaller independent fires joined to form one large catastrophic firestorm.

While Peshtigo's residents gasped for air, flakes of ash covered everything around, including humans, animals, plants, and inanimate objects. Many residents went about their daily business, working in the mills, stores, and hotels and tending to their families and farms. A few prepared their storm cellars for the worst. Most went to bed on Saturday, October 7, expecting the worst but hoping that this fire, like so many in the past, would either burn itself out or be contained by citizen action. The sound of the approaching firestorm on Sunday, described by some as the sound of a thousand trains racing at full speed or as a deafening persistent roar, alerted residents to flee from the town to the Peshtigo River for safety. By then, the raging fire had become a firestorm with a temperature of 200°F (93°C) making its own winds of 100 mph (160 km/h) in some locations. "When a firestorm erupts in a forest, it is a blow-up, nature's nuclear explosion, generating the same heat and devastating power as an atomic bomb. The only precedent for a fire of such magnitude, the only frame of reference for a firestorm, was the Great Fire of London in 1666."[33]

A terrifying account by one resident caught in the firestorm describes the efforts of those struggling to escape the enveloping blaze:

> The air was no longer fit to breathe, full as it was of sand, dust, ashes, cinders, sparks, smoke, and fire. Some [people and vehicles] were hastening toward the river, others from it, whilst all were struggling alike in the grasp of the hurricane. A thousand discordant deafening voices rose . . . The neighing of horses, falling of chimneys, crashing of uprooted trees, roaring and whistling of the wind, crackling of fire as it ran with lightning-like rapidity from house to house – all sounds were there save that of the human voice.[34]

By evening the town of Peshtigo lay in ruins and as many as 800 of its residents had perished. The fire destroyed 14 towns and much of the "Great Woods" forest in three states. With about 640 trees in a square acre (0.4 km), it is reasonable to claim that about one billion trees were destroyed by the firestorm. It burned nearly 2,400 mi^2 (3,800 km^2) and killed many more than the figure given for Peshtigo. Although lacking in specific details, because there remained no trace of some of the people consumed by the firestorm, those attempting to calculate the losses have suggested that approximately 1,500–2,400 died. Many loggers lived in the forests; transient laborers were a seasonal workforce and left no temporary address or next of kin, so accuracy was replaced with estimates of those dead.

Relief efforts

Soon after his inspection trip to the devastated towns and villages, Lucius Fairchild, governor of Wisconsin, led the relief effort seeking donations in cash and kind from in-state citizens. As news of the disaster appeared in papers across the country, donations of food and clothing streamed into Wisconsin. Perishables were distributed immediately, while relief workers packed canned goods, salted meat, and flour into crates for distribution later. Local relief committees organized by the governor with two central agencies in Milwaukee and Green Bay used all forms of transport, including horses, open wagons known as buckboards, and agents on foot to deliver relief supplies of food and clothing to remote farms. Steamboats and wagons with teams of drivers carried out the bulk of the distribution work. Fairchild, a veteran officer in the Union Army during the Civil War, proved to be a skilled strategist in organizing the statewide relief and a shrewd tactician in making a national appeal for donations through writing letters to local newspapers across the country.

In nineteenth-century America, the limited role of the federal government excluded disaster relief. No one expected assistance from Washington DC and no one asked until Governor Fairchild wrote to the Secretary of War, William Belknap. On the same day, he sent out his appeal across the state and country, arguing that what had happened in Peshtigo and communities across Wisconsin was no ordinary calamity. He targeted his requests to assist Wisconsin's farmers who had lost wagons and harnesses. "Has the USA any common harness and ordinary Army wagons to spare?" He offered that "the State will account for them at their value if required to do so." He asked for one hundred of each, as well as one thousand army coats and pants, and offered to pay for them.[35]

Honoring Fairchild's military service and his status as governor, Lieutenant General Philip Sheridan sent him a telegram five days after his appeal, asking: "Can I be of any service to the sufferers from fire in the burnt district of your state, if so what do you want? Please ask me only for what you know is necessary."[36] Two days later, Secretary of War Belknap wrote to Fairchild that he had instructed Sheridan to send the wagons, harnesses, coats, and pants that he, Fairchild, had requested, but had also included blankets, 200,000 military rations of hard bread, beans, bacon, dried beef, pork, sugar, rice, tea, and coffee.[37]

Rebuilding

With the same fervor that guided the relief effort, city and state officials, along with the lumber baron William Ogden, vowed to rebuild the town, and revive and modernize the lumber industry. His optimism inspired survivors and newcomers to build new housing, boarding houses, and the town's major architectural landmarks. These included the Catholic and Congregational churches and the Peshtigo Company Sawmill. As part of the rebuilding and revitalization, several memorials were created to honor the fire's victims. The town established a Fire Museum in 1926, and a Peshtigo Fire Cemetery in 1951 with a perpetual flame acknowledging the sacrifices of the town's residents. Since 1992, corporate sponsors have held a 5-kilometer fire tower run and walk on October 8 to commemorate the date of the fire and to honor those who lost their lives.

Conclusion

A number of factors contributed to the success of the relief effort, including the executive leadership of Governor Fairchild in making appeals to citizens and the federal government in creating a structure for distributing aid to survivors of the firestorm. The tireless effort of individual relief workers also warranted an acknowledgment. Yet, complaints from victims and their advocates tarnished the relief effort. Many of them were familiar complaints, even today when there are more clearly defined roles for government at the local, state, and federal levels.

Establishing priorities about who should be assisted first would become a common problem with communications technology in its infancy. Slow access to food, clothing, and medical attention were legitimate complaints during the aftermath of the worst catastrophe to strike these communities. For some victims, the response of aid workers seemed punitive, not helpful. One administrator of relief, obviously not sympathetic to the plight of victims, complained that some overreached in their appeals for help. To him, many had, "lost a fence and wanted a farm."[38]

Another explanation for the causes of the Chicago and Peshtigo fires

It was unknown at the time, but each fire erupted within a few minutes of each other despite the fact that both sites had been plagued for days or even weeks by local, seemingly containable, fires. The Chicago fire destroyed $200,000,000 (1871 dollars) worth of property and resulted in the deaths of at least 300 people. The major fires that began in upstate Wisconsin and Michigan, of which the fire in Peshtigo was the most devastating, causing the death of upwards of 2,400 farmers and their families, loggers, mill workers, shop- and hotel keepers. It has been suggested that these two conflagrations were not coincidences but occurred as a result of the breakup of a comet in deep space.

The comet was named Biela's Comet after the Austrian astronomer Wilhelm von Biela, who observed it in the night sky on February 26, 1826.

With a complete solar orbit taking six years and nine months, the comet's orbit took it so close to Jupiter that it broke into two comets. According to theory, one of these comets entered Earth's atmosphere on October 8, 1871, and broke into several pieces, the main piece crashing into Lake Michigan while other fragments ignited fires on both sides of the lake – in Peshtigo, the upper, middle, and lower Sugar Bushes, Menekaune, and Williamsonville in Wisconsin, Manistee in Michigan, and Chicago.

Although we have no direct evidence in the form of comet fragments, observations at the time of the fires reveal a pattern that suggest an aerial bombardment. "Basements exploded." "Entire blocks seemed to ignite at once." "There was very little smoke; it burned too rapidly." "During all this time the fire was falling in torrents. There was literally a rain of fire."[39] The smaller comet fragments would consist of frozen comet gases such as methane (CH_4) and acetylene (C_2H_2) that melted upon entering Earth's atmosphere, then vaporized and ignited in the presence of oxygen (O_2). These chemical reactions are consistent with another observation reported often, that "fire balloons" typically four inches (10 cm) in size rained down from the sky and exploded upon contact with Earth's surface, consuming everything in sight. With current research exploring the probability that a comet or meteor might strike Earth, "little attention has been given to the possibility that it has already happened in modern times."[40]

Summary

Despite the horror of Peshtigo's death toll, Chicago's fire during the same week received much more national attention, despite its comparatively modest casualty rate. In all urban cases, including those of Rome and London, the fires created opportunities to re-engineer the natural and built environments.[41]

Advocates of renewal proposed plans for wider streets and thoroughfares, green spaces to separate buildings that were formerly close together, and more structures of stone, and brick with iron support beams to replace the ubiquitous wooden buildings. Government and charitable assistance were key aspects of the renewal process, even though private capital was instrumental in urban redevelopment. This dimension of the renewal process turned out to be a mixed blessing, however. Candidates ran for office pledging their support for enforced building codes using nonflammable materials. The same was true for Rome and especially for

London, where rebuilding commenced immediately after the fire. Within four months, the city had been largely rebuilt in wood.[42] It was not until the twentieth century, with its more powerful urban political systems, that building codes became more acceptable and enforceable.

In Rome, Nero's status as emperor gave him license to rebuild the city as he liked without the consent of the governed. Slaves provided an available labor pool. Although slavery existed in seventeenth-century London, slaves, limited in number, could not be called upon to clear the city's rubble after the fire. The blazes in Peshtigo and Chicago occurred in a post-slavery world. However, in most instances, Peshtigo being the exception, devastating fires created the conditions to alter the spatial and physical environments of Rome, London, and Chicago. New central corridors and districts emerged, residential districts grew, some by removing slum dwellers to the city's outskirts. Beneath the ground, infrastructures of sewer and water pipes, which had previously been limited to the business district and to more upper-class areas before the fires, were extended outward as an integral part of urban revitalization.

Notes

1 Tacitus (2005), "The Burning of Rome, 64 AD," *The Annals of Imperial Rome*, 116 CE. Translated by Alfred John Church and William Jackson Brodribb (Stilwell, KS: Digiread.com Publishing).

2 Stephan Dando-Collins (2010), *The Great Fire of Rome: The Fall of The Emperor Nero and his City* (Cambridge, MA.: Da Capo Press), 56.

3 Ibid., 92.

4 Ibid., 96. and Tacitus (2005), "The Burning of Rome, 64 AD."

5 Miriam T. Griffin (1984), *Nero: The End of a Dynasty* (New Haven: Yale University Press), 130–131.

6 James Leasor (1961), *The Plague and the Fire* (New York: McGraw-Hill), 221.

7 Thomas Vincent (1811), *God's Terrible Voice in the City* (Bridgeport: Lockwood & Backus), 16.

8 Neil Hanson (2001), *The Great Fire of London: In That Apocalyptic Year, 1666* (Hoboken, NJ: John Wiley & Sons), 49–50.

9 Ibid., 32.

10 Ibid., 94–95.

11 Harold Priestley (1966), *London: The Years of Change* (New York: Barnes & Noble), 166.

12 Neil Hanson (2001), *The Great Fire of London*, 168.

13 Ibid., 56.

14 James Leasor (1961), *The Plague and the Fire*, 256 and John Bedford (1966), *London's Burning* (London: Abelard-Schuman), 278–279.

15 Stephen J. Pyne (1997), *Vestal Fire: An Environmental History, Told through Fire and Europe's Encounter with the World* (Seattle, WA: University of Washington Press), 60.

16 Ibid., 228.

17 Adrian Tinniswood (2004), *By Permission of Heaven: The True Story of the Great Fire of London* (New York: Riverhead Books), 239.

18 Ibid., 61.

19 Hilda Polacheck (2011), "American Memory," US Library of Congress, circa 1938–39. At http://memory.loc.gov/ammem/today/oct08.html.

20 William Cronon (1991), *Nature's Metropolis: Chicago and the Great West* (New York: W.W. Norton & Co.), 8.

21 Ibid., 159.

22 Mel Waskin (1985), *Mrs. O'Leary's Comet: Cosmic Causes of the Great Chicago Fire* (Chicago: Academy Chicago Publishers), 70.

23 Stephen J. Pyne (1982), *Fire in America: A Cultural History of Wildland and Rural Life* (Princeton, NJ: Princeton University Press).

24 Mel Waskin (1985), *Mrs. O'Leary's Comet*, 46.

25 Paul Bennie (2008), *The Great Chicago Fire of 1871* (New York: Chelsea House Publishing), 79.

26 Karen Sawislak (1995), *Smoldering City: Chicagoans and The Great Fire, 1871–1874* (Chicago: University of Chicago Press), 29.

27 Ibid., 101.

28 *Ibid.*, 168–169.

29 Peter Pernin (1971), "The Great Peshtigo fire: An eyewitness account," *The Wisconsin Magazine of History*, 54(4), 256.

30 Kurt R.F. Geyer (1921), "History of the Peshtigo Fire, October 8, 1871," *Peshtigo Times*, October 6, 3.

31 Denise Gess and William Lutz (2002), *Firestorm at Peshtigo: A Town, Its People and the Deadliest Fire in American History* (New York: Henry Holt and Company), 83.

32 Ibid., 90.

33 Ibid., 101.

34 Peter Pernin (1971), "The Great Peshtigo fire," 256.

35 Denise Gess and William Lutz (2002), *Firestorm at Peshtigo*, 239.

36 Ibid., 180.

37 Ibid.

38 Ibid., 183.

39 Robert M. Wood (2004), "Did Biela's Comet cause the Chicago and Midwest fires?" American Institute of Aeronautics and Astronautics, Planetary Defense

Conference: Protecting Earth from Asteroids, February 23–26, Newport Beach, California, 3.

40 Ibid., 10.

41 Ross Miller (1990), *American Apocalypse: The Great Fire and the Myth of Chicago* (Chicago: University of Chicago Press), 106–108.

42 Christine Meisner Rosen (1986), *The Limits of Power: Great Fires and the Process of City Growth in America* (New York: Cambridge University Press), 107.

Further Reading

Peter Charles Hoffer (2006), *Seven Fires: The Urban Infernos That Reshaped America* (New York: Public Affairs).

Beginning with the Great Fire of Boston in 1760, and going on to discuss the Pittsburgh fire of 1845 that destroyed 2,500 buildings, Baltimore's 1904 fire that led to the redevelopment of its Inner Harbor, and the inferno in New York City caused by an attack by terrorists on September 11, 2001, the author chronicles these catastrophic events, illustrating how disasters, if they are handled properly, can help us better understand our society.

David Cowan (2001), *Great Chicago Fires: Historic Blazes That Shaped a City* (Chicago: Lake Claremont Press).

There have been several Chicago fires, ranging from the burning of Fort Dearborn in 1812, to the Iroquois Theater disaster, and Our Lady of the Angels school fire. The author describes them in ways that connect each to the other, offering a perspective on city life visited often by fire.

Neil Hanson (2002) *The Great Fire of London: In That Apocalyptic Year, 1666* (Hoboken, NJ: John Wiley & Sons).

The narrative about the outbreak of the Great Fire of London is well known. What this volume adds is a through description and analysis of the mechanism and chemistry of combustion.

Chapter 5

Floods

Most remarkable of all this is the fact that the astonishing picture the nation [Britain] is now witnessing – whole towns cut off, gigantic areas underwater, mass evacuations, infrastructure paralyzed and grotesquely swollen rivers, from the Severn and the Thames downwards not even at their peaks yet – has all been caused by a single day's rainfall. A month's worth [fell] in an hour. It is obvious that the government and the civil powers from [British Prime Minister, 2007–10] Gordon Brown down to the emergency services, are struggling to cope, not only with the sheer physical scale of the disaster itself, but with the very concept of it. It is entirely unfamiliar. It is new.[1]

Introduction

Flooding is the most fatal natural disaster: more lives and property are lost in floods than in any other natural disaster. The majority of devastating floods are flash floods caused by intense rain for a period of hours to days. Many negative effects are associated with floodwaters: injuries and casualties of people and animals, physical damage to structures, contamination of water supplies, pestilence, crop failure, transportation of large amounts of sediment and other material, the spread of pollution, and profound economic loss.

However, humans have been drawn to rivers since the dawn of civilization. Rich nutrients and sediments are spread routinely across floodplains during a flood. This cyclical replenishment of nutrients and sediments makes for superior topsoil and agricultural yields. Rivers are also a source of drinking water, a sink for flushing waste, a source of food (both the fish that live in the river and the animals that are drawn to rivers for

Natural Disasters in a Global Environment, First Edition. Anthony N. Penna and Jennifer S. Rivers.

drinking), energy, recreation, and transportation. When humans attempt to capitalize on the benefits of living near a river, but settle too close to a dynamic and powerful natural system, they place themselves in an unpredictable environment, one in which large and devastating floods occur without warning.

This chapter examines three major floods: the twentieth-century floods of China's rivers, which were the most deadly natural disaster in the history of humanity, the flood disaster of 1953 in the Netherlands, showcasing both the resourcefulness and the fallibility of an engineered city, and the Bangladesh floods of 1987–88, with an eye towards the future and as an example of a poor coastal country living both on a floodplain and in the path of major cyclones.

Central China Floods (1931)

> There is probably no river in the world which is of so little use to mankind as the Yellow River, considering the populous district through which it flows. Thus far, people have been only partly successful in protecting themselves from its ravages. Even as a communication artery it is unimportant. The river is an enemy instead of a helpful agent.[2]

Introduction

One of the deadliest natural disasters in human history was a series of floods in 1931 along the Huang He (Yellow River), the Chang Jiang (Yangtze River), and the Huai River in China, which killed approximately four million people by drowning, flood-related disease, and, later, by famine due to crop failure. Over 51 million people were affected, one-quarter of China's population.[3] Ironically, these floods followed a two-year drought. A winter of abnormal snowfall and a spring with heavy rains ended the drought with catastrophic results caused by excessively rising water levels through July and August, 1931. Seven cyclones in one month contributed to the pending disaster by producing intense rainfall that covered 41,313 mi^2 (107,000 km^2). Over 80 million people lost their homes. Nanjing, one of China's largest cities, became an island, completely cut off from other areas. The 1931 floods caused the collapse of agriculture in the region, and destroyed the social fabric of Chinese society on such a scale that it is difficult to effectively portray the magnitude of this catastrophe.

Geography

Three main rivers, along with their many tributaries, are responsible for most of the flooding in China: the Chang Jiang (Yangtze), the Huang He (Yellow) and the Huai Rivers. The Chang Jiang, one of the world's largest rivers by discharge, flows through its 660,000 mi^2 (1.7 million km^2) drainage basin for 3,988 mi (6,418 km). For scale, Mexico covers an area of 759,530 mi^2 (1,967,000 km^2). The Chang Jiang extends from the glaciers on the Tibetan Plateau to the East China Sea in Shanghai. For thousands of years, humans have used the river for irrigation, transportation, energy, and for political and linguistic boundary-marking. It serves as the dividing line between north China where Mandarin is spoken and south China where Sinitic dialects are used. The recently built and newly opened Three Gorges Dam on the Chang Jiang is the largest hydro-electric power station in the world.

The Huang He, China's second largest river, serves as the artery into the heart of north China, by whose waters 60 million human beings live.[4] When the Huang He floods, it floods catastrophically, as it drains an enormous 290,520 mi^2 (745,000 km^2) basin (for scale, Texas is 269,000 mi^2). Its reach extends from the Tibetan highlands, through grasslands, to a massive plateau of fine-grained yellow silt (loess) blown by wind from the Gobi Desert in Mongolia. Prior to the development of agriculture on this plateau, forests covered the region and retained the sediment so that silt in the river would have been one-tenth the current volume.[5]

But since humans removed the trees to grow crops, the sediment has become destabilized and easily eroded. The river currently carries huge volumes of loess – up to 50% by weight of Huang He water. Downstream from the plateaus is a densely populated region: The Huang He is called "the cradle of Chinese civilization" as its basin is the birthplace of ancient Chinese societies. It was the most prosperous region in early Chinese history, despite frequent devastating floods. Its unenviable names, "China's Sorrow" and "Scourge of the Sons of Han," reflected the ongoing experience of flood victims.[6]

The Huang He has devastated lands around it throughout human history: 4,300 years ago a flood lasted for thirteen years. Four thousand years ago, Emperor Yu dredged the channel and dug nine diversion channels to divert the floodwaters. Two and a half thousand years ago, the Chinese began building a series of earthen levees in an attempt to reclaim land, but those levees have failed many times over the centuries.[7] In 1887, over a million people were killed by drowning and famine when the river overtopped its levees.

The Huai is a 1,000-mile (1,610 km) long tributary to the Chang Jiang, and is a major waterway. Originating in the Tungpo Mountains of the Honan Province in central China, it passes through Honan, Anwhei, Kiangsu, and part of Shantung Provinces.[8] This river flows eastward between the Chang Jiang and Huang He, and is comparatively small, but it is doubtful whether any other river of its size has ever inflicted as much damage as has this so-called "River without a mouth." Although its basin area is only 50,000 mi^2 (130,000 km^2), its discharge is 250,000 ft^3 (7,000 m^3) per second: roughly equal to the normal flow of the Huang He.[9] The Huai also wends its way through an alluvial plain, which has no higher elevations during floods for people to seek refuge. It is also the most densely settled agricultural area and the Grand Canal and Lunghia railways run through the Huai Valley.[10]

As with the Huang He, crops such as wheat, beans, and rice are grown along the floodplains of the Huai, though the productivity has been temperamental and linked to the river's instability. Heavy rains bring floods; light rain causes waterlogging, and no rain means drought. Under the threat of these calamities, the peasants lived in misery along the Huai, which suffered more than 900 floods in 2,000 years.[11] The Huai is the river that turned Nanjing into an island during the 1931 floods.

The floods

The 1931 floods came on the heels of many other massively devastating floods in this region. For centuries, the farmers living near the river have built levees to contain rising waters caused by silt accumulation in the riverbed. Back in 1887, the rising river, coupled with days of heavy rain, breached the levees in Huayankou, Henan Province, causing a massive flood.[12] Despite the accumulation of silt, the region's low-lying areas caused the flood to inundate over 50,000 mi^2 (130,000 km^2) of cities, towns, farms, and commercial centers in a short period of time. After the flood, two million Chinese were left homeless.

The floodwaters became tainted with pollution and sewage, and this contaminated water contributed to the unraveling of the region's social fabric and the resulting outbreak of cholera and typhus. Cholera is caused by a bacterium that is transmitted through contaminated drainage water. It is characterized by violent diarrhea which can lead to death by dehydration within one day. The spread of typhus (a louse-borne infection, not to be confused with typhoid fever which is a bacterial disease carried in water that is contaminated with fecal matter) is also due to bacteria in water, and symptoms include back, joint, muscle, and head pain accompanied by a very high fever, sensitivity to light, and a cloudy or hazy state of mind. These diseases, combined with a lack of basic essentials in food, clothing, and shelter, claimed as many lives as those lost directly to the flood.[13]

Along the Huai, loss of life was tremendous – estimated to be in the millions. Many people were saved by the system of canals as inhabitants sought refuge in small boats normally used to transport grain. Many peasants who had not evacuated prior to the flood hastily constructed rafts or emptied coffins of their dead in desperation to escape the rising waters.[14]

Floods in the region had an impact on agriculture, causing crop yields to decline between 8–56%. Over the next five years, yields became unpredictable.[15] This collapse of agriculture resulted in mass starvation on an unprecedented scale. The Chinese government began receiving vivid reports of people resorting to cannibalism rather than face death by starvation. As the situation deteriorated further, men began to sell their wives and daughters. Some desperate women who gave birth during the floods killed their newborns because of their inability to care for them.

Floodwater exceeded 53 ft (16 m) above the normal level in the Huai River, and the towns of Hubei, Hunan, Jiangxi, Hankou, Wuhan, Hanyang, and Chongqing were inundated and destroyed. In mid-August 1931, the floodwaters rose so high in the Beijing–Hangzhou Grand Canal that levees failed and another 200,000 people died by drowning, with many dying while they slept at night.

In the 1931 flood of the Huang He, between 1,000,000 and 3,700,000 people perished. The human misery associated with the flood resulted in social collapse, with people resorting to violence and retreating to primitive ways of life. A public health crisis much like the one that overwhelmed Chinese society in 1887 occurred as the area became a hotbed of disease.

In the Chang Jiang, from July to August, 2 ft (0.6 m) of rain caused a 53-ft (6 m) flood stage that killed two million people and displaced nearly 30 million more. Overflow from the Chang Jiang flooded the capital, Nanjing (Figure 5.1), and turned it into an island.[16]

Figure 5.1 The Central China floods of 1931.
Source: Mary Evans Picture Library Ltd.

Relief efforts

Early relief efforts were local in nature. In Hankou, local residents raised the equivalent of 800,000 Yuan for immediate relief aid and set up camps that serviced 300,000 people.[17] Public agencies, the provincial reconstruction commissions, initiated relief efforts quickly, though all with limited resources. Private organizations such as the Buddhist Society and the Red Swastika Society and international agencies including the Red Cross and International Famine Relief Commission provided aid in the form of medical supplies, food, and temporary shelters.[18] Government aid came from the USA, the UK, and Turkey in the form of food and money.

In the days following the 1931 floods, China decided that the best way to combat the flood was with a coordinated central planning effort. Executive Yuan, the executive branch of the government in China, ordered the hasty organization of a National Flood Relief Commission in an attempt to address the immediate problems of repairing nearly 3,000 mi (4,800 km) of dikes, caring for refugees, and enlisting support from abroad. China lacked the resources in 1931 to provide much aid to a stunned population. The high death tolls suggest that inadequate amounts of food, medicine, and shelter exacerbated the spread of infection from floodwaters.

When the Huang He flooded again in June 1938, between 500,000 and 900,000 people perished. War added to the misery created by flooding. The Japanese had invaded China, and Chiang Kai-shek, the military head of the Republic of China, decided that a planned flood might stop Japan's advancing troops. He ordered the military to blow up the levees on the Huang He. The resulting flood slowed the Japan's invasion momentarily, but its impact upon China's civilian population was devastating, as the estimated dead toll ranged from 200,000 to 900,000.[19]

> The vicious reactionaries often used the Huang He as an instrument to slaughter the people and maintain their reactionary rule. They deliberately created disasters by breaking the dykes and making the river change course. Adopting a policy of non-resistance towards the aggression of Japanese imperialism, the Kuomintang and Chiang Kai-shek went out of their way to break the Huang He dike at Huayuankou near Chengchow, Honan Province, in 1938 in order to cover their flight. This made the river change course to the south and flooded 54,000 km^2 of land in 44 counties in eastern Hunan, northern Anhwei and northern Kiangsu. A total of 12.5 million people were affected and 890,000 of them died. In addition, it created the vast silt-covered desolate stretches of land known as the flooded Yellow River region.[20]

Rebuilding

In general, the dikes and levees built or repaired after the 1931 flood appear to have afforded substantial protection in 1935 when a flood again inundated 38,000 mi^2 (98,000 km^2).[21] Starting in 1949, much work was done to renovate the river's infrastructure by excavating river channels, by constructing detention and storage reservoirs on the river's upper reaches, and in setting up diversion works for flood detention on the middle reaches. Finally, construction was begun to enlarge the capacity to discharge floods on the lower reaches of rivers.[22] In the 1970s, the government put forth much propaganda, under Chairman Mao Zedong, to suggest that China had turned these destructive rivers into positive, beneficial parts of the landscape.

In 1960, the government constructed the San-men Gorge Dam in an attempt to control floodwaters and also to generate electricity, but the reservoir behind the dam quickly filled with silt, rendering the dam useless. As the river gradient flattens and widens as it travels downstream, much sediment is deposited on the riverbed and levees, causing the channel bottom to increase in elevation by up to 4 in (10 cm) per year. This requires the Chinese to raise the levees in a constant, self-perpetuating cycle. The bed of the river is currently 33 ft (10 m) higher than the adjacent floodplain, with no way of stopping this cycle in sight.

Despite China's efforts, a superflood in 1954 with a recurrence interval of 200 years covered almost the entire area of the Chang Jiang River. Though this flood was greater in magnitude than the 1931 flood, it only killed 30,000 people. In 1991 a flood affected 260 million people and in 1998 a severe flood caused the evacuation of 7.54 million people.[23] China now acknowledges its frequency of serious flooding, and seeks to monitor and control natural disasters, assess damage, and provide relief to its citizens.[24] A combination of flood mitigation strategies are now employed, including engineering, ecological, monitoring, and evacuation planning.

Since 2000, a national integrated system using remote sensing, global positioning, and geographic information systems has monitored and evaluated flood disasters. These systems play an important role in flood mitigation to the point of becoming a key part of the flood management system at China's National Flood Control Headquarters.[25]

Control of the rivers, especially the Huang He, has always been a major function of the government, and throughout history, China has carried out the construction and maintenance of river works with mixed results. The fact that the Huang He was kept in the same channel for 500 years prior to 1852 is evidence that the system operated with some success.[26]

Conclusion

In the floods discussed above, between 2.5 million and 6 million people died. Flooding is not over in China and efforts are underway to examine the causes of flood disasters and to provide practical solutions to mitigate them. The results from recent studies indicate that both historical and more recent recorded data point to an increasing frequency in flood disasters, with damage and losses from flood disasters increasing significantly in the region.[27] In 2010, floods caused damage costing US$21 billion. They destroyed seven million hectares of farmland and 645,000 houses. More than 700 people were killed and eight million were evacuated (a number equaling the entire population of New Jersey in the USA). In total, 110 million people were affected by floods.[28]

By analyzing the physical geographic factors and human activities, a recent study found that the main factors contributing to increasing flood disasters are landform/topography, climate elements, and the reduced drainage capacity of rivers. A low level of flood protection (some levees can only protect against floods with a 10-year recurrence interval) and efforts by humans to reclaim lakes and riparian areas are also causes of floods.[29]

Climate change and intensified industrial activity in China have caused more frequent floods along the rivers, and as a result the country has suffered tremendous economic losses, despite its growing economic prominence, during the last decade.[30] China has long tried to tame her rivers, yet time and again these rivers have won. In this highly populated country, global climate change is likely to further shift the balance in favor of rivers and away from engineered flood control structures, so planning and response is an absolute must along major rivers.

The Dutch Flood Disaster (1953)

> At the village of Tholen, a man saw his wife and twelve children drown as he was trapped helplessly in an upstairs room. A young engaged couple spent 36 hours marooned on a dike. When rescuers arrived the young woman had died from exposure and the young man had become delirious. One man hung on telegraph wires for over 48 hours. Another, caught under the arms by a radio antenna, was still alive 27 hours later when rescued.[31]

Introduction

Since 1014 CE, the Dutch have used windmills to pump water over levees, and since the fifteenth century, they have used the polder system of land reclamation by building dikes and employing pumps to exclude sea water. The polder system currently comprises a large part of the Netherlands. Land elevation differs for each tract of land within the polder system. Each individual tract of land, or cell, is enclosed by dikes that have no hydraulic connection to other areas. The polders vary in height from 11.5–20 ft (3.5–6 m) below sea level and are maintained by dikes, windmills, and pumping systems.

During the weekend of January 31, 1953 a storm surge raged across the northwest European shelf and flooded low-lying coastal areas of the countries around the North Sea.[32] For two weeks in January, the Dutch fought but ultimately lost their battle with the North Sea as it caved in the system of levees. Extremely high spring tides combined with gale-force winds caused massive destruction, resulting in the week-long evacuation of over 100,000 people. Belgium, England, and Scotland were also impacted, though nowhere near the extent to which the Netherlands suffered.[33]

Geography

The Netherlands is a low-lying, delta-type region, where three large rivers, the Rhine, Meuse, and Schelde discharge into the North Sea.[34] A long line of natural dunes stretches along the coast at places intersected by the river inlets that are part of the deltas. Without the present dikes and other flood protection measures, approximately half of the country would be vulnerable to flooding.[35] For much of the history of this region, people lived with these floods, but eventually local populations built dikes out of clay and sand, or even peat to keep agricultural areas dry.[36] This system grew into the polder system of dike construction, particularly in the delta region.

In the twentieth century, the Dutch government created "polder boards" responsible for the cost and dike maintenance for their particular polder. Steam pumping stations replaced windmills used for drainage, although in many places, windmills can still help when needed.[37] The prevailing sentiment in regions below sea level where flooding occurred was either that it was an act of nature or the will of God.[38]

The Netherlands' storm tide warning service was created in 1921 as part of the Royal Netherlands Meteorological Institute. If a weather forecast gave reason to expect a water level significantly higher than the tabulated astronomic tide levels, the Dutch Storm Surge Warning Service (SVSD) became operational. As the storm developed, a warning telegram and radio bulletins were sent out to the public. But since broadcasts stopped at midnight, mayors and other officials who received telegrams had no way of effectively disseminating the warning.[39] In 1921, since private telephones were not yet widespread, floods still came as a surprise to the millions of mostly sleeping Dutch citizens.

In the 1940s, World War II military bunkers and even whole complexes were built into the dikes as part of the military defense system against attack from the sea.[40] Machine gun units and manholes were dug, and piping was laid through the dikes. Since they were closed due to military operations, tunneling by muskrats and moles increased. Following the war, insufficient attention was given to the repair of these rodent holes.[41]

The flood of 1953

The storm and its surge were different from previous floods in that they moved slowly and curved sharply southward prior to making landfall.[42] Rain pounded the area and a storm surge of 9 ft (2.75 m) coincided with spring-tide high water, creating water level heights exceeding any in the historical record.[43] Over 150 sea dikes were breached and many more inland dikes failed. The dike failures caused the flooding of over 136,000 hectares (525 mi^2), an area in which 750,000 people resided. The night and day of the storm are best characterized by chaos and on the spot improvisations.[44] Approximately 2,074 people died and around 100,000 residents were evacuated.[45] Estimates range from between 30,000 and 60,000 livestock drowned. The storm and flooding destroyed between 20,000 and 48,000 houses. Total damage topped US$250,000,000 in 1950 terms (or 1 billion Dutch guilders, the equivalent of $450 million euros today).[46]

The Netherlands was decimated by these dike failures. Zuid (South) Holland, Zeeland and Noord (North) Brabant were largely submerged once the dikes had been breached by the storm and high tide. The hardest-hit areas included the low-lying islands of Alblasserwaard, Goeree-Overflakkee (which suffered an extremely high death rate), the Hoeksche Waard, Ijselmonde, Land van Altena, Nieuw-Vossemeer, Noord-Beveland, Pernis, Rozenburg, Schouwen-Duiveland (where many people drowned), Sint Philipsland, Tholen, and Voorne-Putten, Walcheren, Willemstad, Zeeuws-Vlaanderen and Zuid-Beveland.[47]

The situation was grave. Thirty-five ships off the coast made radio calls for help. Ocean cutters, coasters, and cargo vessels were washed ashore; fishing fleets were torn adrift from their moorings. In the seaside resorts of Scheveningen and Noordwijk boulevards and hotels were turned into rubble.[48] An immense dike protected the central part of the country where over 3 million people lived, and thankfully, this held overall, with only one small breach occurring.

Relief efforts

By the morning of February 1, the scope of the disaster gradually became clear to the outside world and the regional and national authorities started to take stock of the situation by setting up larger-scale coordination efforts.[49] People poured in from surrounding areas to assist with rescue, the distributing of food, water, and medicine, and the removal of corpses. The Dutch army arrived in amphibious vehicles and began to sandbag the dikes while the French and American military shuttled food and people by helicopter to and from remote areas.[50]

Helicopters and boats evacuated survivors for several days. Fishermen were able to use radios to communicate, but overall communication was problematic. None of the radio stations and weather stations in the Netherlands broadcast or operated at night or on weekends. The flood occurred on a Saturday night, so the brunt of the flood came without warning, leaving those affected without the opportunity to prepare to evacuate.[51]

Though the death toll in the 1953 floods topped 2,000, the Dutch dodged a proverbial bullet when the integrity of the main dike withstood the rising waters. With the main dike remaining intact, it protected the inner portion of the country during the highest flood stage, thereby saving the lives of nearly three million people. That the main dike withstood these waters is a testament to mankind's engineering. After this flood, investigations that focused on the efficacy of emergency response and communications systems concluded that virtually no flood emergency plan existed. The flood destroyed telephone lines, so communication was left to ham radio operators on a voluntary basis. In short, for a country that lay largely below sea level with a history of flooding and surrounded by clay dikes, its lack of coordinated evacuation and relief efforts contributed to the many lost lives.

In the absence of a master plan for coping with national disasters, it was left to individual polder boards to maintain the dikes, with local mayors responsible for coordination in emergencies.[52] Neither board members nor mayors had coordinated their responsibilities in the event of a dike failure. In some areas, individuals assumed the role of watchful wardens, staying awake throughout the night to alert neighbors. In other places, no one took on this role, and as a result many people perished who may not otherwise have died.

Rebuilding

Just 17 days after the floods, the Dutch government, seeking to understand the causes of flooding and to protect its people, set up the Delta Committee "to develop measures in order that such a disaster could not happen again."[53] It was soon learned that a series of reports produced by the 1939

Flood Tide Committee, 14 years earlier and written for scientists and senior staff, had highlighted insufficient planning for floods in many parts of the delta area.[54] The reports, however, were never circulated to local polder boards or municipal mayors. The 1953 floods triggered a number of policy-making decisions by the Delta Committee.

Its most important recommendation resulted in the decision to undertake a large engineering project called Deltawerken (Delta Works). As a major addition to the Netherlands' infrastructure, it strengthened existing dikes, and added many new dikes that closed off the estuaries around the most severely flood-impacted regions from the Rhine, Meuse, and Scheldt Rivers. Deltawerken also called for the creation of a robust storm surge barrier, called Maeslantkering, in the Nieuwe Waterweg (New Waterway), a canal near Rotterdam. This project took almost 50 years to complete, making the country safer from flooding.[55]

Queen Juliana and Princess Beatrix toured the flood-impacted towns to raise morale and to view first-hand the devastation. Radio solicitations brought in generous contributions from home. International assistance was also swift and exceedingly generous, so much so that a surplus of money and materials was later donated to industrializing nations abroad.

This flood serves as an engineering success story as well as a cautionary tale. Currently, the Netherlands is engaged in a $144 billion-dollar construction project to strengthen its levee system. With a state-of-the-art system, it hopes to prevent a recurrence of the 1953 disaster.[56]

If the storm and flood had occurred during daylight hours, the peak water levels would have surprised few people. With residents at work or in school, making it easier to mobilize them, daylight would have made it easier to assess the impending danger. Local and national authorities would have been actively functioning, radio could have been used for disseminating warnings, and a central coordinated response system would have started earlier.[57] The number of casualties and failed relief efforts were likely caused by the storm hitting the mainland during the evening and on a weekend. Monitoring and disseminating information are crucial activities during a pending disaster and for a country below sea level they may be instrumental in saving lives.

Conclusion

The Netherlands is a low-lying country, with approximately 25% of its area below sea level, 21% of its residents living below sea level, and 50% of its land lying less than 3.25 ft (1 m) above sea level.[58] Though the polder system has worked well for most of the Netherlands' history, the catastrophic, widespread failure of dikes associated with a storm and a spring high tide in 1953 underscores the precarious nature of regions such as these around the world. These regions may be test cases for more of the terrestrial portion of Earth as changes anticipated by the warming of the planet increasingly imperil low-lying regions with severe storms and rising sea levels. Estimates are that the dikes can be strengthened to accommodate a 20-in (50-cm) rise in sea-level, but after the next five decades, with an expected sea-level rise of 59 in (150 cm), fundamental changes and a completely new infrastructure will be required in the Netherlands to prevent rivers from flooding and to deal with a rising sea.[59]

The Bangladesh Floods (1997–98)

> If you will never come, if you will ignore me
> How can I bear these days of endless rain?
> My gaze lifted afar, I listen eagerly
> My soul rushing restless in the gusting winds,
> O the clouds keep stacking up so high![60]

Introduction

Bangladesh is a low-lying, river-dominated country that has long been plagued with floods: six large events occurred in the 1800s when it was part of India (1842, 1858, 1871, 1875, 1885, and 1892). There have been 18 deadly floods in the twentieth century with four, 1955, 1970, 1987, and 1988, being particularly deadly. Floods continue, and catastrophic floods have most recently occurred in 2004 and 2010. As with the floods in China and the Netherlands, humans have played a major role in the catastrophic floods by inappropriate agricultural techniques creating large areas of unprotected soil which increases runoff.

One can expect that Bangladesh will be increasingly vulnerable to floods in the face of global climate change. Whether the government will have the resources to successfully protect its people from these natural disasters remains to be seen. After the 1971 war liberating it from Pakistan, Bangladesh suffered from famines, floods, cyclones, and widespread poverty, as well as political turmoil and military coups. These events have made

Bangladesh ill-equipped to care for its people during and after flooding. Global climate change challenges existing institutions to adopt policies that ease the potential hardship faced by its people.[61] Due to inherent institutional deficiencies and weaknesses in managerial capacities to cope with anticipated flood-related disasters, it would be extremely difficult for this country to reduce its vulnerability to climate change.[62]

Geology/geography

Bangladesh is perhaps one of the most ill-situated countries in the world from a natural disasters point of view. It is a largely flat, low-lying country along the coast of the Indian Ocean. Virtually all of the land area is only 40 ft (12 m) above sea level; 75% of Bangladesh is less than 33 ft (10 m) above sea level, and 80% of the country is considered either delta or floodplain.[63] It is crisscrossed by rivers, including 57 trans-boundary rivers, and has a flat, wetland-dominated coastline bordering the northern portion of the Bay of Bengal. Bangladesh is a delta plain at the confluence of three major rivers: the Padma (Ganges), the Jamuna (Brahmaputra), and the Meghna, each of which possesses many tributaries. Less than 10% of the drainage basin of these rivers actually lies in Bangladesh, so rainfall in Nepal, Bhutan, China, and snowmelt in the Himalayas determines the flow of water through Bangladesh.[64] The highly fertile alluvial soil is largely created by rivers and results in superior agricultural land. As we will see in Chapter 8 on tropical storms, Bangladesh's tropical climate is characterized by intense heat, high humidity, and seasonal rainfall,. Cyclones, floods, and tornadoes frequently strike the region.[65]

The floods

Given the geography of Bangladesh, its people expect frequent flooding every year. In the 1980s and 1990s, however, floods of a different kind visited the country; floodwaters were higher and remained for a much longer time than usual. The flood of 1997, with a recurrence interval estimated at once every 100 years, became a destructive force throughout July and August and affected over 40% of the country or 22,000 mi^2 (57,300 km^2) of land.

The 1997 flood turned out to be merely an opening act, with Bangladesh falling prey to the most severe flooding in modern world history in 1998. Waters inundated nearly 32,000 mi^2 (82,000 km^2) of land. It coincided with flood stages in the Jamuna, Padma, and Meghna Rivers. Two-thirds of the country was underwater for over 20 days. Over 1,000 people drowned or succumbed to flood-related diseases such as typhoid and cholera, and 135,000 head of cattle also drowned. The flood also destroyed nearly 7,000 mi (11,000 km) of roads. The flood left 30 million people homeless. Since most rural Bangladeshis live in structurally vulnerable homes with walls made of jute, bamboo, or mud, with earthen or bamboo floors, they are particularly vulnerable to flood damage.[66]

Both natural events and human actions exacerbated the flood conditions of the late 1990s. Deforestation, both for logging and to free land for agriculture, removed trees that would promote the absorption of water on steep slopes, and whose roots would help hold soil together, lessening fast runoff. Other human activities, including agricultural techniques such as row cropping and the creation of large tracts of land devoid of vegetation, weakened the soil. The irrigation of steep slopes caused topsoil erosion that destabilized vegetation and destroyed the infiltration capacity of the land.[67] As was the case in China's Huang He, irrigation also caused the silting of the river channels that decreased the area available for flowing water. With monsoon rains and melting snow from the Himalayas, the 1998 floods began a once-in-a-century catastrophe.[68]

Relief efforts

The two main problems facing Bangladesh once the floodwaters subsided were the collapse of agriculture and the spread of disease. Over 98% of the population developed health problems due to drinking and bathing in contaminated floodwaters. Though many of the agricultural products of Bangladesh are resistant to floods, this chronic inundation caused 2,702 mi^2 (700,000 hectares) of crop failure (Figure 5.2).[69]

With a skyrocketing birthrate and few resources, Bangladesh could not afford appropriate rescue and relief efforts once the floods had inundated the land and ravaged its people:

> The Nation is faced with a disaster of the highest order. All signs, as they become more and more visible, lead to one conclusion: we are faced with a national disaster of catastrophic dimensions. . . it is not just another flood, it is THE FLOOD, which all Bangladeshis will remember for generations to come . . . this will be our reference point for many of our national events. This will set the standard of our capability or incapability. We'll measure

Figure 5.2 Flood conditions in Dhaka, Bangladesh, in 2007.
Source: © Rafiqur Rahman/Reuters/Corbis.

> ourselves with this standard in the future. So will the rest of the world. (Professor Mohammad Yunu, quoted in the *Daily Star*, September 11, 1998).[70]

During the peak of the 1998 floods, Abdus Samad Azad, the Bangladeshi Foreign Minister, made an international plea for aid on behalf of his country. He cited the 2,702 mi^2 (6,998 km^2) of destroyed crops as proof of a pending food crisis and potential famine threatening millions of Bangladeshis. The country also lacked the currency to purchase the amount of food necessary to save his people from starvation.[71] Substantial humanitarian relief in food, clothing, medicine, and temporary shelters came quickly. It accepted immediate offers of technical assistance from major aid donors including the UK, France, the United Nations Development Program (UNDP), and the USA. In addition to the immediate crisis, these countries offered to help the government of Bangladesh find a lasting solution to the country's chronic flood problem.[72]

The government did succeed in preventing starvation. Mass flood relief efforts began in August 1998 through the provision of 20,400 tons of rice, and 30,800 tons more arrived in September.[73] The government also began a large-scale program involving distributing 1.3 million Vulnerable Group Feeding (VGF) cards, each entitling the holder to 282 oz (8 kg) of rice per month. This program succeeded in distributing 27,500 tons of rice and feeding over 1.35 million households in August and 2.13 million households in September.[74] In late September, the World Food Programme (WFP) strongly urged the government to expand the card program to include wheat and extend it through September and October. The expansion was necessary since shipping delays resulted in the arrival of only 53,000 tons of food by the end of October. This meant that 71,000 tons less arrived than was anticipated.[75]

Bangladesh's commercial imports of 224,000 tons of wheat arrived and were distributed during November and December, feeding over 4.2 million households. In January 1999 the government used international food donations to create the program Food for Work, with the dual purpose of the construction of infrastructure and the distribution of food to the poor.[76] The government began to encourage private-sector imports of rice to keep the price of rice low.[77] Over 200,000 tons per month of rice were imported by the private sector through March. This action undoubtedly saved lives, because prior to 1994, the Bangladesh government banned private companies from importing food.

Today, the government of Bangladesh remains ill-equipped to deal with floodwaters, given its developing economy. Researcher Barbu Alam at the Bangladesh Center for Advanced Studies stated the country's poverty also hampers its ability to cope with floods:

> Its weak economy and low levels of technology and infrastructure combine to make matters worse. With more money, Bangladesh could install early-warning systems that alert people to flooding four or five days in advance, instead of the current four or five hours. During floods lives could be saved by providing clean water more quickly, along with food, shelter and healthcare. And after the deluge, more funds would mean quicker rehabilitation for those affected. But more strategic planning ahead of time and better information sharing with Bangladesh's neighbors is also required, so that the country does not continue to be caught unawares.[78]

Rebuilding

The government implemented numerous programs to meet the immediate and long-term needs of flood victims by providing food, clothing, and shelter and rehabilitating agriculture. Bangladesh avoided a food crisis.

Many died in the floodwaters but no one died later due to lack of food. Food prices remained low so there was no large migration of people to urban areas in search of food.[79] In addition, long-term public investments in roads, bridges, electricity, and telephones contributed to the efficient marketing systems that enabled the private sector grain trade to supply the country with enough food.[80]

Conclusion

The floods of 1997 and 1998 showed that the Bangladesh government, though ill-equipped financially, provided ingenious, effective, and well thought-out plans to prevent starvation on a mass scale and to rebuild after these floods. Government, donors, nongovernmental organizations (NGOs), and households themselves, together with private trade operating in well-functioning markets, succeeded in mitigating the effects of the 1998 floods. This example illustrates the importance of coordinated actions in ensuring food security following major flood events.[81]

Today, Bangladesh suffers from floods of increasing intensity. In 2004, floods submerged roughly 75% of the country and the following year 25 villages flooded when both the Ghanghara and Atrai Rivers overtopped their levees. Preliminary estimates indicate that the number of people at risk from flooding and sea-level rise in Bangladesh could be 26 million.[82] Major disruptions loom for low-lying, shoreline areas in Bangladesh, regions that will be submerged.[83] Similar to the 1971 Bhola cyclone discussed in detail in Chapter 8, in 1995, half of Bhola Island in Bangladesh became permanently flooded, with its 500,000 inhabitants made homeless, described as the world's first climate-change refugees.[84] Scientists predict rising sea levels may ultimately swallow more than 20% of Bangladesh's land.[85]

Summary

Flooding has historically been among the most devastating and deadly of natural disasters. As these case studies illustrate, humans have proved powerless in the face of rising waters. In the future, the link between flooding and global climate change will become obvious to scientists, and will not be limited to low-lying tropical countries such as Bangladesh. Floods in the

UK in 2007 are entirely consistent with repeated predictions of what climate change will bring, according to the country's Climate Impacts Programme. It gave its first detailed forecast recently of what global warming had in store for the UK in the twenty-first century. It predicted intense and frequent rainfall.[86]

The UK's forecasts of increased flooding are supported by recent events. In 2011, Hurricane Irene tore through the Caribbean, up the eastern seaboard of the USA, and into the Atlantic Provinces of Canada, causing more than US$10 billion in damage and causing up to 60 deaths. This hurricane caused massive flooding along rivers in states not accustomed to hurricanes. The New York City shut down – businesses closed and public transportation ceased.[87] In Vermont, many small dams were breached, and water covered low-lying areas, resulting in at least four deaths. Extensive road damage isolated towns that required helicopters to airlift supplies of food and medicine in the days following the storm.[88] In Montreal, Canada, roads and cars were swept away as the Yamaska River overflowed its banks, forcing evacuations.[89]

New Orleans in the USA, with its elevation below sea level and proximity to the mouth of the Mississippi River, may serve as a test case for coastal eastern cities. Pumping, floodwalls, levees, and dams may need to be increasingly maintained and reinforced to keep out rising rivers and storm surges. Some towns, ravaged by flooding rivers, have relocated historic buildings and houses to build new homes in safer locations. For example, the town of Valmeyer, Illinois made the decision to relocate, requiring a strong commitment from residents, careful planning, FEMA (Federal Emergency Management Agency) home buyouts, and US$45 million in federal, state, and local funding.[90]

The citizens of the Lockyer Valley town of Grantham in Queensland, Australia, which was devastated by the January 2011 floods, have also moved to a new location on higher ground. Under the plan, residents of five flooded towns will be given the option to move to the new site by a voluntary swap of equivalent-sized homes, in a $40 million project.[91] This may be the beginning of a change in flood-control policy, where once residents with government support rebuilt on the same locations when the floodwaters receded. Now, moving to a new location may become an option for those living in the developed world.

In Bangladesh, where flooding is increasing in duration, frequency, and severity, such a forward-thinking strategy may not be available. Coastal plains and rivers have drawn people to their shores for millennia to live, fish, and to move from one location to another. In developed countries, the amenities of coastal living continue to attract residents and vacationers. However, the dynamics of a changing climate, with sea levels rising and an increase in volatile weather conditions, may serve as a deterrent to coastal living.

Notes

1 Michael McCarthy (2007), "A 21st century catastrophe," *The Independent*, July 24. At www.independent.co.uk/environment/climate-change/a-21st-century-catastrophe-458457.html.
2 Burt A. Bolt, William L. Horn, and Greg A. MacDonald (1977), *Geological Hazards* (London: Springer-Verlag), 268.
3 Shuming Cai, Ngai Weng Chan, Hsiang-te Kung, and Pin-Shuo Liu (2001), "Management of flood disasters in the Jianghan Plain, China," *Disaster Prevention and Management*, 10(5), 340.
4 Burt A. Bolt, William L. Horn, and Greg A. MacDonald (1977), *Geological Hazards*, 270.
5 Yoshiki Saito, Zuosheng Yang, and Kazaki Hori (2001), "The Huang He (Yellow River) and Chang Jiang (Yangtze River) deltas: a review of their characteristics, evolution, and sediment discharge during the Holocene," *Geomorphology* 40, 219.
6 Jim Yardley (2006), "A troubled river mirrors China's path to modernity," *New York Times*, November 9, 3. At www.nytimes.com/2006/11/19/world/asia/19yellowriver.html?pagewanted=all&_r=0>.
7 Society for Anglo-Chinese Understanding, "About China: the Yellow River." At www.sacu.org/pic10.html.
8 Hung Nung (1972), "Twenty years' work on the Huai River," in *China Tames Her Rivers* (Peking: Foreign Languages Press), 15.
9 Edward Lockwood (1935), "Floods and flood prevention in China. Far Eastern survey," *American Council, Institute of Pacific Relations*, IV(21), 167.
10 Robert Carin (1962), "River control in communist China" (Hong Kong: Union Research Institute), 9.
11 Ibid., 17.
12 Angus M. Gunn (2007), "Yellow River China flood 1887," in *Encyclopedia of Disasters: Environmental Catastrophes and Human Tragedies* (Westport, CT: Greenwood Publishing Group), 141–144.
13 Stanley Wayne Trimble (ed.) (1997), *Encyclopedia of Water Science* (Boca Raton, FL: CRC Press), 383.

14 David A. Pietz (2002), *Engineering the State: The Huai River and Reconstruction in Nationalist China, 1927–1937* (London: Routledge), 63.

15 Yak-yeow Koeh (1995), *Agricultural Instability in China 1931–1991: Weather, Technology, and Institutions* (Oxford: Clarendon Press), 48.

16 David Pietz (2002), *Engineering the State: The Huai River and Reconstruction in Nationalist China 1927–1937* (London: Routledge), xvii, 61–70.

17 George Stroebe (1932), "The Great Central China flood of 1931," *The Chinese Recorder*, 63(11), 669.

18 National Flood Relief Commission (1933), "Report of the National Flood Relief Commission," The National Flood Relief Commission, The People's Republic of China, 65.

19 Society for Anglo-Chinese Understanding (SACU) "About China: the Yellow River." At www.sacu.org/pic10.html.

20 Huang Chun (1972), "A new chapter in taming the Yellow River," *in China Tames Her Rivers* (Peking: Foreign Languages Press), 5.

21 Edward Lockwood (1935), "Floods and flood prevention in China," 168.

22 United Nations (1983), "Experiences in flood prevention and control in China," in *Flood Damage Prevention and Control in China* , Natural Resources/ Water Series No. 11, (New York: UN), 36.

23 Marilyn Beach, "Floods of summer 1998 in northeast China," *Sinosphere*, 2(3), 8–11.

24 Jiqun Zhang, Chenghu Zhoub, Kaiqin Xua, and Masataka Watanabe (2002), "Flood disaster monitoring and evaluation in China," *Global Environmental Change, Part B: Environmental Hazards*, 4(2–3), 33–43.

25 Ibid.

26 Edward Lockwood (1935), "Floods and flood prevention in China," 166.

27 Shuming Cai, Ngai Weng Chan, Hsiang-te Kung et al. (2001), "Management of flood disasters in the Jianghan Plain, China," *Disaster Prevention and Management*, 10(5), 339–348.

28 Gus Lubin (2010), "Stunning photos of China's worst flood in a decade," *Business Insider*, July 21. At www.businessinsider.com/stunning-photos-of-chinas-worst-flood-in-a-decade-2010-7?op=1>.

29 Quan Wang, Masataka Watanabe, Yoshikazu Hayashi, and Misaki Murakami (2003), "Using NOAA AVHRR data to assess flood damage in China," *Environmental Monitoring and Assessment*, 82, 122.

30 Weihong Qian and Yafen Zhu (2001), "Climate change in China from 1880 to 1998 and its impact on the environmental condition," *Climatic Change*, 50, 449.

31 Ibid.

32 Herman Gerritsen (2005), "What happened in 1953? The big flood in the Netherlands in retrospect," *Philosophic Transactions of the Royal Society*, A363, 1271.

33 Hubert Lamb and Knud Frydendahl (1991), *Historic Storms of the North Sea, British Isles and Northwest Europe* (Cambridge, UK: Cambridge University Press).

34 Herman Gerritsen (2005), "What happened in 1953? The big flood in the Netherlands in retrospect," 1271.

35 Ibid.

36 Ibid.

37 Ibid.

38 Kees Slager (1992), *The Disaster* (Amsterdam: Uitgeverij Atlas), 557.

39 Herman Gerritsen (2005), "What happened in 1953? The big flood in the Netherlands in retrospect," 1271.

40 Ibid.

41 Ibid.

42 Ibid.

43 Ibid.

44 Kees Slager (2003), *How Was Reconstruction Organized?*, (Gouda, Netherlands: CUR), 37–52.

45 Hilda Grieve (1959), *The Great Tide: The Story of the 1953 Flood Disaster in Essex* (Chelmsford, UK: Essex County Council Publisher), 896.

46 See www.deltawerken.com/The-Flood-of-1953/1523.html; "The flood of 1953," *Deltawerken Online*.

47 Ibid.

48 Burt A. Bolt, William L. Horn, and Greg A. MacDonald (1977), *Geological Hazards*, 268.

49 Kees Slager (1992), *The Disaster*, 557.

50 Herman Gerritsen (2005), "What happened in 1953? The big flood in the Netherlands in retrospect," 1271.

51 Deltawerken Online (2004),"Rescue and consequences. The flood of 1953," *Deltawerken Online*. At www.deltawerken.com/Rescue-and-consequences/309.html.

52 Herman Gerritsen (2005), "What happened in 1953? The big flood in the Netherlands in retrospect," 1271.

53 Ibid.

54 Ibid.

55 *Deltawerken Online*. At www.deltawerken.com/23.

56 "Dutch draw up drastic measures to defend coast against rising seas," *The New York Times*, August 3, 2008. At www.nytimes.com/2008/09/03/news/03iht-03dutch.15877468.html.

57 Herman Gerritsen (2005), "What happened in 1953? The big flood in the Netherlands in retrospect," 1271.

58 Eupedia (1994), Netherlands Guide – Interesting facts about the Netherlands. At www.eupedia.com/netherlands/trivia.shtml.

59 Marjolijn Haasnoot (1986), "Impact of climate change and anticipating flood management strategy on floodplain ecosystems of the river Rhine, The Netherlands," in Gjerrit P. Hekstra, *Will Climatic Changes Flood the Netherlands? Effects on Agriculture, Land Use and Well-being* , *Ambio*, 15, 315–326.

60 Poonam Khetrapal Singh (2007), "Flood fury: a recurring hazard," *World Health Organization* Report Focus, 1, 43. At www.searo.who.int/LinkFiles/Publication_&_Documents_EHA_FOCUS.pdf.

61 Saleemul Huq, Mohammad Asaduzzaman, and Zahurul Karim, et al. (eds.) (1999), *Vulnerability and Adaptation to Climate Change in Bangladesh* (Dordrecht, The Netherlands: Kluwer Academic Publishers), 147.

62 Akhtar Ahmed, Mohammad Alam, and Ahmed Rahman (1988), "Adaptation to climate change in Bangladesh: future outlook," in Saleemul Huq, et al. (eds.), *Vulnerability and Adaptation to Climate Change in Bangladesh* (Dordrecht, The Netherlands: Kluwer Academic Publishers), 125–143.

63 Norman Myers and Jennifer Kent (1995), "Environmental exodus: an emergent crisis in the global arena," 134, Climate Institute, Washington, DC. At www.climate.org/PDF/Environmental%20Exodus.pdf.

64 Carlo del Ninno, Paul Dorosh, Lisa Smith, and Dilip Roy (2001), "The 1998 floods in Bangladesh: disaster impacts, household coping strategies and response," IFPRI Institute Research Report 122 (IFPRI: Washington, DC), 24.

65 David E. Alexander (1999), "The Third World," in *Natural Disasters* (Dordrecht, the Netherlands: Kluwer Academic Publishers), 532.

66 Mitra & Associates (2011), "Bangladesh demographic and health survey 2011", National Institute of Population Research and Training, Dhaka, Bangladesh. At www.measuredhs.com/pubs/pdf/PR15/PR15.pdf.

67 Tracey Logan (2004), "Why Bangladesh floods are so bad," BBC News South Asia, July 27. At http://news.bbc.co.uk/2/hi/south_asia/3929217.stm.

68 Peter Haggett (ed.) (2002), "The Indian subcontinent," *Encyclopedia of World Geography* (New York: Marshall Cavendish), 2, 634.

69 Octave Kunii, Shin-Ichiro Nakamura, Rehman Abdur, et al. (2002), "The impact on health and risk factors of the diarrhoea epidemics in the 1998 Bangladesh floods," *Public Health*, 116(2), 68–74.

70 Carlo del Ninno et al. (2001), "The 1998 floods in Bangladesh," 24.

71 Francis Harrison (1998), "Bangladesh Floods Rise Again," *BBC World News South Asia*, August 24. At http://news.bbc.co.uk/2/hi/south_asia/157254.stm.

72 H. Brammer (1990), "Floods in Bangladesh Part I: Geographical background to the 1987 and 1988 floods," *The Geographical Journal*, 1569(1), 12–22.

73 Carlo del Ninno et al. (2001), "The 1998 Floods in Bangladesh," 24.

74 Ibid.

75 Ibid.

76 Nurul Islam (2007), *Reducing Rural Poverty in Asia: Challenges and Opportunities for Microenterprises and Public Employment Schemes* (New Delhi, India Teri Press, and Food Products Press/The Haworth Press), 113.
77 Carlo Del Ninno et al. (2001), "The 1998 Floods in Bangladesh," 24.
78 Tracey Logan (2004), "Why the Bangladesh floods are so bad."
79 Ibid.
80 Ibid.
81 Ibid.
82 Bonnie Docherty and Tyler Giannini (2009), "Confronting a rising tide: a proposal for a convention on climate change refugees 2009," *Harvard Environmental Law Review*, 33(11), 349–403.
83 Norman Myers and Jennifer Kent (1995), "Environmental exodus: an emergent crisis in the global arena," 134.
84 Emily Wax (2007), "In flood-prone Bangladesh, a future that floats," *Washington Post*, September 27, A1.
85 Norman Myers and Jennifer Kent (1995), "Environmental exodus: an emergent crisis in the global arena," 134.
86 Michael McCarthy (2001), "A 21st century catastrophe," *The Independent*, July 24.
87 James Barron (2011), "New York City shuts down amid flooding fears," *New York Times*, August 27, A18.
88 Phil Gast (2011), "Crews reach far corners of Vermont cut off by Irene," CNN, September 1. At www.cnn.com/2011/US/08/31/irene.vermont.towns/.
89 Hatchet Man (2011), "Hurricane Irene sends windows crashing in downtown Montreal," *The Montreal Gazette*, September 2, 5.
90 Emma Graves Fitzsimmons (2008), "Town relocated after 1993 flood watches rising Mississippi with calm," The Utah Daily Herald, June 18. At www.heraldextra.com/news/world/article_fb17f2a9-7bf7-5997-b3ce-746dd7725288.html#ixzz1eB1Z9Tck.
91 Georgia Waters (2011), "Flooded Queensland town to be relocated," Forbes Advocate, May 5. At www.brisbanetimes.com.au/environment/weather/flooded-queensland-town-to-be-relocated-20110505-1e925.html.

Further Reading

Jeffrey H. Jackson (2011), *Paris Under Water: How the City of Light Survived the Great Flood of 1910* (New York: Palgrave Macmillan).

This text provides a narrative account of the Paris flood of 1910.

Jim E. O'Connor and John E. Costa (2004), *The World's Largest Floods, Past and Present: Their Causes and Magnitudes* (Washington, DC: US Department of the Interior, Circular No. 1254, US Geological Survey, 2004).

This document is an extensively researched, scientific account of several historical floods.

M. Monirul Qader Mirza, Ajaya Dixit, and Ainun Nishat (eds.) (2010), *Flood Problem and Management in South Asia* (New York: Springer).
This book details the floods in South Asia from an integrated scientific, policy, historical, and societal approach.

Bruce Vaughn, Pervaze A. Sheikh, and K. Alan Kronstadt (2010), *Flooding in Pakistan: Overview and Issues for Congress – CRS Report* (Washington DC: Congressional Research Service, November 18)
This document details the Pakistani floods of 2010 in the context of their humanitarian and geopolitical significance.

Chapter 6

Landslides

The women were already there, like stone they were, clawing at the filth – it was like a black river – some had no skin left on their hands. Miners are a tough breed, we don't show our feelings, but some of the lads broke down. (Miner in the Aberfan disaster where a school was buried and 116 children perished.)[1]

Introduction

Landslides are defined as the movement of rock and soil down a slope under the effect of gravity. The effect of gravity is distinguished from that of erosion (sediments carried by moving wind and water). Though gravity is the only force causing landslides, a variety of different factors can contribute to it, including the volume of water contained in sediments, the steepness of a slope, and geology. Here, geologic aspects include mineralogy, rock fractures, jointing (regularly spaced fractures similar to those on a checkerboard), bedding planes (layers indicating separate conditions of formation, between which there is usually a discernable difference), climate (freeze–thaw cycles), the amount of vegetation present, and vibrations from mining or earthquakes.

In the USA, landslides occur in all 50 states in many geological settings. They are potentially deadly and can be responsible for the destruction of homes and buildings, blocked infrastructure, ruptured utility lines (gas, oil, water, and electric), and ensuing economic and trade losses. In the USA, landslides cause 25–50 deaths per year, and economic losses costing $1–2 billion per year. Globally, the death toll averages 600 people per year, and

Natural Disasters in a Global Environment, First Edition. Anthony N. Penna and Jennifer S. Rivers.

catastrophic landslides can kill up to 70,000 people at a time as was the case in the 2008 landslide in Sichuan, China.

Landslides, more than the other types of disasters discussed in this book, are not always simply geophysical events. They occur in locations where mining activities make miners and their families vulnerable to the destabilization of the surrounding land. Deforestation for logging and agriculture also weakens slopes and makes the population more susceptible to the dangers of landslides.

Here, we investigate four major landslide events, including the devastation of Turtle Mountain in Alberta, Canada, where coal mining blasts may have loosened over a billion ft^3 (28 million m^3) of material; the Aberfan tragedy in Wales where a school was buried; the Ancash (Peru) landslide occurred along with an earthquake, a flood, a dam bursting, a dust storm, and an anticipated tsunami, all of which made for the worst catastrophe in modern-day Peru; and a recent Philippine disaster on the island of Leyte where, following heavy rains and an earthquake, 1,200 people perished in a mudslide.

The Turtle Mountain Landslide, Canada (1903)

Introduction

The province of Alberta in Canada has long been known for its energy resources. Alberta is known as the "energy province," with the largest tar sand deposit in the world, the Athabasca Tar Sands, which are also the only tar sands deposits shallow enough to mine. Alberta alone has 70% of Canada's coal reserves, and 48% of the province is underlain by coal.[2] Alberta also has vast reserves of oil and natural gas, making this province the energy capital of North America.

In 1903 a rock fall in Alberta sent 1 billion ft^3 (30 million m^3) of materials roaring down the side of Turtle Mountain, perhaps as a result of coal mining, killing 70 people, though only 12 bodies were ever recovered. The town of Frank was founded at the base of Turtle Mountain as a mining town in September 1901. Conveniently located for the miners and its population of 600, the geology of this unstable mountain included massive limestone overlying weak shale and sandstone. Fissures at the top of the mountain allowed water to infiltrate its limestone core. Natural waters are weakly acidic, but capable of dissolving limestone. Thus, this booming coal town and productive coal mine were geological time bombs, and the use of explosives to dislodge the mine's coal, located beneath the fractured limestone in the weak shale and sandstone, undermined the integrity of the mountain without the knowledge of the mine operators, the miners, or their families.

The rockslide

On April 29, 1903 a massive rockslide originating at the top of the north peak of Turtle Mountain crushed the town and buried residents in its path. The slab of limestone that broke free was approximately 0.4 mi (650 m) high, 0.55 mi (900 m) wide, and 492 ft (150 m) thick.[3] Debris from the slide measured just short of 100 ft (30 m) deep and was shy of 2 mi (3 km) wide. The size of the debris pile was overwhelming when one considers that the landslide lasted 90 seconds, moving that amount of rock so far and so fast.

Seven miners' cottages (six inhabited at the time), a dairy farm, ranch, shoe store, livery stable, cemetery, 1.25 mi (2 km) of road and the Grassy Mountain Railway (CPR), and 1.85 mi (3 km) of the town were all buried in the slide. In addition, the slide destroyed a construction camp and all of Frank's surface mine buildings.[4] It trapped 17 miners below ground, toiling on the 11 p.m. to 7 a.m. graveyard shift. They spent 13 hours digging through 9 ft (3 m) of limestone rubble and boulders to escape. One could consider them fortunate since the miners working above ground were crushed by the slide.[5] "Grandfather and 16 other men including his brother George were all trapped in their coal mine. They never said nothing. Ask them, but they don't tell you anyway. You had to drag it out of them."[6]

Debris completely covered the railroad tracks coming through Frank. A brakeman became a local hero after climbing as far as he could over the boulders to alert the Spokane Flyer, a train scheduled to arrive in Frank just hours after the slide occurred. The Spokane Flyer's engineer successfully stopped the train in time, saving the lives of many and possibly all of its passengers.[7]

Theories abounded as to the cause of the slide. Some scientists thought it was due to Turtle Mountain's inherently unsound geology. Others believed that the blasts associated with coal mining deep within the mountain caused, or more likely, contributed to, the slide. Some believed an earthquake in the Aleutian Islands of Alaska two years before in 1901 had weakened the mountain to the point where it was ready to fail (though this theory has since been discounted). Still others thought that a rapid freeze and thaw due to fluctuating weather conditions caused the slide. Perhaps it was a combination of these factors. Turtle Mountain was an unstable structure exposed to several factors known to cause landslides. "There was nothing to see. The air was full of dust, and minutes later the dust was still hanging everywhere. We didn't know what had happened."[8]

Stories, both true and false, emerged about the slide, and fact became indistinguishable from fiction. Two such fictional accounts claimed that a baby girl was the only survivor, and that a vault of gold was buried in the rubble. Indian legend going back centuries said that Turtle Mountain was cursed, and cursed it turned out to be:

> [A Canadian] Blackfoot Indian legend . . . forewarns of the disaster. The legend began in 1853 when the Blackfoot Indians fought a battle at the base of Turtle Mountain with the Crow Indians of Montana. In the midst of the battle, a huge rock the size of a three-story building broke away from the mountain. The rock killed about 200 Native Canadians. The battle ended abruptly as the Indians believed that some spirit within the mountain had given a warning. The spirit was "Napi", whom the Indians believed to be their God and Creator. They tell that "Napi" had created the world and when he was through, he climbed to the top of Turtle Mountain and vanished. They believe that he had taken the mountain as his final resting-place.[9]

Relief efforts

Following the slide, the state government ordered the evacuation of Frank, located at the base of the South Peak of Turtle Mountain, but by the end of April residents and miners were permitted to return to their homes. Three days after the slide, Alberta's Premier, Sir Frederick Haultain, visited the town of Frank and learned that fissures in the mountain had caused the slide. He ordered the evacuation of the town but cancelled this order on May 10, after geologists from the Geological Survey of Canada had examined the site.[10]

Rebuilding

The Alberta government rebuilt rail lines within three weeks and mine operators reopened the mine a month later. Despite this calamity, the people of Frank remained there until 1911, most likely because the Alberta provincial government concluded an analysis and issued a report on the mountain's instability. The government ordered the closure of the south portion of Frank when it became clear that the mountain was still unstable. People moved to a region at the base of the North Slope, known as Crowsnest Pass, and many settled there, naming the town New Frank.[11] The town is once again thriving, with many of the descendants of survivors and of those killed in the 1903 slide living in New Frank.

Geologists have determined that the conditions which caused the slide at the South Slope were almost exactly the same as those currently existing on the North Slope, and that a landslide could come at any time and with equal ferocity. The belief that another slide may happen is supported by the detachment zone (the area of weakness susceptible to future failure), which experiences small yet consistent movement on the order of approximately 0.5 in (1 cm) per year. Dr. John Allan, founder of Alberta Geological Survey, said the area known as South Peak may fail next, and if it does, 6.5 million yd^3 (5 million m^3) of rock could fall.[12]

In 2005, the Alberta Geological Survey undertook a detailed review of the near real-time data stream from a sensor network installed on the South Peak of Turtle Mountain. The government study seeks to provide an understanding of the type and rate of movement of this slowly moving rock mass. The goals of the newly built Turtle Mountain laboratory include the sharing of data gained from the network of sensors with the international geotechnical research community. In this way, the laboratory's scientists hope to develop a better understanding of the mechanics of slowly moving rock masses and to develop and apply more sophisticated technologies for measuring these movements.[13] The first priority of the monitoring system, however, is to provide an early warning to residents of a possible catastrophic rock avalanche.[14] However, some residents are fatalistic about the possibility: "It's not going to bother us; if it falls on me, I won't feel it. What are you going to do?"[15]

Today, an unforeseen environmental consequence from this century-old slide that created the extensive rock field is home to many fauna including pikas, ground squirrels, spiders, and birds. As many as 5,000 golden eagles have been spotted in this area during their fall migration. The century-old trail that meanders through the boulders is a reminder that although nature can be volatile, humans and animals emerge from the ruins.[16]

"There are walking paths around the integrative center with some really good interpretive signs, and then you can walk through the rocks on our Frank Slide Trail, which is 1 mi (1.5 km). We also have a new offering that will be a community walking trail that goes from the Leitch Collieries in the east to Crowsnest Lake in the west. We finished our leg of it last summer, so we now have a beautiful walking trail all along the rim of the slide to the northeast to Bellevue."[17]

Conclusion

The residents of Frank lived next to Turtle Mountain, an unstable landform. Nearly 200 people live in its shadow today, knowing that another landslide may happen. The memory of this disaster exists in the minds of Frank's residents today and the mountain's physical scar is still very visible. Both memory and this enduring scar are reminders of the colossal landslide that killed 70 people in less than 90 seconds more than a century ago.

This disaster reminds all of us of the world's voracious appetite for fossil fuel energy. This thirst for energy comes at a cost that is borne by those regions with the fortune – or misfortune – to have vast reserves of fossil fuel resources underlying their towns. In future, effective policies on mining techniques, evaluation, and oversight as well as emergency management and disaster response plans would lower the risk to residents of such regions.

The Aberfan Landslide, Wales (1966)

> I was standing on the edge of the depression, sir; I was looking down into it, and what I saw I couldn't believe my eyes. It was starting to come back up. It started to rise slowly at first, sir. I still did not believe it; I thought I was seeing things. Then it rose up after pretty fast, sir, at a tremendous speed. Then it sort of came up out of the depression and turned itself into a wave, that is the only way I can describe it, down towards the mountain . . . towards Aberfan village, sir. . . . And as it turned over, I shouted: "Good God, boys, come and look at this lot". . . . I was looking down in the crevice, sir, down at the drop, and it seemed to me like as if the bottom shot out.[18]

Introduction

Wales, one of the four countries including England, Scotland, and Northern Ireland that form the UK, has a long and bitter coal mining history. Wales was a major source of the UK's energy derived from coal in the nineteenth and twentieth centuries. Mining, as the basis of Wales's economy, wrought havoc on the country's environment and took a major toll on its people. Women and children, the latter as young as six, were sent underground to mine coal. They suffered from many ailments, including silicosis, a fatal lung disease. Working conditions led to major labor unrest and to some uprisings in the mid-1800s. Miners called for action in response to conditions in the mines. Parliament acted to protect the health of workers and to end child labor in the mines. However, mine operators ignored these laws and labor strife continued with strikes, violence, and reprisals. Labor unrest continued until the 1980s when mining operations exhausted coal deposits in Wales.

Removing muddy clay material during mining makes the process easier. These extracted mine materials (called tailings or slag) are piled into giant hills, called "tips," that become a blight on the surrounding environment. The Merthyr Vale Coal Company piled coal mining debris into seven large tips directly above the village of Aberfan. This geologically unsound land consisted of sandstone underlying coal. The sandstone and the coal tips became saturated with groundwater from springs. Slides had occurred from 1916 to 1966, causing authorities to terminate the tipping of waste at the two most vulnerable tips. Local authorities raised specific concerns in 1963 about clay and tailings being tipped on the mountain above the village's primary school. The management of the National Coal Board, a national public corporation established in 1946 by the UK to oversee coal mining, largely ignored these warnings.[19]

The slide

> It was a tremendous rumbling sound and all the school went dead. You could hear a pin drop. Everyone just froze in their seats. I just managed to get up and I reached the end of my desk when the sound got louder and nearer, until I could see the black out of the window. I can't remember any more but I woke up to find that a horrible nightmare had just begun in front of my eyes.[20]

At 9:15 a.m. on October 21, 1966, Aberfan was thrown into the global spotlight when a tip composed of coal waste became saturated with rain, causing a large landslide. The leading edge of the tip liquefied and roared downslope, dislodging 4,250,000 ft^3 (120,345 m^3) of slag. By the time it reached Aberfan, it deposited a 40-ft-deep (12 m) mass of 1,420,000 ft^3 (40,000 m^3) of debris.[21] The liquefied debris buried up to 50 houses, a farm, and most tragically, Pantglas Junior School and part of the senior school (Figure 6.1).

Figure 6.1 The Aberfan disaster rescue effort.
Source: www.walesonline.co.uk.

We are so used to having coal tipped near the school and this noise sounded just like coal being tipped, only much more noise than usual; it was a heavy sound . . . I was going towards the school, and I suddenly realized the sound was coming nearer all the time, and the feeling it was the tip came to my mind straight away; so I ran back to the house; my little girl was in bed, so I got her and the wife outside and I went back to the school . . . The north side of the school was completely down, and the tip had come right down the road, Moy Road. I went straight into the boiler house of the junior school and raked out the fire . . . I came out of the boiler house and saw in the classroom next to the boiler house some children there and they were unable to get out, so I tried to smash the window to get the children out, but there was not enough space to get them out that way. The teacher managed to open the door somehow . . . I went in through the door and the children came out past me, out to the yard. Then I went round to the front of the school where Mrs. Williams' class was. I saw she was in there and she could not breathe . . . I got up on the tank and got her down.[22]

Relief efforts

After the slide, residents of Aberfan were justifiably hysterical. The death toll totaled 144 people, including 116 children and five teachers from Pantglas Junior School. People rushed to the site of the school and began digging to try to rescue children. Police arrived and secured the site, aiding in attempts to rescue children, but water and mud continued to pour into the destroyed schoolhouse. As word spread, miners from neighboring towns arrived to aid the search and rescue mission. These miners, travelling in open lorries with shovels in their hands, could do little. They pulled a few children out alive in the first hour, but no survivors were found after 11 a.m.[23]

> Up until then [Friday, 7 p.m.] I had hoped that the chapel was a hospital, but as I went into Bethania people were coming out who had been told their children had gone. Until I went in I still had hope that they were just lost. When I went in all the pews were covered with little blankets and under them lay the little children. They picked up the blankets and showed me every girl until I came to [her] and said she was mine. There wasn't a mark on her except a little scratch over her mouth, even her clothes were clean. What I missed most was the noise and fun around the house. [My daughter] was boisterous and full of fun. Our house was as quiet as a mouse after she'd gone.[24]

Rescue efforts continued in vain. Despite mud and water pouring downslope, emergency workers searched for survivors for several days. Bethania Chapel, 820 ft (250 m) from the disaster site, was used as the temporary mortuary and missing persons bureau for nearly a month. Volunteers and stretcher-bearers used the Bethania Chapel vestry, while the Aberfan Calvinistic Chapel was used as a second mortuary for the victims before their funerals.[25] Death certificates most commonly listed asphyxia and fractured skulls as the cause of death.

Rebuilding

Few laws protected people from coal mining activities prior to the Aberfan slide, and laws that did exist were not enforced. Directly in response to the landslide in Aberfan, Parliament wrote new laws to govern mining spoilage. The act was entitled the Mines and Quarries (Tips) Act 1969, and was intended "to make further provision in relation to tips associated with mines and quarries; to prevent disused tips constituting a danger to members of the public; and for purposes connected with those matters."[26] This act replaced the Mines and Quarries Act 1954, which did not address mine tailings and hardly mentioned public safety.

This new act was a response to a tribunal ordered by both Parliament and the Secretary of State for Wales, Gwilym Lloyd George, called the Davies Inquiry. The inquiry, which lasted two months, involved the examination of exhibits, the interviewing of witnesses, and touring of the region. Its findings placed blame on the National Coal Board due to its lack of policy on public safety for coal tipping. The inquiry found that the mistakes were ones of ignorance, not malice: ". . . the Aberfan disaster is a terrifying tale of bungling ineptitude by many men charged with tasks for which they were totally unfitted, of failure to heed clear warnings, and of total lack of direction from above. Not villains, but decent men, led astray by foolishness or by ignorance or by both in combination, are responsible for what happened at Aberfan."[27]

Conclusion

Residents of Aberfan, understandably, took many years to recover from the tragedy. One study found that 46% of the landslide's survivors suffered from anxiety and depression (later termed post-traumatic stress disorder). They experienced nightmares or difficulty sleeping due to thoughts about the disaster. The study concluded that traumatic episodes, initiated in childhood, persist into adulthood.[28] Despite the terrible tragedy of 1966, Aberfan remains a very small town. Two schools are now located nowhere near the site of the original disaster.

The Ancash Earthquake and Landslide, Peru (1970)

President General Juan Velasco Alvarado said, after the disaster: "We believe that at least 300,000 are gone, just based on the estimates of the population in the areas surveyed by air today. We need help."[29] The death toll eventually reached 100,000.

On May 31, 1970, Peru suffered from an earthquake, flood, landslide, dam burst, massive dust storm, and a tsunami that was anticipated but never arrived. A massive undersea earthquake of 8.0 magnitude (M_w) struck 21 mi (34 km) off the coast of Peru. Though Peru escaped a tsunami, the shaking caused a dam to break, and subsequently triggered a colossal avalanche which was 3,000 ft (915 m) wide and one mi (1.6 km) long, made up of rock, ice, and snow, on Mt. Huascarán, one of the highest peaks in the Andes Mountains, which killed 100,000 people.[30] Lima lost several thousand residents to the earthquake and the subsequent disease epidemics. This combination of natural disasters is considered one of the worst catastrophes ever to hit Peru.

Geology and snowpack

Peru is a rugged, mountainous country, home to over 70% of Earth's tropical glaciers. The area of the landslide, the Ancash Department of North-Central Peru, is located on the junction of the South American and the Nazca tectonic plates, where the Nazca plate is subducting under the South American plate. Subduction zones, deep within Earth, cause the most devastating earthquakes.

Ancash is a rugged, mountainous area with rock debris in the form of glacial outwash deposits. Glaciers appear on the upper reaches of the mountains, including Mt. Huascarán. Two large valleys separate the mountain ranges of Cordillera Negra and Cordillera Blanca (the black and white mountain ranges). Glaciers, snow, and ice cover the latter. Sandy beaches cover the other side of the valleys. This area is noted for its copper and zinc resources, the largest known such deposits, with an estimated mineral reserve of 618 million tons (561 million metric tons).[31] Additionally, bedded limestone deposits overlie copper and zinc metamorphic rocks.

Previous landslides

The geology of the Ancash region is conducive to landslides, especially following earthquakes occurring along the subduction zone. In history, the 1746 earthquake–tsunami that struck Lima and Callao was among the most destructive natural disasters in the history of colonial Latin America. The 1746 earthquake, tsunami, and landslide combination claimed over 5,000 lives – fewer than 4% of the local population survived.[32] In 1962, an avalanche occurred without an earthquake. It began as ice and snow that picked up rocks and water as it travelled down the mountain towards the valley. In 1946 an earthquake of magnitude (M_w) 7.3 triggered a large number of landslides, though very few details exist in published scientific papers.[33]

The avalanche and rockslide

In his work *Remembering The Worst Earthquake In Latin America: The Day The Apus Turned Their Backs On Peru*, Jesús Angel Chávez Machado says: "The Apus, ancestral gods of the Andean peoples, were not just symbolized but rendered physical by their tutelary mountains. Huascarán–at 22,200 ft (6,768 m) above sea level, the tallest mountain in Peru – was the tutelary god of the Ancash people. Its majesty and power made them feel secure. But on May 31, 1970, its force was destructive rather than protective, unleashing the worst seismic catastrophe ever experienced."[34]

At 3:23 p.m. local time the 8.0 M_w magnitude earthquake struck, and lasted nearly one minute. During the shaking, the Northern portion of Mt. Huascarán became unstable and a gargantuan 80 million ft^3 (2.3 million m^3) of ice and rock, 1 mi (1.6 km) long and 3,000 ft (914 m) wide, began to slide, gaining momentum on the steep slopes and gathering more and more debris. At Yungay, the mass roared downslope at incredible speeds – in excess of 200 mph (322 km/h), where it had turned into a jumbled mass of more than three billion ft^3 (85 million m^2) of rock, snow, water, and ice flowing in a viscous manner on very steep slopes. It buried an area slightly larger than the state of Maine (32,000 mi^2 or 83,000 km^2).

> A mud flow of such proportions, originating from an ice flow, represented a geologic process never before recorded . . . the destruction was almost unbelievable, possibly surpassing in magnitude such catastrophic events as the Mt. Pelée eruption of 1902 on the Island of Martinique, and the eruption of Vesuvius in the year AD 79 that buried Pompeii.[35]

The landslide buried Yungay, the first town to be hit. Only 2% of the total population survived: 400 people out of a population of over 20,000. Those who were visiting a cemetery located at a high elevation, and a group of 300 children who were out of town at a circus in a local stadium, were the only survivors. Only the tops of the four tallest palm trees in the plaza of Yungay remained visible above the mass of debris.[36]

Ranrahirca was directly downhill from Mt. Huascarán, and the landslide completely covered it and the village of Huarascucho. Dust from the avalanche created a massive dust storm and completely blocked out the sun, even as earthquakes and slides continued for the next few weeks. Pilots reported the dust storm to be over 18,000 ft (5,500 m) high over parts of the affected region, which made surveying the area and dropping off supplies impossible.[37] Chimbote, a mining and fishing community, was also hit hard, destroying nearly all of the primitive dwellings in the village. It leveled the resort area of Huaras as well.

Officials doubted that the full magnitude of the disaster would ever be known in isolated Quechua and other Indian communities where Peruvians live in adobe houses that frequently collapse in wind or rainstorms.[38] There, villagers traditionally avoid contact with authorities.

In the region, commerce, transportation, and trade were brought to an absolute standstill. Infrastructure was so devastated that the extent of the disaster could not be estimated in Peru's capital of Lima for many days. Peruvian Air Force pilots surveying the flooded valleys caused by burst dams with towns buried under landslides radioed headquarters that "scores of communities are no longer on the map, while raging rivers and roads have been hidden by tons of rocks."[39] Economic losses approached US$750 million. Immediately following the disaster, reports painted a picture of death and desolation, with material damages appearing incalculable. Destruction of villages was described as total, with an estimated 95% of homes destroyed or damaged.[40] When the landslide ended and the dust cloud subsided, the death toll was estimated at 80,000. Homelessness affected over a million people, with an additional three million people losing all their belongings, including personal possessions and animals.

Relief efforts

> The people of Peru are the victims of the worst natural disaster of our time; I was deeply moved by the magnitude of their suffering. Determined efforts will make it possible to rebuild, in time, the homes, schools, and churches, but there is no remedy for the tragic loss of life. I shall never forget the awesome sight of the thousands of new graves, and the faces of the orphans. The only bright spot in the picture of grief was the heartwarming outpouring of assistance, from within Peru, from the Americas, and from overseas.[41]

The Peruvian government was slow to issue figures of people dead, homeless, and impacted. Widespread looting was reported in Ancash where 10 violent criminals made a mass jailbreak in the panic and confusion that followed the quake.[42] Had these disasters, especially the initial earthquake, occurred on a weekday, the loss of life would have been much greater.

The Junta de Asistencia Nacional (the National Disaster Organization) went into operation and the Minister of Health, General Rolando Caro, was named the overall coordinator. His efforts were heroic as he successfully coordinated rescue missions. The president, Juan Velasco Alvarado, immediately visited the area by naval cruiser and returned to Lima with 180 seriously injured people.[43]

The government tried, initially, to downplay this disaster. When Augusto Zimmerman, the Chief of the Office of Information, was asked to explain the conflicting death tolls, and a perceived reluctance to give numbers, Zimmerman said "the military did not want to be alarmist," and when pressed, he replied to reporters:

> Certainly, the numbers of victims are in the thousands, unofficially. There are no official figures. There are estimates from reports that have arrived and that have been corroborated this morning. Let us make an unofficial estimate – God grant that this won't be actually confirmed because it would be the most frightful tragedy that any country in any part of the world has suffered from an earthquake – we would reach a figure of near 30,000 deaths.[44]

With its functioning port and airfields, Chimbote, the town closest to the devastated region, became a command central for rescue workers and the distribution point for food, clothing, and medicine. As time passed, Peruvian paratroopers landed closer to the disaster site to prepare the area so that air drops and helicopter landings could bring essential supplies once the dust had settled. Seasonal fog from the cold waters of the Pacific became trapped by the warm moist air from the Amazon rising from the eastern slopes of the Andes. Combined with the dust, these natural coastal climatic conditions worsened visibility.[45]

Since mud from the landslide made roads impassable for more than a month, 144 planes from the 23 countries which gave aid airlifted supplies, including 14,000 lb (6,350 kg) of food. Many of the flights tested the endurance of pilots, who crossed the Andes Mountains in a 200-mi (322 km) round trip.[46] The media recognized countless acts of heroism by people on the ground as well as those in the air. They included the airmen and women who were lost when their planes struck mountains and the limeños (natives of Lima) in the poorer sections of the capital who queued up to donate clothing and money.[47]

Relief poured in from neighboring countries. While it assembled medical teams to enter the disaster zones, Chile sent several planeloads of medicine and food.[48] Near the end of the relief effort it sent relief in the form of money, clothes, blankets, medicines, and construction materials including sheet metal for roofing. National and international voluntary agencies made generous contributions, and international organizations including the Pan-American Health Organization, United Nations Educational, Scientific and Cultural Organisation (UNESCO), the Inter-American Development Bank, and the Organization of American States all sent money, supplies, and experts.[49]

Rebuilding

After the disaster, the town of Yungay was pronounced sacred ground, similar to a cemetery, and a small memorial (Figure 6.2) as well as extensive memorial gardens cover the debris that overlies the former town. Any digging or excavation to exhume the dead or recover artifacts is expressly forbidden by law. The government has also named May 31 as Natural Disaster Education and Reflection Day, and exercises are conducted in schools and workplaces to ensure that when the next natural disaster strikes this geologically active region, the death toll will be as low as possible. The children who were watching the circus that fateful day never made it home. They were put up for adoption and now live with families in countries around the world.

Figure 6.2 The landslide memorial in Yungay, Peru.
Source: Photo: Jon White. Used by permission.

Conclusion

> For a society predisposed to forget its own history, it is always useful to be reminded of the consequences of natural disasters, especially when they are so devastating that they cry out for a more effective response than relief and reconstruction alone. The earthquake that hit northeastern Peru three decades ago can teach valuable lessons, including the need to carefully monitor governments' disaster reduction policies and their effectiveness, and try to promote a culture of prevention throughout all sectors of society.[50]

Due to the geology of the region, with the Pacific and North American tectonic plates pushing against each other and the Nazca plate sandwiched between these two plates, the area remains at high risk for landslides, earthquakes, floods, and combinations of such disasters. As recently as April 2010, the Peruvian government declared a state of emergency for parts of Ancash. An ice block broke from a glacier and created a massive wave that flooded nearby towns. Nestled between the foothills of the Andes Mountains and the Southern Pacific Ocean, this dangerous area remains breathtakingly beautiful despite the hazards.[51]

The Southern Leyte Landslide, the Philippines (2006)

Introduction

Nearly 1,200 people perished on February 19, 2006 in a landslide following ten days of soaking rain and a 2.6-magnitude earthquake in Southern Leyte, Philippines. Mining and legal and illegal logging for the last 30 years may have either caused or contributed to this slide. As was the case in Aberfan and Frank, deforestation and sub-surface mining destabilized the slopes. Geologists believe that mining in the Philippines as well as in other countries should become more regulated in light of this disaster.

Immediately prior to the landslide, soaking rains saturated slopes and caused gravity to act on the hill slope. Although an earthquake would not cause a landslide by itself, it became the catalyst for the landslide on land compromised by days of rain. Although the government successfully halted illegal logging activities and imposed a 10-year-old ban on legitimate logging, tens to hundreds of years are required for forests to regrow and stabilize the land.

Mining operations came under increased scrutiny by the Mines and Geosciences Bureau (MGB) of the Department of Environment and Natural Resources (DENR) in the Philippines because mining may have played a role in this disaster. The Philippines is one of the world's most highly mineralized countries, with untapped mineral wealth estimated at more than $840 billion, including copper, gold, nickel, silver, coal, gypsum, sulfur, clay, limestone, marble, silica, phosphate, and natural gas. Its chromate deposits are among the largest in the world.[52]

In 1995, President Fidel V. Ramos signed into law the Philippine Mining Act, which gave the government power to grant exploration and extraction permits to foreign companies, allowing these companies to extract up to 100% of the minerals in the permitted area.[53] In December 2004 the Philippine Supreme Court upheld the constitutionality of the 1995 Mining Act, thereby allowing up to 100% foreign-owned companies to invest in the large-scale exploration, development, and utilization of minerals, oil, and gas. Some local government units have enacted mining bans in their territories, however.[54] Specifically, two mining companies, the Buena Suerte Mining Corporation, and Orophilippine Ventures, Inc., currently operate mines for gold, silver, and other minerals in Southern Leyte. The USA and other countries currently claim mining rights in the Philippines, mining for gold, silver, bauxite, nickel, copper, and many other minerals.

The landslide

Rainfall of over 80 in (200 cm) in ten days loosened the soil so much that the resulting sludge and rocks liquefied and thundered down the slopes of nearby Mt. Can-abag, virtually destroying everything in its path. The landslide, more appropriately termed a debris avalanche or mudslide, took less than four minutes. It was estimated that between 530–706 million ft^3 (15–20 million m^3) of rock and soil reached speeds of 90 mph (140 km/h). The slide roared down the slopes of Mt. Can-abag and killed between 1,126 and 1,200 people.[55] It obliterated an entire village and killed nearly all of its inhabitants: "Our village is gone; everything was buried in the mud. All the people are gone."[56]

Relief efforts

The New York Times began an article on this disaster with: "The village of Guinsaugon disappeared Friday. So did nearly every man, woman, and

Figure 6.3 US Marines and sailors digging for survivors after the Leyte Island landslide in the Philippines.
Source: US Marine Corps photo by Cpl. Will Lathrop (Released).

child who lived in this eastern Philippines farming community of 1,857 people. Only a few jumbles of corrugated steel sheeting, sticking up from 30 ft (9 m) of sludge, indicate Guinsaugon ever existed."[57]

Despite the lack of hope that survivors would be found, rescue efforts continued apace for weeks:

> On Sunday afternoon after three days of digging in the shifting sea of mud from massive avalanches that buried the village, rescuers using sophisticated audio sensors heard scratching sounds that seemed to be coming from the

> site of an elementary school that had been buried – along with 246 students and teachers – beneath 100 feet of mud and debris. Hope swept through members of the rescue team as workers in rubber boots and macs [raincoats] crawled gingerly toward the sound across the reddish sucking mud. Then there was a sudden thud, like stone hitting a roof, and the mud started caving in. The scratching stopped . . . the stench of rotting bodies began to envelop the area. Volunteers buried the first group of bodies in a mass grave. And rescue workers, equipped with only shovels or their bare hands, grimly continued to dig in a light rain, finding only the dead.[58]

Sadly, five days after this landslide, geologists and physicists came to a disturbing conclusion: search teams were probing for survivors in the wrong place.[59] Victims trapped in air pockets sent text messages from their cell phones, which grew more frantic as the hours passed. One sent on Sunday, February 19 said simply, "Hurry, the waters are rising."[60] This call may not have saved many, but emergency response personnel excavated 22 people from the debris.

Relief efforts

The Philippine government put out an immediate and optimistic message. Governor Lerias said, "We're still very hopeful." President Gloria Macapagal Arroyo said, "All the efforts of our government continue and will not stop while there is hope to find survivors. The nation is grateful for the continued prayers and concern [and] help from our world allies." She also called for people to "all join hands in the preservation of our environment and protect what is left behind for the sake of the generations to come." Other than these appeals, the government remained largely mute in the face of criticism over the absence of warning systems and hazard maps, as well as the mismanagement of forest and the open-mining policies granted to companies from other nations.

According to official records, the government of the Philippines knew as early as May 2005 that the village was in grave danger and implemented policies to avert the disaster. It evacuated villages in the area in 2005 and banned logging. Residents who had been evacuated, however, returned to their homes despite the government's edicts. "According to government officials and environmental groups, problems ranging from government corruption, the lack of money and the political will to enforce the laws contributed to the collapse of the mountainside causing a large-scale human tragedy."[61]

Von Hernandez, the campaign director of Greenpeace in Southeast Asia said, “This is a failure of the implementation of laws and a failure of policy.”[62] Despite all the warning signs that the government saw, when people moved back into the village after an evacuation, the government did nothing. Also, only 0.1% of the national budget was allotted to disaster funds, so when this tragedy happened, little money had been set aside for disaster relief and reconstruction. Although the government had placed a ban on logging, it was ineffective due to political corruption. The failure to budget proper funds for law enforcement allowed illegal logging to continue.[63] Corruption in government made matters worse since many officials in the presidential palace as well as elsewhere made money and accumulated power from logging enterprises. In late 2005, for instance, the DENR allowed a company owned by a senator who was an ally of the president to resume logging over the objections of the town's residents and religious leaders.[64]

Immediately following the mudslide, Dick Gordon, the chairman of the Philippine Red Cross, made an international plea for supplies and money. As a result of this solicitation, Mr. Gordon raised over US$1.5 million which was used to purchase food, shelter, medical supplies, personal hygiene materials, and water purifying equipment. The USA sent three Navy ships, mobilized 6,000 army and Marine troops who were in the Philippines for an exercise, donated $100,000 of disaster equipment, and gave $560,000 of food, clothing, and other supplies through the US International Development Agency (USAID). South Korea, China, and Australia each donated $1,000,000, New Zealand donated $133,000, Taiwan gave $100,000 and approximately $500,000 in medicine, Malaysia sent a medical assistance team and a search and rescue team, and Spain, through the organization Unidad Canina de Rescate y Salvamento (UCRS), sent rescue dogs and personnel.[65]

Rebuilding

Although the area has been extensively replanted with trees, the trees chosen were coconut trees – which are great as food, but have notoriously shallow roots. So, the problem of repeated landslides continues to plague the island. For example, in December 2003, rains saturated slopes which caused a landslide killing over 200 people and destroying the town of San Francisco.[66] In May 2006, Typhoon Caloy (Chanchu) tore through the Philippines and caused both flash flooding and mudslides in 10 Leyte villages (called barangays), though no one was killed in these floods and slides. In December 2006 the massive Typhoon Durian triggered mudslides that killed over 1,000 people. No rebuilding followed the destruction of the towns, though people still live on these steep slopes.

Conclusion

There remains much debate as to whether logging played a role in this disaster and, if so, to what extent deforestation was also responsible. Indeed, the government seems to be unable to admit that illegal logging is ongoing. Congressman Roger Mercado said that both mining and logging in the past half century were to blame: "The logging stopped around 10 years ago, but this is the effect of the logging in the past."

Other government officials as well as environmental groups stated that the area was completely forested and that the rains were responsible for the mudslide. It will never be known what caused the slide, and reports often contradict each other. According to Archbishop Gaudencio Rosales of Manila, "The real reason for this terrible tragedy is that forests have been badly denuded and no serious replanting has been done. It is time for the powers that be to address strongly these issues."[67]

Global climate change may have played a role in this landslide. The La Niña weather phenomenon caused non-stop rains in 2005 in the province. Dave Petley, Professor at the International Landslide Centre, Durham University, South Africa, stated that: "This sort of rainfall and landslide action in the Philippines at this time of year is quite unusual. The month of January in a typical year would normally see 60 landslide deaths worldwide, whereas January this year [2005] saw 283 landslide fatalities, many in Asia."[68] The Philippines weather bureau similarly stated that adverse conditions since November might be linked to La Niña – a natural cyclical meteorological phenomenon which strikes Southeast Asia in certain years, bringing heavy rainfall.

In 2008, experts from all over the world came together to study and discuss this disaster and to implement a new set of policies and regulations. Experts included geologists from the Philippines, Taiwan, Canada, the USA, Japan, New Zealand, and Hong Kong. Geologists disagree, however, on the extent to which seismic activity played a role in the slope's failure.

The role of the natural environment and human activities such as past and current mining as well as legal and illegal logging still baffle geologists studying this region. They were unable to agree at the 2008 meeting about the causal factors leading up to the calamity, so they focused on discussing the importance of an early warning system:

> There were signs that the village was prone to landslides. But the residents were not aware of the cracks in the ground, muddy water coming out of holes in the ground, and irregular water flow from the mountain. There have to be ways to get people to report signs of a landslide to authorities. For landslides, we don't have a warning system. We can only warn people by way of monitoring.[69]

Residents need to be trained on what to look for, especially after heavy rains and earthquakes that destabilize slopes. Increased rigor of forest management in the region would serve to further stabilize slopes, thus mitigating landslide hazards. Proper land-use planning, including moving villages away from the base of sensitive slopes, could cut down on casualties, as these natural phenomena occur with regularity. It is only when people inhabit dangerous areas that landslides become catastrophes in the Philippines and elsewhere:

> More precise hazard maps and better community outreach, for instance, prompting people to quickly report potential warning signs such as rivers suddenly drying up will enable officials to react more nimbly to disaster and to perhaps even prevent casualties. And there's one message that governments around the world should heed. In the event of a future calamity, any rescue operation should be scientific from the start.[70]

Summary

Landslides, more than any other natural disaster, can be facilitated by human activities such as logging and mining. Slopes, by nature, tend to become unstable through time. Living at the base of mountains, either by choice or for reasons necessitated by family structure or employment, put people in harm's way. These landslides underscore the need for proper land-use planning, for geologic surveys, and for early warning and emergency response mechanisms to be in place in areas prone to landslides.

Emergency response teams in every case study showed their dogged commitment to rescue those injured or lost.

The disaster at Aberfan has become part of its history, and a memorial garden reminds visitors of this tragic landslide. These landslides are commemorated in different ways, including not memorializing the event at all. At Turtle Mountain, no memorial exists to remember its tragic history. Although the Welsh government has assured the residents of Aberfan that such a disaster will never occur again, the governments of Leyte and Ancash are unable to make such promises to the vulnerable residents living on slopes prone to landslides.

Notes

1 Iain McLean, Martin Johnes and the individual sources (1999), *The Aberfan Disaster: 21 October 1966* (Cardiff: Welsh Academic Press), 119. At www.nuffield.ox.ac.uk/politics/aberfan/home.htm.
2 Foreign Affairs and International Trade Canada (2006), "Canadian Energy Facts." At www.canadainternational.gc.ca/eu-ue/policies-politiques/energy-energie.aspx?lang=eng&view=d.
3 Brian Dawson (1995), *Crowsnest: An Illustrated History and Guide to the Crowsnest Pass* (Alberta, Canada: Altitude Publishing), 54.
4 David M. Cruden (2002), "Report on the great landslide at Frank," *Alberta History*, 50(2), Spring, 16–21.
5 SOS! Canadian Disasters Library and Archives Canada (2006), "Frank Rockslide – April 29, 1903". At www.collectionscanada.ca/sos/002028-2300-e.html ?PHPSESSID=gjc8q31s0iq0rurk1v815uqg66.
6 "On this day, April 29, 1903: The Frank rockslide: 90 seconds of terror," CBC Digital Archives. At www.cbc.ca/archives/categories/environment/natural-disasters/natural-disasters-general/the-frank-rockslide-90-seconds-of-terror.html.
7 Ibid.
8 Ibid.
9 Norm Pringle (1974), "The legend of Turtle Mountain: a synopsis." At www.cybercloud.com/turtle/synopsis.html.
10 SOS! Canadian Disasters Library and Archives Canada (2006), "Frank Rockslide – April 29, 1903." At www.collectionscanada.ca/sos/002028-2300-e.html ?PHPSESSID=gjc8q31s0iq0rurk1v815uqg66.
11 David M. Cruden and James Krahn (1978), "Frank Rockslide, Alberta, Canada," in Barry Voight (ed.), *Rockslides and Avalanches* (Amsterdam: Elsevier), vol.1, 97–112.

12 CBC Digital Archives (1967), "On this day, April 29, 1903: The Frank rockslide: 90 seconds of terror." At www.cbc.ca/archives/categories/environment/natural-disasters/natural-disasters-general/the-frank-rockslide-90-seconds-of-terror.html.

13 Alberta Geological Survey (2010), "Turtle Mountain Monitoring Project and Field Laboratory." At www.ags.gov.ab.ca/geohazards/turtle_mountain/turtle_mountain.html.

14 Francisco Moreno & Corey R. Frosese (2008), "Earth Sciences Report 2006–07, Turtle Mountain Field Laboratory Monitoring and Research Summary Report, 2005," Alberta Geological Survey. At www.ags.gov.ab.ca/publications/abstracts/ESR_2006_07.html.

15 David M. Cruden and James Krahn (1978), "Frank Rockslide, Alberta, Canada."

16 Glynis Fediuk (2011), "Stop Rock and Roll," RV West. At www.rvwest.com/index.php/article/alberta_south/stop_rock_and_roll.

17 Ibid.

18 Iain McLean, Martin Johnes and the individual sources (1999), *The Aberfan Disaster: 21 October 1966*, 62.

19 Ibid.

20 Gaynor Madgewick (1996), "Aberfan: Struggling out of the darkness." At www.diggingupthepast.org.uk/disasters.html.

21 Iain McLean, Martin Johnes and the individual sources (1999), *The Aberfan Disaster: 21 October 1966*, 83.

22 Ibid., 21.

23 Ibid., 99.

24 Ibid., 162.

25 "The Aberfan disaster." At http://en.wikipedia.org/wiki/Aberfan_disaster#cite_note-south-wales.police.uk-1.

26 Ibid.

27 Edmund Davies (chairman) (1967), Report of the Tribunal appointed to inquire into the Disaster at Aberfan on October 21 1966, HL 316, HC 553 (London: HMSO), 131–132. At www.nuffield.ox.ac.uk/politics/aberfan/sum.htm.

28 Louise Morgan, Jan Scourfiel, David Williams, et al. (2003), "The Aberfan disaster: 33-year follow-up of survivors," *British Journal of Psychiatry*, 182, 532–536.

29 Iain McLean, Martin Johnes and the individual sources (1999), *The Aberfan Disaster: 21 October 1966*, 119.

30 Harold J. Maidenberg (1970), "Peru estimates 30,000 died in a quake that wiped out scores of towns in North: aid is requested," *The New York Times*, June 2, 39.

31 Juan de Onis (1970), "In Peru, a 40-mile tour of devastated valley," *The New York Times*, June 9, 52.

32 David A. Love and Alan H. Clark (2004), "The lithologic, stratigraphic, and structural setting of the giant antamina copper-zinc skarn deposit, Ancash, Peru," *Economic Geology*, 99(5), August, 887–916.

33 Mark A. Burkholder (2008), *Review of Shaky Colonialism: The 1746 Earthquake–Tsunami in Lima, Peru, and its Long Aftermath* (Durham, NC: Duke University Press), 65–69.

34 Tanya Sandra Kampherm (2009), "Landslides triggered by the 1946 Ancash earthquake (Peru) and geologic controls on the mechanisms of initial rock slope failure," University of Waterloo doctoral dissertation, January 22. At http://uwspace.uwaterloo.ca/handle/10012/4233.

35 Jesús Angel Chávez Machado (2000), "Remembering the worst earthquake in Latin America: the day the Apus turned their backs on Peru," Newsletter ISDR Inform – Latin America and the Caribbean. At www.eird.org/eng/revista/No1_2001/pagina23.htm.

36 Dorothy V. Whipple and Flora L. Phelps (1970), "The town that was . . . until . . . May 30, 1970," *Américas*, 22, 16–26.

37 Ibid.

38 Harold J. Maidenberg (1970), "Area devastated by quake in Peru appeals for help: but blocked roads and fog hamper efforts to send in food and medicine, only one airport open" *The New York Times*, June 3, 1.

39 Ibid.

40 Harold J. Maidenberg (1970), "Peru estimates 30,000 died in a quake that wiped out scores of towns in north: aid is requested," *The New York Times*, June 2, 112.

41 United Press International (1970), "Earthquake death toll may reach 30,000: 2 Peru towns vanish as dam bursts [and] landslide danger mounts," *Boston Globe*, June 3, 7.

42 Dorothy V. Whipple and Flora L. Phelps (1970), "The town that was . . . until . . . May 30, 1970," *Américas*, 22, 16–26.

43 United Press International (1970), "Earthquake death toll may reach 30,000," *Boston Globe*, June 3, 3–6.

44 Dorothy V. Whipple and Flora L. Phelps (1970), "The town that was . . . until . . . May 30, 1970," 16–26.

45 Harold J. Maidenberg, "Area devastated by quake in Peru appeals for help," *The New York Times*, 5.

46 Ibid.

47 Dorothy V. Whipple and Flora L. Phelps (1970), "The town that was . . . until . . . May 30, 1970," 16–26.

48 Ibid.

49 Harold J. Maidenberg (1970), "Peru estimates 30,000 died in a quake that wiped out scores of towns in North," *The New York Times*, 12.

50 Dorothy V. Whipple and Flora L. Phelps (1970), "The town that was . . . until . . . May 30, 1970," 16–26.

51 Jesús Angel Chávez Machado (2001), "Remembering the worst earthquake in Latin America," Newsletter ISDR Inform – Latin America and the Caribbean, 47.

52 *Andean Air Mail and Peruvian Times* (2000), "State of emergency declared in parts of Ancash after ice block breaks from glacier," April 13, B–4.

53 US Department of State Bureau of East Asian and Pacific Affairs (2011), Background Note: Philippines, June 3. At www.state.gov/r/pa/ei/bgn/2794.htm.

54 Alejandro Ciencia, Jr. (2006), "The Philippine Supreme Court and the Mining Act ruling reversal," East–West Center Working Papers, International Graduate Student Conference Series November 9, 2.

55 Ibid.

56 Richard Stone (2006), "Too late, earth scans reveal the power of a killer landslide," *Science*, 311(31), 1844–1845.

57 Associated Press (2006), "1,800 feared killed by landslide in Philippines village," *The New York Times International*, February 18, A3.

58 Ibid.

59 Carlos Conde (2006), "As hopes fade, Filipinos recall signs of a slide," *The New York Times*, February 20, A1, A6.

60 Richard Stone (2006), "Too late, earth scans reveal the power of a killer landslide," 1844–1845.

61 Ibid.

62 Carlos Conde (2006), "Danger of Philippine landslides often ignored, critics say," *New York Time International*. At http://cassiopaea.org/forum/index.php?topic=445.0.

63 Ibid.

64 Ibid.

65 Ibid.

66 BBC News (2006), "Mud wipes out Philippine village," February 17. At http://news.bbc.co.uk/2/hi/asia-pacific/4722702.stm.

67 *The Philippine Daily Inquirer* (2006), "Storm triggers landslides; thousands stranded," May 12, 1.

68 Carlos H. Conde (2006), "Danger of Philippine landslides often ignored, critics say," *New York Time International*, February 21, 34–35.

69 Sarah Buckley (2006), "What caused the Philippine landslide?" BBC News, February 17, 22.

70 Richard Stone (2006), "Too late, earth scans reveal the power of a killer landslide," 1844–1845.

Further Reading

Keith Turner and Robert L. Schuster (1996), *Landslides: Investigation and Mitigation*, National Research Council (US) Transportation Research Board Special Report) (Washington, DC: National Academies Press).

This book is useful reading for those working or studying in the field of engineering geology.

Kyoji Sassa and Paolo Canuti (eds.) (2008), *Landslides – Disaster Risk Reduction* (New York: Springer).
This book was jointly organized by the International Consortium on Landslides (ICL), eight UN organizations (UNESCO, WMO, FAO, UN/ISDR, UNU, UNEP, World Bank, and UNDP) and four NGOs (International Council for Science, World Federation of Engineering Organizations, Kyoto University, and Japan Landslide Society) in Tokyo in 2008.

Derek Cornforth (2005), *Landslides in Practice: Investigation, Analysis, and Remedial/Preventative Options in Soils* (Hoboken, NJ: John Wiley & Sons, Inc.).
This book is an authoritative guide to landslide investigation, evaluation, and mitigation design.

Mannava V.K. Sivakumar, Raymond P. Motha, and Haripada P. Das (eds.) (2010), *Natural Disasters and Extreme Events in Agriculture: Impacts and Mitigation* (New York: Springer).
This book discusses ways to reduce the vulnerability of agriculture to disasters by timely warnings and by impact-reducing countermeasures.

Chapter 7

Pandemic Diseases

There was a crowd of us, now we are almost none. We should make new friends, but how, when the human race is almost wiped out; and why, when it looks to me as if the end of the world is at hand? Why pretend? We are alone indeed. You see how our great band of friends has dwindled. Look, even as we speak we too are slipping away, vanishing like shadows. One minute someone hears that another has gone, next he is following in his footsteps.[1]

Introduction

The study of invading microorganisms, including bacterial and viral agents, is a relatively new field of study.[2] In an effort to understand changing infectious diseases and their role as major natural disasters in human history, this chapter focuses on the bubonic plagues in the pre-modern world, the Great Influenza Pandemic of 1918–20, and the AIDS (Acquired Immune Deficiency Syndrome) pandemic that bridges the last and present centuries. The intentional or accidental introduction of species (alien invaders) into a new environment by humans usually results in adverse consequences. These biological invasions pose a number of questions for the reader. How did the invader get there? Did it succeed in gaining a foothold, and how are we able to explain its ability to spread and persist, while other biological invaders failed to establish themselves? Unlike most other disasters discussed in this volume that have a temporal dimension, pandemic diseases are processes whose dimensions are not confined to a place or time. Their impact is sudden, survivors assess the extent of the devastation, and relief and responses occur based upon history and culture.

Natural Disasters in a Global Environment, First Edition. Anthony N. Penna and Jennifer S. Rivers.

Each of these devastating pandemics struck unsuspecting populations who possessed neither the knowledge nor the material resources to combat their introduction and rapid spread to others. The pre-modern world of burgeoning congested cities, nonexistent or faulty sanitation, poor hygiene and contaminated food stocks provided ideal environments for the incubation and spread of disease. Many pre-modern cities were connected to global trading partners across Eurasia. While adding to the wealth of both, they opened themselves to unknown hazards with unintended devastating consequences. Along with these connections came the Asian black rat and its fleas, *Xenopsylla cheopis*, who hitched a ride on ships carrying wares across the continent. In the process, they infected millions of vulnerable Europeans with bubonic plague.

Before the twentieth century, health and sanitation professionals knew little about vector-borne viral diseases. The same can be said for the absence of medical knowledge among professionals who failed to combat the spread of influenza in 1918. In this latter case, breathing, not an insect bite, spread infection. Vulnerability to the plague spread across Eurasia; influenza spread across the globe. One had continental consequences, while the other proved to be boundless. Both ran rampant across time and space before dying out yet, as we know, influenza reappears again and again, changing its signature each time. The origin of AIDS, a sexually transmitted disease and the final case in this chapter, remains a controversial topic. Similar to influenza, its global spread went unchecked until vaccines and public health information began to slow its spread. Eradication seems unlikely since the viruses change quickly, allowing them to resist existing forms of treatment.

Organized relief efforts for victims did not exist in many pre-modern pandemics. Relatives, friends, and neighbors may have offered some comfort but many out of fear simply fled to places as yet unaffected and unknowingly spread the disease. The increasing numbers of the afflicted overwhelmed charities and places of worship.

The Bubonic Plague (1347–51 and After)

In the minds of most people, the bubonic plague is confined to history as a disease of disastrous proportions that killed millions of people. Yet, the disease is not confined to a far distant past. It erupted in Guangzhou and Hong Kong, China in 1894 and spread to Calcutta and Mumbai in 1895–96.

A massive plague epidemic swept across India in the early twentieth century, killing millions of citizens. Current reports by the World Health Organization (WHO) state that 1,000 to 3,000 cases of plague appear each year. The Plague Commission of India and A. E. J. Yersin identified the plague as disease of wild rodents in which the pathogen, *Yersinia pestis*, is spread by infected fleas.[3]

More alarming for the present are surveys that indicate the widespread existence of bubonic plague among wild rodent populations across the world and more specifically in the USA, southern Asia, southern Africa, and South America. Although these areas have suffered no recent outbreaks of plague among humans, the potential is there. To make the point about the potential likelihood of such occurrences is the evolution of drug-resistant strains of the bacterium and prolonged outbreaks in recent decades in Surat, Mozambique, and Madagascar. Although these developing-world locations remain geographically removed from the modern world, the potential for outbreaks in modern urban centers remains real.

The last epidemic in the USA occurred in Los Angeles in 1924. In New York City, the rat population approximates the human population in numbers, meaning that there is on average 4,500 rodents for every third of a square mile. Such high concentrations make the appearance of the disease the potential trigger for a large-scale outbreak.[4] To gain a better understanding of the relationship between the human and animal world, the history of communicable diseases helps us to understand the ecological complexity of the past. Some of that history is contained in the unexpected and unpredictably lethal appearance of a bubonic plague.

The Justinian Plague (540–547 CE)

Although the precise dates regarding the origins of infectious diseases are difficult to pinpoint, the expansion of Roman trade across the Eurasian landmass between 500 BCE and 500 CE is pivotal to our understanding. "Today archaeology and zoology draw a picture of rats and their history that differs from even a decade ago. Tiny bones and DNA are yielding glimpses of the rat's migration from Southeast Asia into the Roman Empire and medieval Europe. The diffusion of the rat across Europe looks increasingly like an integral part of the Roman conquest."[5] The biological exchange of animal and human microbes, the consequences of which could not have been known by ancient trading partners, shaped the course of human affairs for centuries to come.

Pushing at the boundaries of existing trading networks, the search for new commodities opened markets linking the Upper Nile in Africa to ports in the Mediterranean basin. The routes across Central Asia to India and China, the most famous of which became known as the Silk Road, gave Europeans access to spices, primarily pepper, and fine porcelains from China and woven cloth from India. In the process of trading for these products, another exchange was taking place: the transfer of pathogens from one ecosystem to another.

For our purposes, the origin and transmission of bubonic plague decimated populations across Eurasia a number of times, but especially during the reign of Justinian. He consolidated the power of the Eastern Roman Empire of Byzantium in 532 CE. Having secured the borders of his empire by making an unstable peace with the Goths in the west and the Persians in the east, Justinian pursued the establishment of a commercial empire with its focal point, the flourishing capital of Constantinople (modern Istanbul). Its advantageous location at the entrance to the Black Sea gave it primacy over the Aegean archipelago, the Levant, Syria, and Egypt and access to the commercial riches of India and China.

The city thrived on its trading networks and its growing population. An estimated one-half million people lived on a diet of mostly coarse bread and the looked forward to government-sponsored circuses. To satisfy the growing demands for food and drink, Justinian built a massive granary to hold wheat from Egypt. He located other granaries, at least four in all, in cities within the boundaries of his empire. Alexandria, Egypt possessed one such massive storehouse, and all became excellent breeding grounds for rats.

As zoologists have pointed out, rats are omnivores but given a choice of what to eat, black rats, in particular, prefer grain to all other foods. Modern examples prove the point. Evidence from modern Turkey suggests that rats consume or render inedible 5–15% of stored grain and legumes, contaminating much more with their urine and feces.[6] In the ancient world, rats followed the supply chain, hitching a ride on ships transporting grain across the Mediterranean basin to all the port cities of the Roman Empire and eventually to Constantinople during Justinian's reign. During both periods, once uncovered grain was off loaded by hand and carried to large granaries, it was eventually distributed across the broad expanse of the European continent by Roman carts and pack animals to civilian and military bakeries.

Large staples in grain sustained the urban populations of ancient Roman cities and its successors in Byzantium. The congestion and unsanitary conditions of the poorer sections of these growing cities served as breeding grounds for rats. "A single breeding pair of stowaway rats among the grain could produce one thousand offspring per year. Granaries form excellent flea nurseries – the Oriental rat flea, *Xenopsylla cheopis*, does not feed on blood in its larval form, but rather on the debris from grain or rice."[7] These explosive breeding conditions created dense rat populations that "threatened ecological equilibrium and disposed the rodents to disease."

Recent mathematical modeling estimates the critical density for the disposition at 3,000 rats per 0.19 mi^2 (0.5 km^2). Judging from 143 rat contexts of the ninth to the fifteenth centuries, medieval Europe's rat colonies were extensive and abundant.[8] Although data about the concentrations of rat populations in Byzantium are elusive, the plague that struck Justinian's empire in 540 CE and did not run its course officially until 590 CE was catastrophic. An estimated 100 million Europeans, one-half of the continent's population, died during this 50-year period and allegedly brought economic growth to a halt. At the height of the affliction, death rates in Constantinople reached 5,000 a day, according to Procopius, a prominent Byzantine scholar who described the plague as follows:

> A bubonic swelling developed; and this took place not only in the particular part of the body which is called the "boubon" [the groin], that is, below the abdomen, but also inside the armpit, and in some cases also beside the ears, and at different points on the thighs.[9]

Other observers provided a nuanced description of the plague's spread:

> Whereas some cities were stricken to such an extent that they were completely emptied of inhabitants, there were parts where the misfortune touched more lightly and moved on . . . there were places where it affected one part of the city but kept clear of other parts, and often one could see in a city that was not diseased certain households that were completely destroyed. And there are places where, although one or two households were destroyed, the rest of the city remained unaffected.[10]

Where did the plague come from, and what was its source? The trading routes of Byzantium provided an obvious geographical outline for its spread. An intermediary juncture, then, would be located in East and

Central Africa, spreading along the Nile River from Ethiopia to Egypt into the Mediterranean basin. Many scientists believe that earlier strains of *X. cheopis*, the genus of fleas, emanate from the various kinds of gerbils and marmots that inhabit a vast geographical region of dry grasslands and mountains stretching from Central Asia to Central Africa. In reaching the latter region, the infection moved on to rats, in this instance, the Nile grass rat.

Increased precipitation and humidity contributed to the outbreak of plague. Because of changing climatic conditions, gerbils, marmots, and rats may have overpopulated their natural habitats. Later a cooling occurred during the Age of Justinian as noted by increased levels of CO_2 and SO_2 located in the Greenland ice cores. Tree ring data support the conclusion that the growth of trees was slowed by the limited sunlight penetrating Earth's surface. These findings support the hypothesis that a massive volcanic eruption somewhere in the East Asian Arc of Fire in the period around 535 CE created clouds of ash particles that enveloped Earth and cooled it.

Biologists have verified the observed link between increased precipitation and the outbreak of plague.

> At the local level, above-normal precipitation produces increased plague outbreaks; conversely, above-normal dryness diminishes plague. In an arid or semi-arid ecology, precipitation that increases two to six months before rodent breeding peaks launches a "tropic cascade." An explosion of plant and insect growth bolsters the food chain and fosters a surge in the rodent population. In this kind of ecology, increased precipitation followed by a cool dry climate that created drought conditions may well be the sequence most favorable to plague transmission. Drought decreases the food supply for the newly swollen rodent colonies, which then disperse in search for food.[11]

Without predators to limit the spread of rodents, survival rates accelerate from one generation, eventually outstripping their food supply and local habitat. Overcrowded conditions lead to the dispersal of the rodent population causing wild rural and domestic urban rat populations to mix. "Bubonic plague is actually widespread throughout the wild rodent population."[12]

Based on newer scientific research, however, plague remained endemic in large towns and cities for as long as 100 years without imports from wild rodent populations. The biggest threat to humans occurs when a dense rodent population, stressed by the conditions described above, becomes vulnerable to the previously latent bacterium, *Yersinia pestis*, which is carried from rats to humans via fleas. There will be more about the process of transmission later in this chapter, but suffice it to say that diseases of animals that can be carried to humans are categorized as zoonoses.

Each time a rat dies from the plague, a free infected flea is released to infect another rat and when it decimates the rat population it finds human hosts. These multiple ecological dislocations lead to a bubonic plague pandemic. Although the medical narrative about the transmission of the disease usually refers to infected rats arriving by ship, the explanation provided here may suggest an alternative mode of dispersal.

For example, earthquakes struck Constantinople in 525, 533, 548, 554, 557, and 740 CE. The one in December 557 CE was followed by an outbreak of the plague the following year, in July 558 CE. Quite possibly, the earthquake destroyed the storage facilities for grain, making the contents available to a scattered rat population. Feasting on these newfound sources of energy, a population explosion among rodents could have taken place. Under normal conditions, breeding polygynous rats produce eleven litters a year that in turn are capable of producing their own litters within three to five months. More food means more rats at an ever-increasing rate.

Since population growth quickly outstripped the formerly unlimited food source, malnourished rats in which dormant plague bacillus live become symptomatic. Rat fleas bite the infected rats. Biting causes them to become digestively blocked; that is, unable to digest and metabolize the blood meal. So, they remain hungry and continue to bite live rat hosts until the rat population is decimated. "Free infected fleas are released into the environment every time an infected rat dies."[13] During this phase of the contagion, a ready supply of human hosts replaces the diminishing rat population. If this scenario is plausible, then the importation of rats by ships may seem unnecessary. Earthquakes and their disruptive aftermath became intimately linked to the spread of the bubonic plague during Justinian's reign.

Conclusion

The impact of Justinian's plague in Byzantium must be weighted within the context of a Western Europe disintegrating under the onslaught of infectious diseases including measles, smallpox, tuberculosis, and influenza. In addition, with the fall of Rome, continued violence was followed by decades of malnutrition and the widespread lack of any semblance of sanitation.

As a result, the population dropped precipitously during the sixth and seventh centuries, with some areas losing as much as one-half to two-thirds of their inhabitants. The virtual disappearance of trade with the West caused by the emergence of hostile Muslim states in southwest Asia made matters worse. In contrast to Roman Europe with an estimated population of 50–70 million people, by the Early Middle Ages in 600 CE, the European population had plummeted to approximately 25 million people. The comingling of people and rats in the congested filthy cities of this early period accelerated the spreading plague and caused the death of millions.

The Black Death (1347–51 CE)

A change in the climate beginning sometime between 950 and 1000 CE, called the Medieval Warm Epoch, resulted in a turnabout in the fortunes of early Europeans. The warming took place first in European Russia and Greenland between 950 and 1200 CE and later in most of Europe from 1150 to 1300 CE.[14] Land clearing accelerated as increasing agricultural productivity fed Europe's malnourished population. Milder winters and longer and drier summers continued for centuries, making more and more food available. A population explosion created conditions whereby some farm workers were released to occupations in growing cities.

Farm inventions, such as the heavy wheeled plow pulled by horses fitted with innovations such as horse collars and horseshoes, made previously impenetrable soils available for cultivation. One of the unintended consequences of land clearing to feed this growing population, however, may have been a reduction in birds of prey, including owls, and rat-eating foxes and weasels. Combined with increased cereal production and the concentration of a growing population in cities, a favorable environment was created for the multiplication of rats.[15]

Supported by a favorable climate, agricultural productivity and technological innovations including the increased use of windmills and watermills to produce energy for grist mills, lumber mills, and many others, the economy kept pace with Europe's growing population. Although both began to stagnate beginning about 1250 CE, suggesting that the boom years for economic and population growth were over, no widespread depression followed until the early 1300s with the onset of the Little Ice Age that stretched across the centuries from 1300 to 1850 CE.

A reversal in climate for a Europe dependent on a bountiful agricultural economy turned growth into collapse. Years of longer winters and shorter, cooler, and wetter summers resulted in devastating food shortages. By 1315 CE, Europe's Great Famine had commenced, bringing to the forefront all of the sicknesses associated with failed harvests, food spoilage, and the spread of fungi. Starvation caused the deaths of millions: one-half million in England alone, with countless dead throughout the European countryside. By 1325 CE, the steep decline in food production ended, followed by stability in produce and prices.

"It has often been suggested that the overpopulation of the early fourteenth century created persistent malnutrition, making the population as a whole more susceptible to the microorganism that cause the Black Death (1347–51). In fact, what appears to be the case is that, if anything, the quality of nutrition improved over the period 1322–46 or at least held steady."[16] As a result, the hypothesis that a link between the Great Famine and the Black Death existed and that the impact of the former on the deficient immunity of millions of adults and their offspring may have made them more vulnerable to the ravages of *Yersinia pestis* remains an unsubstantiated one.

It was initially described in history as "the Great Mortality," but in 1824 it was referred to as "the Black Death". Although the origins of this pandemic were located in the distant lands of the Mongolian plains, it reached the shores of European settlements by the global trading routes that connected Eurasia, from China to the Mediterranean city-states. It struck with deadly force in 1347 CE, on Genoese ships carrying cargo that unknowingly included black rats (*rattus rattus*) and their "cargo" of infected fleas. They set sail from the Black Sea port of Caffa destined for Messina, Sicily. The etiology of the disease will be described in greater detail later in this chapter but suffice it to say that this voyage and its unaccounted "cargo" changed the demography of Europe in the short run and transformed the social, economic, and political structure of the continent.

It may not be an exaggeration to describe the global effects of the Black Death as one of the greatest natural disasters in human history. In the absence of accurate census data for the century under discussion, an estimate of 40% mortality in Europe alone seems plausible. This pandemic killed on a scale not seen before or since. If we include Palestine, Syria, and large parts of Egypt, the Ottoman Empire, and Azerbaijan, death came to as many as 50 million persons (Figure 7.1).

As noted earlier in this chapter, outbreaks of plague battered Byzantium and the early medieval world until about 750 CE. The second major outbreak brought Europe's centuries of progress (the decade-long Great Famine being the exception) to a standstill with the outbreak of plague in

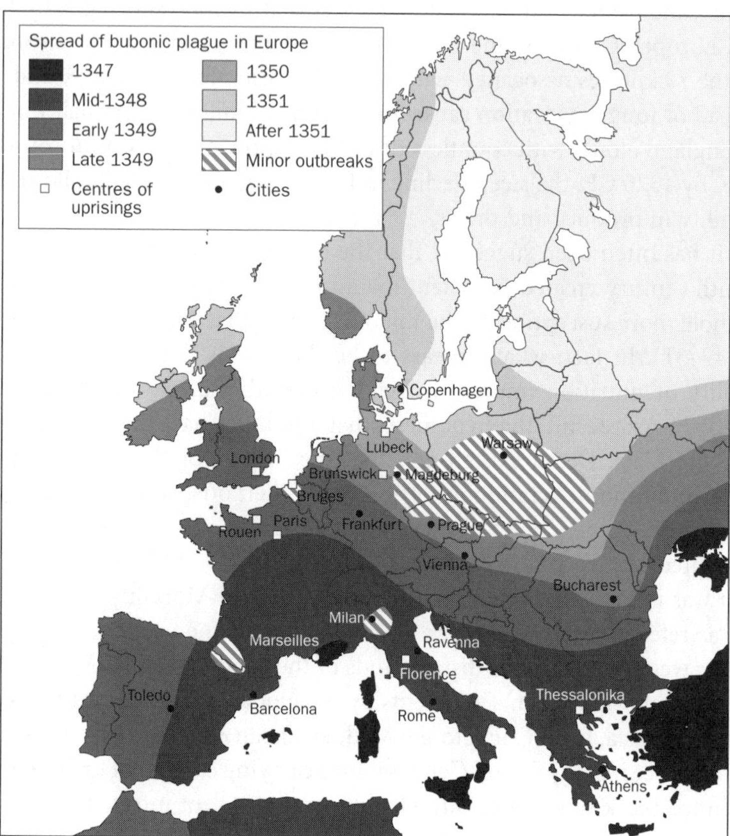

Figure 7.1 Map highlighting the spread of the Black Death in Eurasia, 1347–51. *Source:* Adapted from Wikimedia Commons, the free media repository.

1348 CE and continued to infect populations to varying degrees until the eighteenth century. Spreading from Italy northward into central Europe, its effects became commingled with an earthquake of approximate moment magnitude (M_w) 9 on January 25, 1348 as measured by the Mercalli-Sieberg scale,* with its epicenter located in Friuli, Italy.

* The Mercalli scale was a revision of the simple ten-degree Rossi-Forel scale by Italian volcanologist Giuseppe Mercalli in 1884 and 1906. Rewritten by the German geophysicist August Heinrich Sieberg, it became known as the Mercalli-Sieberg scale. Modified again by Charles Richter, the father of the Richter magnitude scale that measures the amount of seismic energy in an earthquake. The scale is known today as the Modified Mercalli Scale and commonly abbreviated MM and measures the intensity of the quake.

A link may exist between these two natural disasters, the earthquake and the outbreak of plague. The latter would have caused a breakdown in hygiene (taking into consideration that under the best of circumstances it did not meet modern standards), exacerbating conditions for survivors also struggling with the effects of landslides and floods. Under the best of conditions, it is unlikely that people either washed frequently or changed clothing more than one or twice a year. Under these conditions, malodorous humans would attract bites from infected fleas.

Although the latent bacillus, *Yersinia pestis*, in black rats may have been unleashed by a catastrophic earthquake and caused this second pandemic, a more likely culprit may have been the emergence of global Eurasian trade and travel and the faster communication of a pony express invented by the Yam, also known as the Mongolian Tartars. Within a few decades the disease, with its origins in the distant regions of Mongolia, spread swiftly by way of the Crimea across Asia into China, and from Russia to Sicily on merchant ships in late September 1347 CE. Moving quickly northward to the Italian city-states of Genoa, Florence, and Venice, it spread to Spain and France. By the summer and autumn of 1348 CE, the plague had moved northward to England and Ireland and westward to Austria and Germany.

The Rand Corporation has ranked the Black Death as one of the world's greatest natural disasters, killing an estimated 20 million people in Europe between (1347–51), or approximately 40% of Europe's population. In Britain alone, 1.5 million died. According to Emmanuel Le Roy Ladurie, it was the first outbreak of the "microbian unification of the world" between 1300 CE and 1650 CE that would be followed by other global pandemics of smallpox, measles, and syphilis as humans and their microbes traversed the globe on missions of conquest, trade, and travel.[17] Many more millions would succumb to the disease as it traveled across the Eurasian landmass.

Conclusion

In 2007, DNA extracted from the bones and teeth of its victims, dead for almost 500 years, proved that a strain of the bacterium, *Yersinia pestis*, had caused the plague. The findings also answered the question about the possible link between the Justinian Plague and the Black Death. According to researchers from McMaster University in Ontario, Canada and the University of Tubingen in Germany, no link existed.

A now extinct strain of *Yersinia pestis* or something else caused the Justinian Plague. Conversely, modern plague, which kills about 2,000 people annually, has its origin in the medieval Black Death. The virulence of the Black Death may have been caused by its interaction with climate, cramped living conditions, the weak immune systems of its victims, and the outbreaks of other lethal diseases, such as influenza and tuberculosis, either simultaneously or in response to the outbreak of plague.[18]

The Great Influenza Pandemic (1918–20)

> Last fall and winter we were confronted with a new condition, if not a new disease. I believe that we have as much to support this diagnosis in pigs, as the physicians have to support a similar diagnosis in man. The similarity of the epidemic among people and epidemic in pigs was so close as to present a close relationship between the two conditions. It looked like the "flu" and until proven it was not the "flu," I shall stand by that diagnosis.[19]

Introduction

The evolutionary history of humans may be viewed as a continuous battle for survival against microbes that have the ability to mutate and evolve much more quickly than humans. The history of this ongoing battle is written in our genes. Throughout our evolutionary history, infectious attacks have killed the most susceptible, leaving the survivors with immunity acquired to fight off the next attack. As each generation of humans found itself under siege from pathogenic microbes, its survivors slowly acquired genetic resistance. Also, some virulent microbes lost their "killing power" over time. Historically, nursing mothers have passed on their immunity to their children. Although mother's milk remains a safeguard against some diseases, the intervention of modern medicine and the discovery of vaccines also provide immunity to a host of potential lethal viruses.

This pandemic infected a third of the world's population and may have killed as many as 50 million people worldwide. Once the pandemic ended, however, it received little attention from scholars, public officials, and journalists. The pandemic proved to be so lethal and its memory so painful that survivors tried their best to forget about it. Reminders only caused fear, especially since the causes of the outbreak and its spread were unknown until recently.

When a lethal strain of avian flu emerged in south Asia in 2003, public health officials took notice and considered its relationship to the 1918–20 pandemic. Fortunately, it did not spread and remained confined to birds. In 2009, however, an influenza strain that moved from birds and swine to humans and became known as swine flu emerged in Mexico and moved north into the USA, infecting as many as 90 million persons and hundreds of millions worldwide. Known as H1N1 influenza, its lethality thankfully did not compare to the 1918 outbreak. Although it was a mild form of influenza, it alerted health officials to the fact that the potential spread of pandemic disease would require constant vigilance.

The pandemic's origins

The outbreak was identified first by J. S. Koen, a veterinarian and inspector for the US Bureau of Animal Industry in Fort Dodge, Iowa in 1918 who described an illness that afflicted hogs. Although hog farmers treated this description with skepticism, his diagnosis proved to be disturbingly accurate. It would strike next army recruits at Fort Riley, Kansas on March 11, 1918. As the history of the 1918–20 pandemic unfolded, the "flu" that afflicted hogs struck an overcrowded military base preparing young men for traveling to fight in the Great War in Europe (1914–18; it was only named World War I after the outbreak of World War II in 1939). Once the USA entered the war in 1917, they would experience "Over there"* the spreading pandemic and carnage on the muddy battlefields of northern France.

As the number of ill soldiers soared and deaths mounted, hospital and field barracks facilities and personnel became overwhelmed by the workload of caring for the sick. It was one of the deadliest pandemics in world history. "Singlehandedly, flu thrust the year of 1918 back into the previous century."[20] Epidemiologists now believe that influenza may have caused as many as 100 million deaths worldwide. In the USA, they calculated the death totals as 675,000 out of a population of 105 million in 1918–19. Life expectancy dropped from 51 to 39, back to the average lifespan in 1868. As influenza spread from one military post to another, a young physician at Fort Devens, Massachusetts wrote about its lethal symptoms:

* "Over there" is a 1917 song popular with US soldiers in both world wars. It was written by George M. Cohan during the Great War.

> These men start with what appears to be ordinary attacks of influenza [but] very rapidly develop the most vicious type of pneumonia that has ever been seen. Two hours after admission they have mahogany spots over the cheek bones, and a few hours later you can begin to see the cyanosis extended from the ears and spreading all over their faces. It is only a matter of a few hours until death comes, and it is simply a struggle for air until they suffocate. It is horrible.[21]

To add to the horrific symptoms, the following described the condition of dying patients at Fort Devens, Massachusetts. "[I] glanced in at the wards with their lines of cots and prostrated soldiers, whose linens were often stained with bloody sputum and the sudden nosebleeds that were symptoms of Spanish influenza. Soldiers with a tint of blue were almost certainly dying."[22] Autopsies revealed blue swollen lungs filled with a thin bloody fluid. One-quarter of the country's population of 103 million would become infected and, of those, 2.5% would die. Today that would mean 1.5 million deaths, more than the combined deaths from cardiovascular disease, cancers, AIDS, and Alzheimer's disease for a single year in the USA.

Although many accounts of the outbreak of the pandemic began with the outbreaks at US Army camps in Kansas and in Massachusetts, they may only have been the North American examples of a pandemic that had been developing around the world years before its lethal outbreak (Figure 7.2). To support this hypothesis, many virologists argued that the influenza virus (viruses were unknown to medical science in 1918) needs a period of time after it jumps species (in this instance from hogs to humans) to rearrange its genes and become the mass murderer that we know from history. The history of influenza extends backward hundreds and possibly thousands of years.

In a hundred-year time frame, epidemics killed thousands in London alone with symptoms that would become eerily reminiscent of influenza. Rheumatic pain, the coughing up of blood, and high fevers were afflictions described by London's physicians as the epidemical catarrhal fever in 1830–33, 1847, 1855, and 1890.

What would become a more recent harbinger of the Great Influenza Pandemic of 1918 occurred in 1889–90. It allegedly surfaced in Bokhara, Turkistan in the summer of 1889 and struck populations across Europe. In heavily populated regions in and around Paris and London, it caused headaches, muscle pain, weakness, and mental depression. Although lethal by any standards, killing an estimated 250,000 Europeans (Asian estimates are

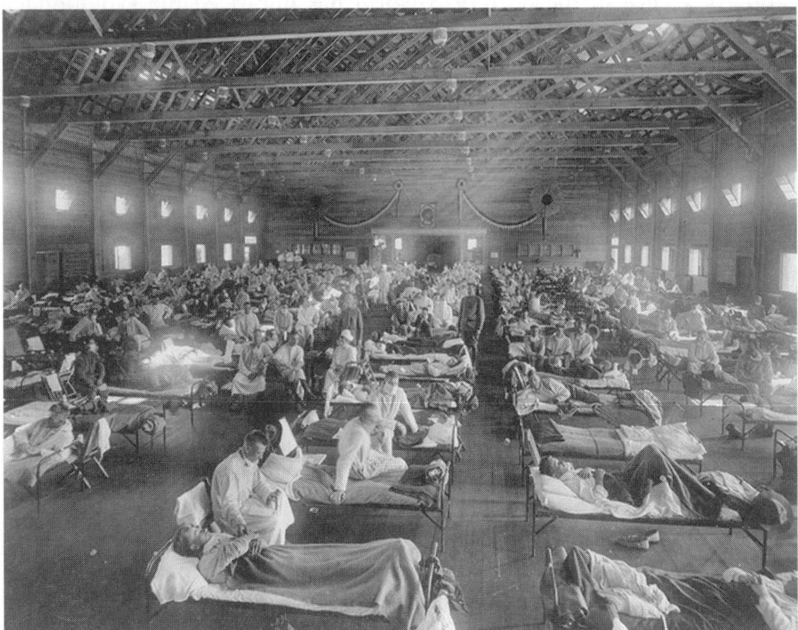

Figure 7.2 Emergency hospital in Funston, Kansas, USA, during the Great Influenza Pandemic in 1918.
Source: The United States Office of the Public Health Historian, Washington, DC.

unknown because census data for many regions did not exist), the symptoms associated with this pandemic suggest that the virus, having successfully jumped from one species (animal) to another (human), was mutating and probably gaining in strength. Influenza epidemics had broken out in 1900, 1908, and again in 1915 and with each outbreak in England, France, and the USA it mutated, gaining in virulence by 1918.

In its postscript to the 1918 pandemic, the UK Ministry of Health concluded that its path could be traced back to 1889. Its success, the report concluded, resulted in "the phase of complete victory in which infective power is maintained, even enhanced, and to this added a toxicity surpassed by few epidemiological competitors."[23]

As the Great War entered its first full year in 1915, Germany reported outbreaks of pneumonia at its military bases, while influenza continued to infect citizens on both sides of the Atlantic. Respiratory diseases ranging from pneumonia, bronchitis, and inflammation afflicted humans and horses alike. The source of these most recent outbreaks is unknown but modern science in the post-1918 world has unraveled the evolutionary history of influenza viruses.

Although not known in 1918, influenza proved to be a deadly virus. It mutated from birds through their droppings to pigs and then to humans, causing the catastrophic pandemic. Although the exact sequence of these events is unknown, the following descriptions provide a reasonable hypothetical explanation for the outburst of infection across the world. The dormant virus exists in the guts of wild fowl potentially everywhere. For the outbreak at Fort Riley to occur, the following sequence of events was possible:

> A bird, probably a wild duck, rose from a lake in Canada. Flying south towards its winter nesting ground, the duck passed over Kansas. The duck sojourned, or perhaps simply defecated, in the pond. Perhaps a pig was wallowing in the pond. Perhaps children were playing there. A chance encounter occurred. Perhaps between a duck and a pig. Perhaps between a duck and a man, woman and child. Perhaps between a pig and a man. Most probably between all three. From this a virus was spawned, a submicroscopic creature which, with all the innocence and cunning of nature herself, created the incalculable human tragedy of influenza 1918.[24]

The pandemic

While the illnesses at Fort Riley were duplicated across military camps in the USA during the spring of 1918, few beyond the medical staff attending to those afflicted took any notice. Soldiers recruited from the rural areas of the USA, tightly packed into makeshift encampments with poor sanitary facilities, without the immunity to infection acquired by living in cramped urban tenements, became the country's first victims. The army would swell to over two million by the end of the Great War, with the first wave of 84,000 in March and another 118,000 arriving in France in April. This transition to Europe represented the second and most virulent wave of influenza. Transport ships moving American soldiers to Bordeaux, France in April 1918 carried the infection to the continent. By May, this spreading contagion reached the British Expeditionary Force and spread to French forces. Although it moved fastest among the closely quartered soldiers, by June an estimated eight million citizens in military neutral Spain had caught the flu. The term "Spanish flu" became shorthand for what we know now as an H1N1 virus.

With the Bolshevik Revolution in Russia in October 1917 and Russian Premier Lenin's decision to withdraw from the war, abandoning the Czarist government's alliance with France, England, and other allied powers, Germany moved its entire fighting force from the Eastern front and began a massive assault on the Western front in the spring of 1918. Its army of one million men and 3,000 large artillery guns turned the Western front into a raging battlefield. By May, the fall of Paris seemed inevitable and the outcome of the war had swung in favor of Germany. By June 1918, soldiers in each of Germany's 37 divisions had caught the flu. The offensive stalled and the advance turned into retreat and ultimate failure. Although the flu had also infected French, British, and American troops as well, its impact did not affect the war's outcome. Combined with deficiencies in German supply lines to provide food and fuel to the Western front and the addition of the two million soldiers in the American Expeditionary Force, the debilitating effects of the influenza pandemic sapped the German army and contributed to its retreat and surrender on November 11, 1918.

Despite the absence of air travel, airborne influenza along with highly infectious pneumonia had spread around the world in less than five months. In addition to the hundreds of thousands of troops who landed in France carrying the virus, troops in the UK also became infected. The British Navy had a major coaling station in Sierra Leone on Africa's west coast. Workers caught the flu from British seamen and passed it on to those with whom they came in contact, including East, West, and South Africans and Australian soldiers traveling to and from the campaigns in Europe. By September, 3% of Sierra Leone's population had died. It spread across Africa with the same speed that it traveled elsewhere. It reached Bombay (Mumbai) and Calcutta, India in June 1918 and Chungking (Chongqing), China in July. New Zealanders caught it from travelers to their island home, probably from the Pacific island countries of the Philippines and Hawaii. Infected New Zealanders landing in Samoa brought the flu with them. "Within three months over 20% of the Samoan population had died. Similar figures for deaths occurred in Tahiti and Fiji . . . influenza had spread worldwide and death followed in its wake."[25]

By some conservative estimates, as many as a fifth of humanity suffered the fevers, aches and nausea of influenza from 1918–20. With a global population of 1.8 billion people, this number would mean that 36 million people had symptoms of influenza. Many millions more who did not exhibit flu symptoms suffered from sub-clinical cases of infection.

The world totals have risen with the accumulation of more and better data and improved statistical methods. Originally the data for deaths in India gathered in the 1940s was put at approximately 20 million but revised upward in 2002 by epidemiologists "in the order of 50 million . . . even this vast figure may be substantially lower than the real toll [of as many as 100 million].[26] Estimates that flu infected one-fifth of the world's population seem plausible. Globally, death toll estimates of 5% seem more than possible.

Although the death tolls in the Western world were high by most standards, those in rural underdeveloped countries exceeded those in the urban developed world. Educational levels, sanitation, and nutrition played a role, and living in the urbanized West also exposed its inhabitants to earlier influenza viruses that gave them some protection against the virulence of 1918–20. In the USA, about 2.5% of the population died, but double that percentage aged between 21 and 30 died, many of them soldiers living in the close quarters of barracks, transport ships, and the battlefield trenches of France. More than 80% of the US Army casualties were influenza-related. "From July 1917 to April 1919, this virus killed 43,000 soldiers in the American Expeditionary Forces."[27] In France, which had a population of 36 million, nearly 200,000 civilian influenza deaths were recorded. Its military deaths were three times higher. In the UK, 240,000 civilian deaths occurred, of which more than 20,000 were military deaths caused by influenza. In Russia, there were 450,000 casualties from the flu and in Italy 500,000, representing 1% of its population. In Mexico conservative estimates were of the deaths of 2.3% of its population, with other estimates over 4%.[28]

Once the Great Pandemic dissipated, a researcher at the Harvard Medical School compared its mortal impact on the military to two other great plagues:

> This fatality has been unparalleled in recent times. The influenza epidemic of 1918 ranks well up with the epidemics famous in history. Epidemiologists have regarded the dissemination of cholera from the Broad Street well in London as a catastrophe. The typhoid epidemic of Plymouth, PA, of 1885, is another illustration of the damage that can be done by epidemic disease once let loose . . . Compared with epidemics for which we have fairly accurate statistics the death rate at Camp Sherman in the fall of 1918 is surpassed only by that of the plague in London in 1665 and that of yellow fever in Philadelphia in 1793. The plague killed 14% of London's population in seven months time. Yellow fever destroyed 10% of the population of Philadelphia in four months. In seven weeks influenza and pneumonia killed 3.1% of the

> population at Camp Sherman. If we consider the time factor, these three instances are not unlike in their lethality.[29]

As quickly as the Great Influenza Pandemic arrived in 1918, it had disappeared by 1920. With the death and trauma it created in the minds of its survivors, erasing it from their memories became instinctive. With the exception of analyses of its causes, symptoms, and lethality in medical journals, generations of schoolchildren and their parents learned little about it. Much of this response or lack of one can be explained by an unconscious effort to put the ravages of the pandemic out of one's mind. Also, no one knew the causes in 1918, even Robert Johnson, a Philadelphia physician who made the first detailed description of the affliction in 1793. With the benefit of more detailed public health statistics in America's cities in the years after the Great Pandemic, it became clear that other influenza outbreaks had occurred in 1833, 1837, 1847, and 1889–90.[30]

The influenza's etiology

Unlike other viral infections, including measles, mumps, and chickenpox, in which infection results in lifetime immunity, influenza viruses circulate continuously among the human population causing outbreaks each year that kill between 250,000 to 500,000 globally. Although the causes of the 1918 pandemic were unknown then, we now know how influenza spreads and how to combat its viruses, that have caused previous epidemics and pandemics. These viruses contain fifteen H (hemagglutinin) and nine N (neuraminidase) proteins that exist on the surface of the virus.

Once infected by a flu virus during "flu season," a person develops antibodies directed against the H and N proteins of that particular virus. Not to be deterred, however, the virus changes the particular combination of its H and N genes, defeating our immunity and causing another outbreak of the flu. None of this was known, of course, when Spanish journalists whose country remained neutral during the Great War began writing about the wartime outbreaks in their uncensored reports.

It was not until 1933 that scientists isolated human influenza and not until the 1950s that they produced tissue cultures using embryonated eggs. Influenza viruses were then divided into three types: A, B, and C. Influenza A afflicts humans but also, pigs, horses, seals, and a wide variety of wild water birds, including ducks, geese, terns, gulls, and domestic birds, including chickens and turkeys, that carry a variety of flu viruses in their guts that become dispersed in their droppings. Influenza B produces the winter flu primarily in children, while C causes the common cold in humans.

As noted above, the H and N genes change their signature, creating new strains of the virus. Although birds usually lack the protein needed to infect human cells, pigs and horses are agents capable of being infected and passing the infection on to humans. "So gene swapping between human and bird strains often occurs in pigs and horses, causing a major genetic change in the virus make-up called a genetic shift."[31] This mixing, by creating a new strain, can cause a pandemic. Once a pandemic has run its course, the virus will remain in the environment, mutating as it moves about, changing its signature and eventually becoming unrecognizable to humanity's immune system.

Once a genetic shift has occurred, the new virus is ready to strike again. In 1998, researchers using lung material from two 1918 victims, a US Army soldier and a woman buried in the Alaskan permafrost, discovered that one of the virus's mutations in its NS_I gene prevents the production of cytokine (interferon), one of the body's defenses against infection. Without a defense, the virus duplicates itself 39,000 times in human lungs. "The body reacts to this rampant infection with a massive and inappropriate inflammatory [immune] response called a 'cytokine storm' and the unfortunate victims literally drown as the air sacs of their lungs fill with blood and fluid."[32] This finding may explain why so many young and healthy adults succumbed to the 1918 influenza pandemic. Previous pandemics attacked the young and the old, presenting us with a U-shaped curve representing mortality. The 1918 pandemic exhibited a W-shape, indicating the addition of a healthy adult population, ranging in age from 21–35 years, in the mortality tables.

The etiology of the influenza virus became known through a convoluted series of episodic outbreaks involving pigs, hunting hounds, and ferrets. An epidemic struck London in 1933 and infected medical research staff at Wellcome and Medical Research Council of Molecular Biology (MRC) laboratories. As part of the experimental protocols of the laboratory, a researcher infected ferrets with the nasal mucus from infected humans. The ferrets became victims of the influenza virus. A model for understanding viral infections, their replication and transmission, was discovered by experimenting with genetic manipulation. The discovery of H and N glycoproteins and the classification of influenza A, B, and C discussed earlier represented the medical breakthroughs that would guide future viral research.

The antigenic shift and drift in the viral proteins, hemagglutinin (H) and neuraminidase (N) are what medical researchers look for in determining the structure of future strains of influenza. In this way, future outbreaks would be classified based upon the changing genetic structure of the virus and the distribution of H and N proteins. As a result, the 1933 virus was labeled H1N1, the 1957 as H2N2 (Asian flu), 1968 as H3N2 (Hong Kong flu) and 1977 as H1N1 again. Medical research focuses on the composition of avian and human influenza viruses as they replicate in pigs and recombine to make a new strain that infects humans. Its goal is to develop vaccines of inactivated viruses that prove more effective in increasing immunity for some people.

Relief efforts

Many references to hospitalization appear in this case study. Of the thousands who were cared for, few survived. The medical establishment did not know what we know today about influenza and its rapid spread from one person to the next by contact through touch or by breathing, sneezing, and coughing. Keeping the afflicted quiet and comfortable was all that doctors and nurses could accomplish. The outbreak, its spread and lethality, stymied them. For the millions of victims globally, hospitalization brought few, if any, rewards. Death arrived for those at home, in civilian transit, in military service, and in hospital wards.

Conclusion

Increased immunity does not protect all people, as the following statistics bear out. By mid-January 2010 about 11,700 Americans had died from the recent H1N1 swine flu and about 257,000 had been hospitalized. Between 41 million and 84 million caught the virus, while about 70 million have been vaccinated. Most of the hospitalized and the dead were aged between 18 and 64. A year before, the WHO confirmed the outbreak of more than 6 million cases worldwide by November 2010, with more than 6,500 deaths. With little seasonal flu in the USA that year, children did not need to make up a jingle to mask the terror of widespread death. In 1918, Boston schoolchildren assuaged their fears by “jumping rope” and singing the following jingle:

I had a little bird
And its name was Enza
I opened the window
And in-flew-Enza.[33]

HIV/AIDS (1985–)

Introduction

In the spring of 1981, the Center for Disease Control (CDC) in Atlanta, Georgia reported the outbreak of *Pneumocystis carinii* pneumonia (PCP) and Kaposi sarcoma (KS) among young homosexual men and intravenous drug users in San Francisco and New York City. Both illnesses were associated with a human immunodeficiency virus (HIV) not previously known by the medical profession. Within a few years, this virus and the illnesses associated with it became known as AIDS (acquired immunodeficiency syndrome).[34]

Medical knowledge did not lead to a public policy response, however. Ignoring the findings of the CDC, the nation's federal agency responsible for protecting the public health, the administration of President Ronald Reagan (1981–89) interfered both directly and indirectly with agency efforts to both publicize the dangers of unprotected sex between homosexual partners and to begin a publically financed campaign to combat this HIV/AIDS epidemic in the USA and to treat its victims. The administration's lack of leadership has been unflatteringly described as "negligent homicide" and "public health malpractice."[35]

Only when President Reagan's good friend, actor Rock Hudson, died of AIDS did he ask the nation's Surgeon General, C. Everett Koop, for a report on the disease. Dr. Koop argued persuasively for active educational programs in the nation's schools, the use of condoms, voluntary serologic testing, and more. Because of the years of inaction, 15,000 people had died of AIDS in the USA by 1987, the year the report became public, with a projected 12-fold increase by 1991. Exhibiting no symptoms, an estimated 1.5 million men, women, and children were already infected. While the administration remained silent, many infected adults in this growing population spread the disease to others at an alarming rate. Thousands, possibly millions, died unnecessarily.[36] Although the Surgeon General lacked the authority to implement his recommendations, he used his position as the nation's public health officer to begin a public information campaign. In May 1988, he sent his eight-page AIDS pamphlet to the nation's 107 million households. As the largest public mailing in the country's history, it provided for the first time explicit information about sexual behavior.

In 2008, the last year in which we have reliable statistics, the WHO estimated that 33.4 million people had been infected with HIV. The high estimated range is 35.8 million and the low range was 31.3 million. The newly infected in 2008 ranged from 2.4 to 3.0 million, while AIDS-related deaths claimed the lives of approximately two million adults and children in that year.

The downward trend, in terms of those infected and those succumbing to the deadly virus, shows a measure of success in prevention, diagnosis, and treatment. During the 1980s, the mean number of months from diagnosis to death was less than 24 months and 80% of those diagnosed with the disease for three years or more died. Today, the conversion from asymptomatic HIV status to symptomatic AIDS disease has declined to about 60%. So, although the battle against HIV/AIDS goes on, the impact of education, detection, and treatment with a new generation of drugs has resulted in higher survival rates and movement in a positive direction.[37]

The question of origins – competing theories

Despite the favorable direction of recent trends, understanding the origins of the disease may be the way to prevent the outbreak of other emerging diseases. Emerging diseases are integral to human history. Learning about their origins and the thresholds that they need to achieve in order to infect large numbers of humans remains a vital concern. Without a threshold population, an infection will fade out. For example, the population necessary to sustain infectious measles is about 300,000. It, along with human smallpox, rubella, and pertussis (whooping cough) became emerging diseases with the advent of agriculture and the beginning of settled societies about 10,000 years ago. Once human populations in these settlements exceeded the numbers necessary to maintain infection, those diseases mentioned here, and many more, persisted through the millennia. The controversies about the origins of HIV/AIDS, however, may not result in a consensus about its detection, spread, treatment, and lethality.

The account of its origin that gained widespread currency once the HIV/AIDS pandemic became headline news after 1981 is described simply as "the cut-hunter theory: direct non-human–primate–human transfer followed by human-to-human amplification."[38] This theory underlies the generalization that simian immunodeficiency viruses (SIVs) from non-human primates are transferred to humans where they become human immunodeficiency viruses (HIVs). This transfer happens in a number of different ways: for example, a hunter cuts himself while butchering a monkey, getting blood from the primate into his wound. A person is bitten or scratched by a monkey or eats undercooked monkey meat.

Virologists know about the dangers of eating the meat of dead monkeys, gorillas, chimpanzees, porcupines, scaly anteaters, cane rats, and others. Bush meat, as it is called in tropical Central Africa, has been consumed by native people for millennia and today represents a major source of protein for the region's growing population. Annually, about two million tons of bush meat is consumed. Mangabeys, a monkey found in the dense forests of the Cameroon, among others, "are viral warehouses, carry(ing) many viruses that infect humans, including one that may cause a rare form of T-cell leukemia and another, simian foamy virus, the ultimate impact of which is not yet known."[39]

According to the cut-hunter theory, the infection probably began at least a century ago in a lush forest, much like those located in Cameroon, when a hunter killed and butchered a chimpanzee, ate the meat himself or gave it to someone else to consume. Living in remote and isolated villages, the virus did not begin its lethal spread until populations began to soar in the twentieth century and road-building began to link hinterlands to population centers. Tourism, global trading, and transcontinental air traffic transformed a local health risk into one of enormous proportions, spreading infection and death across the globe.

To support the non-human–primate–human transfer hypothesis, HIV's closest non-human host is *P.t. troglodytes*, a sub-species of chimpanzee living primarily in the Democratic Republic of the Congo (the DRC, formerly Zaire). This chimpanzee possesses the simian immunodeficiency virus (SIVcpz) that is closer to HIV than any other SIV found in other non-human primates. A long low level incubation period in isolated villages shifted from low-risk to high-risk populations either slowly or quickly through unspecified events. Since many pathogens move between non-human and human populations, it does not necessarily follow that an epidemic transmission occurs within the new species.

However, one body of research suggests that the number of HIV infections in the DRC increased exponentially after an initial transfer and continued to increase exponentially through time. If the first transfer of the virus occurred either decades or centuries ago, the failure to detect AIDS may be accounted for by a number of factors, including the existence of a scattered population living in isolated villages. More importantly, AIDS is a complicated disease that suppresses the immune system, providing an opening for other diseases to gain a foothold and to kill its human host. With a ten-year latency period from infection to AIDS, detection of an emerging disease would be problematic.[40]

The publication of *The River: A Journey Back to the Source of HIV and AIDS* by Edward Hooper in 2000 popularized a competing theory about origins. In it, Hooper renewed an argument that a massive vaccination effort in Africa in the 1950s to prevent the spread of polio caused the AIDS pandemic. The polio vaccine was cultured in the harvested kidneys of monkeys, possibly infected by SIV, unknown until 1985. Since monkeys showed no symptoms of illness while carrying the infection, medical staff took no precautions as they vaccinated more than a million people in central and Western Africa from 1957–60. Furthermore, this line of argument contends that the first known AIDS cases and HIV-positive blood samples coincide with this vaccination program in Africa.

To buttress this argument, its supporters contended that the cut hunter theory was implausible because hunters had been butchering and consuming bush meat for thousands of years, probably longer. As noted earlier, however, a virus can travel only as far as its host travels and in past time that was not very far. So, diseased bush meat could have wiped out an entire isolated village without anyone either acknowledging this disaster or knowing about its causes. "A more realistic period for human–primate predation is one to two million years, but the presence of SIVs over this period is speculative."[41]

So, the conclusion that SIVs emerged as a disease in the twentieth century seemed unreasonable. In addition, supporters contended that their detractors demanded "direct evidence" that chimpanzee kidney tissue was used in the preparation of the polio vaccine. They replied that these detractors provided no "direct evidence" from proponents of the "cut hunter" theory. In the absence of "direct evidence" from either theory, a third theory was proposed for the transfer of SIV to humans causing the human immunodeficiency virus (HIV).

This theory claims that a modern event such as the use of non-sterile injections in Africa from 1950 to 1970 provided the mechanism for SIV infections in humans to emerge as epidemic HIV. The cumulative effect of such injections repeated over and over allowed partially adapted

SIV to produce mutations, leading to epidemic HIV infections. Facts and assumptions support this line of reasoning. First, a group of SIVs predate the appearance of AIDS by thousands of years. SIVs existed as five or six distinct genetic types in mangabeys, African green monkeys, and chimpanzees. So, SIVs are ancient in Africa and all five or six genetic types pre-date AIDS.

Even with a population event as catastrophic as the African slave trade, which lasted for over 400 years and violated the lives of millions, no evidence existed of HIV in Africa or among slaves in Europe or the Americas. Not until the twentieth century, long after these horrific events, did we witness the emergence of the AIDS pandemic. According to this third theory, the other theories about its spread in the twentieth century seem unsatisfactory. As noted before, the first theory suggested that infectious HIV evolved in Africa from the ancient and separate transmissions of multiple SIVs to humans but remained latent in isolated human locales until population growth, migration, and increased hunting changed during the twentieth century. These events allowed HIV to emerge as an epidemic that soon became a global pandemic. A second possible explanation suggested that "new ecological factors," as yet unspecified, caused mutations that led to the multiple transitions of SIVs to HIVs. Without specificity regarding ecological factors, the third theory searching for a "biologically plausible event" remained a viable one.

As noted earlier, the massive use of non-sterile injections in sub-Saharan Africa from the 1950s until 1970 met the test of a biologically plausible event that significantly increased the transfer of partially adapted SIV infections to humans. To support this theory, its authors described the history of technological advances made in injection equipment. These included hypodermic syringes invented in 1848 but not used widely until the end of the twentieth century.[42] Made individually of glass and metal and identified as precision medical instruments, syringes remained expensive and supplies limited until the 1920s. Each unit cost about $50 in 1900 (adjusted to current cost) and global production never exceeded 100,000 units per year.

Between the two world wars in the twentieth century, the manufacture of interchangeable parts and mass production methods accelerated the distribution of syringes. Worldwide production grew from two million units in 1930 to eight million in 1950, while per unit costs dropped by 80%. The number of clinical uses grew, particularly for the increased injection of insulin in the USA and throughout Europe in the 1930s and 1940s.

Despite these changes, sterilization equipment in the form of expensive autoclaves limited access and availability.

Not until the manufacture of penicillin in the 1950s and the mass production of antibiotics did the demand for syringes explode globally. Despite increases in the production of glass and metal syringes, worldwide demand exceeded supply as the efficacy of new drugs, including insulin, penicillin, chloroquine, the polio vaccine, malaria injections, and the smallpox vaccine, became widely used. In anticipation of this change in the demand curve, the pharmaceutical company that came to dominate the industry's production, Becton-Dickinson, initiated a strategy of acquiring smaller manufacturers of glass and metal syringes. By 1960, the company made more than 50% of the world's supply. Having achieved a comparative advantage not only in manufacturing but also in the innovative technologies of the recently acquired companies, Becton-Dickinson developed an inexpensive plastic, single-use, disposable syringe.

The global market felt the impact of this invention almost immediately as production led to a 100-fold increase in use globally to about one billion units annually, with a 56-fold decline in the price to $0.18 per unit. As disposable units made of polypropylene plastic, they could not withstand the high temperatures of an autoclave. If disassembled, they could be sterilized in temperatures of not over 176°F(80°C) and reassembled under sterilized conditions. Of course, this procedure would be time-consuming, cumbersome, and counter to the intended use of these new syringes.

As the proponents of this theory pointed out, these new syringes flooded the developing world's market in the 1950s. As more injectable antibiotics became available, the reuse of disposable plastic syringes became widespread, especially in sub-Saharan African countries recently freed from former colonial (British, French, and Belgium) status. There, Western medical practices suffered as newly independent countries faced decades of migration to cities that overwhelmed fragile infrastructures with burgeoning populations, increasing poverty, and national debt. Accordingly, the reuse of disposable syringes became one of the many ways to economize – but this had disastrous effects.

Combined with the UN's initiatives to begin national health campaigns to eradicate diseases using injectable antibiotics, public health workers created a fertile environment for the spread of other diseases by reusing single-use disposable syringes. In fact, reuse was so prevalent that a "striking finding [was] that 80% of African households had experienced needle use in a two-week period by the 1960s."[43] As a result, the non-sterile massive use of syringes during these eradication campaigns was the single most effective way of causing the serial passage of SIV among humans. The risk of needle transmission of HIV is 0.25% or more, so the prospect of transferring SIV would become especially high with the increased reuse of syringes.

Conclusion

Regarding competing theories to explain the spread of HIV infections, the proponents of this explanation offered the following rebuttal. Social upheaval and disruption have characterized much of African history, with more than 30 million of its people enslaved and removed from their rural environments to plantations in the western hemisphere over a 400-year period. The geographical area of the slave trade coincided with the emergence of epidemic HIV in the second half of the twentieth century. "Had HIV existed, even in small numbers of people, it is likely that HIV would have spread as a sexually transmitted virus. In contrast to HIV, the human T-cell leukemia virus appears to have spread during the period of the slave trade, showing that retroviruses were disseminated during those voyages."[44]

The second theory identified an eradication campaign, in this case one that targeted polio (the Oral Polio Vaccine) as the primary source for HIV transmission. It focused not on the reuse of disposable syringes as the transfer agent but on a process whereby the vaccine was produced in the harvested kidneys of Asian macaques and African green monkeys. Neither, however, contains SIVs closely related to HIV. As a result, the proponents identified mangabey monkeys and chimpanzees as the agents for transfer.

The third theory, somewhat akin to the second, proposed that carriers of the AIDS virus spread it through the misuse of disposable syringes, a technological innovation misused through human ignorance. It demonstrated once again the vulnerability of underdeveloped societies facing a public health crisis, compounded by their poverty, compromised hygiene, contaminated water, and recurring and intermittent public health crises (Figure 7.3).

Summary

Biological agents in the form of a bacterium and two viruses meet the criteria of causing natural disasters that shaped the course of human history. The bubonic plague of the Justinian era in post-Roman Europe

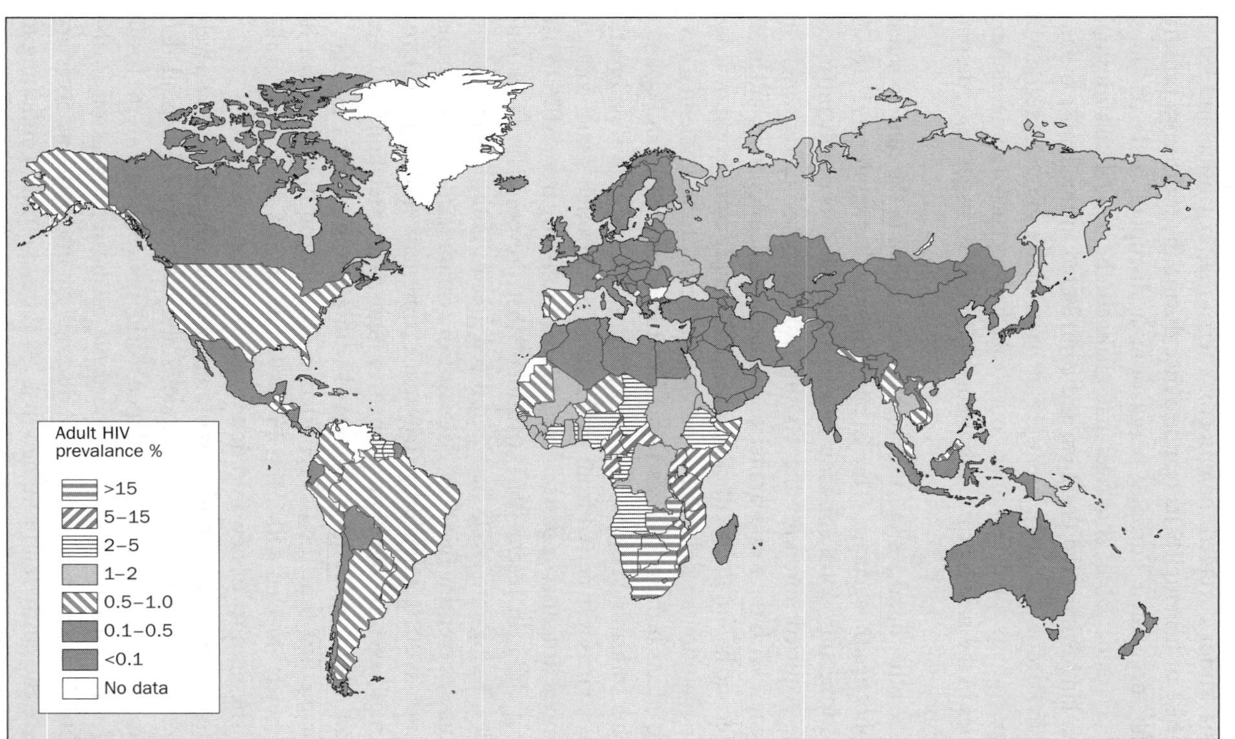

Figure 7.3 World map showing people living with AIDS.
Source: Adapted from Wikimedia Commons, the free media repository.

and Asia Minor curtailed the emperor's territorial expansion and led to the demise of his empire. Its reappearance during the fourteenth century not only decimated Europe's population; it disrupted trade relations, caused a major labor shortage that changed the feudal relationships between landowners and peasants, and contributed to the demise of feudalism in Europe. Although latent plague bacteria live in the subterranean world of rodents today and major outbreaks have occurred in developing countries in the past century, less attention is given to its lethality, despite this history.

On the other hand, retroviruses remain uppermost in the consciousness of public health agencies. The Great Influenza Pandemic of 1918–20 receded from our global consciousness in the wake of its deadly intrusion and the acquired immunity that its survivors harbored unknowingly in their genes. With the reappearance of influenza epidemics and pandemics in the second half of the twentieth century and a more complete knowledge of their evolution and mutability, public awareness of their potential devastating effects brought us back to the Great Pandemic again and again.

Neither transmitted by the host to its victims by a bite or by their breath, AIDS is a virus transferred from victim to victim through sexual contact, intravenous drug use, or passed from a woman suffering from AIDS to her newborn child. In recent years, treatment that prevents HIV infections from developing into AIDS have improved greatly, both delaying and in many cases preventing this deadly disease from claiming additional victims. As recently as 2010, a new drug, Truvada, a combination of two antiretroviral drugs taken by men and women in high-risk populations, reduced infection rates by 44% when compared with a group taking a placebo.[45] And for the first time the UN reported in 2010 a drop in the number of people newly infected with AIDS in 2009, almost 20% fewer than in the 1990s. The number of new infections was 2.6 million people.

Death continues to visit millions of men, women, and children in developing countries where medical diagnosis and treatment lag behind that found more commonly in the developed world. In the meantime, the battle to find more effective and more affordable medications goes on in the expectation that medical science will discover the interventions necessary to reduce the costly toll in human lives. At the same time, continuing to misuse disposable syringes will allow unknown infective agents to enter the bloodstreams of unsuspecting victims and begin the spread of diseases, some of which will become epidemic and pandemic in nature.

Notes

1 Gabriele de Mussis (1999), *Historia de Morbo,* trans. Rosemary Horrox in *The Black Death* (Manchester: Manchester University Press), 248–249.
2 Alfred Crosby (2004), *Ecological Imperialism: The Biological Expansion of Europe, 900–1900* (New York: Cambridge University Press), and John Robert McNeill (2010), *Mosquito Empires: Ecology and War in the Greater Caribbean, 1640–1914* (New York: Cambridge University Press).
3 Christopher Duncan and Susan Scott (2005), "What caused the Black Death?" *Postgraduate Medical Journal*, 81, 315–320.
4 Matt J. Keeling and Chris A. Gilligan (2000), "Bubonic plague: a metapopulation model of a zoonosis," *Proceedings: of the Royal Society of London Series Biological Sciences*, 267(1458), 2219 and 2226.
5 Michael McCormick (2003), "Rats, communications, and plague: toward an ecological history," *Journal of Interdisciplinary History*,34(1), 1.
6 Ibid., 3.
7 Wendy Orent (2004), *Plague: The Mysterious Past and Terrifying Future of the World's Most Dangerous Disease* (New York: Free Press), 73–74.
8 Michael McCormick (2003), "Rats, communications, and plague," 14.
9 Wendy Orent (2004), *Plague*, 77–78.
10 Robert Sallares (2007), "Ecology, evolution, and epidemiology," in Lester K. Little (ed.), *Plague and the End of Antiquity: The Pandemic of 541–750* (Cambridge, UK: Cambridge University Press), 259–260.
11 Michael McCormick (2003), "Rats, communications, and plague," 20.
12 Matt J. Keeling and Chris A. Gilligan, "Bubonic plague," 2225.
13 Ibid., 2221.
14 Hubert H. Lamb (1977), *Climates of the Past, Present and Future*, Vols. I and II (London: Metheun).
15 Michael McCormick (2003), "*Rats, Communications, and Plague,*" 22.
16 William Chester Jordan (1996), *The Great Famine: Early Modern Europe during the Fourteenth Century* (Princeton, NJ: Princeton University Press), 185.
17 Emmanuel Le Roy Ladurie (1981), "A concept: the unification of the globe by disease," in Le Roy Ladurie, *The Mind and Method of the Historian* (Chicago: University of Chicago Press), 28–83.
18 Kirsten I. Bos, Verena J. Schuenemann, and G. Brian Golding (2011), "A draft genome of *Yersinia pestis* from victims of the Black Death," *Nature*, 478, 506–510.
19 Joseph S. Koen (1919), "A practical method for field diagnosis of swine disease," *American Journal of Veterinary Medicine*, 14, 468.

20 Alfred W. Crosby Jr. (1976), *Epidemic and Peace, 1918* (Westport, CT: Greenwood Press), 311.
21 Edwin D. Kilbourne (1987), *Influenza* (New York: Plenum), 15.
22 Alfred W. Crosby Jr. (1989), *America's Forgotten Pandemic, The Influenza of 1918* (Cambridge, UK: Cambridge University Press), 7.
23 Pete Davies (2000), *The Devil's Flu: The World's Deadliest Influenza Epidemic and the Scientific Hunt for the Virus That Caused It* (New York: Henry Holt & Co), 50.
24 Lynette Iezzoni (1999), *Influenza 1918: The Worst Epidemic in American History* (New York: TV Books), 19.
25 Irwin W. Sherman (2007), *Twelve Diseases That Changed Our World* (Washington, DC: American Society for Microbiology Press), 167.
26 John M. Barry (2004), *The Great Influenza: The Epic Story of the Deadliest Plague in History* (New York: Viking Penguin), 396–397.
27 Michael B. A. Oldstone (2000), *Viruses, Plagues, & History* (New York: Oxford University Press), 173.
28 Ibid., 398.
29 Ibid., 175.
30 Ibid., 179.
31 Dorothy H. Crawford (2007), *Deadly Companions: How Microbes Shaped Our History* (New York: Oxford University Press), 205.
32 Ibid., 207.
33 E. Fuller Torrey and Robert H. Yolken (2005), *Beasts of the Earth: Animals, Humans, and Disease* (Piscataway, NJ: Rutgers University Press), 118.
34 Harold W. Jaffe, Dennis J. Bregman, and Richard M. Selik (1983), "Acquired immune deficiency syndrome in the United States: the first 1000 cases," *The Journal of Infectious Diseases*, 148(2), 339.
35 Donald P. Francis (1987), "Commentary, Surgeon General's report on acquired immune deficiency syndrome," (Washington, DC: Public Health Reports, US Public Health Service), 121, 286.
36 Ibid., 287.
37 Theodore C. Eickhoff (1988), "The acquired immunodeficiency syndrome (AIDS) and infection with the human immunodeficiency virus (HIV)," *Annals of Internal Medicine*, 108, 273.
38 Brian Martin (2001), "The burden of proof and the origin of acquired immune deficiency syndrome," *Philosophical Transactions of the Royal Society: Biological Sciences*, 356(1410), 939.
39 Michael Spector (2010), "Letter from Cameroon: the doomsday strain," *The New Yorker*, December 20–27, 50.
40 Karina Yusim, Martine Peeters, Oliver G. Pybus, et al. (2001), "Using human immunodeficiency virus type 1 sequences to infer historical features of the

acquired immune deficiency syndrome epidemic and human immunodeficiency virus evolution," *Philosophical Transactions of the Royal Society: Biological Sciences*, 356(1410), 855–866.

41 Brian Martin (2001), "The burden of proof and the origin of acquired immune deficiency syndrome," 941.

42 Preston A. Marx, Phillip G. Alcabes, and Ernest Drucker (2001), "Serial human passage of simian immunodeficiency virus by unsterile injections and the emergence of epidemic human immodeficiency virus in Africa," *Philosophical Transactions of the Royal Society: Biological Sciences*, 356(1410), 911–920.

43 Ibid., 918.

44 Ibid., 917.

45 Donald G. McNeil, Jr. (2010), "UN reports decrease in new HIV infections," *The New York Times*, November 24, A4.

Further Reading

William H. McNeill (1976), *Plagues and Peoples* (New York: Anchor Books).
This seminal work offers a new interpretation of world history, focusing on the impact of epidemic disease on the political, demographic, ecological, and psychological development of society.

John M. Barry (2005), *The Great Influenza: The Story of the Deadliest Pandemic in History* (New York: Penguin Books).
This comprehensive and highly readable book describes in great detail the world's deadliest twentieth-century pandemic, the Great Influenza Pandemic of 1918–20.

George C. Kohn (2001), *Encyclopedia of Plague and Pestilence: From Ancient Times to the Present* (New York: Facts on File).
For a shorthand reference to the world's known diseases, this volume is a valuable starting point.

Jo N. Hays (2005), *Epidemics and Pandemics: Their Impacts on Human History* (New York: ABC-CLIO).
Written by a historian of science and medicine, this book describes the impact of pandemics and epidemics throughout the world from ancient times to the present.

Helen Epstein (2008), *The Invisible Cure: Why We Are Losing the Fight Against AIDS in Africa* (New York: Picador).
Epstein is a public health specialist and molecular biologist who has worked on AIDS vaccine research. Her book about the AIDS pandemic disputes many theories about why AIDS is rampant in Africa and how to combat it.

Part 3

Atmospheric Processes

Chapter 8

Hurricanes, Cyclones, and Typhoons*

> *I had eight children and a wife. Four of my children were boys; four were girls. The eldest, my daughter, was 11, and the smallest, my son, 6 months old. When we heard the water and the wind, I tried to think of what to do. But there was no time. It seemed only a moment before we were in the water. My wife was carrying the baby. I caught hold of one of her hands. I told the children to hold each other's hands. The force of the wave was terrible. I tried to brace my feet and stand fast, but it lifted me like a child and threw me hard against something solid. For a moment I was stunned. It was so dark I could not see and because of the noise of the wind I could not hear. When I recovered I had my arms around a tree. But my hands were empty. God forgive me. I did not try to look for my family but clung to the tree until daybreak. I have not seen any of them since.*[1]

Introduction

A changing climate is a naturally occurring phenomenon, but during the last few decades it has become apparent that the emission of greenhouse gases has accelerated this process. In 1750 the carbon dioxide (CO_2) concentration was 280 parts per million (ppm) in the atmosphere; in 2010 it was 389 ppm – we have experienced a one-third increase in just a few

* These are organized tropical storms that become named storms when their rotating winds exceed 39 mph. When wind speeds exceed 74 mph, the system is called a cyclone. They are called "cyclones" in the Indian Ocean, "hurricanes" in the Caribbean, Atlantic and northeastern Pacific, and "typhoons" in the northwestern Pacific.

Natural Disasters in a Global Environment, First Edition. Anthony N. Penna and Jennifer S. Rivers.

centuries.* According to the United Nations Intergovernmental Panel on Climate Change (IPCC), "most of the warming over the last 50 years is attributable to human activities."[2]

These emissions continue to increase and show no signs of stabilizing anytime soon. Since CO_2 remains in the atmosphere for decades, we can assume that climate change will continue quite possibly into the next centuries. Its effect on the global hydrological cycle and on the intensity of weather events is the subject of this chapter. Although there will be differences between regions of the globe, on average it will become a wetter world. For the millions of people living in coastal regions, the probability of wet weather extremes will result in severe flooding.

Tropical cyclones, hurricanes, and typhoons are extreme weather events that occur when strong winds with a central "eye" with a diameter of 12–93 mi (20–150 km) circulate around a low-pressure system. They form above warm ocean temperatures of at least 89.6°F (26.5°C). Worldwide, the destruction caused by tropical cyclones has intensified during the last 30 years, with the number of category 4 and 5 cyclones (sustained winds of 135 mph (215 km/h) and upward) nearly doubling since 1970.[3] Without the availability of data drawn from longer-term time series, whether rising temperatures will affect these more destructive storms in the short term remains a question to be answered. "In the short term, such changes remain very difficult to detect in the context of high inter-annual and multi-decadal variability in tropical cyclone occurrence (linked to, for instance, the El Niño/Southern Oscillation [ENSO], the stratospheric quasi-biennial oscillation and multi-decadal oscillations in the North Atlantic)."[4]

This chapter focuses on twentieth-century events in light of the paucity of research material on cyclones in previous centuries, with a few exceptions.[5] The stories told here include the Caribbean hurricane of 1935 in the Florida Keys that led to considerable destruction and loss of life. The Bhola cyclone in the Bay of Bengal in 1970 served as a catalyst for the movement to establish a nation state, Bangladesh. Mortality rates mostly among poor coastal residents, in the hundreds of thousands, were exceeded only by the death, destruction, and escape to India by Bengali refugees during the subsequent Indian–Pakistani War. Despite the massive differences in casu-

* A unit of concentration used to measure levels of pollutants in air, water, body fluids, etc. One ppm is 1 part in 1,000,000. The common unit mg/liter is equal to ppm. Four drops of ink in a 55-gallon barrel of water would produce an "ink concentration" of 1 ppm. One part per billion is 1 part in 1,000,000,000.

alty rates for these two cases, the poor were victimized by ineptitude on the part of officials in the first case and by direct attacks by government in the second. The last case, a super-typhoon named Typhoon Nina, struck the People's Republic of China in 1975, a year in which the number of typhoons exceeded all other years. In this case, lack of preparedness and bureaucratic bungling led to death, homelessness, and property losses for millions of Chinese. In addition, the extent of the environmental damage and the loss of life to thousands of unsuspecting peasant farmers make for a compelling story.

The Labor Day Hurricane in the Florida Keys (1935)

> The sea swirled and the wind threw the cars around like straws. One by one the windows burst, spraying seawater through the cars as if from a fire hose, pressing everyone against the opposite wall. Huge waves continued rocking the train while rain blew in, cutting visibility to zero. The engine remained upright but the seawater had doused the fire in the firebox.[6]

Introduction

The Florida Keys are among the most vulnerable islands in the world, stretching out from the southern tip of Florida into the Caribbean, some 170 mi (275 km) from Miami to Key West, the country's southernmost city. With the Atlantic Ocean splashing on its east side and the Florida Bay on the other, most of its 400 islands, including Key Largo, Matecumbe Key, Long Key, Grassy Key, Boot Key, No Name Key, Big Pine Key, and Key West are but slivers of land on average just 5 ft (1.5 m) above sea level. The highest above sea level is Windley Key at 18 ft (5.5 m).

Geologists note that many of these "Keys" surfaced in the last 30,000 years, after millennia of rising and receding sea levels, caused by advancing and retreating glaciers in the northern hemisphere. The bedrock was layered with limestone covered by reefs composed of the calcified remains of sea urchins. Key West, the island famous for being the home of celebrated writer, Ernest Hemingway, and a winter retreat for President Harry S. Truman (1945–53) is only 4.5 mi (7.2 km) long and 0.5 mi (0.8 km) wide. Historically, the island's economy thrived on cigar making (employing thousands of Cuban workers), sponge fishing, and a government naval station.

Transportation from one island to the next by boat continued until Henry M. Flagler built the extension of his Florida East Coast Railroad from Homestead, Florida to Key West in 1912. Ten years of constructing roadbeds across the islands, through jungle swamps and mangroves, battling the sweltering heat, mosquitoes, and snakes resulted in the completion of the railroad. His original line had been laid from Jacksonville to Homestead earlier in the decade to promote settlement and tourism. Detractors scoffed at his plan to build a railroad that would "go to sea" as Flagler's Folly, since connecting the chain of islands would require constructing concrete pillars and arches anchored in solid bedrock some 30 ft (9 m) below the water's surface. As one of the decade's engineering marvels, at an estimated cost of $50,000,000, the 153 mi (246 km) of railroad tract linked the near-sea-level archipelago from Miami to Key West. For some the feat was "the Eighth Wonder of the World."

Background

The success of Flagler's railroad accelerated a real estate boom in the Keys in the 1920s. However, the global Depression that began with the collapse of the New York stock market in October 1929 triggered a crisis in banking with lost savings, mortgage foreclosures, factory bankruptcies, and massive unemployment. One-third of the nation's workforce was unemployed when the election of 1932 ended Republican domination of national politics and ushered in the New Deal of the newly elected president, Franklin Delano Roosevelt. Putting the unemployed back to work became a New Deal priority. A work program for the nation's youth, the Civil Conservation Corps (CCC), placed men in the nation's wilderness areas building infrastructure for the nation's campgrounds, trails, parks, and roads. One such work project envisioned the construction of a road system adjacent to the railroad built by Henry Flagler to revitalize the faltering economy of the Keys.

As part of the Federal Emergency Relief Administration (FERA), a program for unemployed World War I veterans who had been denied the early payment of their federal bonuses (i.e. pensions) by a Republican-controlled Congress in the 1920s, was created to establish work camps to build roads, bridges, and public buildings. Key West had been Florida's largest city with 25,000 residents in the last decade of the nineteenth century and at one time the country's richest city per person. By 1934, however, of its remaining 12,470 residents, more than one-half were destitute and on the relief rolls when FERA entered with a plan to revitalize the economy of the city and the islands. Five work camps, located on and around Upper and Lower Matecumbe Key, would employ 700 veterans. They were assembled there to build US Highway One, making the mainland accessible to the Keys by motor vehicle.

The hurricane

Many of these veterans would become victims of the most intense storm to make landfall in the USA. On Labor Day (September 2) 1935, a category 5 hurricane, with maximum winds of 140–150 mph (225–240 km/h) with winds gusting at above 200 mph (320 km/h), struck the Florida Keys. Typical of tropical hurricanes, a storm surge measuring 15–20 ft (4.5–6 m) swamped most of the Keys, destroying almost everything including buildings, vegetation, and much of the Florida East Coast Railroad built by Henry Flagler. In the event of a destructive storm, it was assumed that the railroad would enable the 12,470 residents and the 700 veterans to reach the mainland safely.

Until Hurricane Sandy in October 2012, this hurricane held the Atlantic record for the lowest barometric pressure ever recorded. At Craig Key, a barometer measured a pressure of 892 millibars/26.35.[7] The American Red Cross calculated that at least 423 persons lost their lives and assumed that many more disappeared, blown into the sea and drowned. Among them were scores of veterans living in bunkhouses and tents that had been hastily built by FERA. With the absence of anything resembling the weather forecasting capabilities of today, local residents, vacationers, and the veteran workforce were unaware of the storm's destructive capacity. The National Weather Bureau operated without the technology of satellite imaging, Doppler radar, and offshore weather buoys. Without television, there was no Weather Channel. Coastal weather observation centers and ships at sea tracked the storm as best they could and reported their information to FERA officials who were part of a command structure, responsible for makeshift evacuation plans in the event of an oncoming hurricane.

These personnel failed miserably in their assigned tasks by ignoring the warnings identified by local residents as evidence accumulated of an impending disaster. Locals, as well as veteran workers, noticed the mass migration of crabs and the large schools of tarpon swimming from the Atlantic side of the islands to the Gulf side. Fishermen, knowledgeable about such movements and their meaning, were clear about what was happening. FERA decision-makers dismissed these warnings as the ravings of panicking locals. Convinced that trains were at the ready on the mainland awaiting a call from FERA officials to rescue veteran workers and their bosses, these officials ignored evidence that the hurricane was gaining strength and bearing down on the Keys. In their stubborn refusal to hear appeals to change direction, they exacerbated their ineptitude by giving orders to confiscate the keys to cars and trucks owned by FERA, to prevent an *ad hoc* evacuation. In addition, they stationed National Guardsmen at a camp near Tavernier for the same purpose.

In defense of the officials responsible for the safety of the men in their employ, the storm that would become the hurricane of the century measured only 40 mi (65 km) across, with an eye that was only 8 mi (12.8 km) in diameter on the evening of September 1, and remained stationary about 200 mi (320 km) from the Keys. Why it stalled and why no upper atmospheric winds ripped it apart remains a mystery 75 years later. While it remained fixed in place, however, the heated sea surface waters of the Caribbean, the heat engine that fuels hurricanes, caused it to intensify rapidly, changing it into a deadly monster. Given the warm waters, the direction of the hurricane had two possibilities: following the Gulf Stream through the Keys up the East Coast of the USA or following a westerly direction into the Gulf of Mexico. At noon on September 2, and without the knowledge of the National Weather Bureau, the storm took a sharp turn to the northwest and headed directly toward the Keys.[8]

By mid-afternoon on September 2, hurricane winds began to rip apart the shacks, barracks, and tents housing the veterans. Homes and hotels for residents and vacationers fared no better as shelter from the storm. With tidal waves of 15 ft (4.5 m) and higher, the punishing storm surge inundated the low-lying Keys: "A surge always achieves its greatest height in shallow water, like that surrounding the Keys, because the water has no place else to go."[9] The railroad bed built to accommodate Flagler's trains served as a barrier to the rushing water. Instead of allowing the water to wash over the Upper Keys islands, it was held back while the hurricane kept pushing more of it forward, each time raising the wall of water. To provide some sense of the destructive power of the ocean whipped up by the force of hurricane winds, a cubic yard of water weighs 1,700 lb (770 kg).

To further compound the folly, FERA and Flagler railroad officials failed to communicate with each other about the time required to prepare the train for dispatch and decide who would pay the required $300 service charge. As a result, the rescue train arrived late in the afternoon of September 2 at the middle Key islands. By then, the hurricane's brutal force, with 200 mph (320 km/h) wind gusts, had enveloped the islands and derailed the train. The storm ripped railroad tracks from their bed and scattered them like matchsticks in the adjacent mangrove swamps.

For the island's inhabitants, forced as they were into the open, it was not only high-velocity winds and raging water that they had to contend with, but also flying debris including sand that lacerated their skin. Flying tree limbs, lumber from the hastily built shelters, flooring ripped from foundations, roofing, machinery, tools, and even railroad ties loosened by the storm surge and rushing surface waters exposed everyone regardless of rank to the hurricane's fury.

At 6:30 p.m. the rescue train approached the lodge (which had been turned into a hospital) at Windley Key without stopping to pick up its occupants including veteran workers, instead proceeding to the camps further out on the Keys before returning to Windley. During the intervening time, water flooded the first floor, requiring everyone to move to an upper floor. Occupants broke windows on both sides of the lodge to reduce the air pressure and to prevent the wind from overturning the structure. To no avail: the roof blew off and the lodge collapsed. Frantic and chaotic mayhem aptly describes the plight of the victims, whose survivor stories reveal much about the will of humans fighting for their lives against nature's fury.

Eyewitness accounts of the horror facing the veterans in the wake of the hurricane and the storm surge tell a frightening story of monumental hubris on the part of decision makers and injury and death to its victims. "I was washed out by the tide to a spot near the infirmary. Near the infirmary stood a shack. The storm kept getting worse and worse and the trees around my shack began popping. Then all of a sudden it broke and the tidal wave came in and my shack started floating around. The shack next door rose up, crashed into my shack, and split it in two. I was struck by two timbers, but I managed to pull my arm out from between them." This man noted that another was not so lucky. "The timbers broke his arm and crushed his ribs."

In abandoning another shack, destruction and death followed. " As soon as we got out the door, seawater rose up to our waists. We grabbed one another and leaned against the shack for protection. The roof came down on us. It must have hit every one of us. Finally I got hold of a beam that was drifting around with the wreckage. Another beam came around and I was caught between them. One slammed into another survivor, snapping his hip and breaking his pelvis. He managed to grab part of another roof and held on; it washed up against some brush and trees and stayed there."[10]

Officials and veterans regarded the train from Homestead, Florida as their lifeline to the mainland. Miscalculating the forward speed of the hurricane compromised the train's objective of reaching the camps, loading its cargo of men and material, and returning to Homestead safely. By the time it crossed the narrow strip of land connecting the mainland to Key Largo, seawater was splashing two to three feet over the tracks, an ominous beginning for "Old 447" on the initial part of its mission of collecting and returning stranded people to safely. The mission unraveled after the relief train picked up camp administrators at Islamorada station at Matecumbe Key and began its trip to Camp 3.

At 8:20 p.m. a storm surge blew the boxcar off the tracks, causing the emergency brake to engage. To the passengers on the forward cars, the train seemed to be still moving. In fact, the movement was not forward movement but the movement of the passenger cars being rocked by a huge wave on the crest of a storm surge. Although the railroad bed was 7 ft (2.1 m) above sea level and the floor of the cars were 5 ft (1.5 m) above that, the surge lifted the cars off the tracks. When it was over, one amazed observer noted that all eleven of the railroad cars had been thrown off the tracks and that the rails were bent like hairpins. Although exaggerated, the wreckage was a jaw-dropping sight (Figure 8.1).

Failed in its rescue mission, the train and its occupants became observers to this rolling disaster, unable to provide assistance to those left to fend for themselves. The account that had unfolded in one camp was repeated in another. The only difference was that in some of the camps material that veterans believed would offer some protection failed them as well. In Camp 3, a water tank car sat alone on a railroad siding. With no drinkable water at the five work camps, water arrived from the mainland in tank cars to meet the daily needs of workers. The plight of those who sought protection on the tank car was as follows: "It began to roar in your ears just like a faraway rumble, that wind and water, and the water when it came over the reef just like that, and we began to mount the (tank) car. Seventy to 100 men sought shelter on the tank car. A wall of water at least 25 ft (7.6 m) high slammed into them and washed some off, and the wind blew more off, and then the car began tipping over and others leaped rather than be squashed under its weight."[11]

Most of Camp 3's casualties occurred during this frightful episode. These eyewitness accounts were reinforced by the news reports written after the

Figure 8.1 Relief train derailed at Islamorada by the 1935 hurricane.
Source: Photo courtesy of Monroe County (FL) Public Library.

fact by magazine and newspaper reporters who canvassed the Keys once the hurricane had lost much of its velocity and moved northward toward the mainland of Florida.

Government response

Much of the public, made aware of the circumstances leading to the death of veterans and local citizens, were outraged. Investigations followed. In one, Harry Hopkins, President Roosevelt's chief administrator of the Works Progress Administration (WPA) and FERA, accused the National Weather Bureau of laxity. The Bureau claimed that its warnings were "timely, intelligent, definite. Lack of initiative elsewhere is key to tragedy."[12] Another investigation by Florida's attorney general, George Ambrose Worley, stated that, "We will follow this thing relentlessly and let the chips fall where they may. If any of our men are to blame we want to know it."[13] The American

Legion, on behalf of veterans, carried out a third investigation. Both government investigations concluded quickly after only a few days, finding that the strongest hurricane, a category 5 one, was an "Act of God." Veterans groups, including the American Legion and the Veterans of Foreign Wars, regarded the hastily concluded investigations as a "whitewash."

Ernest Hemingway, the celebrated American reporter, essayist, and novelist lived on Key West, as mentioned above, and had witnessed the comings and goings of tropical storms and hurricanes. In preparation for this one, he had shuttered his stone and concrete home and secured his boat, the *Pilar*, at the US Naval Station. Within days of the storm and the investigations, the anger that he felt about the mismanagement and miscalculations by FERA officials that had led to the death of so many innocent veteran workers was poured out in an essay titled "Who Murdered the Vets?" and published in the leftist journal, *New Masses* on September 17, 1935. Hemingway's anger was palpable, as evident by the following excerpts:

> The total of the dead may well pass a thousand as many bodies were swept out to sea and never will be found . . . The veterans had been sent there; they had no opportunity to leave, nor any protection against hurricanes; and they never had a chance for their lives . . . Who sent nearly a thousand war veterans, many of them husky, hard-working and simply out of luck, but many of them close to the border of pathological cases, to live in frame shacks on the Florida Keys in hurricane months? Camp Five was where eight survived out of 187, but we only find 67 of those plus two more along the fill makes 69. But all the rest are in the mangroves. It doesn't take a bird dog to locate them . . . You're dead now, brother, but who left you there in the hurricane months on the Keys where a thousand men died before you when they were building the road that's now washed out? Who left you there? And what's the punishment for manslaughter?[14]

In response to the charge of a government "whitewash," the Veterans Administration (VA) conducted its own investigation, interviewing surviving veterans and asking each a number of questions including the most significant one: "Who do you think is responsible?" The VA's conclusion, highlighted in its 400-page report, placed the blame for the disaster squarely on the administrators responsible for protecting the workers. Unfortunately, the report resulted in neither punitive action against those responsible nor corrective actions. In the chain of command from the agency's director, General Frank Hines to the president, this timely report never reached Franklin D. Roosevelt.

As a result, a Congressional hearing before a special House of Representatives Committee was called to study "a bill for the relief of widows, children and dependent parents of World War veterans who died as a result of the Florida Hurricane at Windley Island and the Matecumbe Keys on September 2, 1935."[15] After six weeks of testimony, the committee concluded that no one was to blame; the hurricane was an Act of God. Its bill became law on June 1, 1935, however, awarding $217 per month to the families of every veteran killed by the Labor Day hurricane. In the aftermath, the WPA completed the highway from Miami to Key West on March 29, 1938 and by 1943 the solid ramparts through the Upper Keys that had caused walls of water to erode coastal areas were replaced with bridges that allowed water to pass through the Keys.

Conclusion

The idea that the Labor Day hurricane was an "Act of God" absolving humans of any fault was a fiction on at least three counts. First, the calamity reflected the exposure of workers to the storm's fury and their helplessness during the height of the storm. Second, the culpability of the administrators responsible for the safe evacuation of their worker veterans was carefully documented in the testimony before the VA investigation and further acknowledged in the House of Representatives hearing. Third, the Florida Keys were and remain today a high-risk environment waiting for disasters to happen.

As noted at the beginning of this case study, the Keys are but a sliver of land whose composition of limestone and reefs rises only slightly above sea level. But for the climate and its geographical location at the tip of Florida, it would be an unlikely candidate for land development and economic growth. However, the Keys became such a candidate with the construction of Flagler's Overseas Railroad and its replacement with a highway. The highway gave tourists the opportunity to travel by motor vehicle to the resorts extending from Key Largo to Key West. The construction of Flager's Overseas Railroad transformed the Keys into a manscape (a landscape transformed by human activity including real estate development) that obscured its natural beauty. The hurricane destroyed much of the islands' built environment and returned it to a more rustic state. With the completion of the highway and the development that followed it, evidence of the calamity that destroyed the railroad and the surroundings in 1935 disappeared from sight.

The Bhola Cyclone (1970)

Cyclones and floods wreck havoc on the people of East Pakistan (now Bangladesh), with regularity. As part of an extended delta system located at the foothills of the Himalayan Mountains, monsoon flooding is a common occurrence during June through September because of heavy rainfall upstream and the inability of its estimated 300 rivers including the three largest ones, the Ganges, the Brahmaputra, and the Meghna, to drain the excessive amount of water into the Bay of Bengal. With as much as 93% of the rivers' flood plain within the borders of Bangladesh, the flow washes over the country destroying croplands, housing, and the mostly primitive infrastructure of roads and canals.

Looking south from the mountains, these annual floods bring sediment that enriches the land for peasant farmers and makes low-lying areas highly desirable for cultivation, attracting large numbers of landless people. However, this remaking of the coastal landscape over time is built up into islands, making the inhabitants, their livestock, and housing vulnerable to the destructive forces of cyclones and storm surges.

These islands are no more than 20 ft (6 m) above sea level. Densely populated, they are home to many thousands of Bengali fishermen and their families. They, along with those who live on marginal coastal land in the southern part of the country, suffer the highest incidence of poverty. Bangladesh has a vulnerable section of its southernmost border about 440 mi (710 km) long. It runs along a continental shelf that is up to 164 ft (50 m) deep. The path of repeated devastating storms from the Bay of Bengal strikes first along the coastal plains and the mainland. The region possesses a highly diversified ecosystem composed of these islands, tidal flats of muddy and sandy beaches, and naturally occurring mangroves, some of which are degraded mangrove forests. In addition to the most vulnerable section, this entire coastal area covers 1,841 mi^2 (4,660 km^2) or 32% of the country's size, serving nearly 40 million of the country's 160 million people.[16]

The coast is funnel-shaped with a vast network of rivers discharging sediment into the Bay. High levels of rainfall with strong currents and wind action from the sea make the region particularly dangerous for millions of its poverty-stricken landless population, with over 2,070 people per mi^2 (800 people per km^2). Since 1820, when statistics on cyclone activity began to be collected, about one million people have died due to cyclone and storm surge activity. During 1891–1990, 700 cyclones made landfall, with 64% occurring before the advent of the monsoon season (April–May). Over 25% happen after the season (October–November).

During the monsoon season, the main river system carries about 1.7 billion tons of sediment to the Bay, causing severe turbulence and massive erosion of riverbanks and the displacement of people. Erosion is not restricted to riverbank communities, however, as island communities are also affected. Bhola Island has suffered a net loss of about 88 mi^2 (227 km^2) in the last 50 years, while other vulnerable islands have suffered a similar fate.[17] The prospect of additional erosion of coastal zones from rising sea levels as glaciers melt will only diminish the fragile environment of these marginal coastal regions and weaken the communities of people dependant on the flora and fauna of the area for sustenance. Over the last 100 years, the sea level in the Bay of Bengal has risen 1.64 ft (0.5 m). The World Bank has estimated that about 16% of the coastal region will become inundated within the next 100 years, covering an area of about 3760 mi^2 (23,000 km^2) and displacing millions of people.[18]

Since the coastal plain of Bangladesh is shaped and reshaped by sediments moving south along the intricate river systems from the foothills of the Himalayas, the flow is magnified by annual monsoons. Most of the plain is low-lying, mostly at sea level or below, and under the best of circumstances is subject to flooding during higher than normal tides. Cyclones, caused by low-pressure systems and the warm ocean waters in the Bay of Bengal, pummel the coastal plains of the region annually. Some are stronger than others and the amount of damage they inflict depends on the velocity of the wind and the rising sea. Since 1970, four major cyclones have battered the coastal plain, with the 1970 Bhola cyclone the most destructive in terms of lives lost and property damaged.

For each killer cyclone, storm surge is the most terrifying element, exacerbated by the triangular shape of the shallow bay that funnels high waters into the highest point of the triangle along the coast. Since early warning systems and shelters were either non-existent or ineffective by more modern standards, the impact of the Bhola cyclone was the most severe. For example, the wind's speed during this cyclone was about 141 mph (227 km/h), while the cyclones that struck the coast in 1991, 1999, and 2007 were 159 mph (257 km/h), 147 mph (237 km/h), and 153 mph (247 km/h), respectively. The storm surges whipped up by the high-velocity winds were recorded at 26 ft (7.8 m), 29 ft (8.8 m), 27 ft (8.1 m), and 28 ft (8.4 m) for the 1970, 1991, 1999, and 2007 storms, respectively.[19]

Seen in a larger context, about 10% of the world's cyclones develop in the Indian Ocean, particularly the Bay of Bengal, considered an "ideal breeding ground for tropical cyclones."[20] During the twentieth century as many as 180 severe cyclones formed in the Bay, killing millions of people and wrecking havoc on the region's fragile infrastructure, disrupting economic activity, and creating irreversible coastal changes to the region's flora and fauna. Many of the four most destructive storms, noted above, crossed the Meghna estuary and caused death and destruction in the Sandwip, Hatia, and Bhola islands and a number of coastal *chars* (small uplifted deposited islands in the sea).[21]

The cyclone

> "Then an immense and deafening wall of water, which some peasants have said was 50 ft (15 m) high, thundered down on the offshore islands. Houses, people, animals, trees vanished under it. As the wave roared on coastward, a blinding, driving, killing wind followed it over the wrecked islands. Wave and wind now exploded on the mainland shore. They rushed onward, unchecked and uncheckable, cutting out a swath 50 mi (80 km) across which all villages and living creatures were ploughed under. The wave halted, and then came a new terror. All waves, once they had broken on land, receded into the sea. The titanic mass of water was in fact a wave, and it obeyed this principle. It swept back seaward the way it had come. The survivors of the villages in its forward path now found themselves enveloped in choking, muddy water as it returned. Thousands of people, together with dead cattle, the wreckage of houses and boats and uprooted trees, were swept helplessly out into the open sea.[22]

The Bhola cyclone of November 12, 1970 was the worst recorded cyclone of the twentieth century, resulting in the deaths of an estimated 225,000–500,000 people. The estimates vary so widely because of census data, that tend to undercount the poorest in a large population, and the large numbers of highly mobile people living and fishing on the threatened coastal plain and its adjacent islands. Also, many of the dead were lost in the raging sea and were never seen again. The estimated loss of 280,000 cattle and property losses of $63 million only begin to describe the destructive reach of this devastating cyclone.[23]

The November catastrophe was preceded by a less destructive cyclone on October 23. That cyclone, like all such weather events, began as a low barometric pressure event in the Malay seas off the Andaman Islands, moving swiftly northward at speeds of under 10 mph (16 km/h) but with increased swirling wind velocity into the Bay of Bengal. It was tracked by Pakistan's Cox Bazar radar station near the city of Chittagong. As the storm approached, Radio Pakistan sent out warnings to people to prepare for the onslaught. It was a familiar pattern of detection, monitoring, forecasting, and warnings to the population living on the coast and its adjacent islands. Although loss of life and property damage always accompanied these cyclones, this one failed to live up to its destructive potential.

With so many cyclone warnings over the years, some catastrophic, others destructive and a few false alarms, people living in the area became accustomed to warnings and responded either in a matter-of-fact way or not at all. In the people's defense, however, the Pakistan government provided no flood control system and no shelters sufficient to protect them. Their substandard living conditions and education ill-equipped them to make adequate preparations. The November 12 cyclone followed the same path, was monitored by the Cox Bazar radar station, and was responded to in similar fashion by the population as the October event. The only additional warning system was data provided by the US weather satellite (ESSA) to the radar station that focused on the immense size of the swirling mass as it passed over the waves. Unfortunately, this characteristic was not transmitted over Radio Pakistan. Having experienced the weaker cyclone of October 23 after receiving dire warnings from government sources, most people with few or no options remained at home, asleep in their thatched straw huts, somewhat protected against the heavy rains and a swelling sea. Slowly, a distant roar became more intense, drowning out the familiar sounds of night (Figure 8.2).

In the aftermath of this nightmare, the daylight revealed thousands of floating bodies in the ocean, rivers, and streams along the southern tip of Bangladesh. Where once there existed a green landscape of trees and crops dotted with large villages comprised of many straw and bamboo huts, there was now a denuded area of yellow putrid water. Fallen and broken trees littered the land, former symbols of the coastal region's lush ecology. Bhola Island, home to an estimated 900,000 people and located on the country's southern tip, was hardest hit in terms of human and property losses.

As noted earlier, there are no accurate records of the fishermen lost at sea, in the rivers and streams and of the migrant workers who migrate to the offshore islands of Bangladesh annually from the north to harvest crops. Without a proper census, estimates of 300,000 to 500,000 dead and

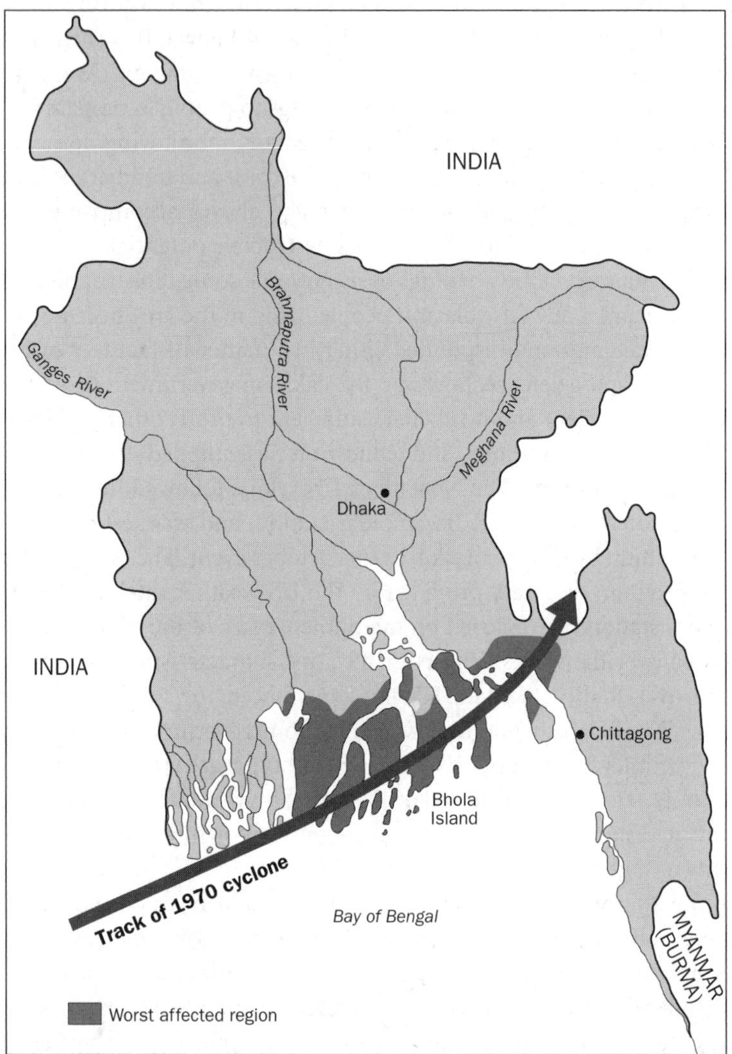

Figure 8.2 Map showing the direction of the Bhola cyclone, 1970.
Source: Adapted from Wikimedia Commons, the free media repository.

2.5 million homeless were followed by the days and months in which the weakened succumbed to disease and starvation.

The government response

A week after the cyclone, Bengalis told heartbreaking stories to Pakistani soldiers and British Marines who were stationed in Singapore but airlifted into Bangladesh to assist in the recovery and aid workers from a number of countries. However, little progress was made in assisting the survivors. Ground transportation remained problematic, though army engineers had begun the task of repairing roads and bridges. Strong currents along many of the rivers and streams prevented boats from moving food and medical supplies for relief. With most of the rice harvest destroyed, food shortages were commonplace. Because of the lack of housing, which had been destroyed by the cyclone, any available materials were gathered up and turned into makeshift lodgings to provide shelter from the scorching sun and the cold nights. Lean-tos made of rags, tin, wood, thatch, and palm leaves became a familiar sight.

The political context is always important in understanding a public policy response to a crisis, and the Bhola cyclone was a crisis of epic proportions. Pakistan was in many ways a hybrid country from its beginning in 1947 with the partition of the former British India into India and Pakistan. The country was divided into West and East Pakistan (Bangladesh), separated by 1000 mi (1,600 km), but joined by a common religion, Islam. There, however, the common link ended. Despite the adoption of Urdu as the national language in 1955, a language spoken mainly in West Pakistan by its 58 million people, in Bangladesh with its 72 million people, Bengali was the dominant language. The official state language became a symbol of the economic and political domination of the East by the West.

Further complicating the frayed relationships between the separated parts of the country was the matter of regional affinity. With the partition of British India, West Bengal was ceded to India and East Bengal became East Pakistan (Bangladesh). These Bengal states shared a common culture, language, and customs, despite the political separation imposed by the partition. In this instance, language rather than religion bound Bengalis together, regardless of their West Bengal Hindu or East Bengal Muslim beliefs.

West Pakistan's motivation in dominating its Eastern part was driven partly by its effort to curtail India's influence in East Pakistan (Bangladesh). The differences between the Punjabis of West Pakistan and the Bengalis of East Pakistan extended beyond differences in population size, with an overpopulated East and an underpopulated West in comparative terms. The Bengalis and the Punjabis are ethnically different, with the former living on a diet of fish and rice, while the latter consume mainly meat and wheat.

Armed conflict between India and Pakistan since partition over disputed territory and hegemony in the region served as a backdrop to the role played by India in its sympathy for the plight of Bengalis in East Pakistan, both before and after the Bhola cyclone. A strained relationship between the West and the East had existed since partition. In 1952, only three years after the formation of the Pakistani state, the Bengali Language Movement attempted to create a separate national unity. It was met with violence, as Pakistani troops and police opened fire on student protesters, killing some and arresting others. As happens with many such violent responses, an equally charged reaction followed.

In this instance, the episode sparked a surge in Bengali nationalist fervor, with the creation of a nationalist political party, the Awami League, dedicated to expanding the national language to include Bengali. Language became a symbol of the irreparable differences between the West and the East. As the Awami League pressed on during the decades that followed, the West engaged in repressive tactics. The Bhola cyclone struck one month before a general election was to be held in December 1970, and the response or lack of one to the devastation caused by the cyclone by the West Pakistani government played a major role in the permanent division of the country into Pakistan (the West) and Bangladesh (the East) in 1972.

The Bhola cyclone created conditions for massive human suffering. The response of the West Pakistani government, which was chaotic and brutal, confirmed to Bengalis and foreign observers that the government regarded East Pakistan as a colony to control and suppress – not as an equal governing partner. The national election, the first in the 23-year history of this geographically and culturally divided country, would serve the cause of Bengali autonomy and eventual secession. Against the backdrop of the devastating cyclone, the election resulted in the Awami League winning a national majority based on its campaign for more self-rule in East Pakistan (Bangladesh). With this majority, it would form a civilian government for the entire country, thereby eliminating military rule, and beginning the process of writing a constitution.

Its efforts were stymied by the reluctance of West Pakistan's People's Party led by Zulfikar Ali Bhutto to accept the election results and the decision by General Agha Mohammad Yahya Khan to postpone indefinitely the National Assembly's opening session on March 3, 1971. Riots, military reprisals, and guerrilla style warfare waged by the Bengalis in response to West Pakistan's army attacks resulted in a full-scale war. The long-term animosity between India and Pakistan brought India into the struggle in December 1971, supporting the plight of Bengalis by invading East Pakistan.

The cyclone and the election served as the origin for a war that caused massacres, cholera epidemics, and the migration of many other Bengalis into India. By June 1971, an estimated 250,000 Bengalis had been killed by Pakistani government troops, with six million more crossing the border into West Bengal, India. In an attempt to capitalize on the chaos, Ali Bhutto and his political party rallied its supporters to the cause of the government, hoping that with victory, he and the People's Party would be in the best position to form a civilian government and take the upper hand in writing the promised constitution. Although he would eventually form a government, it would be one representing a dismembered country.

Despite official support from the US government with arms shipments to the Pakistani government, the secession movement prevailed and the defeat of Pakistan was assured with India's military support. Faced with this outcome, the US government, represented by the administration of President Richard Nixon, recognized the independence of "Bangla Desh," the new Bengal nation, on April 5, 1972.

Recognizing the inevitability of the war's outcome and their defeat, Pakistan and India agreed on a truce in Kashmir in July 1972 and began the process of withdrawing troops from each other's territory. India had captured and held 5,139 mi^2 (13,310 km^2) of Pakistan in the West, while Pakistan held 69 mi^2 (179 km^2) of Indian territory.[24] With the return of 90,000 prisoners captured in East Pakistan during the war, the new nation of Bangladesh demanded and received recognition from West Pakistan as a condition for releasing these prisoners

The Bhola cyclone turned a smoldering political crisis between West and East Pakistan into an outright assault on the fragile sovereignty of this 23-year-old nation. In the end, a civil war, aided by Pakistan's long-term enemy India, led to a truce between them and the secession of East Pakistan and the establishment of a new Bengali nation. The cyclone and civil war added greatly to the human and environmental costs.

Of Bhola Island's 900,000 people, more than 100,000 died. In the 2,300 mi^2 (6,000 km^2) delta region, 2.5 million became homeless. The wind and water destroyed more than 235,000 homes and damaged another 100,000. Hunger and starvation followed as the cyclone's toll included the loss of 250,000 tons of rice, a staple in the Bengali diet. Casualties from the civil war between Bengali guerrilla fighters and Pakistani regular troops and the war between India and Pakistan have never been accurately calculated. Some estimates of the total number of casualties suggest that between 300,000 and one million civilians and military personnel were killed.

Adding to this number, the Pakistani army was accused of genocidal atrocities against Bengali civilians, causing the flight of between six and ten million refugees to camps in India during the war.[25]

Conclusion

The vulnerable seascape of Bangladesh places millions of people at risk who are not there by choice. They are there providing for themselves and their families by fishing and planting. These residents have neither other occupations nor the mobility to go elsewhere. Under the constant threat of cyclones, they need a government that provides early warning systems, shelters, and hope that their lot and that of their children will improve. The latter seems achievable despite warnings at the time of its secession from West Pakistan in 1971 that it was "an international basket case."

In the country today, more girls attend school than boys. The focus on education has helped to improve the economy, reduced population growth rates, and fostered a civil society. The 1970 cyclone dealt a devastating blow to the population but its immediate effect accelerated a protest movement that helped to create the nation state and in the long run put the new country on the path to economic improvement and political stability.[26]

Super-Typhoon Nina (1975)

> The blare of the dam burst sounded like the sky was collapsing and the earth was cracking. Houses and trees disappeared all in an instant. Numerous corpses and bodies of cattle floated in water amid people wailing for help.[27]

Introduction

Typhoons exhibit the same characteristics of cyclones and hurricanes: high winds, storm surges, and flooding that when combined produce near-total devastation. Tropical storms that become typhoons generally begin in the shallow seas of the Federated States of Micronesia where the Pacific Ocean water is easily heated by the penetrating sun. For reasons that still baffle scientists and climatologists, in 1975 there were typhoons year-round. The typhoon season in the northwestern Pacific Ocean coincides with the hurricane season in the Atlantic Ocean, although they are not related. Typhoons battered China three times in 1975, setting a record for the country.

The typhoon season generally begins in June and ends in October. Yet in 1975, the first typhoon formed on January 21 and the last one dissipated on December 29. In all, the Pacific Northwest region and its people faced 20 storms, 14 of which became typhoons. Nina was the first super-typhoon, followed by June, a November category-5 storm with sustained winds of 185 mph (300 km/h). At the time, June was the strongest typhoon on record, one broken by super-typhoon Tip in 1979. Yet, human losses, a lack of preparedness, property damage, and environmental devastation are among the many reasons for choosing Nina as a case study.

In late July, a tropical storm was identified in the Philippine Sea moving southwestward. By the end of the month, it had begun to intensify into a typhoon with the barometric pressure dropping rapidly and wind velocity exploding from 75 mph to 150 mph (120–240 km/h) on August 2. As it approached Taiwan, it weakened into a category 3 storm, moving across the island's sparsely populated central mountain range. Although the damage was limited, 25 people died and 168 were injured. Over 3,000 homes were damaged, 39 fishing boats were lost and the 16,000-ton South Korean freighter, the *Sun Star*, capsized near Koahsiung harbor. Flooding and mudslides were common.[28]

Moving across the Taiwan Straits and making landfall on the southeast coast of mainland China on August 4, Nina was downgraded from a typhoon to a tropical storm. However, it regained its strength over land. A soaking rain of 42 in (106 cm), an extreme amount of rain in a 24-hour period by any measure and 40% more than the heaviest previous rainfall in China, saturated the already wet land. "When the rain continued, the days were like nights as rain fell like arrows. The mountains were covered all over by dead sparrows after the rain."[29] Normally, the average annual precipitation was 31.5 in (80 cm). The evaporation of water from a warm and wet surface probably contributed to the storm's intensification and to the release of more intense rain.[30]

Once-in-a-millennium flood conditions event led to the collapse of the Banqiao hydroelectric and flood control dam in the early morning of August 8. As the largest of the 62 dams in Zhumadian Prefecture in Henan Province, its collapse led to the failure of the Province's other 61 dams, one after the other. Their collapse was caused either by the rushing waters or destroyed by government-authorized air strikes to protect dams and populations further downstream. In total, the collapsing and destroyed dams released 15.7 billion tons of floodwaters into an area of about 3900 mi^2 (10,101 m^2).

Built in the early 1950s to control the flooding in the Huai River basin, the Banqiao Dam was an early technological undertaking during the first decade of the People's Republic of China under Mao Zedong. Despite its height of 387 ft (118 m) with a storage capacity of 130,000 gal (492,000 l) and with 99,000 gal (375,000 l) reserved for flood storage, the Banqiao was no match for this overwhelming flood event. Engineers calculated that its failure to hold back 184,000 gal (697,000 l) of floodwater, almost double its flood storage capacity, led to its collapse. Contributing to its collapse may have been the cracks identified in both the dam and the sluice gates after its completion, the result of construction and engineering mistakes. Although these flaws were corrected with the assistance of engineers from the Soviet Union, the structural integrity of Banqiao had been compromised.

Workers onsite were ordered to open the sluice gates, thereby releasing the rising water behind the dam. However, poor maintenance had left the gates partially blocked by accumulated silt. The dam system's leading hydrologist, Chen Xing, had recommended many more sluice gates than appeared in the design specifications, but was ignored and finally banned from the entire project. The design included the construction of many additional dams in the Huai Basin for hydropower and flood control but without Chen's expertise more flaws were built into the system.

The dam's collapse released 785 million yds^3 (600 million m^3) of water, traveling at almost 31 mph (50 km/h) downward into the valleys below. Entire communes and small towns disappeared in an instant. At 8:00 p.m. on August 9 the Zhumadian Prefecture sent an emergency telegram to the central government outlining to the best of its knowledge the casualties caused by the collapse. "The Banqiao reservoir collapsed at 1:00 a.m. on August 8. Three million people have been engulfed by the flood and have been isolated on the tops of roofs and in trees for three days. Emergency!"[31]

Ten days later, millions of Chinese were still trapped in the water, marooned on the remains of dams and dikes, on rooftops and in trees (Figure 8.3). Many of these survived without food, stricken by infectious diseases including dysentery, typhoid, hepatitis, influenza, malaria, conjunctivitis, and more. Injuries, wounds, and poisoning from eating decaying food afflicted thousands more. Only by dynamiting the

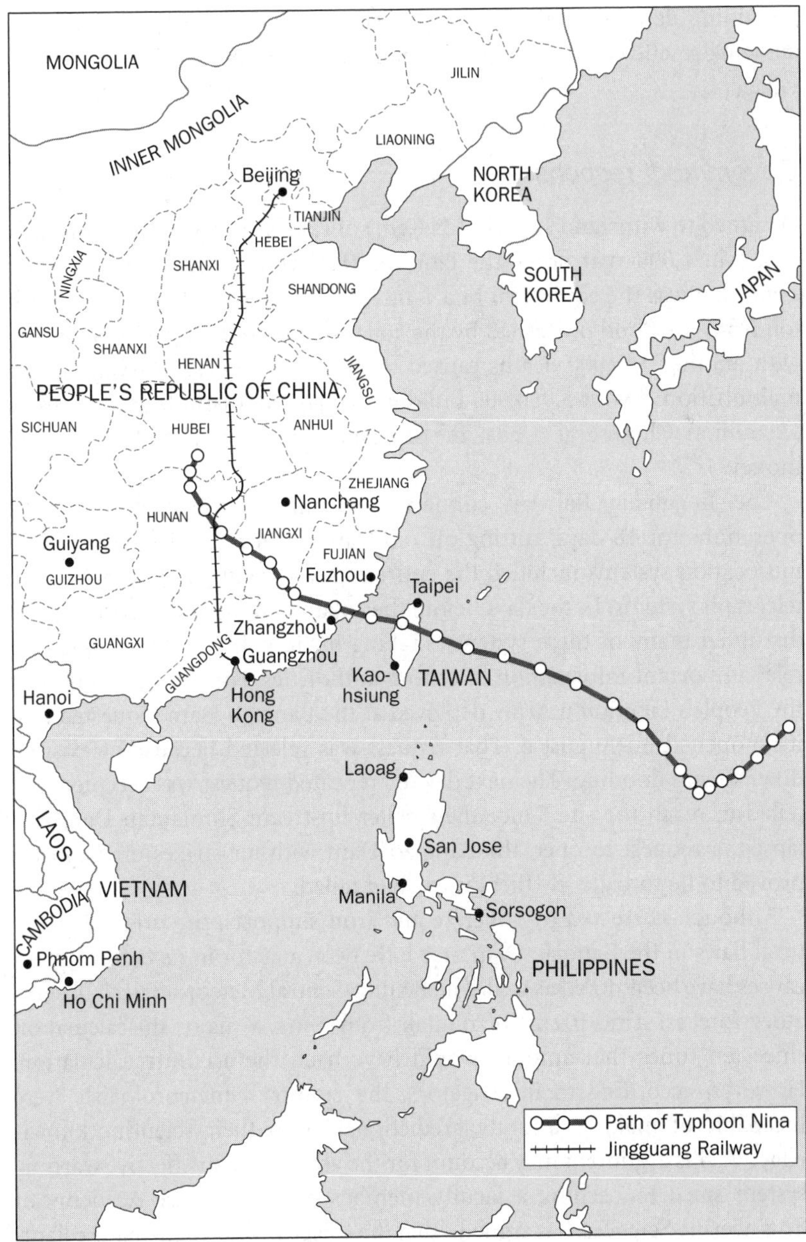

Figure 8.3 Outline of China's provinces affected by Typhoon Nina.

remaining dams were the waters that flooded the entire region released, allowing rescue efforts and relief supplies to reach the millions of trapped villagers.

Government response

Designed to withstand 11.75 in (29.8 cm) of rain each day or the equivalent of a 1-in-1,000-year flood, the Banqiao Dam was assaulted by a weather event that was the equivalent of a 1-in-2,000-year event. The official death toll from the flood unleashed by the collapsing dams was placed at 26,000 with another 145,000 deaths caused by epidemic disease, starvation, and malnutrition. About 5,960,000 buildings collapsed, disrupting the lives of 12 million Chinese at a cost of 10 billion renminbi (RMB) ("people's money").[32]

The Jingguang Railway, connecting Beijing to Guangzhou, ceased operations for 18 days, cutting off rail transportation. Other failed communication systems included the entire roadway network, telephone, and telegraph systems. In the days before the collapse, rains and mudslides had disrupted many of these systems, making it difficult if not impossible to relay important information to central authorities. For example, a unit of the People's Liberation Army deployed at the Banqiao Dam requested that it be opened on August 6. That request was rejected because of existing downstream flooding. The next day the repeated request was accepted, but failed to reach the site. Once the smaller upstream Shimantan Dam collapsed, a request to open the Banqiao Dam with air strikes on August 8 proved to be too late. By then, it too had failed.

Although corrected by concrete and iron supports, the original structural flaws in the Banqiao Dam may have been a factor in its failure. Other causes have been noted as well. The Beijing Central Meteorological Observatory forecast 4 in (10 cm) of rainfall from Nina, a major miscalculation since ten times that amount would have been the accurate calculation. However, according to investigators, the country's meteorologists were incapable of making accurate predictions "given their scientific knowledge."[33] This argument may account for the absence of an effective warning system since Li Zechun, a faculty member of the Chinese Academy of Engineering Sciences, has argued, "that the tragedy was a man-made calamity rather than a natural one."[34] To him, the failure to release water from the Banqiao Dam once it reached capacity was a human failing, one based on the failure to use the knowledge of the dam's carrying capacity. Today, an early warning system with a wireless communication system to alert the millions living in the reservoir areas is in place – sadly, this was not the case in 1975.

Conclusion

Many of the dams destroyed during the August 1975 super-typhoon have been rebuilt, including Banqiao in 1993. In 2005, a year in which the Chinese government declassified documents relating to Nina's destruction, Typhoon Haitang followed a path similar to Nina, dropping torrential rain on the area but causing minimal damage. Although early warnings and storm water releases from the dam systems helped to mitigate potential damage, of China's 28 provinces, ten coastal and six inland provinces are located in the path of future typhoons and their destructive capability. With a population of 250 million in these provinces and the potential loss of 60 trillion renminbi (RMB) in lives, property, and economic production, typhoons pose a continuing threat to China's wellbeing.

Rising sea levels and more frequent and intense storms, a by-product of climate change, will continually challenge the government's ability to respond effectively. In 2006, five deadly typhoons, three of which were super-typhoons, caused 1,600 deaths and affected 66.6 million people. Economic losses included damage to agricultural areas costing 80 billion RMB. Among the worst of these disasters was Typhoon Saomai on August 10, 2006, one of the category 5 storms to strike China's southeast coastal provinces with 25-foot waves before moving inland. It caused 240 deaths and the sinking of 952 ships with damage to 1,594 others in Shacheng harbor. If it had arrived two hours later, during a summer high tide, its waves and storm surges would have flooded much of Zhejiang and Fujian provinces.[35]

Although much work has been completed by the Chinese government to build new flood control systems, and to upgrade the country's infrastructure of sea walls, dams, roads, and bridges, nearly one-half of China's sea walls are incapable of withstanding major typhoons. Several of its dams and reservoirs are vulnerable to typhoon flooding. Mud-rock flows and landslides continue to threaten humans and animals living in the disaster-prone provinces.

Summary

In the North Atlantic, 2005 proved to be a most frightening year in terms of hurricanes. Katrina and Wilma may be the most memorable because of the deaths and property losses they caused, but the year posed particular threats to coastal residents with six major hurricanes, four of which were category 5 hurricanes. As more people chose to move to the coasts and as the government provides incentives to do so, the financial burden on all will continue to rise, as will the continuing vulnerability of residents, including those new arrivals. Because hurricanes in the southern hemisphere were thought to be nonexistent, the event that surprised most, if not all, meteorologists was the appearance of Hurricane Catarina off the coast of southern Brazil in 2004. On March 28, the hurricane's wind velocity peaked at 100 mph (155 km/h), destroying much of the country's banana and rice crops. This development may suggest that it was not a unique event but a response to global changing climatic conditions.

Notes

1 Dom Moraes (1971), "East Pakistan: the wave," *The New York Times*, January 10, 71.

2 Robert T. Watson, Daniel L. Albritten, and Terry Barker, (2002) *Synthesis Report, A Contribution of Working Groups 1, 11, and 111 to the Third Assessment Report of the Intergovernmental Panel on Climate Change* (New York: Cambridge University Press), 5.

3 Kerry Emanuel (2005), "Increasing destructiveness of tropical cyclones over the past thirty years," *Nature*, 436, 686–688. Also Peter Webster, Greg Holland, Judith Curry, and Huan Chang (2005), "Changes in tropical cyclone number, duration, and intensity in a warming environment," *Science*, 309(5742), 1844–1846.

4 Maarten K. van Aalst (2006), "The impacts of climate change on the risk of natural disasters," *Disasters*, 30(1), 13.

5 Matthew Mulcahy (2001), *Melancholy and Fatal Calamities: Natural Disasters and Colonial Society in the English Greater Caribbean, 1607–1786* (Baltimore, MD: The Johns Hopkins University Press) and Steven Biel (ed.) (2001), *American Disasters* (New York: New York University Press).

6 Phil Scott (2006), *Hemingway's Hurricane: The Great Florida Keys Storm of 1935* (New York: McGraw-Hill), 111.

7 Lewis H. Watkins (1939), "Hurricane data, Florida Keys – September 2, 1935," *National Archives*, file no. PE167, March 30, 3.
8 Phil Scott (2006), *Hemingway's Hurricane*, 111.
9 Ibid., 134.
10 Ibid., 141–143.
11 Ibid., 158.
12 *The New York Times* (1935), "3 inquiries start in Florida deaths," September 7, 3.
13 Ibid.
14 Ernest Hemingway (1935), "Who murdered the vets?" *The New Masses*, reprinted in Joseph North (1969) *New Masses: An Anthology of the Rebel Thirties* (New York: International Publishers), 183–187.
15 Phil Scott (2006), *Hemingway's Hurricane*, 217.
16 Shamsuddoha Rezaul Karim Chowdhury 2005), *Climate Change, Disaster and Coastal Vulnerabilities in Bangladesh*, Working Paper of the Research Development & Coastal Livelihoods (Dhaka, Bangladesh: COAST Trust), 1–2.
17 Ibid., 5–6.
18 Ibid., 7.
19 Muhammad Hossain, Mohammad Islam, Tetsuya Sakai, and Mau Ishida (2008), "Impact of tropical cyclones on rural infrastructures in Bangladesh," *Agricultural Engineering International: the CIGR Ejourna*, Invited Overview, X(2), 5–6.
20 Alak Paul and Maksudur Rahman (2006), "Cyclone mitigation perspectives in the islands of Bangladesh: a case of Sandwip and Hatia Islands," *Coastal Management*, 34, 200–201.
21 Ibid.
22 Dom Moraes (1971), "East Pakistan: the wave," 64.
23 C. Emdad Haque (1997), "Atmospheric hazards preparedness in Bangladesh: a study of warning, adjustments and recovery from the April 1991 cyclone," *Natural Hazards*, 16, 184.
24 Masoud Popalzai (1972), "Indians begin withdrawal of troops from Pakistan," *The New York Times*, December 14, 10.
25 Arthur Sulzberger (1971), "Non-limits of disaster," *The New York Times*, June 16, 10; and Arthur Sulzberger (1970), "Disease increases in the region of Pakistan area swept by cyclone," *The New York Times*, November 18, 1.
26 Nicholas D. Kristof (2010), "Pakistan and Times Square," *The New York Times*, May 12, A25.
27 Li Ying and Lianshou Chen (2003), "Numerical study on the impacts of the wet land boundary layer fluxes over wetland on sustention and rainfall of landfalling tropical cyclones," *Chinese Academy of Meteorological Sciences* (Beijing, China), 1.

28 US Fleet Weather Central Joint Typhoon Warning Center (1975), *Annual Typhoon Report 1975* (Guam, Mariana Islands), 21.

29 "After 30 years, secrets, lessons of China's worst dams burst accident surface." At http://english.people.com.cn/200510/01/eng20051001_211892.html.

30 US Fleet Weather Central Joint Typhoon Warning Center (1975), *Annual Typhoon Report 1975* (Guam, Mariana Islands), 21.

31 Yi Si (1998), "The Banqiao and Shimantan dam collapses," in Dai Qing, *The River Dragon Has Come: The Three Gorges Dam and the Fate of China's Yangtze River and Its People* (Armonk: M. E. Sharpe), 34.

32 Defu Liu, Liang Pang, and Botao Xie (2009), "Typhoon disaster in China: prediction, prevention, and mitigation," *Natural Hazards*, 49, 422.

33 "After 30 years, secrets, lessons of China's worst dams burst accident surface." At http://english.people.com.cn/200510/01/eng20051001_211892.html.

34 Ibid.

35 Defu Liu, Liang Pang, and Botao Xie (2009), "Typhoon disaster in China: prediction, prevention, and mitigation," 423.

Further Reading

Cherie Burns (2006), *The Great Hurricane: 1938* (New York: Grove/Atlantic).
This book contains numerous personal accounts of those who lived through this once-in-a-century hurricane. They range in detail from those who survived to those who lost relatives and friends. From the Moore family who were washed into the sea from their attic floor to the actress, Katharine Hepburn, watching her car disappear in the wind, these are human-interest stories at their best.

Ivor van Heerden and Mike Bryan (2007), *The Storm: What Went Wrong and Why During Hurricane Katrina – the Inside Story from One Louisiana Scientist* (New York: Penguin).
In *The Storm*, van Heerden and Bryan describe the failure of government officials at all levels to respond quickly and correctly to the catastrophe that inundated a great American city and changed the lives of the survivors forever.

Louis A. Jr. Perez (2000), *Winds of Change: Hurricanes and the Transformation of Nineteenth-Century Cuba* (Chapel Hill, NC: The University of North Carolina Press).
This short history of hurricanes in Cuba describes their powerful impact on Cuba's economy and culture.

David Longshore (2007), *Encyclopedia of Hurricanes, Typhoons, and Cyclones* (New York: Facts on File).
This encyclopedia contains 400 cross-referenced entries that cover the science and history of these catastrophic storms.

Chapter 9

Famines and Droughts

> *On a typical afternoon the wind on the Great Plains blows at a steady 15 mph [24 km/h] . . . In the spring of 1934, however, the wind suddenly turned demonic. On April 14, a vast black blizzard of earth came rolling out of the north toward Texas, whirling and spinning in a huge bowl, darkening the sun and blanketing the land with drifts up to 20 ft [6 m] high.*[1]

Introduction

Climatologists associate severe weather events with the increasing concentrations of greenhouse gases that raise Earth's global temperature. In a warming world, droughts and floods are natural consequences. Droughts occur because of hotter land surfaces and floods because warmer oceans release more water vapor into the atmosphere, which returns it to Earth as torrential rain. One immediate effect of drought is its impact on agricultural productivity. Without rain, plants wither and die. A failed growing season creates a shortage of plant food, causing rising food prices, especially for wheat, corn, sugar, and oils.

Although other factors contribute to the shortages, especially the increasing global demand for food, clearly severe weather disrupts agricultural production most directly. The price of wheat nearly doubled in 2010 and the bulk of that production decline reflected the sharp decline in Russia where record heatwaves pushed temperatures in Moscow above 100°F (37°C) for the first time ever. Droughts followed there and in Brazil as well. In Australia, record flooding damaged food production while recorded temperatures reached an all-time high in 19 countries, representing a fifth of the world's land area.

Natural Disasters in a Global Environment, First Edition. Anthony N. Penna and Jennifer S. Rivers.

Chapter 5 on floods, examined some extraordinary cases as natural disasters. Despite the vulnerability to coastal areas caused by rising sea levels and the one billion people who live within 25 miles of these coasts, the numbers projected to become affected by drought living in "water-stressed countries" will rise to three billion people in the next 20 years.[2]

This chapter focuses on three case studies that examine the cultural and historical significance of disasters and their impact on society and the environment. The Irish Potato Famine (1845–51) devastated the country's population. About one million people lost their lives in the famine. This case demonstrates the ways in which social and economic developments can cause human suffering and vulnerability. The second case, the Great Plains Dust Bowl (1930–40) illustrates how the weather and destructive farming can create the conditions for an agro-ecological disaster. Both cases focus on the creation of vulnerable environments by human activity and by unpredictable and unforgiving weather. An invasive fungus destroyed Ireland's potato crop while drought and dust upended the livelihoods of Great Plains farmers. The agro-ecological systems developed in both locations made both peasants and farmers vulnerable to opportunistic pests and the weather. The Great Leap Forward Famine in China (1959–61), the last case study, illustrates the many ways in which ideological-driven industrial and agricultural policies not only create unstable and vulnerable ecosystems but can also lead to the deaths of millions of people.

The Irish Potato Famine (1845–51)

> [The children were] like skeletons, their features sharpened with hunger and their limbs wasted, so that there is little left but bones, their hands and arms, in particular, being much emaciated, and the happy expression of infancy gone from their faces, leaving the anxious look of premature old age.[3]

Introduction

The Four Horsemen of the Apocalypse appeared in the last book of the New Testament of the Bible, titled the Book of Revelations by St. John the Evangelist. It identified pestilence, war, famine, and death as harbingers of the Last Judgment. Thomas Malthus, in his famous *Essay on the Principle of Population* in 1798, used the concept of the four horsemen in the following way:

> Famine seems to be the last, the most dreadful resource of nature. The power of population is so superior to the power of the earth to produce subsistence for man, that premature death must in some shape or other visit the human race. The vices of mankind are active and able ministers of depopulation . . . But should they fail in this war of extermination, pestilence and plague [will] advance in terrific array. Should success be still incomplete, gigantic inevitable famine stalks in the rear, and with one mighty blow levels the population with the food of the world.[4]

As applied to nineteenth-century Ireland, Malthus argued that early marriage and increased fertility led to a growing Irish population. According to him, increasing dependence on a single hardy foodstuff made the Irish poor more vulnerable to the unpredictability of weather, climate, and disease. Much of his argument was supported by developments in the country. The population grew an average of 1.3% before the famine. From 1600 to 1845 the total grew from two million to more than eight million people. In addition, the demand for meat and animal products outside of Ireland led landlords to turn their wheat fields and vegetable gardens into pastures. This transformation forced large peasant families, without the capital resources to do the same, to change their varied diets of wheat bread and vegetables.

With wheat fields becoming pastures for livestock, the potatoes previously fed to animals became a staple in Irish peasant diets. Becoming dependent on potatoes, they consumed as much as 12–14 lb (5.4–6.3 kg) per adult male each day. As one commentator noted, "The Englishman would find considerable difficulty in stowing away in his stomach this enormous quantity of vegetable food, and how an Irishman is able to manage it is beyond my ability to explain."[5] With a total population of 8,525,000, as many as three million people depended almost solely on potatoes for protein, calories, and minerals. Millions more landlords, peasants, and craftsmen supplemented their diets with this tuber.

Reduced to eating a bland diet of nutritious potatoes, cultivators placed them too close together. The crop reduced the biodiversity needed for a healthy soil while piles of potato biomass became a breeding ground for the fungus *Phythophthora infestans*, which began to destroy all potatoes planted in 1845; this changed the course of the country's history for the next century and beyond.

Background to the famine

Ireland had coped with potato blight many times in centuries past. "In 1845, however, social and ecological conditions created a situation that allowed this relatively common agricultural pest to destroy an entire society."[6] A number of factors contributed to this catastrophe. They included the decline in cottage industries devoted to weaving linen cloth and their replacement with factories employing hundreds of workers in industrial England. Upwards of 2,000 self-employed weavers in one town lost their means of support. The percentage of weavers, as a share of Ireland's workforce nationally, dropped from 40 to 30%.

As part of the comprehensive exchange of crops, animals, and pathogens, sixteenth-century Spanish explorers brought back to Western Europe the white potato, cultivated and harvested in the Andean Highlands by Native Americans. There, it quickly spread to countries across Eurasia.[7] Irish farmers cultivated approximately two million acres of potatoes, primarily as animal feed prior to the famine, accounting for about one-third of all agricultural lands. Potatoes could be grown on relatively infertile plots of ground without the need for horse or oxen power. Using hoes and spades, peasants cut deep ridges into the soil and added copious amounts of manure to fertilize the land.

With more land turned to pasture, bumper harvests of potatoes fed the three million poor and supplemented the diets of the many millions of not-so-poor as well as barnyard animals, pigs and a host of fowl including chickens, geese, ducks, and pigeons. For the poor, plentiful amounts of satisfying potatoes mixed with buttermilk provided all of the nutrition needed to maintain one's health. Because they were rich in vitamin C, scurvy – a common endemic affliction of the poor in countries dependent on maize – was unknown in Ireland.

In the decades before the famine, however, living standards remained intolerable by modern standards. "The poor were wretchedly housed – two-thirds of the entire population huddled into sparsely furnished, tiny mud cottages or their urban equivalent – and poorly clothed, and often hungry for two or three months of every year."[8] As with all famine disasters, poor hygiene, primitive sanitation, and malnutrition made the millions of poor agricultural workers, farmers, and their families vulnerable to infectious diseases including dysentery and typhus.

The availability of cheap fuel in the form of peat dug from the country's plentiful bogs and consumed in the fireplaces of even the most depressing of dwellings lessened the worst effects of daily life. Before the famine, quality of life measures for the Irish compared favorably with those of many other countries. Life expectancy, at 37 or 38 years, lagged behind only England and the Scandinavian countries but was higher by a few years than in other European countries. Illiteracy was low compared with other countries and the height of men, a proxy measure for wellbeing, was greater than in England and in at least six other European countries.

Despite the condition of Ireland's housing stock, its system of roads linked all major towns. The introduction of steam power increased the frequency and number of Irish Sea ferry crossings. This innovation influenced Irish emigration to England, to where over 419,000 people had moved by 1841, seeking work in the burgeoning factories.[9]

The famine

Neither government action nor voluntary aid was able to prevent this ecological and man-made disaster. From 1846–51, the very young and the elderly succumbed to the ill-effects of malnutrition and eventual starvation more quickly than those aged 10–59. The young accounted for only 13.5% of the population but 29% of the deaths occurred among those aged under four years old. Those aged 10–59 represented 68.5% of the population and accounted for about 40% of the deaths. With a significant 14% drop in birth rates, a by-product of high death rates, an estimated 300,000 births never took place.[10]

The misery caused by the famine is hard to overestimate. The aggressive fungus affliction *P. infestans* appeared in the USA in 1843, having come from the Toluca Valley, southwest of Mexico City. It was first identified in Belgium in June 1845, quickly moving to the Netherlands, parts of northern France, and the English coast. By the middle of September it had appeared in western Germany, southern Denmark, the remainder of England, and eastern Ireland. Shortly thereafter, all of Ireland and parts of Scotland were infected.[11]

The pattern of infection was the same everywhere. The plants' leaves were covered with purple-black lesions and the stems and stocks turned into black slime. Either initially or eventually attacking the skin of the potato with black blotches, incursions into the flesh of the potato turned it into inedible mush. Within days a crop was destroyed.[12] When the blight arrived in Ireland in September 1845, its immediate impact was selective. The potato blight struck a glancing blow to the Irish economy and its people. A decline in yield was evident but not so widespread that it resulted in hunger or starvation. However, the reappearance of the blight in July 1846 resulted in a complete failure of the potato crop.

In 1846–47, the weather intervened, causing the blight to take a far greater toll on the population. Wintry weather delayed spring planting. In Dublin, where farmers and local officials collected and coded time series data on climatic conditions, average temperatures between December and February were nearly 4°F (15.5°C) below the 1830–50 average.[13] Drought during the early spring and summer inhibited the transition from potato seed and bulb to tuber. Heavy rainfall during July and August destroyed the entire crop as water washed the spores of *P. infestans* into the soil, destroying the potato bulbs.

Factors other than the weather also contributed to the blight. It was probably caused by the use of infected tubers for seeds, left in piles from the preceding year or left in the ground where infected spores remained from one growing season to the next. Crop failures from 1847 through 1849 extended food shortages throughout the winter months, heightening the spread and impact of illnesses associated with malnutrition.[14]

Relief efforts

As was common in most countries, regional nutritional differences existed in Ireland. Milk, herrings, oatmeal, eggs, and bread supplemented the diets of many, except for the poorest. With the outbreak of the potato blight, government rations, local charities and landlord supplements sought to stem the tide of starvation. The debate over providing assistance to the most vulnerable in society became a contentious one. Harsh winters, blowing snow, freezing ice storms, impassible roads, and failed relief efforts only added to the misery of the destitute (Figure 9.1).

As one member of the English Relief Service wrote, "A great deal has been written about and many an account given of the dreadful sufferings of the poor . . . believe me, the reality in most cases far exceeded description."[15] Notices posted by landlords became commonplace. One read: "I hereby give notice to the Labourers and Poor Householders on Lord Caledon's Estate, that his Lordship and Lady Caledon have instructed me to open Three Soup Kitchens, in convenient parts of his Lordship's property, to supply Soup and Bread at a very moderate price."[16]

Relief efforts took a number of forms but always in the context of an economic system dedicated to free market principles where, no matter how

Figure 9.1 Famine memorial, Dublin, Ireland.
Source: © Mike Walker/Alamy.

destitute they were, food aid always carried a cost to consumers. Ireland did not gain its independence from Great Britain until 1922, and free food for the starving Irish peasants, it was argued, would negatively impact food prices across England. So the government imposed a minimal cost on Indian corn and meal. Intended to provide relief for the millions without income, it simply added to their frustration and misery.

Appeals for relief met with cold calculating responses. The following, from the first editor of the *Economist*, James Wilson, urged, "it is no man's business to provide for another" and that public relief would upset that natural law of distribution claiming that "those who deserve more would obtain it."[17] Work relief on government-sponsored public works projects had the same frustrating effects. Wages paid never approached the rising cost of food. Not only did the workers remain hungry, but families dependent on them suffered continually.

Charitable associations and government-sponsored soup kitchens failed in their goal of relieving the suffering of the many. A bowl of soup and a biscuit were no substitutes for a population formerly thriving on many pounds of potatoes daily. For those already suffering from the ill-effects of hunger with weakened gastrointestinal systems, watery soup only made matters worse. Exacerbating the frustration was "a market plentifully supplied with meat, bread, fish, in short everything."[18] The lack of money, rather than the lack of food, turned a food crisis into an epic national famine.

Until one reads the riveting eye-witness account by a magistrate of county Cork published in *The Times* on December 24, 1846, one could not imagine the extent of the suffering. He observed the following upon entering the town of Skibbereen.

> I was surprised to find the wretched hamlet apparently deserted. I entered some of the hovels to ascertain the cause, and the scenes that presented themselves were such that no tongue or pen can convey the slightest idea of. In the first, six famished and ghastly skeletons, to all appearances dead, were huddled in a corner on some filthy straw, their sole covering what seemed a ragged horsecloth, their wretched legs hanging about, naked above the knees. I approached with horror, and found by the low moaning they were alive – they were in fever, four children, a woman and what had once been a man.[19]

These deplorable conditions and the fate of millions of citizens would continue without much relief for years to come. As the potato famine in Ireland proved, relief efforts properly conducted and funded could make a difference in the lives of those caught up in a disaster. The endemic poverty facing at least one-third of Ireland's population existed in the geopolitical world of Victorian England with its highly developed political culture, bureaucratic structure, and increasing modern infrastructure of good roads and postal service.

As the quotation above from *The Times* suggests, it possessed a free press, making news about the plight of Irish subjects available to all readers. Absent of civil unrest or outright rebellion, financial and other resources if monitored effectively were available "to relieve distress and keep down mortality."[20]

Too much energy was expended on "blaming the victim" in the daily newspapers and presenting them to the public as unworthy, shiftless, and lacking in gratitude. Many government officials declared the famine to be over years before it actually ended. Cash-for-work programs passed by Parliament to aid famine victims looked promising on paper but displayed utter ignorance of market conditions that drove the price of scarce food ever higher: so high that it denied the poor on work relief the ability to purchase food with their meager incomes.

The following observation speaks to the reality of cash-for-work sponsored programs:

> Yesterday morning at daybreak, I saw a gang of about 150, composed principally of old men, women, and little boys, going out to work on one of the roads near the town. At that time the road was covered with snow, and there was a very severe frost; seeing that they were miserably clad, I remarked to a bystander that it was a miracle that the cold did not kill them . . . In less than half an hour after, one of them, an old man, named Richard Cotter, was brought on a man's back dying . . . In the course of the day, I went out to visit this gang, who were opening a drain inside the fence on the marsh road, and such a scene I hope I may never again be called upon to witness. The women and children were crying out from the severity of the cold, and were unable to hold the implements with which they were at work, most of them declared that they had not tasted food for a day . . . I could not help thinking how much better it would be to afford them some temporary relief in their own homes during the severe weather, than to sacrifice their lives to carry out a miserable project.[21]

Public spending on famine relief between 1846 and 1852 reflected public attitudes and government policies. It totaled less than £10 million (US$48 million). With the blight destroying a projected 50 million tons of potatoes during this period, famine relief would have cost an estimated £50 million ($240 million). Using the higher cost of substitute foods and the reassignment of laborers, increased expenditures would have reduced but not eliminated the famine's deadly outcome. The latter sums would have represented about a national yearly income of 2% from a relatively wealthy England or 20% of its public expenditure. Although these percentages were significant, they were not insurmountable. Yet, many English policy-makers and the Irish landholding class rejected such transfers of wealth.[22]

As with many natural and man-made disasters, those most severely affected fled in hopes of finding food, lodging, and medical attention elsewhere. The Irish exhibited a long historical pattern of migration. "Between 1815 and 1845, about eight hundred thousand Irish people, about two-thirds of them men, had emigrated to North America."[23] Given the costs of passage and the need for some money after landing in America, these immigrants did not come from the ranks of the landless rural population. Migration to England entailed few of these costs, and the Irish and their families accounted for the hundreds of thousands who emigrated there before 1845 in search of work in the country's industrial workshops.

The tragedy of the famine accelerated emigration. More than a million people left between 1845 and 1852. As with earlier migrations to North America, those with cash to pay for passage, mostly small landowners who could sell their property to larger owners, crossed the Atlantic. With more Irish living in New York City than in Dublin, this new wave of immigrants found an already established community willing and able to provide access to lodging and work. If one assumes that voluntary migration during the famine saved thousands of lives, then a government-assisted migration policy that cost an annual sum of £1 million ($4.8 million) for passage would have saved 100,000 famine victims.[24]

Conclusion

Ireland lost one-fifth of its population during the famine years due to starvation, emigration, and falling birth rates. The famine killed about one million people or one-eighth of the population: "This makes it one of the major human disasters in the last centuries, even on a world scale."[25] At the national level, relief efforts failed to address the magnitude of the crisis. Evidence that food exports from Ireland by Anglo-Irish landlords during the famine only added to the legitimate charges that they and government officials made a terrible calamity worse. Exports of one-half million pounds of wheat, however, would never compensate for the loss of an estimated 50 million tons of potatoes to the blight.

By 1854, Ireland's shrinking population created a labor shortage with agricultural employment falling by 45% between 1845 and 1876. With a rebounding economy, the shortage translated into higher wages for laborers. These laborers would work on consolidated agriculture properties gathered together by landlords purchasing the smallholdings of emigrating Irish farmers before, during and after the famine. So, while wages for landless farmers increased, "the potato blight inflicted significant and enduring damage on Irish capital stock. This ecological aspect differentiates the Irish famine from most other famines."[26]

The "Dust Bowl" Drought in the American West (1930–40)

> I saw not a solitary thing but bare earth and a few lonely, empty farmhouses . . . There was not a tree or blade of grass, or dog or cow or a human

> being – nothing whatsoever, nothing at all but gray raw earth and a few farmhouses and barns, sticking up from the dark gray sea like white cattle skeletons on the desert. [It was] the saddest land I have ever seen, this withering land of misery.[27]

Introduction

The Great Plains are large natural grasslands stretching westward from the central region of North America to the Rocky Mountains. As a high plain of more than 2,000 ft (600 m) above sea level, it slopes upward to about 5,000 ft (1,500 m) above sea level as it approaches the Rockies. From the Canadian border in the north to the Texas and New Mexico boundaries in the south, the Great Plains encompass all or parts of nine states. For centuries, if not millennia, the region's native grass (sod) fed millions of north–south migrating bison. Their urine and feces fertilized the grassland as they moved on to greener landscapes.

Howling Arctic winds searching for the warmth of the Gulf of Mexico whistled through the sod without disturbing its fragile soil. Much of this pristine landscape, altered only marginally by Native American tribes, changed with the arrival of European and American settlers. For the southern Great Plains, the focus of much of the 1930s Dust Bowl history, its native grasslands covered over 100 million acres in Texas, Oklahoma, New Mexico, Colorado, and Kansas.

Background

Unknown to farmers, long-term Dust Bowl conditions were part of the Great Plains' history, with the longest one during the last 1,200 years being a mega-drought lasting from 900 to 1300 CE. Coinciding with the Medieval Climate Optimum (800–1200 CE), Great Plains' drying was a natural response to hemispheric warming. Moderate to severe droughts on the Great Plains during the past century are related to both the cooling sea surface temperatures (SST) in the Pacific Ocean and the effects of La Niña. This weather event causes waters in the Pacific Ocean to cool, pushing warm dry air inland. It shifts rain away from Texas, Arizona, and New Mexico, causing severe droughts.[28] In the case of the 1930s Dust Bowl, the drought affected almost two-thirds of the country as well as parts of Canada and Mexico. The duration and severity of droughts with very high temperatures and blowing dust have visited the region once or twice each century during the last 400 years.[29]

Its severity led historian Donald Worster to conclude that the Dust Bowl was one of the three worst socially-caused ecological blunders in history. Human action and the weather turned the parched land into blowing dust, making farmers and their livestock vulnerable to changing climatic conditions. Only China's deforestation of its uplands in about 1000 BCE, which triggered severe flooding and erosion, surpassed it. In the Mediterranean, the destruction of the region's woodlands for shipbuilding to support Rome's empire two thousand years ago and the overgrazing of the landscape in the centuries that followed turned a once fertile land into a barren waste. Whereas these two mankind-induced "natural" disasters took centuries to complete, the Great Plains fiasco of churning up the native sod and making it the victim of wind and drought took a mere 50 years. How did it all happen?

It began with generous land grant federal laws including the Homestead and Morrill Acts of 1862. It gave farmers free land on the condition that they turn grasslands into farmland. Also, states received grants to establish land grant agricultural colleges. Later, the Hatch Act of 1887 brought extension stations, educational agencies affiliated with agricultural colleges and funded by the US Department of Agriculture to bring the latest knowledge about farming. As one farmer noted about these new institutions, they "bring science down out of the sky and hook it to a plow."[30]

With the influx of homesteaders after the Civil War (1861–65), the development of labor-saving tractors and the expansion of a national system of railroads, farmers produced an abundance of grain for an expanding domestic market and a growing foreign one. As another example of the Columbian Exchange, "the varieties of wheat, sorghum, alfalfa, and livestock refined in the western regions of the USA originated in Europe, Asia, and Africa."[31] Turning the "Great American Desert" into cultivated farmland would require the use of advanced dry farming techniques and the cooperation of nature in providing sufficient annual rainfall of 15–20 in (38–50 cm) each year.

The conditions that created the Dust Bowl

In response to the need for food in a Europe ravaged by the Great War (1914–18), grain prices soared as farmers acquired more land, planting wheat almost everywhere in Western Nebraska, Kansas, Oklahoma, and Texas. Tillable cheap land accompanied by the promotion of gasoline tractors and harvesters and soaring grain prices encouraged farmers, homesteaders, and speculators to plow up the southern plains with its 100 million acres (400,000 km^2). With sufficient annual rainfall, homesteaders advanced into the northern and arid Plains states. Planting wheat expanded by 200% and in some counties by as much as 400–1000%. With grain shortages keeping wheat prices high, as high as $2.75 a bushel, unemployed oil-field workers along with others descended on the land, purchasing, leasing, and borrowing money to plant and harvest rapidly maturing spring wheat.

Little or no attention was paid to the findings of agricultural extension station personnel regarding crop rotation, fallowing, and other strategies proven to protect the land from desiccation. Despite the vulnerability of soils to erosion, farmers used disc plows that pulverized the soil, making it susceptible to droughts.[32]

Complicating the European food shortage during the war, Turkey, an ally of Germany and Austria-Hungary, cut off Russia's grain shipments to its British and French allies. Wheat farmers in the Great Plains filled the void, with Kansas, Colorado, Nebraska, Oklahoma, and Texas plowing up an additional 13.5 million acres during the war years, 11 million of which were native grasslands. By the end of the war, farmers had harvested 74 million acres of wheat that yielded 952 million bushels, of which 330 million was shipped to Europe.[33] Speculators in grain planted winter and spring wheat, leaving little fallow land.

Agricultural extension station scientists concluded that only large, efficiently managed farms could survive the drought years. If they used the latest technology in farm equipment and scientifically proven methods of crop rotation, they could weather the lean years. With the acceptance of these methods, farmers would continue to harvest large harvests of bumper crops in the southern plains.

The dust storms

Despite a bumper wheat crop in the spring of 1931, the onset of the Depression caused wheat prices to collapse. Farmers and speculators had borrowed heavily to purchase and cultivate more land, buy more machinery, and mortgage more property. Collapsing incomes in a highly leveraged farm economy produced bankruptcies and foreclosures as the Decade of

Prosperity (1921–29) turned into the Depression (1929–38). Drought followed in the summer and by late January 1932 dust storms swept across the Texas panhandle. Within months, winds turned the pulverized soil into dust storms in much of Oklahoma's panhandle region, much of Texas, western Kansas, southeastern Colorado, and northeastern New Mexico. In mid-November 1933 the wind had deposited blown soil as far east as Lake Superior.

Arthur Rothstein and Dorothea Lange, employed by the Farm Security Administration, photographed migrant worker camps in California. They proved to be some of the nation's strongest Dust Bowl images. Pare Lorentz's pioneer promotional 1936 documentary, *The Plow that Broke the Plains*, portrayed the exploitation of the land by speculators and the role of modern tractors in tearing up the grasslands.

John Steinbeck's 1939 Pulitzer Prize-winning novel, *The Grapes of Wrath*, further strengthened these images in the American mind. He described the escape of Tom Joad and his family from dust-ravaged Oklahoma to the opportunities they believed were awaiting them in southern California. In Steinbeck's view, Tom Joad and his family symbolized a backwardness that blinded them to the march of industrialized agriculture. According to him, it was that force more than the drought that forced them off the land. In John Ford's film version of the novel, however, a happier Hollywood ending greeted the Joads in California. "Though reformers preferred the novel, the masses, migrants included, flocked to the movie."[34]

Photographs, documentary films, movies, and poems captured the reality of the wind that began in 1931 and reached a fury in the spring of 1934 when 20 dust storms that became known as "black blizzards" occurred throughout the Great Plains.

The term came to describe the decade-long social and ecological disaster and entered the American memory as it was portrayed in poems such as Langston Hughes's wistful one, titled simply "Dust Bowl":

> The land wants me to come back
> To a handful of dust in autumn
> To a raindrop
> In the palm of my hand
> In spring.
> The land wants me to come back
> To a broken song in October
> To a snowbird on the wing
> The land wants me to come back.[35]

Reporting on the worst of these storms, the "black blizzard" of Sunday, April 14, 1935, a reporter for the Washington DC *Evening Star*, Robert E. Geiger, used the words "bowl" and "dust" for the first time. It resonated with the news media about the eroding environmental conditions on the Great Plains states.[36]

> On April 14, a vast black blizzard of earth came rolling out of the north toward Texas, whirling and spinning in a giant bowl, darkening the sun and blanketing the land with drifts up to 20 ft (6 m) high. Then, less than a month later, on May 10, another storm moved east toward Chicago. Twelve million tons (10.8 million metric tonnes) of Plains dirt was dumped on that city. Two days later the storm reached the eastern seaboard. Dust sifted into the White House and fell on ships standing out at sea.[37]

It was estimated that the "black blizzards" were 1,500 mi (2,400 km) long, 900 mi (1450 km) across and 2 mi (3.2 km) high. As it raced across the Great Plains, the blizzard displaced about 350 million tons (317 million metric tonnes) of topsoil. Some of it was piled many feet high at different locations on the Plains, while much of it settled elsewhere. It would represent an unprecedented ecological transfer of nature's bounty in topsoil.

The dust storms covered an area larger than France, Italy, and Hungary combined. They continued to blow into 1938. In some locales, storms struck with blinding winds of 50 mph (80 km/h). They interrupted all motorized travel. The winds broke many glass windows. Even windows that were shut tight and sealed with wet cloths could not prevent the intrusion of dust. As people sat out the storms inside, the dust entered through cracks and crevices. As one woman described the aftermath, "Our faces were as dirty as if we had rolled in the dirt; our hair was gray and stiff and we ground dirt between our teeth."[38]

For those who could afford them, dust masks, goggles, and handkerchiefs became a necessity when working outside and traveling. Many rural classrooms closed temporarily due to the amount of dirt that teachers regularly shoveled out of classrooms. Schools shut their doors permanently when local residents moved away as part of the massive outmigration from the region. The storms continued throughout the decade, with some of the worst ones taking place in 1937 (Figure 9.2). By 1940, 250,000 residents had moved out of the Dust Bowl states, with an estimated 200,000 leaving for California.

Figure 9.2 Dust Bowl, Dallas, South Dakota, in 1936.
Source: Photo: US Department of Agriculture.

With each passing year, the battering of the soil by high winds and the dryness due to the lack of rain turned its granular structure into finer dust particles many feet deep. During the seasonal spring storms, fine dust particles reduced visibility in a few places to 5 ft (1.5 m). Wheat crops and ground fodder for cattle and horses, layered with dust, became inedible. Livestock not only suffered: they died from the lack of food and gale-force winds that lacerated their hides, penetrated their lungs, and suffocated them.

Above average rainfall began in July 1938 and dust storms became less frequent and less severe in 1939. In that year, moisture permeated the soil to depths of 48 in (1.2 m) in some Great Plains states. Some 9.5 million acres (38,445 km^2) were still susceptible to erosion, but they represented a considerable decline since the winter peak in 1934–35 when 50 million acres (202,342 km^2) were compromised by wind and drought.[39]

Although many Great Plains writers used humor to alleviate their pain and suffering, many residents, especially the young and old, suffered from dust-related respiratory illnesses. As for humor, Kansans dealt with the unfolding disaster by stating that they knew how to cope with a dust storm. "They take it on the chin, in the eyes, ears, nose and mouth, down the neck, and in the soup."[40] Dust contained silica, the same organic material that caused silicosis in coal miners, cutting into the lining of the lungs and causing an early death. Although found in the soil in infinitesimal amounts compared to coal dust, it still irritated the membranes of the respiratory system and caused laryngitis, bronchitis, and "dust" pneumonia.

As Western writer Timothy Egan has pointed out, "Life without water did strange things to the land."[41] Drought brought out legions of insects in search of water; black tarantulas, centipedes, spiders, and grasshoppers invaded croplands and households. Grasshoppers stripped the remaining farms and gardens of wheat and vegetables in a few days, depriving families of food that would have sustained them for a winter. The victims of a black widow spider's poisonous bite not only suffered severe pain but even died in some cases.

The image of having one's living space overrun by breeding insects only added to the challenge and torment of trying to keep dust from permeating almost every crevice and corner of the household. For many seeking revenge, weekly rabbit hunts provided an outlet for frustration. Like insects, rabbits began to overrun the land in the wake of the drought, eating whatever crops and grasses remained on the depleted land. As competitors for the little that remained, signs announcing, "Big Rabbit Drive Sunday – Bring Clubs," became commonplace.

Government response

The calamity on the Plains coincided with the collapse of the country's financial markets. Distributing dust masks, providing oxygen tents, when they were available, and making nurses and physicians aware of the symptoms of dust-related illnesses were all that could be done given the shortage of material and personnel during the Depression.

The government's response extended beyond the immediate relief of dust-related illnesses. It saw the Dust Bowl disaster as a social and ecological one made worse by the weather. "The Great Plow Up" (1901–30) of the native sod in response to favorable global wheat prices, both during and after the Great War, led to destructive farm practices on semi-arid lands. In both words and actions, the Great Plains Committee commissioned by President Franklin D. Roosevelt in 1936 concluded that the Dust Bowl was a man-made disaster that "imposed upon the region a system of agriculture to which the Plains are not adapted."[42] By the time the Dust Bowl ended and normal rainfall of 15–20 in (38–50 cm) returned, the New Deal farm programs had spent $2 billion on relief, recovery, and reform.

Its first Agricultural Adjustment Act (AAA) on May 12, 1933 (declared unconstitutional by the Supreme Court in 1936) used some draconian measures to bring production in line with consumption in the hopes of creating price stability. Paying farmers for not planting cotton, corn, wheat, and other crops and destroying planned harvests became government policy. A projected surplus of 1.2 billion lb of pork led to a program in August of the same year that resulted in the slaughter of more than six million young hogs and pigs and more than 200,000 sows. All pigs weighing under 70 lb were destroyed and their meat declared unfit for human consumption at a time when many millions of hungry Americans stood in long bread lines.

Although farm prices and income did stabilize temporarily in 1933, one government official remarked ironically that this New Deal program must have been the mark of a "civilized" society. "Indeed, no 'primitive' nation would serve its economic institutions so well and its hungry people so badly."[43] Efforts to stabilize farm prices were coupled with soil conservation plans in the Dust Bowl, some of which were similar to those instituted in the northern Plains after the severe drought and collapse in farm prices in the 1920s.

The Department of the Interior's Soil Erosion Service (SES; later renamed the Soil Conservation Service, SCS) within the Department of Agriculture invested $5 million in demonstration projects. Working with young workers and conservation agents employed by the Civil Conservation Corps (CCC), farmers received payment for accepting a new set of farm practices. Terracing and contour plowing, crop rotation, the strip cropping of drought-resistant feed crops, and extended fallowing were among the most successful of these practices.[44]

Passage of the Soil Erosion Act in 1934 accounted for much of the program's success. It not only included the price and income support provisions of the original AAA but also encouraged states to establish large farm "districts" committed to soil conservation. By 1939, states had established 37 such districts that required farmers to plant grasses, legumes, and feed crops for animals. In addition, the federal government subsidized wind erosion control programs and paid farmers to take additional land out of production. Desperate for work and income, almost all farmers participated in these farm programs.

Ineligible to get loans from private banks, the Resettlement Administration (RA), in April 1935, began making loans to financially distressed farmers. Two years later the Farm Security Administration (FSA) replaced the RA with "standard loans" to farmers who seemed able to become self-sustaining by having access to farm equipment, seed, and livestock. Despite direct cash payments, federal loans, and investments in programs for soil conservation from the AAA, RA, and FSA, farmers continued to face the assault from blizzards of dust, intense summer heat, and drought. With the return of normal Great Plains precipitation in 1939, weather conditions changed, alleviating the crisis on farms.[45]

Conclusion

As Donald Worster has argued, the disaster that struck the southern Plains occurred because "the expansionary energy of the USA had finally encountered a volatile, marginal land, destroying the delicate ecological balance that had evolved there."[46] Over-expansion of wheat farming on marginal lands, the failure to practice soil conservation strategies similar to those employed on the northern Plains a decade earlier, drought, and an unrelenting wind and erosion created the Dust Bowl. Government policies, the heightened awareness of farmers about the benefits of diversification, rotation of crops, the planting of drought-resistant crops, contour farming, irrigation, and the like would, it was hoped, prevent a repeat of a Dust Bowl in the twenty-first century. Yet, we know that despite the knowledge gained from this disastrous decade, dry farming on the semi-arid Great Plains would remain problematic subjected to the complexity of human activities and the unpredictability of the weather.

The Great Leap Forward Chinese Famine (1958–61)

> In those years, starvation became a sort of mental manacle, depriving us of our freedom to think . . . it is strange that hunger can cause so much pain in your body. It seems like a vice pinching all your bones which feel dislocated for lack of flesh and sinews. Your head, hands, feet, even your belly and bowels are no longer where they normally are. You are tempted to cry out

loud but haven't the strength. When experiencing extreme hunger, one can barely utter an audible sound.[47]

Introduction

Less than ten years after defeating the Nationalist Chinese army led by Generalissimo Chiang Kai-shek, an ally of the USA against imperial Japan during World War II, Mao Zedong, the leader of the Communist Party and the People's Republic of China launched his Great Leap Forward. Intended to rapidly transform a poor agricultural society into an industrial powerhouse, Mao's goal of rapid industrialization ignored the process of slow incremental and evolutionary change in favor of a speedy process implied by the term "industrial revolution." Mao's proclamation of the Great Leap Forward on November 7, 1957 in Moscow, claiming that China would overtake the UK in the production of steel within 15 years, occurred at the height of his power. Having purged Communist Party members and intellectuals who questioned the wisdom and timing of his expansionary economic policies in 1957, he announced the plan for the Great Leap Forward at the Communist Party's Supreme State Conference in January 1958.

The Great Leap Forward

As the country's symbol of victory in war and successful leader in the transition to a peacetime communist society, Mao's fervor turned into fantasy as he proclaimed that the catch-up of 15 years could be achieved in the next year! No one in a position of leadership within the Party apparatus challenged him. Those who questioned his judgment recanted soon thereafter, served prison sentences, or suffered a more serious fate.

The Great Leap Forward entailed the rapid communalization of millions of small private farm holdings and larger collectives, established in 1955–56 into "agro-cities." The one located at Chayashan in Henan Province brought together 27 collectives and 9,300 farms with 43,000 people. The government abolished all private property to achieve one of three goals, the first being "a new social organization as fresh as the morning sun above the broad horizon of East Asia."[48] The second and third goals included the Great Leap Forward and a form of socialist construction that would promote China's transition to the ideal communist state.

Each morning, small groups of workers formed production teams while larger groups became brigades. All marched in military fashion to the fields carrying the red flags of revolution. The most disciplined men and women workers formed militarized "shock troops" working 24-hour shifts to prove their superiority and their dedication to Maoist ideals.

Despite the radical transformation of peasant life, China lacked the technology needed to mobilize millions of workers into efficient agricultural producers. In 1958, not a single factory existed for making farm tractors, plows, threshing machines, trucks, engines, or pumps. Such technology was unknown to nearly all peasants. So, combining small plots into large communes without the technology to increase productivity proved to be a fatal flaw. Tractors, trucks, and threshers were absent from the planning process as well as the entire mechanized infrastructure of spare parts, repair shops, fuel delivery, and trained mechanics.

Mao asserted that centralized decision-making and communal living on a grand scale would create new communist citizens out of illiterate peasants who used primitive farming techniques. Experimentation intended to break family bonds became the norm. Leaders placed men and women into separate living quarters. Mao speculated that separation with monthly conjugal visits might improve worker productivity. Segregated brigades began working on building dams, reservoirs, roads, tunnels, and other infrastructure projects. The People's Commune was viewed as the true family of the communist revolution. The elderly were banished to retirement homes, children attended boarding schools and lived separately from their parents. Domestic life, as we know it, including cooking and eating in a nuclear family setting, was replaced by communal eating halls.

In the absence of a developed urban factory system, tens of millions of communal peasants and city workers following plans articulated in the Great Leap Forward were ordered to enter mines, digging for iron ore and limestone. To smelt iron ore, they cut and burned millions of trees to produce charcoal for small clay furnaces. In most cases, these crude backyard furnaces produced useless clumps of brittle iron. In cities, workers melted all metal objects including bowls, pots and pans, cooking grates, eating utensils, iron bedsteads, and doorknobs to make steel, with the goal of tripling the production of steel. In the countryside, some peasants melted the scythes that they used for harvesting wheat. By June 1960 Mao called for an enhanced further leap forward by mobilizing 70 million workers to produce a targeted 22 million tons (20 million metric tonnes) of steel, a giant and unrealistic leap given that only an alleged 11 million tons (10 million metric tonnes) had been produced in 1958. As before, they produced useless clumps of cast iron.

Figure 9.3 The Great Leap Forward famine: backyard furnaces.
Source: Jacquet-Francillon/AFP/Getty Images.

Despite the transfer of peasants from the fields to small backyard furnaces (Figure 9.3), the farms produced a great harvest. As the abundant 1958 harvest came in, communal kitchens encouraged workers and their families to eat well. Slogans became substitutes for statistics. "Open your stomach, eat as much as you wish, and work hard for socialism."[49] Communal leaders seeking favorable responses from the central authorities increased deliveries to state granaries and greatly exaggerated the size of their communal harvests. Gorging on food left the granaries empty by the winter of 1958–59. Public policies in agriculture and in industry, driven by radical economic and ecological experimentation, played a central role in the famine. A driven communist leadership, inspired by a rigid interpretation of communist ideology and enforced by believers in the righteousness of Mao's ideas, created the conditions for this catastrophe. Natural causes, the drought that accompanied the Great Leap, played a contributing role.

The famine

Most historians and scientists regard this famine as the worst in human history, with an incalculable number of deaths. From 1958 to 1962, approximately 30 million premature deaths were caused by famine. At the same time, fertility plummeted, with the number of expected births dropping by 33 million. Taken as a total, the 30 million excess deaths and the 33 million lost to declines in fertility, the famine caused the largest in human history. By 1961, grain output had dropped by 25%.[50] China was unmistakably one of the world's poorest countries when Mao began his grand experiment. The Chinese gross national product (GDP) per person in 1950 was about one-fourth of the UK's GDP per person in 1820 and much less than the GDP per head of Irish citizens at the outbreak of the Irish potato famine. Given the abject poverty of most Chinese, especially those living in rural villages, grand experimentation of any kind was a precursor to calamity.[51]

Implemented soon after the communist victory in 1949, China's First Five-Year Plan sought to increase per capita daily food intake from 2,130 to 2,280 calories. The famine not only erased these gains; it caused per capita food energy to collapse. For China in 1960, per capita calorific intake fell to 1,500. Despite the suffering and the loss of life, the government's decision to export grain during 1959–60 to pay off its debts to the Soviet Union totaled almost 7 million tons (6.3 metric tonnes). They represented almost 22 trillion kilocalories and deprived 16 million Chinese of a diet of 2,000 calories for two years.[52] Statistics do not begin to describe the daily suffering of people caught in this gripping vise of hunger. Needing a daily diet of 2,100 calories to sustain them, the meager food available provided only a semblance of nutrition.

The unpredictability of the weather is also cited as a major factor, with one China expert claiming the following: "80% of their best agricultural area was damaged with everything – from rain, drought, pests. If you name it, they had it. They had all kinds of disasters."[53] Government officials alleged that drought in northern China in 1960 caused many of its rivers to dry up, while the Huang He (Yellow River) became so shallow that people could wade across it. The drought also brought infestations of locusts that destroyed crops.

In other regions of the country, the largest number of destructive typhoons in the last half-century decimated the wheat-producing countryside. In 1960, flooding and wheat stripe rust (a plant fungus that turns green leaf plants into brown, dry decaying stocks, and spreads rapidly during a cool, wet spring) crippled China's agricultural sector and caused the enormous grain losses experienced in 1960–61.

Acknowledging the presence of severe drought on the Loess Plateau and in northern China, the Irish economist Cormac Ó Gráda argued that, based on the meteorological evidence, severe weather events played a less conclusive role in causing the Great Leap Forward Famine. He noted that the 1960 drought was mild compared to those occurring in 1972 and 1997.

According to Ó Gráda, the famine struck with varying severity in 1959–61. Some provinces experienced unseasonably hot weather in July 1959, while others were wetter in August. Others experienced drought during July and August 1959. Two of China's central provinces, in particular, experienced excess deaths. They were the Sichuan province, with a fivefold increase in deaths, and Anhui, with a sixfold increase. Historically, both were centers of major famines in China. Three other central provinces, identified as the weakest economically and with the most fragile ecologies, included Guizhou, where deaths increased fourfold, and Henan and Qinghai, where death rates trebled. "In 1960, the excess death rates ranged from 4 per 1,000 in Liaoning to 35.4 per 1,000 in Guizhou."[54] Low GDP, per capita income, cited earlier, and sizable crop failures explain much of the excess mortality suffered by these Chinese provinces.[55]

National death rates reached 14, 25, and 14 per 1,000 for the famine years of 1959, 1960, and 1961 respectively, while the death rate for the years before the famine averaged 11 persons per 1,000. Fertility rates for women up to the age of 39 also dropped significantly during the famine years from 5.6 births per woman in the pre-famine years to a low of 3.06 in 1961. These data suggest that 33 million lost births as a result of this calamity is a reasonable estimate. Malnutrition and starvation proved to be the main culprits. In the post-famine years after 1961, fertility rebounded dramatically, to five births per woman. This rebound confirmed the presence of traditional Chinese values meaning "more children, more happiness." Despite a belief in the value of more children, pregnant women and their children suffered greatly during the famine years.

Exacerbating local conditions were the activities of government cadres convinced that peasants hoarded food. The following describes the experience of one survivor who lived in the famine-ravaged province of Anhui in the winter of 1959–60.

> The village cadres came to every household to search of food. They searched every street and every building. They took away everything they could find including several bags of carrots and the cotton we had saved to make new clothes. Our family had one jar of sweet potatoes that we had dried and ground up. When the cadres came, Second Aunt sat on the jar pretending to sew clothes and so they missed it. They searched every home for nine consecutive days. Later, we buried the jar underground but the cadres came and poked the ground with iron rods to see if we had buried anything. Then we hid it somewhere else. This went on until February. My legs and hands were swollen and I felt that at any moment I would die. Instead of walking to the fields to look for wild grass [to eat], I crawled and rolled to save energy. Several old women tried to get grass from ponds and rivers but because they had to stand in water their legs became infected.[56]

More than half of the villagers died, mostly between the beginning of 1960 and May. When people died, no one collected the bodies. After people died, their families would not report the death to the production team in order to continue to receive the dead person's food portions. Passive acceptance of their plight may have become the norm across the thousands of communes in China but examples of food riots and attacks on government granaries by starving peasant robber bands were not uncommon.

In a few instances peasants battled each other for food. The number of casualties stemming from these confrontations remains unknown, but observers who witnessed these attacks put the number in the thousands. One such battle between peasants from Hebei and Henan resulted in approximately 3,000 deaths. To protect these grain reserves, the government authorized the placement of armed local militia around facilities that were protected by barbed-wire fences.

Although verified evidence about injuries and deaths associated with attacks on these granaries is lacking, one eye-witness described an attack on a train that was guarded by soldiers with rifles and fixed bayonets. As peasants attacked the train, soldiers "trembled nervously" as the train was looted. In another instance, armed peasants attacked a train carrying grain and were fired upon by armed soldiers. "The station became a battlefield. People had to run away. How could the 'people's army' now shoot its own people? Later, it was said that the military garrison had itself been without food for three days."[57]

Despite sporadic food riots, the public posting of slogans on walls and meetings at universities criticized government policy. The great majority of the population, however, remained silent, intimidated by a ruthless system of surveillance that led to arrests, imprisonment, and death. They suffered in silence. Only a few were courageous enough to act out privately. In response to a slogan affixed to a bathroom wall in Hefei that read "Down with Tyrant Zeng, capture his demon wife alive!," an intense police investigation failed to reveal the name of its author.[58]

During the famine, overall grain yields dropped by 25%, wheat yields alone by 41%, oil-seed production, and a major source of fat in the Chinese diet, declined by 61%. Pigs, the major meat source, dropped from 146 million to 75 million in the four years of the famine. The number of draft animals, especially donkeys, was halved by 1961.[59] At the same time, the government hid the spread of hunger and starvation by expelling the Soviet Union's 1,500 technical advisors, curtailing foreign travel for all but its elite, banning internal travel, and closing off the flow of information in and out of the country.

Government response

A vast network of prisons and labor colonies became filled with dissidents. They rejected the reforms imposed by the Communist Party and criticized the government's failure to relieve the plight of the masses. The highly variable famine conditions in the countryside became uniform in the prison and labor colony systems. Mass starvation turned prisons into death camps.

As the above examples suggest, in China as well as in totalitarian regimes generally, dissent is prohibited. Those who do face imprisonment or a worse fate. Given Mao's suspicions, those who reported empty granaries were regarded as subversives. As he ordered a doubling of grain exports for the three famine years and cut imports, exports to the Soviet Union rose by 50% while free grain was delivered to struggling communist countries including North Korea, North Vietnam, and Albania.[60] In this way, Mao hoped to repay Soviet loans quickly and to prove to the world the success of communism. Although these farm exports amounted to only about 2% of production, they denied Chinese citizens of foodstuffs during a period of great need. When news of famine began to spread, Mao retreated to his study in 1960 and allegedly ate no meat for seven months, while his prime minister Chou En-lai cut his monthly grain consumption by seven kilos.

Relief efforts

The government's failure to act for three years turned a famine into a catastrophe. Mao could have ended it and could have prevented this disaster if food imports had become a priority and peasants were given the means to reinstitute private farm plots. Although the estimates of excess mortality remain controversial (since the government concealed and then denied the existence of the famine), 40 million deaths is the figure recorded in the *Guinness Book of Records*. However, "voluminous secret reports collated by Party committees in the last months of the Great Leap Forward" show the calamity of 45 million deaths.[61] Some reports hostile to the communist government put the figure at 50–60 million.[62] Thirty million deaths seem to be a number accepted by many researchers, with lost and postponed births representing a similar number, as mentioned above.[63]

As information about the spreading famine reached members of the Communist Party's hierarchy, corrective action with Mao's tacit consent took place. Some communal land was contracted out to peasant farmers while others received private plots of land for the purpose of increasing grain yields to 1957 levels. Throughout Anhui province, which was crippled by famine despite its fertile lands, returning the land to peasants saw grain production rise from 6 to 10 million tons (5.4–9 million metric tons) by the end of 1961. Despite this success, Mao tried to subvert efforts to extend these reforms to other provinces. In the meantime and while an internal power struggle was underway, local officials encouraged peasants to produce cash crops for sale in the cities and to encourage their relatives living in foreign countries to send them food parcels.

These successes did not deter Mao from re-exerting his control over the Communist Party hierarchy and apparatus. He condemned these reforms as "capitalist" and "anti-socialist," trying with all his power to marginalize Liu Shaoqi and Deng Xiaoping, the architects of these reforms. Recovery from the famine continued, while the struggle for the hearts and minds of Communist Party members accelerated. Village leaders faced the choice of following Mao's "ten points on agriculture" with the goal of reinstituting the communal system imposed as the centerpiece of the Great Leap Forward. The ten points refers to Mao's central government plan for agriculture, including a return to collective farms and segregated communal living, while reformers put forth a revised ten points that allowed for some private land holdings and a degree of competition.

Despite the successes of the reform group, Mao remained adamant in his support for the failed system of communal agriculture and unrelenting in his opposition to "anti-socialist, rightist" changes that he believed would ultimately bankrupt the communist system. Very few of Mao's opponents lived to challenge him.

The cultural revolution

The one major exception was Deng Xiaoping, who would rise to lead both the Communist Party and the Chinese government after Mao's death in 1976 to embrace capitalist economic principles while at the same time enforcing strict public policies. Before that happened, however, Mao regained absolute control of the government and the Party and launched the Cultural Revolution. Its goal was to impose a strict adherence to Maoist communist principles. It began with re-education campaigns using Mao's "Red Book" of sayings, led by fanatical youth Party members who worshiped him. They were committed to rooting out those who had betrayed the goals of the Great Leap Forward by sending them to rural communes to work in the fields and to study Mao's writings.

Additional millions of Chinese died at the hands of these young zealots called Red Guards who became Mao's private army equipped with armaments raided from Red Army depots located throughout the country. Mao's death in 1976 brought the Cultural Revolution to an abrupt end. The slow renewal of economic reforms began during Mao's declining years in the early 1970s and catapulted Deng Xiaoping to his new position as leader of the government and the Communist Party. His economic reforms, built on a system of state capitalism, eventually made China the world's second largest economy in the opening decades of the twenty-first century.

Conclusion

With a population of 660 million in 1958, the famine caused the death of almost 5% of China's population. Within the short span of two years, death rates doubled from 12 persons per 1,000 in 1958 to 25 per 1,000 in 1960, an astonishing and eye-popping figure. Even though the worst of the famine occurred in four provinces, these figures suggest the extent of humanity's vulnerability when agricultural production plummets.[64] Poor weather, the colossal failure known as the Great Leap Forward, and the wanton destruction of an incentive system in the private economy caused a sudden reversal in agriculture. Taking away farm tools and household pots, pans and woks, and forcing independent peasants into immense communes only added to the misery.

Research conducted on the lives of famine-born and famine-conceived individuals concluded that they suffered serious health and economic consequences. "In the absence of famine, individuals born in the year 1959 would have grown significantly taller, worked longer hours and earned much more income. These empirical findings strongly suggest that the tragedy in 1959–61 has a considerable sustained welfare impact on the survivors more than 30 years later."[65]

Using the 2000 Chinese Population Census, males were 9% more likely to be illiterate, 6% less likely to work if born during the famine years, and 6.5% less likely to be married if exposed to the famine *in utero*. Women were 7.5% more likely to be illiterate and 3% less likely to work and more likely to marry men with less education. Women and men exposed to the famine were 12% and 13%, respectively, more likely to be disabled than the greater population.[66]

Summary

The Nobel laureate in economics, Amartya Sen, has argued that such a closed system of communication can exist only in a totalitarian society. In a democratic society, opposition political parties and a free press would thwart government efforts to manipulate the news and compel it to "abandon its ongoing policies and meet the situation with swift public action."[67]

Misguided government policies exacerbated the plight of Irish famine victims. Work rule requirements for a weakened population weakened it further, causing death to many. Insisting on payment for a meager diet of soup and bread served no purpose. An ideological position, with no verifiable evidence, suggested that providing free food to the needy would cause food prices to rise and upset the fragile economic marketplace. As a result, delays in responding to the need for food caused undo hardship, as nutrition, starvation, and death followed. A famine caused by an adventurous pest from the natural world was made worse by the inaction of humans.

Human agency played a significant role in causing Dust Bowl conditions on the Great Plains. "The Great Plow Up" transformed a stable ecosystem into one made vulnerable to the wind. Unrelenting winds turned soil into dust and scattered it across the mid-western and eastern regions of the country. Government policies had encouraged movement to the Plains with free land and other appealing incentives. Now, in the light of the unfolding calamity, New Deal government policies attempted to end the damage to the land and alleviate the suffering of the drought's victims.

The Great Leap Forward famine differs in some major ways from all others. The famine was a man-made catastrophe made worse by the Chinese Communist Party juggernaut, that suppressed all opposition. The scale of the disaster separated it from all the famines that preceded it. In fact, its colossal number of casualties defies simple explanation.

According to Communist Party rhetoric, the Great Leap Forward in agriculture and industry would allow the People's Republic of China to catch up with the West and create a utopia in which individual rights and private property would disappear and be replaced by the new communist man and woman.[68]

The Great Leap Forward's war on nature delayed the country's attempts to recover. To fuel the misbegotten backyard furnaces to produce iron and steel required tons of wood from adjacent forests. Massive deforestation resulted, with once lush green flora becoming barren deserts. In cities where many of these makeshift furnaces existed, piles of corrugated iron waste covered the land and contaminated groundwater, making the water undrinkable. In rural China, hastily-built irrigation canals and earthen dams to increase the productivity of the land failed to withstand the ravages of nature as floodwaters caused by periodic typhoons overwhelmed these recently completed projects. Further weakening an already fragile ecology, the Great Leap's overuse of pesticides unintentionally poisoned the land. Its wilful policy of slaughtering sparrows that ate grain stocks, however, led to long-term ecological costs that would burden the country long after Mao's death. Although food production began to increase in the years immediately following the famine, the long-term ecological and human costs would continue to burden the country.

Notes

1 Donald Worster (1976), "Grass to dust: the Great Plains in the 1930s," *Environmental Review*, 1(3), 3.

2 Mark Hertsgaard (2010), *Hot: Living Through the Next Fifty Years on Earth* (Boston, MA: Houghton Mifflin Harcourt).

3 Cecil Woodham-Smith (1962), *The Great Hunger: Ireland 1845–1849* (New York: Harper & Row), 158.

4 Thomas Robert Malthus (1970), *Essay on the Principle of Population* (London: Harmondsworth), 118–119.

5 P. M. Austin Bourke (1968), "The use of the potato crop in pre-famine Ireland," *Journal of the Statistical and Social Inquiry Society of Ireland*, 12(6), 76.

6 Evan D. G. Fraser (2003), "Social vulnerability and ecological fragility: building bridges between social and natural sciences using the Irish potato famine as a case study," *Conservation Ecology*, 7(2), 2. At www.consecol.org/vol7/iss2/art9/.

7 Alfred W. Crosby Jr. (1972), *The Columbian Exchange: Biological and Cultural Consequences of 1492* (Westport, CT: Greenwood Press).

8 Cormac Ó Gráda (1995), *The Great Irish Famine* (Cambridge, UK: Cambridge University Press), 30.

9 James H. Johnson (1990), "The context of migration: the example of Ireland in the nineteenth century," *Transactions of the Institute of British Geographers*, 15(3), 276.

10 Phelim P. Boyle and Cormac Ó Gráda (1986), "Fertility trends, excess mortality, and the Great Irish Famine," *Demography*, 23(4), 555–556.

11 Eric Vanhaute, Richard Paping, and Cormac Ó Gráda (2006), "The European subsistence crisis of 1845–1850: a comparative perspective," University College Dublin Center for Economic Research, Working Paper Series, October, 10.

12 Glenn Garelik (2002), "Taking the bite out of potato blight," *Science*, 298(5599), 1702.

13 Cormac Ó Gráda (1999), *Black '47 and Beyond: The Great Irish Famine in History, Economy, and Memory* (Princeton, NJ: Princeton University Press), 36.

14 James H. Johnson (1990), *The Context of Migration: The Example of Ireland in the Nineteenth Century* (Cambridge, MA: MIT Press), 265–266.

15 Cecil Woodham-Smith (1991), *The Great Hunger: Ireland 1845–1849* (New York: Penguin Putnam), 285.

16 Cormac Ó Gráda (1995), *The Great Irish Famine* (the cover).

17 Cormac Ó Gráda (1999), *Black '47 and Beyond: The Great Irish Famine in History, Economy, and Memory*, 6.

18 Cecil Woodham-Smith (1991), *The Great Hunger: Ireland 1845–1849*, 165.

19 Ibid., 162.

20 Cormac Ó Gráda (1999), *Black '47 and Beyond*, 82.

21 T. H. Marmion in the *Cork Constitution*, December 17, 1846 and quoted in Cormac Ó Gráda, *Black '47 and Beyond*, 68.

22 Ibid.

23 Ibid., 228.

24 Ibid., 121.

25 Eric Vanhaute, Richard Paping, and Cormac Ó Gráda (2006), "The European subsistence crisis of 1845–1850: a comparative perspective," 13.

26 Cormac Ó Gráda (1999), *Black '47 and Beyond*, 228.

27 Timothy Egan (2006), *The Worst Hard Times: The Untold Story of Those Who Survived the Great American Dust Bowl* (Boston, MA: Houghton Mifflin), 278.

28 Edward R. Cook, Connie A. Woodhouse, C. Mark Eakin, Savid M. Meko, et al. (2004), "Long-term aridity changes in the Western United States," *Science*, 306(5698), 1015–1018.

29 Siegfried D. Schubert, Max J. Suarez, Phillip J. Pegion, Randal D. Koster, et al. (2004), "On the cause of the 1930s Dust Bowl," *Science*, 303(5665), 1859.

30 Vernon Carstensen (1999), "*The Plow That Broke the Plains:* film legacy of the Great Plains," in John R. Wunder, Frances W. Kaye and Vernon Carstensen (eds.), *Americans View Their Dust Bowl Experience* (Niwot, CO: University of Colorado Press), 305.

31 Sarah T. Phillips (1999), "Lessons from the Dust Bowl: dryland agriculture and soil erosion in the United States and South Africa, 1900–1950," *Environmental History*, 4(2), 246.

32 Ibid., 255–256.

33 Donald Worster (1999), "The dirty thirties: a study in agricultural capitalism," in Wunder et al. (eds.), *Americans View Their Dust Bowl Experience*, 355.

34 Charles J. Shindo (2000), "The Dust Bowl myth," *The Wilson Quarterly*, 24(4), 30.

35 Langston Hughes (1941), "Dust Bowl," *Poetry*, 58(2), 72.

36 R. Douglas Hurt (1981), *The Dust Bowl: An Agricultural and Social History* (Chicago: Nelson-Hall Inc.), 3.

37 Donald Worster (2009), "Grass to dust: the Great Plains in the 1930s," *Environmental Review*, 1(3), 3.

38 R. Douglas Hurt (1981), *The Dust Bowl*, 37.

39 Ibid., 46.

40 Ibid., 58.

41 Timothy Egan (2006), *The Worst Hard Times*, 115.

42 Donald Worster (2009), "Grass to dust," 6.

43 Vernon Carstensen (1999), "*The Plow That Broke the Plains*," 310.

44 Sarah T. Phillips (1999) "Lessons from the Dust Bowl," 256–257.

45 R. Douglas Hurt (1981), *The Dust Bowl*, 95.

46 Donald Worster (1979), *Dust Bowl: The Southern Plains in the 1930s* (New York: Oxford University Press), 5.

47 Jasper Becker (1996), *Hungry Ghosts: Mao's Secret Famine* (New York: The Free Press), 205.

48 Ibid., 105.

49 Gene Hsin Chang and Guanzhong James Wen (1997), "Communal dining and the Chinese famine of 1958–1961," *Economic Development and Cultural Change*, 46(1), 4.
50 Basil Ashton, Kenneth Hill, Alan Piazza, and Robin Zeitz (1984), "Famine in China, 1958–1961," *Population and Development Review*, 10(4), 614.
51 Jasper Becker (1996), *Hungry Ghosts*, 244.
52 Basil Ashton et al., "Famine in China, 1958–1961," 622–623, 629.
53 Ibid., 248.
54 Yuyu Chen and Li-An Zhou (2007), "The long-term health and economic consequences of the 1959–1961 famine in China," *Journal of Health Economics*, 26, 663.
55 Basil Ashton, "Famine in China, 1958–1961," 250–254.
56 Jasper Becker (1996), *Hungry Ghosts*, 135–137.
57 Ibid., 154–155.
58 Ibid., 157.
59 From Frederick W. Crook (ed.) (1996), *Agricultural Statistics of the People's Republic of China, 1949–1986*, in Jasper Becker, *Hungry Ghosts*, 248.
60 Ibid., 81.
61 Frank Dikotter (2010), *Mao's Great Famine: The History of China's Most Devastating Catastrophe, 1958–1962* (New York: Walker & Co.), x.
62 Cormac Ó Gráda (2009) *Famine: A Short History* (Princeton, NJ: Princeton University Press), 95.
63 Judith Banister (1987), *China's Changing Population* (Palo Alto, CA: Stanford University Press).
64 James Kai-sing Kung and Justin Yifu Lin (2003), "The causes of China's Great Leap famine, 1959–1961," *Economic Development and Cultural Change*, 52(1), 5.
65 Yuyu Chen and Li-An Zhou (2007), "The long-term health and economic consequences of the 1959–1961 famine in China," 679.
66 Douglas Almond, Lena Edlund, Hongbin Li, and Junsen Zhang (2007), *Long-Term Effects of the 1959–1961 China Famine: Mainland China and Hong Kong*, Working paper 13384, 3–4, 15. At www.nber.org/papers/w133384.
67 Amartya Sen (1983), "Development: which way now?" *Economic Journal*, 93, 758–759.
68 Xinzheng Shi (2011), "Famine, fertility, and fortune in China," *China Economic Review*, 22(2), 244–259.

Further Reading

Frank Dikötter (2011), *Mao's Great Famine: The History of China's Most Devastating Catastrophe, 1958–1962* (New York: Walker & Co).

A detailed chronicle of a seminal event in Chinese history never before fully documented.

Thomas Keneally (2011), *Three Famines: Starvation and Politics* (New York: Public Affairs).

The author examines the sustained widespread hunger that was the result of government neglect and individual culpability.

Stephan Haggard, Marcus Noland and Amartya Sen (2009), *Famine in North Korea: Markets, Aid, and Reform* (New York: Columbia University Press).

This book reveals the state's role in this tragic event; it is especially critical in the light of the current power transition in North Korea.

Alex de Waal (2009), *Famine Crimes: Politics and the Disaster Relief Industry in Africa* (Bloomington, IN: Indiana University Press).

This book critiques the role of international humanitarian agencies that dominate famine relief in Africa.

Robert Conquest (1987), *The Harvest of Sorrow: Soviet Collectivization and the Terror-Famine* (New York: Oxford University Press).

This book is a study of those who died as a result of the Soviet Union's policies, focusing on a dark side of the twentieth century's history.

Chapter 10

Meteorite Impacts

The first sign of the threat was no more than a speck on a star-streaked telescope image. David Tholen was scanning for asteroids in an astronomical blind spot: right inside Earth's orbit, where the sun's glare can overwhelm telescopes. Tholen, an astronomer from the University of Hawaii, knew that objects lurking there could sometimes veer toward Earth. As he [and colleagues Bernardi and Tucker] stared at a computer, three shots of the same swath of sky, made a few minutes apart, cycled onto the screen. "Here's your guy," said Tucker, pointing at a clump of white pixels that moved from frame to frame. Tholen reported the sighting to the International Astronomical Union's Minor Planet Center, a clearinghouse for data on asteroids and comets. He and Tucker hoped to take another look later that week, but they were rained out, and then the asteroid disappeared from view. When astronomers got a fix on it again that December, they realized they had a problem. The rock, bigger than a sports arena, tumbles menacingly close to our planet every few years. As observations streamed into the Minor Planet Center, the meteor, named Apophis after the Egyptian god of evil, looked increasingly sinister. "The impact hazard kept getting higher and higher," says Tholen. By Christmas, models predicted 1-in-40 odds that Apophis would smash into Earth on April 13, 2029, and a ripple of alarm spread to the public. "One colleague called it the Grinch that stole Christmas."[1]

Introduction

The race to destroy an asteroid before it collides with Earth remains a priority for earth scientists and the citizens who depend on them, since an

---

Natural Disasters in a Global Environment, First Edition. Anthony N. Penna and Jennifer S. Rivers.

extraterrestrial impact could wipe out life on Earth. The threat of such collisions has become the plot of countless science fiction movies and not surprisingly these successful blockbuster films remind us of the growing public awareness of a potential meteorite impact. Although Earth has not recently experienced an extreme impact event that would leave the planet's inhabitants defenseless, the probability of such an event rises with each passing decade. Some scientists believe that they have identified the more dangerous meteorites in our solar system, while others remain skeptical.

Meteorites are extraterrestrial (ET) objects that strike the surface of Earth, while a meteoroid is matter that has not yet hit Earth. Meteoroids travel through space at speeds of 50–60 mi per second (mi/s) (100 km/s) due to the lack of atmosphere in space. When meteoroids encounter Earth's gravity, however, the planet pulls them into its atmosphere. Earth's atmosphere, with its thick blanket of gases, causes a friction that slows the meteoroid's velocity. This slowing of the object causes the motion energy to change to heat energy as the meteorite ionizes. If the object is small enough it will burn up completely in the atmosphere, and if it is not, it will strike Earth.

In 1794, the French chemist Antoine Lavoisier investigated an impact event, and after careful chemical analysis of a meteorite fragment, he reported the object was just an ordinary Earth rock that had been struck by lightning. He came to this conclusion because in his words, "A stone cannot fall from the sky – there are no stones in the sky."

Lavoisier's "ordinary Earth rock" turned out to be of extraterrestrial origin, however. Lavoisier's attitude was not unusual. Although unexplained objects streak through the sky regularly, the scientific community did not widely accept the extraterrestrial origin of these objects until the middle of the nineteenth century.[2]

Between 1794 and 1803, many people in Italy, France, and England witnessed falling extraterrestrial objects. Finally, in 1803, between 2,000 and 3,000 specimens were found following a meteor shower in L'Aigle, France. Their existence offered irrefutable proof that the fragments were of extraterrestrial origin. The history of official meteorite investigation in the USA began on December 14, 1807 when a bright fireball was seen streaking southwards across the sky of western New England. As local newspapers reported, eyewitnesses heard three loud explosions before the meteorite fragments fell to Earth in at least six different locations around the town of Weston, Connecticut. Two Yale professors journeyed to Weston to investigate further: Professors Benjamin Silliman and James Kingsley interviewed several eyewitnesses, visited impact sites and recovered meteorite fragments. They postulated that some meteorites must have weighed 200 lb (91 kg) before being pulverized by impact. The professors published a detailed description of the event, including chemical analysis by Silliman, one of the first analyses of a meteorite ever recorded.[3] Their research led to the founding of meteoritics as new field of study in the USA.

This chapter focuses on three major case studies. The first was a colossal meteorite strike that signaled the end of the age of dinosaurs 65 million years ago and graphically illustrates what happens when a meteorite strikes Earth. The second case examines controversial new evidence that a comet strike in North America may have contributed to the disappearance of the Clovis culture nine thousand years ago. Lastly, eyewitness accounts detail the largest impact event in the twentieth century, located in Tunguska, Siberia (Russia).

We include information on modern meteorite research that hypothesizes about the probability of future extraterrestrial objects colliding with, and possibly destroying, Earth. We begin with a discussion of meteor craters on Earth's moon as well as a colossal impact from prehistory that created Earth's moon. Though the discussion of Earth's moon does not qualify as a natural disaster, as no one was killed, this event is important in that it illustrates the frequent nature of meteorite impacts.

The Creation of Earth's Moon and the Origins of Meteorites

With no atmosphere on the moon, its most prominent characteristic is its pock-marked surface of craters. In fact, craters overlay other craters, which makes it difficult, if not impossible, to find a surface on the moon that remains free of meteorite impacts. Since Earth's atmosphere burns up many meteorites before they make impact and its surface consists of 70% water, few impact craters exist on the planet's surface. Also, Earth's hydrologic and tectonic cycles result in weathering and subduction.

If an impact site occurs at a high elevation, weathering rapidly erodes the depression. If the crater is located at a lower elevation, over time weathering and/or sediment will bury it. Convection cells creating the movement of tectonic plates cause Earth's crust to subduct and be continually recycled. This makes it impossible to find ancient meteorite impacts, some of which may be billions of years old. Where impact craters remain visible on Earth's surface, the impact was likely very large, recent, or located in a stable geologic area.

Of the meteorite impacts Earth has endured, perhaps the most significant caused the formation of our moon.[4] Theories about the moon's origin vary considerably, but one is widely accepted by scientists. It posits that in the early stages of its accretion, a large meteorite struck Earth a glancing blow. Its force dislodged a piece of the Earth's crust and liquefied it. Unable to escape Earth's gravity, it solidified and orbited the planet, becoming our moon.[5]

The asteroid belt in our solar system, located between Mars and Jupiter, is essentially the remains of a failed planet. During the process of planetary accretion that began 4.6 billion years ago, the asteroid belt consisting of millions of asteroids failed to amalgamate into planets. Though these asteroids move within the Sun's equatorial plane (or have a similar orbit as the planets), it is possible for a comet or other extraterrestrial body to knock an asteroid out of its orbit. Thus there exists the potential for a large-sized object similar to the meteorite that hit Earth and created the moon to strike Earth again and extinguish life on our planet.

Meteorite strikes may result in positive outcomes, however. If a meteorite had not smashed into Earth and created the moon, Christian and Chinese calendars would be different, since they are based on the phases of the moon. Also, eclipses contributed to our understanding of Earth as spherical rather than flat. The gravitational pull on the Earth from the moon creates tides and slows the Earth's rotation by approximately 14 hours. This rapid rate of spin would increase the force of wind, would have altered the evolution of more fragile forms of life, and would have made storms much more violent.

The Yucatán Chicxulub Crater, Mexico (65 MYA)

> *Life is a huge blackboard filled with a million marks of chalk. Every thirty million years that chalkboard is forcefully wiped clean, leaving only a few small smudges in the corners.*[6]

Introduction

Why did most non-avian dinosaurs mysteriously disappear from our planet about 65 million years ago? Initially, many scientists believed that an ice age caused their extinction. In the absence of confirming evidence, however, a number of other explanations were put forth. Writers with varying degrees of competence suggested that dinosaurs disappeared because the climate deteriorated. Suddenly or slowly, the climate became too hot or too cold, too dry or too wet. The dinosaurs' diet changed with either too much or too little food or from poisons in water or plants or ingested minerals that caused the loss of calcium or other necessary nutritional elements. Others suggested that disease, parasites, anatomical disorders such as slipped vertebral discs, or metabolic disorders such as the imbalance of hormone and endocrine systems caused declining brain function.

Other explanations included evolutionary drift into senescent overspecialization, changes in the pressure or composition of the atmosphere, excessive oxygen from plants, gene pool drainage by little mammalian egg-eaters, overkill capacity by predators, cosmic radiation, and a shift of Earth's rotational poles, floods, and continental drift.

Tracing the evidence

However, with little evidence to support these hypotheses, geologists studying Earth's history formulated another theory. Since sedimentary rocks record much of the history of Earth, an ice age answer would suggest that the dinosaurs died slowly over a period of thousands, even millions of years, yet scientists examining the fossilized evidence in the sedimentary rock record suggested that dinosaurs died off quickly.

In 1978 the experimental physicist Luis Alvarez and his geologist son Walter first linked the extinction of non-avian dinosaurs to an extraterrestrial impact event when they discovered a centimeter-thick layer of clay in sedimentary rock dated to the Cretaceous–Tertiary (K–T) boundary, 65 million years ago. This clay layer, which coincided with the disappearance of the dinosaurs, contained iridium, a rare Earth element commonly found in meteorites. They determined that the high levels of iridium found in their samples could only be explained by a major impact event. They postulated that a giant extraterrestrial meteorite struck Earth and pulverized on impact. Its dust cloud created from the ejecta encircled the globe, blocked out the sun, and caused the collapse of photosynthesis.

They also found high concentrations of tektites; glass rocks that form when silicate minerals are exposed to extreme heat and pressure caused by an extraterrestrial impact. A layer of soot in the rock provided further evidence that 65 million years ago a giant fireball ripped through the atmosphere on a path to Earth and ignited everything. Further studies of Cretaceous–Tertiary boundary clays, taken from five sites in Europe and New Zealand, contained highly enriched elemental carbon, which proved to be isotopically uniform and the product of soot from a single global fire, a fire triggered by a meteorite impact that began before the ejecta had settled back to Earth.[7]

Further sedimentary deposits resulting from a mega-tsunami that was several thousand feet high, caused by this impact event, were found throughout the Atlantic Ocean up into Alabama and in the Gulf of Mexico.[8] When assembled, these lines of evidence supported the Alvarez hypothesis that the instantaneous dying-off of the dinosaurs was due to a massive impact from space causing one of the three largest mass extinctions in the past 500 million years. This theory hinged on the existence of a crater large enough to suggest such a massive impact.[9]

Though the search for this key piece of evidence occupied many of the world's leading geologists, geophysicist Glen Penfield discovered the crater by accident while attempting to locate oil-trapping geologic features. Examining magnetic survey data recorded off the coast of the Yucatán Peninsula in Mexico, Penfield found a massive, perfectly symmetrical semicircle that spanned 40 mi (65 km). Probing further in the area, he discovered the mirror image of his original semicircle, the other side of a full circle resembling a crater.

However, Penfield was not the first geophysicist to stumble across the crater. In 1966, Robert Baltosser, conducting analysis for another oil company, began to suspect that data anomalies on a gravity map signified the presence of an impact crater. Unfortunately, the company for whom Baltosser worked would not allow him to share his findings with the scientific community.[10] Though the company that employed Penfield also barred him from publishing the results of his field study, it permitted him to give an oral presentation at a national meeting of geophysicists.

Simultaneous with these discoveries, in 1981, Alan Hildebrand and William Boynton, using a myriad of data, suggested that an impact occurred somewhere near the Caribbean, but could not locate the actual crater. The story of the Chicxulub crater did not become public until nearly 10 years later in 1991, when Hildebrand and Penfield joined forces after learning of each other's research through a reporter.[11] Due to the efforts of Luis and Walter Alvarez, Penfield, Baltosser, Hildebrand, and

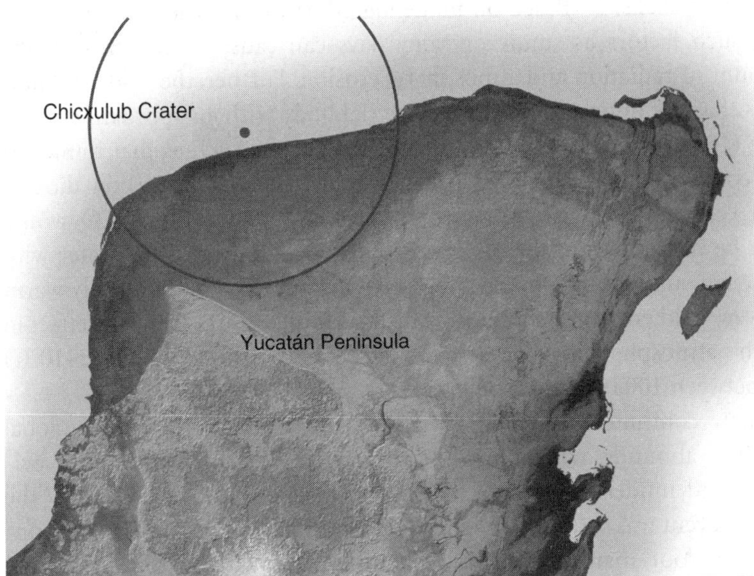

Figure 10.1 The Yucatán Chicxulub crater.
Source: Adapted from Wikimedia Commons, the free media repository.

Boynton, most scientists now agree that a meteorite 6-mi (9.6 km) across slammed into Earth roughly 65 million years ago, creating a crater 100-mi (160 km) across, and caused the sudden extinction of the dinosaurs.[12]

In 2007, a team led by Bill Bottke of the Department of Space Studies at Southwest Research Institute in Boulder, Colorado, identified the probable cause of the Chicxulub impact, a collision between an asteroid named Baptisina orbiting between Mars and Jupiter and a smaller, unnamed asteroid. Computer models indicate that the resulting impact sent a 6.2-mile-wide (10 km) asteroid hurling towards Earth that struck the Yucatán Peninsula (Figure 10.1).[13]

Though there exists substantial evidence linking this meteorite impact to the extinction of the dinosaurs, the true mechanism behind the mass dinosaur die-off still puzzles scientists.[14] Some believe that the resulting nuclear winter may have lasted for as long as 2,000 years. Others blamed acid rain found in the geochemical signature for the extinctions. Normally immobile acid elements such as mercury (Hg) leached into sediments and carbonate shells.[15,16] Based on modeling efforts, some scientists suggested that such factors as sunny or rainy days can cause a difference in the amount of radiation and atmospheric erosion. Further, the evidence indicates that the impact of an extraterrestrial body with an approximate 6.2-mile (10 km) radius onto a carbonate-rich terrain, such as that found off the coast of the Yucatán Peninsula, would increase the carbon dioxide (CO_2) content of the atmosphere by a factor of 2–10. Additional CO_2 would then be released from the ocean's photic zone, an area of the water with sufficient sunlight for photosynthesis.[17] This release would not only warm the very cold environment but would also amplify the greenhouse effect in Earth's atmosphere and increase the temperature from 35–52°F (2–10°C) for between 100,000 and a million years.

Many continue to work in this field, and further evidence of global wildfires abounds, with much controversy.[18,19] Some scientists cited evidence and models suggesting that the thermal radiation released by the impact event was sufficient to ignite local wildfires.[20,21] Regarding the abundance of soot, many scientists rejected the theory that wildfires occurred on a global scale, citing minimal amounts of charred plant remains and abundant uncharred material.[22,23] Plants that went extinct were animal-pollinated flowering plants, while understory vegetation survived the destruction.[24] Scientists speculated that as ash from the impact fell back to Earth, it might have blocked the heat emitted by the later-arriving materials. This self-shielding may have prevented widespread wildfire ignition, although the spike in temperature may have been sufficient to ignite localized fires that killed fauna which lacked temporary shelter.[25]

Conclusion

Based on the discovery that birds are a type of dinosaur, some scientists dispute the claim of a mass extinction. Many groups of animals became extinct, including non-avian dinosaurs, some types of birds and mollusks, and many mammals. In addition, paleontologists discovered the remains of non-avian dinosaurs above the rock record coinciding with the Chicxulub impact. Most scientists dismissed the idea that these dinosaurs survived the impact event, believing that the specimens were reburied in later sediments after washing out of their original locations. Most agree, however, that this first documented large meteorite strike demonstrated that extraterrestrial impact events could significantly affect both the geological and biological evolution of our planet through mass extinction.[26]

The Clovis Extinction (12,500–12,900 BP)

Introduction

Archeologists and paleo-anthropologists agree that the Clovis people flourished in North and South America between 11,000–10,800 Radio Carbon Years Before the Present (RCYBP) (which translates to roughly 12,500–12,900 calendar years Before the Present, BP). Several opposing theories now exist regarding their origin, the route they followed to the Americas from Asia, and their disappearance. Archeologists named them the Clovis people after discovering evidence of their culture at an archeological site in the 1930s near Clovis, New Mexico. Among the artifacts found at the site, now officially known as Blackwater Draw Locality 1, were distinctive fluted Clovis spearheads, discovered along with animal remains. These artifacts confirmed that the Clovis people hunted big game animals such as mammoths, mastodons, bison, camels, saber-toothed cats, and other large mammals.

Between 12,800 and 11,500 years BP, there was a rapid return to glacial conditions in the northern hemisphere that dramatically interrupted the warming transition from the last ice age. Ice core data samples from Greenland and fossil evidence from different sites in the higher latitudes indicate a sudden 45°F (7°C) to 59°F (15°C) drop in temperature over a period of less than 20 years. This onset of a period called the Younger Dryas (named for an Arctic flower) profoundly affected Earth's flora and fauna. This sudden plunge in temperatures radically altered photosynthesis, habitat, growing and reproduction seasons, and diet. During this period, a variety of megafauna, including those hunted by the Clovis people, became extinct across North America.

That the abrupt disappearance of the Clovis culture coincided with the Younger Dryas period has led several climatologists to suggest a link between the loss of megafauna and the Clovis culture. Although this connection remains hypothetical, several theories suggest that the Clovis people and their prey vanished mysteriously. Climate change, overhunting, and the spread of disease are among the most frequently suggested causes but recent evidence gathered in several different fields of study support an extraterrestrial impact hypothesis.

Since 2001, scientist Richard Firestone and archeologist William Topping have searched for evidence that an extraterrestrial impact over North America triggered the sudden drop in temperature during the Younger

Dryas. They posit that this impact event ignited widespread wildfires leading to the extinction of North American megafauna and the disappearance of the Clovis people. Firestone assembled a 26-member team from 16 institutions to investigate the possibility that an extraterrestrial impact caused the Younger Dryas extinction. In 2007, this team made a formal presentation to the American Geophysical Union and published their findings in *Proceedings of the National Academy of Sciences*, in which they proposed "...that one or more large, low-density ET objects exploded over northern North America, partially destabilizing the Laurentide Ice Sheet and triggering Younger Dryas cooling. The shock wave, thermal pulse, and event-related environmental effects (e.g. extensive biomass burning and food limitations) contributed to end-Pleistocene megafaunal extinctions and adaptive shifts among PaleoAmericans in North America."[27]

The article cited evidence collected from several Clovis-era sites. Firestone and his team described detailed evidence of an impact event found in the charred organic-rich layer of peaty soil. Commonly referred to as "black mats," these thick and deep wetland areas flourish in moist to wet conditions, associated with the refilling of these organic areas with water during deglaciation. The largest distribution of black mats date from between 12,800 and 11,500 BP, suggesting that they may have formed in response to the Younger Dryas. Beneath this layer, but not within or below the black mats, Firestone's team found the remains of extinct megafauna and Clovis tools. Also, they discovered that a thin layer located immediately beneath the black mats contained remnants of a extraterrestrial object and evidence of resulting wildfires including high levels of iridium, nanodiamonds, magnetic microspherules (tiny spheres of extraterrestrial material), charcoal, soot, and extraterrestrial helium.

At each site, Firestone's team found nanodiamonds located only in the rock record correlating to the date of the Younger Dryas impact event. They found no nanodiamonds above or below this layer. Nanodiamonds are tiny carbon spherules created when molten carbon atoms cool rapidly in a hexagonal pattern instead of the usual cubic structure. They are only produced under high-temperature, high-pressure conditions associated with an extraterrestrial impact. Only found on Earth in meteorites, these nanodiamonds contain a rare Earth isotope helium-3, commonly found in extraterrestrial objects. Additional evidence of the impact included: titan magnetic microspherules; carbon spherules; magnetic grains; iridium; and nickel. The team found high levels of chemicals associated with wildfires including soot, charcoal, and polycyclic aromatic hydrocarbons (fused aromatic rings found in comets and meteorites) in Younger Dryas period soil samples taken by the team at three different Clovis sites.

Firestone insisted that, taken together, these findings proved that a meteor explosion or extraterrestrial impact sparked catastrophic fires over much of North America, prompting the Younger Dryas. Despite these findings, many scientists remain skeptical of the Younger Dryas Impact Theory, rejecting much of the evidence found by Firestone's group. More recent studies by other researchers, including separate teams led by archeologist C. Vance Haynes, Jr. and paleobotanist Andrew C. Scott, suggest alternative terrestrial explanations for the evidence presented by Firestone.

Haynes's team failed to find iridium in samples collected at the Murray Springs Clovis site. They argued that magnetic microspherules and magnetic grains found at the site are consistent with common cosmic dust unrelated to an impact event. Haynes and his co-authors believe that the chemical by-products presented by Firestone as evidence of massive wildfires are more consistent with smaller Clovis hearth fires.[28] Questions remain regarding the nanodiamonds found by Firestone's group. Scott's team found no nanodiamonds, concluding that Firestone has mis-identified graphite-containing compounds.[29] Scott and his fellow researchers identified the carbon spheres, carbon cylinders, and charcoal pieces described by Firestone as charred biomass created by the massive global wildfires as balls of plant and fungal material, fecal pellets from insects, and wood burned in localized wildfires.[30]

Unlike the conclusive linking of the Cretaceous impact with its identifiable crater, finding the Younger Dryas impact crater remains elusive. Some scientists, who believe that an extraterrestrial impact launched the Younger Dryas, posit that the crater may never be found because it may not exist. They postulate that a meteor or comet exploded into pieces over the Laurentide ice shield, a massive sheet of ice covering much of North America. These cosmic pieces may have left craters in this nearly 2-mile-thick (3.2 km) ice sheet that melted soon after impact.

Extraterrestrial debris levels are highest at the Gainey archeological site in Michigan and decrease as one moves away from this area, leading researchers to believe the extraterrestrial object exploded over the Hudson Bay region of Canada. Firestone's team found anomalies in the Great Lakes and Hudson Bay and suggested that this impact event could create craters. Chemist Wendy Wolbach of DePaul University in Chicago detected by-products of the intense wildfires in sediment taken from the Carolina Bays, thousands of oval depressions along the Atlantic coast oriented towards the Great Lakes region. Firestone team member Allen West believes tornado-like winds caused by the impact created these craters.

Conclusion

Firestone's impact theory would benefit from conclusive evidence of an impact crater. Seven of Firestone's original twelve lines of evidence have yet to be reproduced and support has waned for the Younger Dryas impact theory. Currently, the end-Cretaceous extinction of non-avian dinosaurs remains as the only extinction event that the majority of the scientific community accepts as linked to a extraterrestrial impact. However, many scientists are not entirely ready to rule out a cosmic impact as the cause of other massive die-offs. Firestone's detractors agree that something drastic occurred to trigger the Younger Dryas cooling period and bring about the disappearance of megafauna and the Clovis culture, but they do not accept the impact theory.

The Tunguska (Siberia) Event (1908)

> The sky split in two and fire appeared high and wide over the forest. The split in the sky grew larger, and the entire northern side was covered with fire. At that moment it became so hot that I couldn't bear it, as if my shirt was on fire; from the northern side, where the fire was, came strong heat. I wanted to tear off my shirt and throw it down, but then the sky shut closed, and a strong thump sounded, and I was thrown a few meters. I lost my senses for a moment, but then my wife ran out and led me to the house. After that such noise came, as if rocks were falling or cannons were firing, the Earth shook, and when I was on the ground, I pressed my head down, fearing rocks would smash it. When the sky opened up, hot wind raced between the houses, like from cannons, which left traces in the ground like pathways, and it damaged some crops. Later we saw that many windows were shattered, and in the barn a part of the iron lock snapped.[31]

Introduction

As the only large-impact event witnessed in recent history, the Tunguska event holds special significance for those who study near-Earth objects (NEOs). Interviews with eyewitnesses provided valuable information to researchers looking to unlock the mysteries of space. On the morning of June 30, 1908, people in remote Central Siberia observed a blinding bluish light streaking across the sky, followed by a loud explosion that knocked some of them off their feet.

Witnesses reported what felt like an earthquake and sounded like artillery fire. The following account is a sample of their recollections.

> On the 17th of June, around 9 a.m., we observed an unusual natural occurrence. In the north Karelinski village, the peasants saw to the northwest, rather high above the horizon, some strangely bright bluish-white heavenly body, which for 10 minutes moved downwards. The body appeared as a pipe (i.e. cylindrical). The sky was cloudless; only a small dark cloud was observed in the general direction of the bright body. It was hot and dry. As the body neared the ground (forest), the bright body seemed to smudge, and then turned into a giant billow of black smoke, and a loud knocking (not thunder) was heard, as if large stones were falling, or artillery was fired. All buildings shook. At the same time the cloud began emitting flames of uncertain shapes. All villagers were stricken with panic and took to the streets, and women cried, thinking it was the end of the world.

Size, type, and impact

Although scientists offered conflicting explanations as to the size and type of this object, they agreed it entered the atmosphere just after 7 a.m. and exploded before it reached the ground. This object, traveling at speeds close to 33,500 mph (54,000 km/h), heated the air around it to temperatures as high as 44,500°F (24,700°C) and ignited fires on the ground. The extreme heat caused water to vaporize instantly and enter the atmosphere. Noctilucent (which roughly translates from Latin and means "luminous at night") clouds, Earth's highest clouds, located at an altitude of approximately 47–53 mi (76–85 km), soon formed ice crystals, collecting soot created by the wildfires.

Eyewitnesses say the sky shined brightly for many nights as a result of these noctilucent clouds, and people as far away as London in the UK reported being able to read the newspaper by the light of the night sky. This powerful above-ground explosion propelled seismic waves across the land at the speed of sound, registering on barometric gauges across Europe and Asia. Estimates regarding the power of the explosion vary, but researchers

Figure 10.2 Fallen trees caused by the Tunguska event.
Source: Ria Novosti/Science Photo Library.

agree it was at least 3 to 5 megatons of TNT equivalent energy release (or 300 times the bomb dropped on Hiroshima, Japan, during World War II).

Drastic political changes occurring in Russia, including World War I (1914–18), Russia's withdrawal from the war (1917) and the Russian Revolution (1918), which eventually led to the creation of the Union of Soviet Socialist Republics (USSR), delayed the investigation of the Tunguska event for almost 20 years. Leonid Kulik, a Russian mineralogist, conducted the first official study of the Tunguska event in 1927. His team found millions of scorched and flattened trees radiating hundreds of kilometers from the epicenter (Figure 10.2). His many expeditions established that the Tunguska event leveled 830 mi^2 (2,150 km^2) of forest. However, he found no evidence of an impact crater or fragments of the meteor.

Chemical analysis of the area's peat bog layers uncovered highly enriched iridium. Soil and felled trees also contained metals and elements rare to Earth, but commonly associated with objects of extraterrestrial origin.[32] Modeling by Princeton astro-biologist, Christopher Chyba, demonstrated that an extraterrestrial object would almost instantly explode as soon as the forces opposing its descent become greater than the force holding it together. He postulated that this would explain the widespread devastation coupled with the lack of debris substantial enough to create an impact crater.[33] The discovery of a potential crater in June 2007 has caused a slight revision to Chyba's theory. Although scientists continue to believe that the Tunguska body exploded before reaching the ground, University of Bologna researchers believe that the impact of a fragment created Lake Cheko, 4.9 mi (8 km) north of the epicenter.[34] Recent research supports this theory, and analysis of the sediment layer confirms that the formation of the lake coincided with the date of the Tunguska event. The bowl-like shape of Lake Cheko is similar to the shape of an impact crater.[35]

Conclusion

Some eyewitnesses thought the Tunguska event signaled the end of the world. This was a fanciful speculation, given the amount of damage caused by the blast. However, a blast of this magnitude in a densely populated area would have devastating consequences. The Tunguska investigation provided valuable information about the potential damage that such a near-Earth object would inflict on an increasingly urban world.

Investigating Future Impacts

Introduction

Meteoroids enter Earth's atmosphere at speeds between 22 and 160 mi/s (35–260 km/s). The friction of gases in the troposphere rapidly slows the smaller ones entering Earth's atmosphere to speeds of 50 mph (80 km/h) or less. As such, they strike the surface of Earth with considerably less force. For larger meteoroids traveling at high speeds, however, the friction encountered in Earth's troposphere has virtually no effect and they can thus hit Earth with extremely high velocity, able to cause massive devastation.

A near-Earth object is any extraterrestrial body with an orbit that could bring it within 1.3 Astronomical Units (AU) of our Sun (where 1 AU is equal to 92,955,807 mi (149,597,870 km), the mean Earth–Sun distance). As the scientific community in several nations began to link impact events to mass extinctions, they looked for ways to deal with these potential hazards. In the USA, the National Aeronautics and Space Administration (NASA), in cooperation with the US Air Force and Jet Propulsion Laboratory, created the Near-Earth Asteroid Tracking (NEAT) program. It searches for NEOs using the Ground Based Electro-Optical Deep Space Surveillance (GEODSS) telescope located in Hawaii.

In late 2001, NEAT identified a 1,000-ft-long (305 m) object rapidly hurtling towards Earth. On January 7, 2002, this asteroid, later named 2001 YB5, missed Earth by some 500,000 mi (800,000 km); that is, twice the distance to our moon, but in astronomical terms, considered too close for comfort. With the explosive force of 4,000 megatons, 2001 YB5 had the potential to destroy an area the size of France. That this NEO avoided detection until two weeks prior to passing Earth alarmed the scientific community. Since then, several other objects have been discovered, and they are monitored closely.

1997 FX11

The discovery of asteroid 1997 FX11 in July of 2002 caused quite a stir. Its potential impact date is October 26, 2028. This asteroid could potentially strike Earth at a speed of 17,000 mph (27,000 km/h), creating an explosion two million times greater than the Hiroshima atomic bomb. If it struck in the ocean, tsunamis would be hundreds of feet high and inundate land miles from the shore. Earth would become engulfed in darkness for months as debris, soot, and dust blocked the sun's rays. While the margin of error is 140,000 mi (225,000 km), this asteroid is likely to pass within 30,000 mi (48,000 km) of Earth, so a hit is not completely ruled out.

2002 NT7

NASA found that although the orbit of 2002 NT7, a massive 1.2-mile-wide (1.9 km) asteroid, coincides with Earth's own orbit, colliding with Earth on February 1, 2019 (a date calculated based on the asteroid's travel speed, trajectory, and distance) is unlikely. Scientists are studying the possibility that it will collide on February 1, 2060. The impact of an asteroid this size would wipe out an entire continent. "We are still monitoring 2002 NT7, but it appears that the impact probability might have already started the typical, inexorable decline that we normally see in these cases," says senior engineer Steve Chesley of NASA's NEO program office at NASA's Jet Propulsion Laboratory (JPL). "We picked up more observations yesterday and ran them through the impact probability and risk scales and all have declined." So why was there so much fuss in the media about this hurtling hunk of rock? The news about 2002 NT7 was everywhere yesterday and from some of the accounts it seemed almost as if "the sky might be falling" – rather than the asteroid was on its way, edges blazing. It was picked up from [NASA's web] pages and disseminated and some of the news organizations apparently decided to get a little sensational headline out of the deal, suggests Chesley, "which is really quite inappropriate in this case."

Asteroid 2002 NT7 still tops the list of NASA/JPL's NEO impact risks because of the low-probability Earth impact prediction for 2019. But Chesley and other asteroid experts assure that the sky is not falling, and the rock will, in all probability, at this stage, orbit safely on by 2019. "While this prediction is of scientific interest, the probability of impact is just not large enough to warrant public concern," reassures Chesley. "It is unusual, but it's not anything that would deserve as much attention as it's gotten. We've seen much higher probabilities, but since this asteroid is quite large, its moderately high probability combined with its great size raises it to a higher level on our risk scales. In other words, this one went over the threshold on one of the risk scales we use; someone noticed and said, 'Hey, that's never happened before.' There's your story.'"[36]

2003 QQ47

Asteroid 2003 QQ47 will be closely monitored over the next several years. Its potential strike date is a year away, March 21, 2014. Astronomers say that any risk of impact is likely to decrease as they gather more data, however. A spokesman for the UK government's Near-Earth Object Information Centre told BBC Radio that, on impact, this asteroid would likely produce 20 times the devastating effects of the Hiroshima atomic bomb. "The near-Earth object will be observable from Earth for the next two months and astronomers will continue to track it over this period," said Dr Alan Fitzsimmons, one of the expert team members advising the Centre.

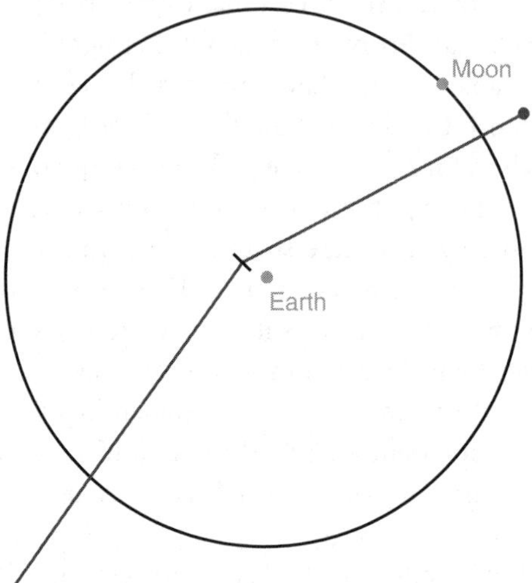

Figure 10.3 Apophis passing Earth.
Source: Adapted from Wikimedia Commons, the free media repository.

99942 Apophis

> Friday, April 13, 2029 could be a very unlucky day for planet Earth. At 4:36 a.m. Greenwich Mean Time (GMT), a 25-million-ton, 820-ft-wide (250 m) asteroid called 99942 Apophis will slice across the orbit of the moon and barrel toward Earth at more than 28,000 mph (45,000 km/h). The huge pock-marked rock, two-thirds the size of Devil's Tower in Wyoming, will pack the energy of 65,000 Hiroshima bombs – enough to wipe out a small country or kick up an 800-ft (245 m) tsunami.[37]

In 2029, the 1,100-ft (335 m) asteroid, Apophis, will swing dangerously close to Earth (Figure 10.3).[38] Observations collected in December 2004 and January 2005, however, provide scientists with enough information to conclude that a direct hit is unlikely. In their continual efforts to process observational data, scientists try to pinpoint the path of this large asteroid. Despite observational data, however, many scientists still think this asteroid will pass dangerously close to Earth. The Planetary Society has offered $50,000 in prize money to any company or school able to complete designs for a space probe or tracking device specifically for Apophis. It is possible that effects of this asteroid will be similar to the eruption of Krakatau. If Apophis struck off the West Coast of the USA, there would be catastrophic tsunami along the length of this coast. The odds of a potential strike on

2029 have been rated at near zero. However, upon passing Earth, at a distance of 20,000 mi (32,000 km) (for scale, this distance is between Earth and our geosynchronous communication satellites), Apophis's presence would cause Earth to bend the asteroid's orbit so that when it came around again on 2036, a direct hit would be virtually guaranteed.

> If NASA eventually does get the nod (to mitigate the threat using technology) – and more important, the budget – from Congress, the obvious first move would be a reconnaissance mission to Apophis . . . a transponder-equipped gravity tractor could be launched for $250 million [to obliterate the asteroid in space to prevent it from striking Earth]. Ironically, that's almost precisely the cost of making the cosmic-collision movies *Armageddon* and *Deep Impact*. If Hollywood can pony up a quarter of a billion in the name of defending our planet, why can't Congress?[39]

2012 DA14

Asteroid 2012 DA4, which was only discovered on February 23, 2012, is approximately 50 yd (45 m) in diameter and weighs approximately 132,000 tons (120,000 metric tons).[40] Calculations show that on February 15, 2013, the distance between the asteroid and Earth will be 21,000 mi (35,000 km), which is closer than human-built satellites in geosynchronous orbit.[41] This asteroid will pass even closer to Earth on February 16, 2020, though the odds of an impact are 1 in 37,037,000.[42] 2012 DA14 rates 0 on the Torino Scale and –3.24 on the Palermo Scale (see next section).[43] If 2012 DA4 struck, it would produce an impact that was the equivalent of 2.4 megatons of TNT. For scale, scientists estimated the Tunguska event at 3–20 megatons. Understandably, scientists and astronomers will be watching this asteroid carefully.

Quantifying the risk

Scientific communities work diligently to improve tracking methods to identify these dangerous NEOs. Important tools in this effort to identify potential threats include the two scales used to classify these objects: the Palermo Technical Impact Hazard Scale and the Torino Scale.

Astronomers communicate the level of danger associated with NEOs to the general public using the Torino Scale. On the Torino Scale an object is given a value between 0 and 10 based on probability of impact and explosive energy potential (expressed in megatons) within the next hundred years. A zero indicates the near impossibility of a collision. Zero also applies to small objects such as meteors that burn up in the atmosphere, as well as small, infrequent meteorite impacts that rarely cause damage.

A 10 indicates the certainty of a collision, causing a global climate catastrophe. Such events occur on average once per 100,000 years or less.[44] An NEO named 2007 VK184[45] has been classified as a level 1 NEO, making it the only object currently listed above 0 on the Torino Scale. A slight chance exists (0.033%) that this asteroid, which measures 425 ft (130 m) in diameter, may strike Earth on June 3, 2048. The highest Torino rating, level 4 out of 10, was assigned to 99942 Apophis in December 2004, though this rating has since been changed to 0.

The scientific community, to provide a detailed risk assessment, uses the more complex Palermo Scale. This scale is the logarithm of the relative risk of the event in question, the time of impact measured in years, and the probability of the impact's energy (in megatons of TNT).[46] The cumulative Palermo Scale value reflects the seriousness of a potential collision.

Preventing a global catastrophe

Early thinking on the possibility of an asteroid strike posited that we should shoot the object with a nuclear warhead to pulverize the rock and eliminate the risk. However, this plan would only make matters worse: imagine the outcome of a huge extraterrestrial object hurtling straight towards Earth at 170,000 mph (274,000 km/h) and then being blown up! Instead of changing the meteorite's course, the nuclear detonation would break the meteoroid into thousands of individual pieces still moving at high velocity toward Earth. At that point, the situation would be changed from one possible impact to several certain impacts. Because meteors pose such a threat to Earth, scientists are developing methods that might be used to throw them off their destructive courses.

One idea involves painting half the meteor black. Since the color black absorbs heat, the painted side would differentially absorb the Sun's energy and potentially re-radiate it enough to nudge the asteroid slightly, possibly pushing it off course. Another idea is to explode a nuclear blast in space, near enough to the meteor to blow it off course. A third idea is to use an electromagnetic slingshot to nudge the meteorite off course. And, a fourth idea, following the same theory as the black paint method, is to use a solar concentrator, or large reflective device, to concentrate the Sun's energy on the meteor and cause the re-radiation of a large amount of heat, which may also nudge the meteor off course.[47] Such ideas, as preposterous as they may seem, are the only line of defense we have against these hazards from space.

Summary

Earth is probably safe from extraterrestrial impacts for the foreseeable future. However, mapping of the sky and understanding of the paths of asteroids, meteoroids, and comets is an important step humans can take to feel safe. The NEOs we have identified are not currently putting Earth in imminent danger of a collision. Past impacts, however, have caused anything from small holes on Earth's surface to devastating impacts that liquefied portions of the crust, causing a fundamental reshaping of Earth. As the human population grows, a meteorite strike in a populated region of the world would have devastating consequences, locally, regionally, and potentially globally. Several mass extinctions of plants and animals in the geologic past were due to meteorite impacts, and the moon's craters remind us that we are at risk of being struck by a rock from space.

If a large meteorite strikes Earth, its explosive power will be felt from days to millennia. Some of the changes would include a dust cloud large enough to envelop Earth. It would take approximately two weeks for huge amounts of dust released into the atmosphere for this to happen. If Earth were covered in dust, photosynthesis would cease and widespread starvation would occur. Dust filling the atmosphere would block the sun's rays and lead to global cooling.

Earth's early atmosphere was missing an essential gas that we require to survive: oxygen, (O_2). Early plants and bacteria slowly excreted oxygen into the atmosphere over the course of about one billion years. If a large meteorite came streaking through our atmosphere, this ionizing fireball would cause nitrogen (N_2) molecules in the atmosphere to break apart and to form monoatomic nitrogen (N). Similarly, O_2 would decouple to yield monoxygen (O). After the meteorite strikes and ionization in the atmosphere ceases, the N_2 and O_2 bonds would create nitric oxide (NO) which, when exposed to oxygen, becomes nitrogen dioxide (NO_2). When nitrogen dioxide comes into contact with water it becomes nitrous acid (HNO_2), a cause of acid rain. If the intensity of this acid rain became strong enough, it would cause the death of terrestrial and aquatic organisms, the acidification of soil, and the deterioration of the built environment.

If a meteorite were to strike the ocean, a likely scenario given that 70% of Earth is water, massive amounts of seawater would vaporize and enter the atmosphere. Water vapor has a great capacity to store the sun's heat, and therefore, after any dust in the atmosphere had settled, extreme global heating would take the place of cold. The potential exists for the release of this water vapor to condense and cause torrential rains and powerful floods.

As a meteorite hurled through the atmosphere, it would ignite global forest fires. Rock records of soot layers on the surface of the planet supports the fact that meteorites have struck Earth through geological time. Scientists found soot from global wildfires in virtually all terrestrial environments dating back to 65 million years ago, when the last great fireball arrived.

Other smaller, localized responses to the vibrations of the impact might include landslides, earthquakes, and volcanoes. The impact would jar locked tectonic faults and bodies of magma would rise to the surface, causing lava to issue forth, potentially in great volumes. Earthquake and shock waves would change the angle of repose of virtually every slope, causing massive landslides in sensitive regions.

This type of natural disaster is the only one capable of destroying Earth as we know it. As such, watching the sky is a worthwhile endeavor so that we avoid a fate similar to that of the Clovis people. Statistically, Earth is long overdue for such an impact event and we would be defenseless against its effects.

Notes

1 Richard Stone (2008), "Target Earth," *National Geographic*, August, 136–149.
2 Nigel Calder (1994), *Comets: Speculation and Discovery* (New York: Dover).
3 Benjamin Silliman and James Dan (1869), *The American Journal of Science and Arts*, second series, XLVII(145, 146, 147), New Haven, CT.
4 Edwin Gnos, Ramachandran Ganapathy, Reid R. Kayes, et al. (2004), "Pinpointing the source of a lunar meteorite: implications for the evolution of the moon," *Science*, 305(5684), 657–659.
5 Ramachandran Ganapathy, Reid R. Kayes, and John C. Laul (1970), "Trace elements in Apollo 11 lunar rocks: Implications for meteorite influx and origin of the moon," *Geochimica et Cosmochimica Acta Supplement*, Vol. 1, in

A.A. Levinson (ed.), "Proceedings of the Apollo 11 Lunar Science Conference, Vol. 2: Chemical and Isotope Analyses," Houston, Texas, January 5–8.

6 Tom Bissell (2003), "A comet's tale," *Harper's Magazine*, February, 33–47.

7 Wendy S. Wolbach, Iain Gilmour, and Edward Anders (1988), "Global fire at the Cretaceous–Tertiary boundary," *Nature*, 334, 665–669.

8 Philippe Claeys, Wolfgang Kiessling, and Walter Alvarez (2002), "Distribution of Chicxulub ejecta at the Cretaceous–Tertiary boundary," *Geological Society of America* Special Paper 356, 55–68.

8 Timothy Bralower, Laurie Eccles, Justin Kutz, et al. (2010), "Grain size of Cretaceous–Paleogene boundary sediments from Chicxulub to the open ccean: implications for interpretation of the mass extinction event," *Geology*, 38(3), 199–202.

9 Peter Schulte (2010), "The Chicxulub asteroid impact and mass extinction at the Cretaceous–Paleogene boundary," *Science*, 327(5970), 1214–1218.

10 Gerrit L. Verschuur (1996), *Impact!: The Threat of Comets and Asteroids* (New York: Oxford University Press).

11 Charles Frankel (1999), *The End of the Dinosaurs: Chicxulub Crater and Mass Extinctions* (Cambridge, UK: Cambridge University Press), 236.

12 David A. Kring (2007), "The Chicxulub impact event and its environmental consequences at the Cretaceous–Tertiary boundary," *Palaeogeography, Palaeoclimatology, Palaeoecology*, 255(1–2), 4–21.

13 Phillipe Claeys and Steven Goderis (2007), "Solar system: lethal billiards," *Nature*, 449, September, 30–31.

14 Gerta Keller, Thierry Adatte, Zsolt Berner, et al. (2007), "Chicxulub impact predates K–T boundary: new evidence from Brazos, Texas," *Earth and Planetary Science Letters*. 255(3–4), 339–356.

15 A.R. Hildebrand (1991), "Chicxulub crater: a possible Cretaceous–Tertiary boundary impact crater on the Yucatán Peninsula," *Geology*, 19, 867–871.

16 David A. Kring (2007), "The Chicxulub impact event and its environmental consequences at the Cretaceous–Tertiary boundary," 4–21.

17 John D' O-Keefe and Thomas J. Ahrens (1989), "Impact production of CO_2 by the Cretaceous–Tertiary extinction bolide and the resultant heating of the Earth," *Nature*, 338, March, 247–248.

18 H. Jay Melosh, John Schneider, Kevin Zahnle, et al. (1990), "Ignition of global wildfires at the Cretaceous–Tertiary boundary," *Nature* (letters), 343, 251–254.

19 David A. Kring and Daniel D. Durda (2002), "Trajectories and distribution of material ejected from the Chixulub impact crater: implication for post-impact wildfires," *Journal of Geophysical Research*, 107(E8).

20 Claire M. Belcher (2009), "Reigniting the Cretaceous–Paleogene firestorm debate," *Geology*, 37(12), 1147–1148.

21 V.V. Shuvalova and N.A. Artemeiva (2002), "Atmospheric erosion and radiation impulse induced by impacts," *Geological Society of America*, Special Paper 356.

22 Mark C. Harvey, Simon C. Brassell, Claire M. Belcher, et al. (2008), "Combustion of fossil organic matter at the Cretaceous–Paleogene (K–P) boundary," *Geology*, 36(5), 355–358.

23 Andrew C. Scott, Barry H. Lomax, and Margaret E. Collinson (2000), "Fire across the K–T boundary; initial results from Sugarite Coal, New Mexico, USA," *Palaeogeography, Palaeoclimatology, Palaeoecology*, 164, 381–395.

24 A.R. Sweet (2001), "Plants, a yardstick for measuring the environmental consequences of the Cretaceous–Tertiary boundary event," *Geoscience Canada*, 28(3), 127–138.

25 Tamara J. Coldin and J. Jay Melosh (2009), "Self-shielding of thermal radiation by Chixulub impact ejecta: firestorm or fizzle?," *Geology*, 37(12), 1135–1138.

26 David A. Kring (2007), "The Chicxulub impact event and its environmental consequences at the Cretaceous–Tertiary boundary," 4–21.

27 Richard B. Firestone, Allen West, James P. Kennett, et al. (2007), "Evidence for an extraterrestrial impact 12,900 years ago that contributed to the megafaunal extinctions and the Younger Dryas cooling," *Proceedings of the National Academy of Sciences*, 104(41), 16016–16021.

28 C. Vance Haynes Jr., Jennifer Boerner, Loiacona Dominik, et al. (2010), "Murray Springs Clovis site, Pleistocene extinction, and the question of extraterrestrial impact," *Proceedings of the National Academy of Sciences*, 107(9), 4010–4015.

29 Tyrone L. Daulton, Nicholas Pinter, and Andrew C. Scott (2010), "No evidence of nanodiamonds in Younger Dryas sediments to support an impact event," *Proceedings of the National Academy of Sciences USA*, 107(37), 16043–16047.

30 "Not a comet, but fungus, fire and fecal pellets," Astrobio.net, June 20, 2010. At www.astrobio.net/pressrelease/3531/not-a-comet-but-fungus-fire-and-fecal-pellets.

31 Mark W. Brazo and Steven A. Austin (1982), "The Tunguska explosion of 1908," *Origins*, 9(2), 82–93.

32 Amir Alexander (2008), "The Tunguska riddle: how powerful was the greatest asteroid impact in recorded history?" *The Planetary Society*, April 15. At http://www.planetary.org/press-room/releases/2008/0129_Planetary_Society_Takes_Aim_at_Target.html.

33 www.hotdocslibrary.ca/uploads/filmAssets/HD_DocLib_EducPkg_TUNGUSKA.pdf.

34 Luca Gasperini, Francesca Alvisi, and Gianni Biasini (2007), "A possible impact crater for the 1908 Tunguska event," *Terra Nova*, 19(4), 245–251.

35 Ibid.

36 A.J.S. Rawl (2002), "Asteroid 2002 NT7 under watch, but probably not coming our way," The Planetary Society: Planetary News: Asteroids and Comets. At http://www.allthingsnow.com/day/astronomy/shared/11473355/Asteroid-2002-NT7-Under-Watch-But-Probably-Not-Coming-Our-Way-Planetary-News-The-Planetary-Society.

37 David Noland (2006), "Five plans to head off the Apophis killer asteroid," *Popular Mechanics*, November. At http://www.popularmechanics.com/science/space/deep/4201569.

38 V.V. Ivashkin and C. A. Stikhno (2008), "On the problem of orbit correction for the near-Earth (99942) asteroid Apophis," *Doklady Physics*, 53(4), 228–232.

39 David Noland (2006), "Five plans to head off the Apophis killer asteroid."

40 Paul Chodas, Jon Giorgini, and Don Yeomans (2012), "Near-Earth asteroid 2012 DA14 to miss Earth on February 15, 2013," NASA/JPL Near-Earth Object Program Office, March 6. At http://neo.jpl.nasa.gov/news/news174.html.

41 Ibid.

42 Ibid.

43 Ibid.

44 The Torino Impact Hazard Scale, NASA. At http://neo.jpl.nasa.gov/torino_scale1.html.

45 2007 VK184 Impact Risk Assessment, NASA. At http://neo.jpl.nasa.gov/risk/2007vk184.html.

46 The Palermo Technical Impact Hazard Scale, NASA. At http://neo.jpl.nasa.gov/risk/doc/palermo.html.

47 Henry Fountain (2002), "Armageddon can wait: stopping killer asteroids," *The New York Times*, November 19. At www.nytimes.com/2002/11/19/science/armageddon-can-wait-stopping-killer-asteroids.html?pagewanted=all&src=pm.

Further Reading

Brigitte Zanda, Monica Rotaru and Roger Hewins (2001), *Meteorites: Their Impact on Science and History* (Cambridge, UK: Cambridge University Press).

The text, with illustrations, shows the connection of the science of meteorites with their different histories.

Vladimir Rubtsov and Edward Ashpole (2009), *The Tunguska Mystery (Astronomers' Universe)* (New York: Springer).

This book is a comprehensive treatment on the mystery of this meteorite, how it landed, how it destroyed parts of Siberia, and how it was discovered.

Paul W. Hodge (2010), *Meteorite Craters and Impact Structures of the Earth* (Cambridge, UK: Cambridge University Press).

This text presents a very recent and technologically advanced treatment of meteorites, possible future impacts, and recent past impacts.

Wolf Uwe Reimold and Roger L. Gibson (2010), *Meteorite Impact! The Danger from Space and South Africa's Mega-Impact, The Vredefort Structure (Geoparks of the World)* (New York: Springer).

This field guide is both a primer on meteorites and also gives a more comprehensive treatment in an understandable narrative.

Ted Nield (2011), *The Falling Sky: The Science and History of Meteorites and Why We Should Learn to Love Them* (Guilford, CT: Lyons Press).

This text presents an account of how life on Earth has been influenced by extraterrestrial impacts.

Epilogue

The human world remains central in our discussions about natural disasters. In this way, we have attempted to avoid separating the "natural" in natural disasters by placing humans squarely at the center of the book's focus on natural hazards. In many instances, humans have contributed to their vulnerability by moving to hazardous locations, in the vicinity of smoking volcanoes, on geological faults, on low-lying deltas and in the known paths of hurricanes. Others, more than one billion inhabitants, live where they must to access food, to use transportation, and find work. Their vulnerability to risks becomes intertwined with their normal daily existence. Human activity based on choices versus actions based on necessities underlies the broader societal patterns of the world's population.

These patterns, rooted in history, show how the inequitable access to resources in food, clothing, housing, medicine, and education place populations at risk. "The crucial point about understanding why disasters happen is that it is not only natural events that cause them. They are also the product of social, political, and economic environments (as distinct from the natural environment), because of the way these structure the lives of different groups of people."[1] The potentially lethal impact of voluntary decisions or those made out of necessity by either individuals or societies suggests the ways in which human actions can create the conditions for turning a natural disaster into a colossal human tragedy with generational implications.

The ability of catastrophic events to alter the course of human history is a reminder of the vulnerability of complex societies with growing urban populations and fragile ecosystems to explosive volcanism. For example, some megacities, including Tokyo, Naples, and Mexico City, share space with active volcanoes including, respectively, Mt. Asama, the Ischia volcano, and Popocatepetl (Aztec for "smoking mountain"). Major eruptions near

Natural Disasters in a Global Environment, First Edition. Anthony N. Penna and Jennifer S. Rivers.

these locations disrupt the normal functioning of civil society. A modern city's complex infrastructure, including sanitation and electronic communication systems, can be either damaged or destroyed. In cities dependent on local agriculture for food and fodder, the danger of hunger further compromises a population that is already vulnerable to the shocks of life-threatening, yet unpredictable, eruptions.

Regarding tsunamis caused by powerful oceanic earthquakes, the Tōhoku tsunami in Japan would have been limited to the massive destruction of its coastal communities if it were not for the political and economic decision to locate the Fukushima nuclear power plant on the coast. Inundated by flood waters, the power plants exploded and their overheated nuclear reactors melted down. A country without reserves in fossil fuels led its elected officials and its industrial elite to construct a nuclear power industry commensurate with the needs of a modern society. Atomic energy became the preferred option of the government, with the support of its citizens, who need electricity to improve urban living standards. Initially, rural Japanese citizens protested against the placement of nuclear power plants along their coastal plains, arguing that their planned location would destroy their fishing industry.

The government prevailed, however, by offering the equivalent of "pork barrel" projects funded by the national treasury including athletic facilities, parks, senior centers, state-of-the-art wastewater treatment plants, and property and income tax relief. The infusion of new capital, economic incentives, and social benefits trumped worries over nuclear power. The new plants provided jobs, stimulating the region's economy, which had formerly been dependent on seasonal employment in the fishing industry. The 2012 earthquake and tsunami crippled Japan's nuclear power industry. This disaster forced Japan to import record amounts of liquefied natural gas and double its imports of petroleum. In hindsight, a trade-off may have saved the country from a nuclear nightmare. Buying fossil fuel from other petroleum-producing countries would make Japan vulnerable to fluctuations in world energy prices but it would not have suffered the miseries caused by the Tōhoku tsunami to this generation and to those that follow.

This case suggests that a complex mix of human actions and forces of nature in the form of an oceanic earthquake and a destructive tsunami together created the conditions for a natural/human disaster. Many more examples show how societal economic decisions, combined with individual choices, create the conditions for catastrophe. In the Haitian earthquake, political expediency created an urban social environment of teeming slums and massive unemployment on a geological fault line.

Elected president in 1971, Francois Duvalier chose to consolidate his grip on this small island country by destroying its regional economies. Without work, residents poured into the capital city of Port-au-Prince where Duvalier ruled with an "iron fist." There was an earthquake along the geological fault beneath the city in 2011, killing thousands and leaving much of the urban population homeless. A crass political maneuver compromised the nation's viability and exposed a vulnerable population to the earthquake's terror. As Greg Bankoff has pointed out (in reference to the Hawke's Bay earthquake that destroyed New Zealand's North Island town of Napier on February 3, 1931; but also applicable to the Haitian earthquake): "Seeing the earthquake as part of a process involves a wider perspective that encompasses not only the present event but its antecedents and consequences."[2]

Seismologists know that earthquakes will happen in geologically fragile zones from Chile to Alaska, along the west coast of the Americas and in China, Iran, Turkey, and Italy. They are inherently vulnerable to disasters, suggesting that what occurs there is a process that "stretches from the past through the present to the future ad infinitum."[3] Despite newly developed seismic equipment that monitors subtle tectonic movements, seismologists know which, but not when, earthquakes will fracture Earth's surface. Our histories, our identities and sense of place (picturesque beaches or scenic views) compel those with choices to live where they will.

On Earth's surface, the evidence of a changing climate appears in many forms, not least of which is the volatility of the world's weather. "Variations in mean average temperatures [have] effects on agriculture, human nutrition, population density, as well as having an important bearing on the intensity and frequency with which people were subject to extreme events at any given location on the Earth's surface."[4] The onsets of rapid and unseasonably high levels of rainfall cause floods that currently represent the highest percentage of all natural disasters. Future projections suggest, however, that this percentage will rise significantly in a warming world. In the UK, massive flash floods in 2007 caused nearly £6 million (US$9.6 million) of property damage, and left 350,000 people without drinking water and 50,000 people without electricity for weeks. Thousands lost their homes to the raging waters. With the exception of the bombing raids that destroyed much of London in World War II, modern Britain has experienced nothing quite like these floods.[5]

Similarly, Missouri/Mississippi River floods have plagued the USA for centuries. With a westward-moving population, government efforts to build dams, levees, and retaining walls in order to hold back the river have proven unsuccessful. In flood stage, the adage reads, "The river always wins." A classic example of the potential plight of the north-central region of the USA to massive flooding occurs in the vicinity of the Red River Valley, which separates North Dakota and Minnesota. A region that is susceptible to flooding, the record floods of the twenty-first century exceeded those kept by forecasters in the last century. Made by a massive glacial lake thousands of years ago, it is the richest farmland in the world. When the lake dried up, it left behind fertile soil. As one of the flattest, most poorly drained river valleys due to its history as a lake, it reverts to a lake-like configuration each spring. Massive blizzards, an indication of recurrent volatile weather in a changing climate, increased the total annual snow accumulations to 117 in (3 m). Snowmelt caused flood crests ranging from 39–49 ft (12–15 m). Ice storms raised the total to 54 ft (17 m). The region's repeated flooding is suggestive of the progression of vulnerability into root causes (the geophysical origins of the flatlands), the dynamic pressures (excessive snowmelt and rising flood waters), and the unsafe conditions (breached, broken, and sinking levees forcing massive evacuations).[6]

Obvious connections and links exist when discussing disasters. Just as volcanoes, earthquakes, and tsunamis are potentially related, heavy rainfall leading to flooding weakens slopes and causes landslides. For example, of the many deadly landslides, we recall the landslide that occurred in December 1999 in Venezuela, when torrential downpours caused flash floods and mudslides. They obliterated the encampments and impoverished towns surrounding Caracas, destroying 20,000 homes and killing 30,000 people. Another landslide struck the Khait region of Tajikistan on July 10, 1949. It destroyed 33 villages, causing the deaths of 28,000 people.

How do we learn about these events in regions far away from our own? Increasingly, the global media responds in real time, alerting people everywhere to an unfolding calamity. In addition, newer electronic media including internet communication signals to the larger public the need for a humanitarian response. A Facebook page alerted citizens to the Southern Leyte landslide by soliciting donations to repair the damages and assist people in need. On a much larger scale, in 2011 the US Congress published a report titled, "Social Media and Disasters: Current Uses, Future Options, and Policy Considerations." It states:

> In the last five years social media have played an increasing role in emergencies and disasters. Social media sites rank as the fourth most popular source to access emergency information. They have been used by individuals and communities to warn others of unsafe areas or situations, inform friends and family that someone is safe, and raise funds for disaster relief. Facebook supports numerous emergency-related organizations, including Information Systems for Crisis Response and Management (ISCRAM), the Humanitarian Free and Open Source Software (FOSS) Project, as well as numerous universities with disaster-related programs.

The connections of natural disasters to each other and the role of human activities is an obvious conclusion to be drawn from this book. Logging and mining may cause landslides. Earthquakes shake slopes; typhoons and heavy rains saturate the land. Global climate change and worsening La Niña events, tsunamis, and dust storms produce particularly lethal hazards. As the impact of climate change become clearer and as more people inhabit disaster-prone areas, the severity and frequency of disasters may become more apparent.

With planning, foresight, and disaster response management, engineering the built environment to withstand shocks and tremors may minimize the loss of life.

For local, regional, and national governments, preparing citizens for hazards requires a number of risk reduction strategies including evacuation plans from the areas immediately affected. In addition, a public information campaign about the risks of living in a hazard-prone area needs to be repeated on a regular basis with recommendations about the role that individuals can play to lessen the effects of disasters on them and their families. Such announcements should provide a sober assessment of the risks and ways to protect yourself and those around you.

Mitigating risk with engineering and technology may save lives. Remaining constantly vigilant by identifying gaps in our emergency disaster response plans could save many more. Yet, millions of survivors of such terror will suffer for many of their remaining years from what we know medically as Post-Traumatic Stress Syndrome (PTSS), recalling with acute anxiety a time when their lives were in danger.

Notes

1 Ben Wisner, Piers Blaikie, Terry Cannon, et al. (2004), *At Risk: Natural Hazards, People's Vulnerability and Disasters* (London: Routledge), 4.
2 Greg Bankoff (2011), "Historical concepts of disaster and risk," in *Handbook of Hazards and Disaster Risk Reduction*, eds. Ben Wisner, J.C. Galliard, and Ian Kelman (London: Routledge), 38.
3 Ibid., 37.
4 Ibid., 34.
5 Michael McCarthy (2001), "A 21st-century catastrophe," *The Independent*, July 24, 21.
6 Greg Bankoff (2011), "Historical concepts of disaster and risk", 31.

Index

Natural Disasters in a Global Environment, First Edition. Anthony N. Penna and Jennifer S. Rivers.